Beginning Fedora Desktop

Fedora 20 Edition

Richard Petersen

apress·

Beginning Fedora Desktop: Fedora 20 Edition

ISBN-13 (pbk): 978-1-4842-0068-1

ISBN-13 (electronic): 978-1-4842-0067-4

Trademarked names, logos, and images may appear in this book. Rather than use a trademark symbol with every occurrence of a trademarked name, logo, or image, we use the names, logos, and images only in an editorial fashion and to the benefit of the trademark owner, with no intention of infringement of the trademark.

The use in this publication of trade names, trademarks, service marks, and similar terms, even if they are not identified as such, is not to be taken as an expression of opinion as to whether or not they are subject to proprietary rights.

While the advice and information in this book are believed to be true and accurate at the date of publication, neither the author nor the editors nor the publisher can accept any legal responsibility for any errors or omissions that may be made. The publisher makes no warranty, express or implied, with respect to the material contained herein.

Publisher: Heinz Weinheimer
Lead Editor: Louise Corrigan
Technical Reviewers: Nikolaos Vyzas and Martin Berg
Editorial Board: Steve Anglin, Mark Beckner, Ewan Buckingham, Gary Cornell, Louise Corrigan, Jim DeWolf, Jonathan Gennick, Jonathan Hassell, Robert Hutchinson, Michelle Lowman, James Markham, Matthew Moodie, Jeff Olson, Jeffrey Pepper, Douglas Pundick, Ben Renow-Clarke, Dominic Shakeshaft, Gwenan Spearing, Matt Wade, Steve Weiss
Coordinating Editor: Christine Ricketts
Copy Editor: Michael G. Laraque
Compositor: SPi Global
Indexer: SPi Global
Artist: SPi Global
Cover Designer: Anna Ishchenko

Distributed to the book trade worldwide by Springer Science+Business Media New York, 233 Spring Street, 6th Floor, New York, NY 10013. Phone 1-800-SPRINGER, fax (201) 348-4505, e-mail orders-ny@springer-sbm.com, or visit www.springeronline.com. Apress Media, LLC is a California LLC and the sole member (owner) is Springer Science + Business Media Finance Inc (SSBM Finance Inc). SSBM Finance Inc is a Delaware corporation.

For information on translations, please e-mail rights@apress.com, or visit www.apress.com.

Apress and friends of ED books may be purchased in bulk for academic, corporate, or promotional use. eBook versions and licenses are also available for most titles. For more information, reference our Special Bulk Sales–eBook Licensing web page at www.apress.com/bulk-sales.

Any source code or other supplementary material referenced by the author in this text is available to readers at www.apress.com. For detailed information about how to locate your book's source code, go to www.apress.com/source-code/.

To Mark and Lauren,
best wishes always

Contents at a Glance

Contents

About the Author

Richard Petersen holds an M.L.I.S. in library and information studies (UC Berkeley). He is the author of numerous books on C programming, UNIX, and Linux. Currently, he is the publisher of Surfing Turtle Press, specializing in books for Fedora and Ubuntu Linux. His research background includes artificial intelligence applications to information retrieval. He has taught computer science programming and Unix at UC Berkeley.

About the Technical Reviewers

 **Martin Berg** has been using Linux on the desktop since 1999 and has been using Linux as the only desktop platform both professionally and at home since 2003. Martin has introduced Linux as a server platform (running Oracle databases) for several companies over the years.

Nikolaos Vyzas is a lead database consultant at Pythian and an avid open source database engineer. He began his career as a software developer in South Africa and then moved into technology, consulting for various European and US-based firms. After having worked at Accenture as a senior consultant, implementing automated DSL, VoIP, and IPTV Ethernet service-provisioning solutions for several years, he moved into the world of open source technology, working within the areas of MySQL, Galera, Redis, MemcacheD, and MongoDB on many OS platforms, including RHEL, Fedora, Debian, Solaris, and FreeBSD. He gets his inspiration and energy from his loving family.

Acknowledgments

I would like to thank all those at Apress who made this book a reality, particularly Louise Corrigan, the Apress open source editor, who initiated and oversaw the project; Christine Ricketts, the coordinating editor, for her support and analysis, as well as management of such a complex project; and Nikolaos Vyzas and Martin Berg, the technical reviewers, whose analysis and suggestions proved very insightful and helpful. Special thanks to Linus Torvalds, the creator of Linux, and to those who continue to develop Linux as an open, professional, and effective operating system accessible to anyone.

Introduction

This book examines Fedora for the user. Although administrative tools are covered, the emphasis is on what a user would need to know to perform tasks. The focus here is on what users face when using Fedora, covering topics such as installation, applications, software management, the GNOME and KDE desktops, shell commands, and the Fedora administration and network tools. Desktops are examined in detail, including configuration options. Applications examined include office suites, editors, e-book readers, music and video applications and codecs, e-mail clients, web browsers, FTP clients, microblogging, and IM applications. This book is designed for the Fedora 20 desktop, with all the latest features of interest to users.

Part 1 focuses on getting started, covering Fedora information and resources, Fedora Live DVDs, installing and setting up Fedora, and the basic use and configuration of the desktop. The GNOME 3 System Settings configuration tools, such as power, background, privacy, network, and display, are examined. Also covered are software management using the YUM software manager and its desktop front ends, the GNOME Software and PackageKit, along with repositories and their use, including the RPM Fusion repository.

Part 2 keys in on such applications as office, multimedia, mail, Internet, and social networking. This part includes coverage of the PulseAudio sound interface and music and video applications. New GNOME applications are included, such as GNOME Music, GNOME Weather, and GNOME Maps.

Part 3 covers the two major desktops, GNOME and KDE, discussing GNOME 3 features, including the activities overviews, the dash, and the top bar. Unique KDE 4 features such as the dashboard and activities are also explored. In addition, the shell interface is examined, including features such as history, file name completion, directory, and file operations, among others. Additional desktops are also discussed, including Xfce, LXDE, Sugar (SoaS), Mate, and Cinnamon.

Part 4 deals with administrative topics, first discussing system tools, such as the GNOME system monitor, the Disk Usage Analyzer, the Disk Utility storage manager, temperature monitors, and SELinux configuration. Then a detailed chapter on Fedora system administration tools such as those for managing users, authorization controls, and Bluetooth, along with service management and file system access, is included. The network configuration chapter covers a variety of network tasks, including configuration of wired and wireless connections, firewalls, and Samba Windows access. Both the GNOME 3 network tool and the older Network Manager editor application are covered. Finally, a chapter on printing examines both the GNOME 3 printers tool and the older `system-config-printer` application and their support for personal and remote printers.

CHAPTER 1

■ ■ ■

Fedora 20 Introduction

The Fedora release of Linux is maintained and developed by an open source project called the Fedora Project (http://fedoraproject.org). The release consists entirely of open source software. Development is carried out using contributions from Linux developers. The project is designed to work much like other open source projects, with releases keeping pace with the course of rapid online development. The Fedora Project features detailed documentation of certain topics, such as installation and desktop user guides, at http://docs.fedoraproject.org (see Table 1-1).

Table 1-1. *Fedora Sites*

Web Site	Description
http://fedoraproject.org	Fedora resources
http://download.fedoraproject.org	Fedora repository site
http://docs.fedoraproject.org/en-US/Fedora/20/html/Installation_Guide/	Fedora installation guide
http://docs.fedoraproject.org/en-US/Fedora/20/html/Release_Notes/index.html	Fedora release notes
http://fedoraproject.org/wiki/Overview	Fedora project overview
http://fedoraproject.org/wiki/FAQ	Fedora FAQ
http://fedoraproject.org/wiki/CommunityWebsites	Fedora community web sites
http://docs.fedoraproject.org	Documentation and support tutorials for Fedora releases
http://fedoraproject.org/en/get-fedora	Fedora download page
http://fedoraproject.org/get-fedora-all	Fedora download page for all download methods and Fedora versions
http://download.fedoraproject.org	Fedora repository, mirror link
http://mirrors.fedoraproject.org	Fedora mirrors list
http://fedoraforum.org	User discussion support forum, endorsed by the Fedora Project; includes FAQs and news links
www.linuxfoundation.org	The Linux Foundation, official Linux development

(continued)

1

Table 1-1. (*continued*)

Web Site	Description
http://kernel.org	Latest Linux kernels
www.redhat.com	The Red Hat web site
http://magazine.redhat.com/	*Red Hat Magazine,* with specialized articles on latest developments
www.centos.org	Community Enterprise Operating System, CENTOS (Red Hat–based)

This chapter covers the information about the Fedora release, where to obtain informaion on it, and what versions are available for download. You can also download and try out the Fedora release on a Live DVD without installing it, even running it from a USB disk.

Fedora Documentation

Documentation for Fedora can be found at http://docs.fedoraproject.org (see Table 1-1). The Fedora installation guide provides a detailed description of all install procedures. The Fedora desktop user guide covers basic desktop operations, such as logging in, using office applications, and accessing the Web. Several dedicated Fedora support sites are available that provide helpful information, including http://fedoraforum.org and http://fedoraproject.org. The http://fedoraforum.org site is a Fedora Project–sponsored forum for end-user support. Here you can post questions and check responses for common problems.

Your Firefox browser will already be configured with links for accessing popular documentation and support sites. On the Firefox Bookmarks toolbar, click the Fedora Project button to display a menu with entries for Fedora Project, Fedora Forum, Fedora Solved, Fedora Weekly News, Planet Fedora, and Join Fedora. The Red Hat menu displays entries for Red Hat, jBoss, OpenSource.com, and The Open Source Way (you may have to set the bookmarks toolbar to display; choose View ➤ Bookmarks Toolbar).

Fedora maintains detailed specialized documentation, such as information on understanding how udev is implemented or how SELinux is configured. For much of the documentation you must rely on installed documentation in /usr/share/doc or on the man and info pages, as well as the context help button for different applications running on your desktop. Web sites for software such as GNOME, KDE, and LibreOffice.org provide extensive applicable documentation. For installation, you can use the Fedora installation guide at http://docs.fedoraproject.org/en-US/Fedora/20/html/Installation_Guide/.

Fedora 20

The Fedora versions of Linux are entirely free. You can download the most current version from http://fedoraproject.org or http://download.fedoraproject.org. The http://download.fedoraproject.org address will link to the best available mirror for you. You can update Fedora using the software update (PackageKit) to access the Fedora repository. Access is automatically configured during installation.

The Fedora distribution is also available online at numerous FTP sites. Fedora maintains download sites at http://download.fedoraproject.org, along with a mirrors listing at http://mirrors.fedoraproject.org, where you can download the entire current release of Fedora Linux, as well as updates and additional software.

Fedora 20 Desktop Features

Fedora releases feature key updates to critical applications as well as new tools. The following information is derived for the official Fedora release notes. Consult these notes for detailed information about all new changes. The Fedora release notes are located on all the Fedora spins as an HTML file on the top directory. You can also find the release notes at http://docs.fedoraproject.org/en-US/Fedora/20/html/Release_Notes/.

Fedora 20 uses GNOME 3.10 and KDE 4.11.

Fedora provides the Mate and Cinnamon desktops. Mate is a traditional desktop based on GNOME 2, and Cinnamon is the Mint Linux desktop derived from GNOME 3, but with many traditional features, such as the panel and applets.

GNOME Software has replaced PackageKit as the primary front-end software management application. GNOME Software (gnome-software) is designed to work with applications rather than just specific packages. You can still install and use the older PackageKit software manager (Packages and Software Update).

The lock screen displays the time, date, and username. From the lock screen, you can adjust the sound, configure your network connection, and check your power. Press the ESC key to display the login screen.

The System Status Area has been combined into one menu showing sound volume, brightness, network connections, the current user, battery power, and buttons for Settings, lock screen, and power off. The user item is only shown if more than one user is set up for the system. The user menu item expands to Log Out and Switch User entries.

For systems with wireless devices, there is a Wi-Fi entry in the System Status Area menu that expands to a menu with options to select a network, turn off the wireless device, and to open the GNOME Network system setting dialog at the wireless tab (Wi-Fi Settings).

For systems with a battery, such as laptops, a Battery entry is displayed on the System Status Area menu showing the power level. The Power menu item expands to a menu with an entry to open the Power Settings dialog in System Settings.

GNOME windows and workspaces can be displayed easily and accessed quickly from the overview.

Sound volume and screen brightness (laptops) are adjusted using sliders on the System Status Area menu.

A search box at the top of the overview allows you to search directly for applications and files. It is also configured to search GNOME Contacts, Documents, and Keys, as well as to conduct a web search. Use the System Settings Search dialog to select the applications that can be searched. You can also add other applications.

The GNOME Tweak Tool lets you perform common desktop configurations, such as placing your home folder on the desktop, changing the theme for icons and windows, changing and adjusting fonts, choosing startup applications, configuring how the date is displayed on the top bar, and setting up static (fixed number) workspaces.

The GNOME Network dialog for System Settings has been enhanced and is now the primary network configuration tool. As with the system-config-network (Network Connections), it is a front end to Network Manager. The older system-config-network can still be installed and used. Both use similar dialog entries.

Several System Settings dialogs have been redesigned, including Date & Time, Power, Displays, Background, and Region & Language.

Several new System Settings dialogs have been added: Notifications, Privacy, Search, and Sharing. Screen Lock is now managed by Privacy.

The Privacy dialog in System Settings lets you configure Screen Lock, Usage & History, and to Purge Trash & Temporary Files.

The Sharing dialog in System Settings lets you allow screen sharing, media sharing in specified folders, and remote logins.

The Notification dialog in System Settings lets you select applications that can display notices.

Chat messages can be responded to on the message tray.

On GNOME Help, the Getting Started page displays animations for common tasks, such as starting applications or accessing files.

Though GNOME workspaces are generated automatically (dynamic) from the overview, you can also use the GNOME Tweak Tool to set up static (fixed-number) workspaces instead.

The GNOME overview features a dash (Activities) that lists icons for your favorite applications and opened applications, letting you access them quickly. You can add applications to the dash. An Applications icon on the dash opens the applications overview. A search box at the top lets you search for applications and files. A Frequent button at the bottom lets you display only frequently accessed applications. A pager to the right lets you move through the icons by page.

In the GNOME-shell, notifications are displayed in the message tray at the bottom of the screen (they are automatically hidden). Use the Super+m key to display it (Windows key+m), or move the mouse forcefully to the bottom edge of the screen.

On all GNOME windows, the toolbar and the title bar have been combined into a header bar, with a single close box on the right side.

The GNOME Files file manager has buttons for two views: icon and list. A button for a View menu lists tasks such as zooming and sorting, and a tool button displays a menu for folder tasks such as a new tab, item selection, and bookmarking. A Files menu on the GNOME applications menu on the top bar contains tasks such as connecting to an FTP site, opening a new window, and configuring bookmarks.

The GNOME Files file manager (Nautilus) features a sidebar with Places, Devices, Computer, Bookmarks, and Network sections. You can quickly access any file system on removable devices, remote networks, and internal drives, as well as your home folders.

The file manager supports a preview of file contents, displaying text, video, images, and PDF files. Select the file and press the spacebar.

In System Settings, you can configure use of Online Accounts, such as Google and Facebook. Configuring the Online Accounts sets up configuration for mail and chat (Empathy).

GNOME supports an integrated onscreen keyboard for both access and tablets and the integration of keyboard layouts and input methods.

GNOME Contacts (gnome-contacts) provides integrated management for all your contacts on Empathy, Evolution, and online accounts.

GNOME Documents supports local and cloud-based documents (Google docs and Microsoft SkyDrive), letting you quickly search and access your documents (text, PDF, presentations, and spreadsheets).

systemd and its unit files have replaced System V and its init scripts. Upstart is no longer used. The GNOME Log Viewer is a front end to journald.

journald has replaced syslogd as the logging daemon. You can use `jouralctl` to access the logs.

The GNOME print manager (System Settings ➤ Printers) features full support for configuring printers.

KDE provides several desktop improvements, including the system tray, notification area, desktop file indexing, and a reworked activities interface, which makes it easier to manage desktop widget collections.

The GNOME Classic mode (gnome-classic-session package) lets you use a GNOME 2–like interface.

Fedora ISO Images

Fedora disks are released as a set of spins that collect software for different purposes. Currently, there are three major Fedora distribution spins available: the Install DVD for desktops, workstations, and servers; the Desktop Live DVD (GNOME Desktop); and the Fedora KDE Live DVD. The Install DVD spin includes a collection of workstation and server software, but not the entire collection. Spins are created with Revisor, which you can use to develop your own customized spins. You can find out more information about spins at `https://fedoraproject.org/wiki/SIGs/Spins`.

Fedora Desktop Live DVD: The Fedora GNOME Desktop Live DVD, available in i386 and x86_64 versions

Fedora KDE Live DVD: The Fedora KDE desktop Live DVD, available in i386 and x86_64 versions

Fedora Install DVDs: The Fedora Install DVD, with a more complete selection of software, available in i386 and x86_64 versions; only performs an installation or rescue

Fedora Custom Spins

Custom spins are also available and can be downloaded from `http://spins.fedoraproject.org`. The official spins are listed at `https://fedoraproject.org/wiki/Releases/20/Spins`.

Fedora XFCE Desktop Spin: Features the XFCE desktop instead of GNOME

Fedora LXDE Desktop Spin: The Lightweight X11 Desktop Environment

Fedora Mate-Compiz Desktop Spin: The Mate Desktop Environment. Mate is an updated version of the GNOME 2 interface

Fedora SoaS Desktop Spin: Sugar on a Stick spin for USB drives featuring the Sugar desktop (OLPC)

Fedora Games Spin: Games available on Fedora

Fedora Design Suite: Image applications available on Fedora

Fedora FEL Spin: Fedora Electronics Lab spin

Fedora Security Spin: Fedora Security Lab spin, a safe environment for security testing and recovering a system

Fedora Robotics Spin: Robotic simulation environment

Fedora Scientific-KDE Spin: Scientific research

Fedora Jam Audio Spin: Audio and music applications and tools

Multimedia

Although licensed multimedia formats such as MP3 and DVD are still excluded, open source formats are all included, including Vorbis, Ogg, Theora, and FLAC. Multimedia codecs with licensing issues can be directly downloaded with PackageKit, once you have configured YUM to use the RPM Fusion repository on your system. (Just install the `http://rpmfusion.org` configuration package for Fedora 20, which is available from that site.) The RPM Fusion repository is *not* configured by default.

Fedora Live DVD

The Fedora Live DVD lets you run Fedora on any computer using a DVD-ROM drive. You can save files to removable devices such as USB drives. You can temporarily install software, but the install disappears when you shut down. You can also mount partitions from hard drives on the system you are running the Live DVD on. Find out more about the Fedora Live DVD at `http://fedoraproject.org/wiki/FedoraLiveCD`.

The Live DVD provided by Fedora includes a limited set of software packages. Servers are not included. For desktop support, you use GNOME (there are KDE, LXDE, and Xfce versions). Other than these limitations, you have a fully operational Fedora desktop. The Live DVD enables Network Manager by default, automatically detecting and configuring your network connection. You have the full set of administrative tools, with which you can add users and change configuration settings while the Live DVD is running. When you shut down, the configuration information is lost.

You can log out, but this will display a login screen with a simple login dialog for automatic login and a language menu. The bottom panel of the login screen has menus for setting the language and keyboard. You can shut down or restart from the shutdown menu on the right side of the panel.

Fedora provides GNOME and KDE desktop Live DVD spins, as well as those for LXDE, Xfce, Mate-Compiz, and SoaS, each in 32-bit and 64-bit versions.

Fedora 20 Desktop Spin: Available for i868 and x86_64; includes GNOME desktop and productivity applications

Fedora 20 KDE Spin: Available for i686 and x86_64; includes KDE desktop

Fedora 20 XFCE Spin: Features the XFCE desktop instead of GNOME

Fedora 20 LXDE Spin: Features the lightweight LXDE desktop instead of GNOME

Fedora Mate-Compiz Desktop Spin: The Mate Desktop Environment. Mate is an updated version of the GNOME 2 interface

Fedora SoaS Desktop Spin: Sugar on a Stick spin for USB drives featuring the Sugar desktop (OLPC)

Starting the Live DVD

When you first boot, you can press the spacebar to display the boot options. These include booting up the Live DVD directly (the default), booting with basic video, verifying the disk media first, performing a memory test, or booting to another OS already on your hard disk. If you press nothing, the Live DVD starts up automatically. After your system starts up, you will be presented with the standard login screen (the KDE Live DVD will boot directly to the desktop). You will be automatically logged in. The GNOME desktop (see Figure 1-1) will then start up.

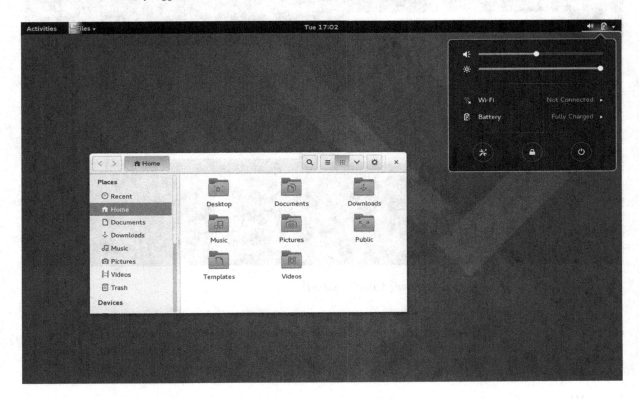

Figure 1-1. *Fedora Live DVD*

Click the Activities button on the upper-left corner to enter the overview mode, where you can access windows, search for applications and files, and open applications (Applications icon on the Favorites sidebar). From the Favorites sidebar, you can quickly open applications (see Figure 1-2). The Favorites sidebar contains, as its last icon, an Install to Hard Drive icon, which you can use to install Fedora on your hard drive.

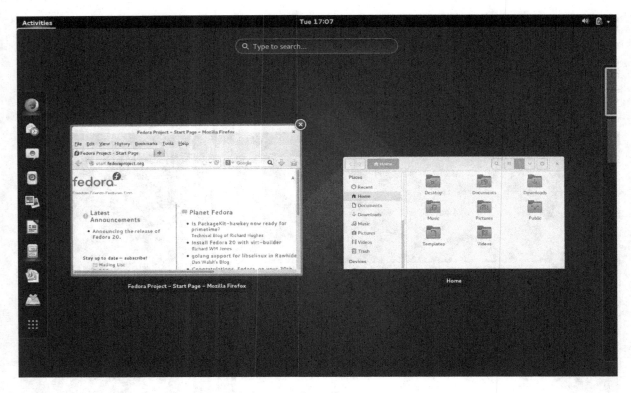

Figure 1-2. *Fedora Live DVD overview mode (Activities button)*

An easy way to save data from a Live session is to use a USB drive. On GNOME, the USB drive will appear as an entry on a file manager window sidebar. Double-click it to open a file manager window for the USB drive. You can then copy files generated during the session to the USB drive. Remember to eject the drive before removing it (click the eject button next to the USB drive entry on the file manager sidebar).

Installing Fedora from a Live DVD

The Live DVD can also be used as an installation disk, providing its limited collection of software on a system, that can be expanded and updated from Fedora online repositories (see Chapter 2). In this case, you don't have to download a complete set of Fedora install CD disks or the install DVD, just the Live DVD. Later, you add packages from repositories. Double-click the Install to Hard Drive icon on the overview dash to start the installation (see Figure 2-4 in Chapter 2).

USB Live Disk

You can also install Fedora Live ISO images to a USB disk. The procedure is not destructive. Your original data on the USB disk is preserved. To create a Live USB drive, you can either use the `liveusb-creator` application (`liveusb-creator` package), or the `livecd-iso-to-disk` command (`livecd-tools` package).

liveusb-creator

The `liveusb-creator` application is a GNOME application with an easy-to-use interface for creating a Live USB image from a Live DVD ISO image file. Once it's installed, you can start `liveusb-creator` from Utilities ➤ Fedora LiveUSB Creator to open the Fedora Live USB Creator window. Use the Browse button to locate the USB image or download one using the Download Fedora pop-up menu. The selected image will appear in the pane. Use the Target Device pop-up menu to select the USB drive to use, if there's more than one. The Persistent Storage slider allows you to create an overlay memory segment on which changes and added data can be saved. When you are ready, just click the Create Live USB button at the bottom of the window.

livecd-iso-to-disk

You can also install Fedora Live images to a USB disk using the `livecd-iso-to-disk` command to install the image (part of the `livecd-tools` package). This is a command-line tool that you enter in a terminal window. Use the Live image and the device name of the USB disk as your arguments.

```
/usr/bin/livecd-iso-to-disk Fedora-20i686-Live-Desktop.iso /dev/sdb1
```

Each Live DVD also provides a `livecd-iso-to-disk` script in its LiveOS directory.

Live USB Persistence Storage

If you want to make changes to the Fedora OS on the USB Live version, set up an overlay memory segment on the USB drive. To do this, use the `--overlay-size-mb` option with the size of the overlay in megabytes. Be sure your USB drive is large enough to accommodate both the overlay memory and the CD image. The following allows for 512MB of persistent data that will be encrypted:

```
livecd-iso-to-disk --overlay-size-mb 512 Fedora-20i686-Live-Desktop.iso /dev/sbd1
```

Persistent Home Directory

If you want to save data to a /home directory on the USB Live version, set up a home directory memory segment. To do this, use the `--home-size-mb` option with the size of the home directory segment in megabytes. Be sure your USB drive is large enough to accommodate the home memory and the CD image, as well as a memory overlay, if you also want to enable changes to the operating system. Your /home directory memory segment will be encrypted by default, to protect your data in case it is lost or stolen. Upon creating your overlay, you will be prompted for a passphrase. Whenever you boot up your USB system, you will be prompted for the passphrase. The following allows for a 1024MB /home directory that will be encrypted:

```
livecd-iso-to-disk --home-size-mb 1024  Fedora-20-i686-Live-Desktop.iso /dev/sbd1
```

If you do not want the data encrypted, add the `--unencrypted-home` option when creating the disk.

Combining the overlay and the /home memory would require a command such as the following. In all, about 3GB of disk space would be required.

```
livecd-iso-to-disk --overlay-size-mb 512 --home-size-mb 1024 Fedora-20-Live-i686-Desktop.iso /dev/sbd
```

Fedora Logo

The Fedora logo depicts an *f* encased in a blue circle (see Figure 1-3). The logo is designed to represent three features of the Linux community and development: freedom, communication, and infinite possibilities. The *f* stands for "freedom," which melds into the infinity symbol, both encased in a speech bubble evoking communication (voice). The logo, then, represents free and open software with infinite possibilities developed through global communication. The idea is to evoke the spirit and purpose of Linux development as one of infinite freedom given a voice. The logo incorporates the four basic ideals of Fedora: open, free, innovative, and forward vision. See http://fedoraproject.org/wiki/Logo for more details.

Figure 1-3. *Fedora logo*

Linux

Linux is a fast, stable, and open source operating system that features development tools, desktops, and a large number of applications, ranging from office suites to multimedia applications. Linux was developed in the early 1990s by Linus Torvalds, along with other programmers around the world. Technically, Linux consists of the operating system program, referred to as the *kernel*, which is the part originally developed by Torvalds. But it has always been distributed with a large number of software applications. Linux has evolved as part of the open source software movement. Currently, hundreds of open source applications are available for Linux from the Fedora software repository and the Fedora-compliant third-party repository RPM Fusion (http://rpmfusion.org). Most of the GNOME and KDE applications are incorporated into the Fedora repository, using software packages that are Fedora-compliant. You should always check the Fedora repository first for the software you want.

Linux is distributed freely under a GNU General Public License, as specified by the Free Software Foundation, making it available to anyone who wants to use it. GNU (the acronym stands for "GNU's Not Unix") is a project initiated and managed by the Free Software Foundation to provide free software to users, programmers, and developers. Linux is copyrighted, not public domain. However, a GNU public license has much the same effect as the software being in the public domain. The GNU General Public License is designed to ensure that Linux remains free and, at the same time, standardized.

Open Source Software

Most Linux software is developed as open source software. This means that the source code for an application is distributed free with the application. Programmers can make their own contributions to a software package's development, modifying and correcting the source code. Linux is an open source operating system. Its source code is included in all its distributions and is freely available. Much of the software provided for Linux are also open source projects, as are the KDE and GNOME desktops, along with most of their applications. The LibreOffice office suite is an open source project based on the StarOffice office suite. You can find more information about the open source movement at www.opensource.org.

Open source software is protected by public licenses. These licenses prevent commercial companies from taking control of open source software by adding a few modifications of their own, copyrighting those changes, and selling the software as their own product. The most popular public license is the GNU General Public License provided by the

Free Software Foundation. This is the license that Linux is distributed under. The GNU General Public License (GPL) retains the copyright, freely licensing the software with the requirement that the software and any modifications made to it always be available for free. Other public licenses have also been created to support the demands of different kinds of open source projects. The GNU Lesser General Public License (LGPL) lets commercial applications use GNU licensed software libraries. The Qt Public License (QPL) lets open source developers use the Qt libraries essential to the KDE desktop.

Linux is currently copyrighted under a GNU public license provided by the Free Software Foundation, and it is often referred to as GNU software (see `www.gnu.org`). GNU software is distributed free, provided it is distributed to others for free. GNU software has proved both reliable and effective. Many of the popular Linux utilities, such as C compilers, shells, and editors, are GNU software applications. Installed with your Linux distribution are the GNU C++ and Lisp compilers, Vi and Emacs editors, and BASH and TCSH shells. In addition, there are many open source software projects that are licensed under the GNU General Public License. Chapter 4 describes in detail the process of downloading software applications from online repositories and installing them on your system.

Under the terms of the GNU General Public License, the original author retains the copyright, although anyone can modify the software and redistribute it, provided the source code is included, made public, and provided free of charge. Also, no restriction exists on selling the software or giving it away free. One distributor could charge for the software, while another could provide it free of charge. Major software companies also provide Linux versions of their most popular applications. For example, Oracle provides a Linux version of its Oracle database.

Linux Documentation

The Linux Documentation Project (LDP) developed a complete set of Linux manuals, available at `www.tldp.org`. The documentation includes a user guide, an introduction, and administrative guides. These are available in text, PostScript, or web page format. You can also find briefer explanations, in what are referred to as HOWTO documents. The Linux documentation for your installed software is available in your `/usr/share/doc` directory. As previously noted, some Fedora-specific documentation is available at `http://docs.fedoraproject.org`. The `www.gnome.org` site holds documentation for the GNOME desktop, while `www.kde.org` holds documentation for the KDE desktop.

■ ■ ■

Installation and Upgrade

This chapter describes the installation and upgrade procedures for Fedora 20 Linux. Fedora uses the Anaconda installation program. Designed to be simple and fast, it installs a core set of applications. A Fedora 20 installation guide is available online. First check the new Fedora installation guide at `http://docs.fedoraproject.org/en-US/Fedora/20/html/Installation_Guide/index.html`.

You can also link to this guide from the Fedora download page (right-side links) at `http://fedoraproject.org/en/get-fedora`.

If you are upgrading your system from Fedora 19, check the section for upgrading at the end of this chapter. There are several methods you can use, including a direct upgrade from the online repositories or upgrading using the Install DVD. A clean install, if possible, is always recommended over an upgrade, as conflicts can occur with some software if configuration file formats and supporting software libraries change too much. You can only upgrade to Fedora 20 from a Fedora 19 install. If you want to upgrade from Fedora 18, you first have to upgrade to Fedora 19, before you can upgrade to Fedora 20.

Obtaining the DVDs

To download Fedora 20 for installation from a DVD/CD-ROM drive, you download either the Fedora Install DVD image or a Fedora Live image. The Fedora Install and Live images are large files that have an `.iso` extension. Once they are downloaded, you burn them to a disk using your CD or DVD writer and burner software, such as the Brasero or K3b on Fedora.

There are ISO images for 64-bit system support and for the standard x86 (32-bit) support. Download the appropriate one. You cannot run a 64-bit version on an x86 (32-bit) system.

To obtain the current version of Fedora, go to the Fedora Project web site and click the Download tab (`http://fedoraproject.org`) to open the Get Fedora Main tab. There are several tabs you can use. The first holds a download button for the Fedora Live `iso` images. Desktops tab lists alternate spins, such as the KDE and LXDE versions. The Formats tab lists the DVD ISO image. At the bottom of the page, under the Download heading, the Full Download List link opens a page with other methods for downloading, such as BitTorrent and Jigdo.

Fedora 20 is also available on mirror sites. You can directly access a Fedora mirror site by entering the following URL: `http://download.fedoraproject.org`. You then need to navigate through the releases and the version directories (in this case 20) to find the Fedora and Live directories where the Fedora Install and Live `iso` images are kept.

You can also access a specific mirror at the following URL: `http://mirrors.fedoraproject.org/publiclist/`. The current Fedora mirror and their addresses are listed there. The addresses include web and FTP addresses. You can use an FTP client such as gFTP or Filezilla to perform a direct download.

Install Strategies: Making Use of Repositories

With Fedora 20, for installation, you can use either the Fedora Install DVD or one of two Live DVDs: Live Desktop with GNOME or Live KDE with KDE. The Fedora Install DVD allows you to download from specified repositories during installation, as well as to select the packages you want installed. It also includes a more extensive set of packages on disk than the Live DVD.

One major advantage of the Install DVD is its flexibility in the selection of software packages during installation. The Live DVDs install only a predetermined set of packages. The Fedora Install DVD allows you to select the packages you want to install, offering a much larger selection to choose from. The Fedora Install DVD is an extensive collection of the more popular applications (servers, development, and desktop).

The Fedora Install DVD also allows you to install packages from the Fedora repository, as well as from any associated repository you choose, such as http://rpmfusion.org. With the Fedora Install DVD, you can choose to download additional packages from the Fedora repository that are not included on the Fedora DVD.

Live DVD Advantages

Quick download of small install disk (about 900MB)

Ability to check out the desktop operations on a Live DVD interface

Quick installation of basic desktop (cannot select packages)

Ability, after installation, to add current packages from online repositories, as needed

Fedora Install DVD Advantages

Larger collection of initial software packages: servers, administration, multimedia, office (much larger initial download of Fedora DVD image: 3GB)

Ability to install more packages without having a high-speed connection for downloading from repositories

Ability to specify which packages to install

More extensive set of installation packages on hand for later installations

Installation Issues

Before you install, you should be aware of certain installation issues, such as dual-booting on a system with Windows, basic hardware requirements, storage options, and installation sources. Most of these concerns do not apply to a normal installation.

Installing Dual-Boot Systems

If you have another operating system already installed on the same computer as your Linux system, your system will be automatically configured by GRUB, the bootloader, for dual booting. Should you have Linux and Windows systems installed on your hard disks, GRUB will let you choose to boot either the Linux system or a Windows system. Manually configuring dual boots can be complicated. If you want a Windows system on your computer, you should install it first, if it is not already installed. Otherwise, Windows would overwrite the bootloader that a previous Linux system installed, cutting off access to the Linux system. You would then have to use the rescue option on the Install DVD disk to access your Linux system and then reinstall the GRUB bootloader.

Storage Configuration

Fedora Linux is very flexible, using a minimum of about 1GB RAM and 9GB hard disk space for everything. The minimal install uses as little as 100MB.

Linux usually runs on its own hard drive, although it can also run on a hard drive that contains a separate partition for a different operating system such as Windows. You can also install Fedora on specialized storage devices, such as Storage Area Networks (SANs).

If you want to install Linux and Windows on the same hard drive, and you have already installed Windows on your hard drive and configured it to take up the entire hard drive, you can choose to resize its partition to free up unused space during installation. The freed space can then be used for a Linux partition. See the Fedora installation guide for more details. You can also use a partition management software package—such as fdisk, Parted, or Partition Magic—to free up space before installation.

Install Sources (Install DVD)

Fedora supports several methods for installing Linux. You can install from a local source, such as a DVD/CD-ROM or a hard disk, or from a network or Internet source. For a network or Internet source, Fedora supports NFS, FTP, and HTTP installations. With FTP, you can install from an FTP site. With HTTP, you can install from a web site. NFS enables you to install over a local network. For a local source, you can install from a CD-ROM or a hard disk. You can start the installation process by booting from your DVD-ROM or from boot disks that can then use the DVD-ROM or hard disk repository. Fedora documentation covers each of these methods in detail.

To select an install source, you have to boot the install kernel, either from a Fedora 20 Install DVD or CDs, or from a Fedora Install DVD image file (you can also use USB disks and PXE servers). Press the ESC key to display the boot prompt. At the boot prompt, you enter the option linux askmethod, as shown following:

```
boot: linux askmethod
```

After you configure your language and keyboard, a dialog appears with options for local DVD/CD/hard drive, NFS directory, and URL (FTP and HTTP installations).

Basic Install with Fedora Live Desktop DVD

If you want to download and install Fedora quickly, you can simply install it from the Fedora Live Desktop DVD, which allows you to see what Fedora is like, without having to install it. Should you then want to install Fedora on your system, you can do so using just the Fedora Live Desktop DVD. You can then later download and install software you want to add from the Fedora repository.

The Fedora Live Desktop DVD includes the GNOME desktop. If you want to use the KDE desktop, you can use the Fedora Live KDE CD. The Fedora Live Desktop and Fedora Live KDE have i686 (32-bit x86 systems) and x86_64 (64-bit systems) versions.

The Fedora Live Desktop DVD installs a basic set of applications. Should you want to install a more complete set or install applications from other software repositories during the install process, you can use the Install DVD. The Install DVD is also a Live disk, and it allows you to run Fedora first. The Install DVD is much larger, though—about 3GB.

Once the installation program begins, you follow the instructions, screen by screen. Most of the time, you need only make simple selections. The installation program progresses through several phases. You perform some basic configuration, set up Linux partitions on your hard drive, configure your bootloader, then install the software packages.

Once you download and burn the Fedora Live Desktop DVD, place it in your DVD/CD drive, and boot your system from it. The system starts up automatically and displays the following menu (see Figure 2-1).

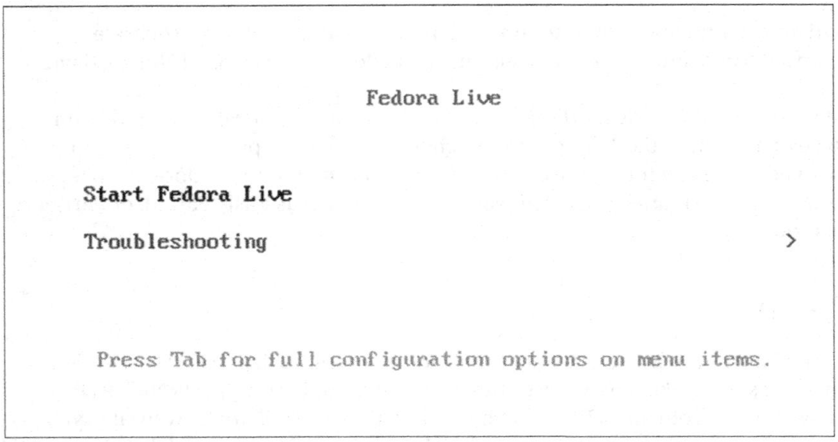

```
                              Fedora Live


 Start Fedora Live

 Troubleshooting                                              >



     Press Tab for full configuration options on menu items.

```

Figure 2-1. Install menu

By default, the first entry, Start Fedora 20, is selected. Press Enter to start Fedora. Should you need to add options directly to the boot command, press the Tab key. A command line is displayed on which you can enter the options (see Figure 2-2). Current options will already be listed. Use the Backspace key to delete and the arrow keys to move through the line. Press the ESC key to return to the menu.

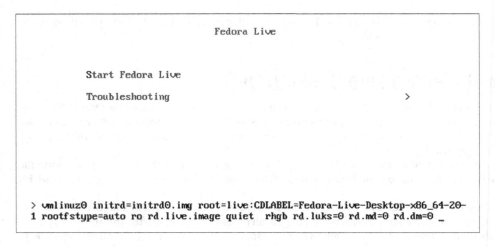

Figure 2-2. Install menu with boot options

For more startup options and testing, use the arrow key to move to the Troubleshooting entry. The Troubleshooting menu enables you to use the basic graphics mode, test the media, test the memory, and boot from a hard drive (see Figure 2-3). Use the arrow keys to move from one menu entry to the next, then press Enter to select the entry.

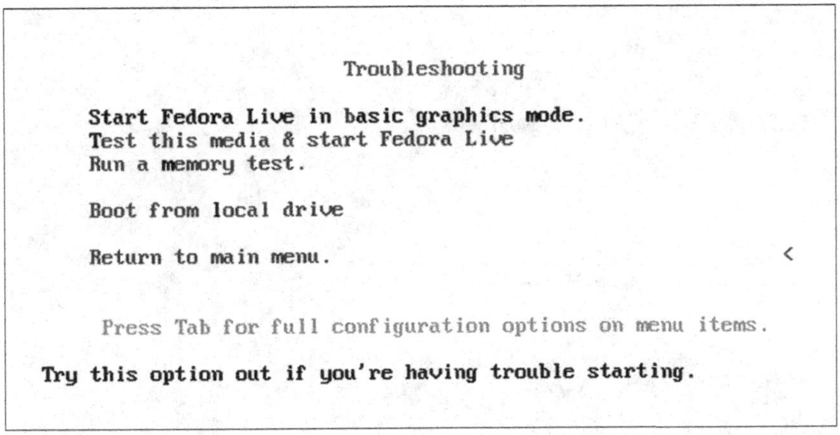

```
                   Troubleshooting

   Start Fedora Live in basic graphics mode.
   Test this media & start Fedora Live
   Run a memory test.

   Boot from local drive

   Return to main menu.                              <


      Press Tab for full configuration options on menu items.

   Try this option out if you're having trouble starting.
```

Figure 2-3. *Install menu's Troubleshooting options*

The first option (Start Fedora Live in basic graphics mode) starts up with basic video. The second (Test this media & start Fedora Live) will test if your DVD/CD media is okay. The third (Run a memory test) performs a hardware memory test. The last (Boot from local drive) will boot a local OS on a connected hard drive, if there is one.

When you first start the Live disk, you can choose whether to try Fedora or to install it (see Figure 2-4). If you want to install Fedora directly on your system, click the Install to Hard Drive icon to start the standard install procedure (Anaconda), as described in this chapter. You will be installing Fedora just as you would from the standard Fedora Install DVD. The only difference is that only the small subset of applications already on the Fedora Live Desktop DVD will be installed. You cannot choose applications during the install process.

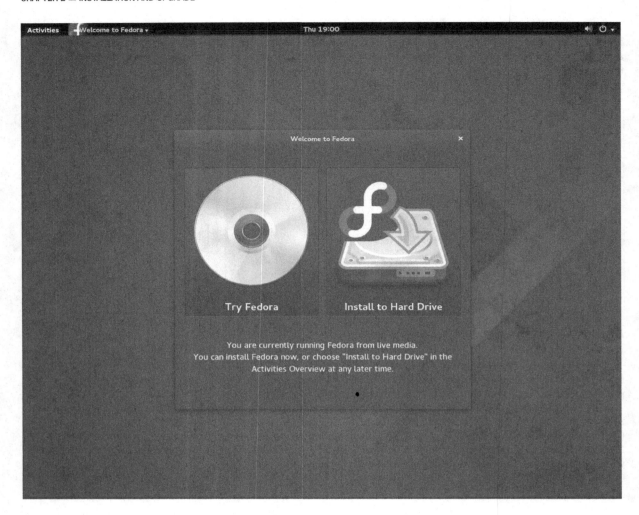

Figure 2-4. *Fedora Install window on Fedora Live Desktop*

You can also install Fedora at any time while you are using the Fedora Live Desktop. On Activities, there is an icon showing the hard disk and Fedora logo image with the label "Install to Hard Drive" (see Figure 2-5).

Figure 2-5. *Fedora Install icon on Fedora Live Desktop overview*

The install process has fewer options than the DVD install process but performs all necessary tasks. The screens shown are as follows:

Language: Select your language.

Installation Summary: Configure your installation. The Fedora Live install has four options: Date & Time, Keyboard, Installation Destination, and Network Configuration. A warning emblem is displayed on those options that require configuration. Ordinarily, only the Installation Destination option has a warning emblem. You cannot continue until all options with warnings are configured.

Date & Time: Select your city from the map or the pop-up menu or click the time zone on the map. This option may not have a warning on it but could still be incorrect. Be sure to check it.

Keyboard: Select and configure your keyboard, if you need to.

Installation Destination: Choose the hard drive to install on and set up your partitions. You have the option to manage your own. Once you finish configuring your installation summary items, the installation begins, showing a progress bar.

Network Configuration: Normally, this is automatically configured.

Configuration: As your system installs, you can set up a root password and configure a user.

Root Password: You are prompted to enter a password for the root user. This is your administrative password.

User Creation: Create a user for you to log in as. This should be the administrative user.

When the installation finishes, a simple Quit button will be displayed with a message to restart, to complete the installation. You can close at this point, to return to the Fedora Live Desktop, and then restart, to reboot to your installed system.

On reboot, you enter the Fedora Setup Agent procedure, where you can set the date and time and create a standard user, which you can use to log in for normal use (not as root). More users can be created later. After Setup, your login screen appears, and you can log in to your Fedora system.

Initially, you will have only the same software available as was on the Fedora Live Desktop DVD, but you can use the software manager to install other applications, such as LibreOffice. You may also have to update many of the applications installed from the Fedora Live Desktop DVD. Click the update notification icon on the message tray (lower right), which will appear automatically, to start the update process. Applications and updates are downloaded from the Fedora repository and installed.

Quick Install with the Install DVD

If you are installing from the Install DVD, installation is a straightforward process. The graphical installation is very easy to use. It provides full mouse support and explains each step with detailed instructions on a Help pane (you can also use the Install CDs).

> Most systems support booting a DVD-ROM or CD-ROM, although this support may have to be explicitly configured in the system BIOS.

> Also, if you know how you want Linux installed on your hard disk partitions, or if you are performing a simple update that uses the same partitions, installing Fedora 20 is a fairly simple process. Fedora 20 features an automatic partitioning function that will perform the partitioning for you.

> If you choose package collections from one of the preconfigured packaging installations, you will not have to select packages.

For a quick installation, you can simply start up the installation process, placing your Install DVD in your optical drive and starting up your system. Graphical installation is a matter of following the instructions in each window as you progress. Many of them are self-explanatory. The steps involved are the same as for the Fedora Live install, but with more options at the Installation Summary stage:

> **Language**: Select your language.

> **Installation Summary**: Configure your installation. The Install DVD has several options with three categories: Localization, Software, and System. For Localization, you can configure the Date & Time, the Keyboard, and Language Support. For Software, you configure the Installation Source and Software Selection. For Storage, you configure the Installation Destination and Network Configuration. A warning emblem is displayed on any options that require configuration. Ordinarily, only the Installation Destination option has a warning emblem. You cannot continue until all options with warnings are configured.

> **Date & Time**: Select your city from the map or the pop-up menu or click the time zone on the map. This option may not have a warning on it but could still be incorrect. Be sure to check it.

> **Keyboard**: Select and configure your keyboard, if you need to.

> **Language Support**: Install additional languages.

> **Installation Source**: Choose the install source, DVD, or network.

Software Selection: Choose the environment to install: a desktop (GNOME, KDE, Xfce, and LXDE), web server, development workstation, infrastructure server, or minimal install. With each option, you can also choose to install additional packages.

Installation Destination: Choose your hard drive to install on and set up your partitions. You have the option to choose from several default configurations or mange your own. Once you finish configuring your installation summary items, the installation begins, showing a progress bar.

Network Configuration: Configure your network connection. Configuration is the same as with the Live DVD. There are items for the root password and user creation.

Root Password: You are prompted to enter a password for the root user. This is your administrative password.

User Creation: Create a user for you to log in as. This should the administrative user.

After the installation, you will be asked to remove your DVD and click the Reboot button. This will reboot your system (do not reboot yourself).

On reboot, you will enter a Fedora Setup Agent procedure, where you will be able to set the date and time and create a standard user, which you can use to log in for normal use (not as root). More users can be created later. After the setup, your login screen will appear, and installation will be complete.

Installing Fedora Linux

First check the Fedora 20 installation guide before installing Fedora 20. It provides detailed screen examples.

```
http://docs.fedoraproject.org/en-US/Fedora/20/html/Installation_Guide/
```

The installation process used on Fedora is a screen-based program that takes you through all installation steps as one continuous procedure. You can use the mouse or the keyboard to make selections. When you finish with a screen, click the Continue button at the bottom to move to the next screen. If you have to move back to the previous screen, click Back. You can also use Tab, the arrow keys, the spacebar, and Enter to make selections. You have little to do other than make selections and choose options. Some screens provide a list of options from which you make a selection. The installation process will first install Linux on your system. It will then reboot and start a Setup process to let you set the time and date and create a user to log in as. The steps for each part of the procedure are delineated in the following sections.

As each screen appears in the installation, default entries will be selected, usually by the auto-probing capability of the installation program. Selected entries will appear highlighted. If these entries are correct, you can simply click Next to accept them and go on to the next screen.

Starting the Installation Program with the Install DVD

If your computer can boot from the DVD, you can start the installation directly from the Install DVD (or the Install CD). The installation program on the DVD Install disk presents you with a menu listing the following options:

Install Fedora 20

Test this media & install Fedora

Troubleshooting

Use the arrow keys to move from one menu entry to the next and then press Enter to select the entry. Should you need to add options, press the Tab key. A command line is displayed on which you can enter the options. Current options will be listed. Use the Backspace key to delete and arrow keys to move through the line. Press the ESC key to return to the menu.

The following Troubleshooting menu enables you to use the basic graphics mode, rescue a Fedora system, test the memory, and boot from a hard drive:

Install Fedora in basic graphics mode

Rescue a Fedora system

Run a memory test

Boot from local drive

Return to main menu

The install program (Anaconda) will automatically detect and configure your video card so that it can run a graphical interface for the install procedure. If it has difficulty configuring the video card, you can choose to use a basic video driver instead, which means you can still use the graphical install. Choose Install Fedora in Basic Graphics Mode from the Troubleshooting menu.

If you already installed Fedora 20, but the system fails for some reason, you can start up from the Install DVD and then choose Rescue a Fedora System from the Troubleshooting menu.

Check Disk Media

If you have doubts about the integrity of your DVD, you can choose to perform a check of the media before installation. This check can take several minutes. On the Install DVD, this option is on the first screen, and on Fedora Live, it is on the Troubleshooting screen. You can stop the check at any time by pressing the ESC key to enter a shell. Then type the exit command and press Enter to continue with the installation.

Initial Setup

If your basic device and hardware configuration were appropriately detected, a Welcome screen is displayed, with a Continue button on the lower-right corner. Once you've completed a step, you click Continue to move on. In some cases, you can click a Back button to return to a previous step.

■ **Tip** Your mouse will be automatically detected. If you have a USB mouse that is not being detected, try reinserting the USB connector several times. If you cannot use your mouse for some reason, you can use the Tab key to move to different components and buttons. Use the arrow keys to select and enter a list. Press the Enter key to click a selected button or entry. The Tab key will cycle through entries on a screen sequentially. To return to a button or component, just continue to press the Tab key.

On this screen, you are asked to select your language. A default language is already selected, usually English (see Figure 2-6).

Figure 2-6. *Welcome and language selection*

You are then presented with an Installation summary screen with categories for Localization and System (see Figure 2-7). For Localization, you can configure the Date & Time and the Keyboard. For System, you can configure the Installation Destination and Network Configuration. For Network Configuration, see the section "Network Configuration with the Fedora Install DVD/CDs," later in this chapter A warning emblem appears on options that have to be configured, usually only the Installation Destination, although you should also check that the date and time are correct. A Quit button at the bottom-left of the screen lets you quit the installation. A Begin Installation button at the bottom right remains grayed out as long as there are warnings. When all options are configured and the warning emblems disappear, this button becomes active, and you can click it to continue the installation.

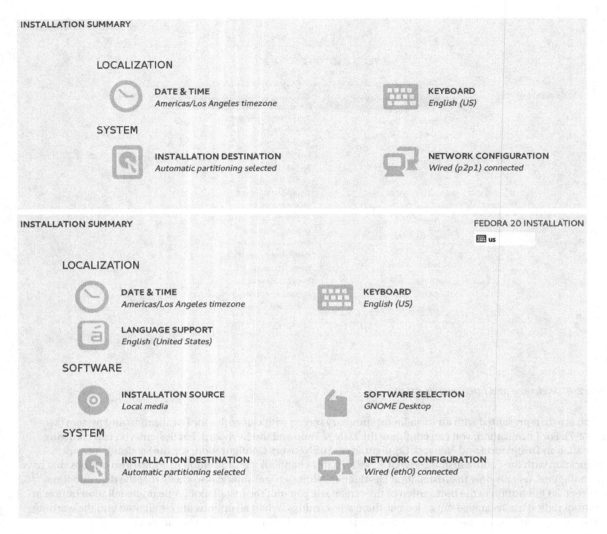

Figure 2-7. *Installation Summary screen (Fedora Live DVD and Fedora Install DVD)*

For the Install DVD, the Installation Summary screen shows a Software category with Installation Source and Software Selection (see Figure 2-7). On the DVD install, Localization also has a Language Support icon. See the section "Software Installation Configuration with the Fedora Install DVD/CDs," later in this chapter.

With warning emblems present, a warning appears at the bottom of the screen, as follows:

⚠ Please complete items marked with this icon before continuing to the next step.

To check and configure your time, date, and time zone, click the Date & Time icon. On the Date & Time screen, you have the option of setting the time zone by using a map or pop-up menu to specify your location (see Figure 2-8). The selected city will appear as the pop-up menu selection. There is a switch that lets you turn off network time (the time obtained from NTP servers). A configure button next to this switch opens a dialog that lets you specify the NTP time servers to use. Click the Done button in the upper-left corner when finished.

24

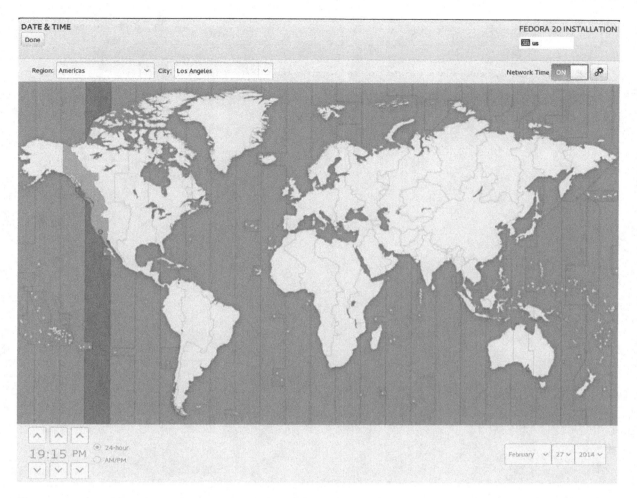

Figure 2-8. *Time zone selection*

On the Installation Summary page, click the Keyboard icon to configure your keyboard (see Figure 2-9). Keyboard layouts are listed on the left scroll box. Clicking the plus button at the bottom of this box lets you add another language layout. The Keyboard button displays an image showing all the keys. A text box to the right lets you test the keyboard. The Options button lets you specify which keys to use to switch layouts.

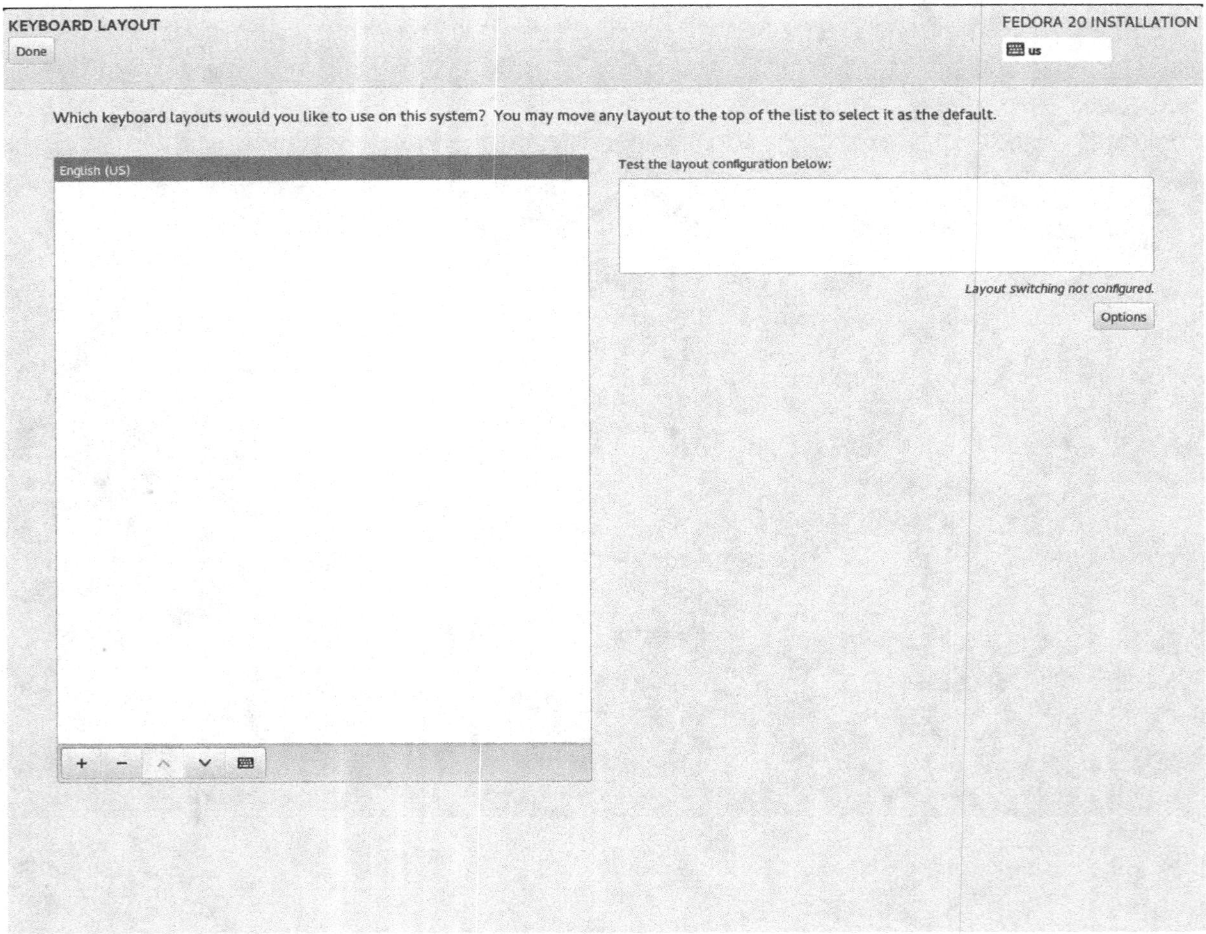

KEYBOARD LAYOUT

Done

FEDORA 20 INSTALLATION

us

Which keyboard layouts would you like to use on this system? You may move any layout to the top of the list to select it as the default.

English (US)

Test the layout configuration below:

Layout switching not configured.

Options

+   −   ∧   ∨

Figure 2-9. *Keyboard selection*

On the Installation Summary screen, click the Installation Destination icon to open the Installation Destination screen, where you can choose the hard disk device on which to perform the installation (see Figure 2-10).

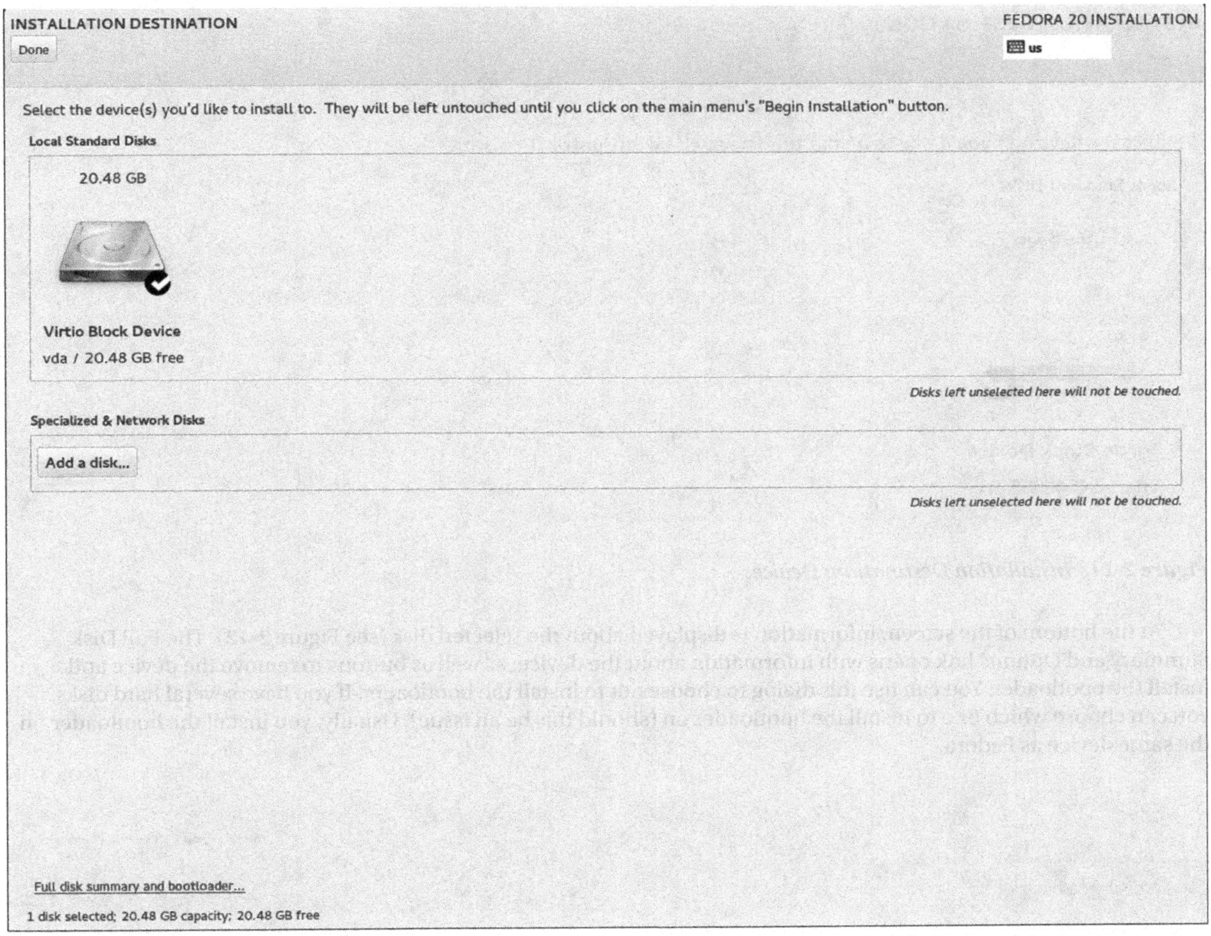

INSTALLATION DESTINATION

FEDORA 20 INSTALLATION

Done

⌨ us

Select the device(s) you'd like to install to. They will be left untouched until you click on the main menu's "Begin Installation" button.

Local Standard Disks

20.48 GB

Virtio Block Device
vda / 20.48 GB free

Disks left unselected here will not be touched.

Specialized & Network Disks

Add a disk...

Disks left unselected here will not be touched.

Full disk summary and bootloader...

1 disk selected; 20.48 GB capacity; 20.48 GB free

Figure 2-10. *Installation Destination*

The top icon bar shows your installation devices. The local drives are shown under the Local Standard Disks heading (see Figure 2-11). If you have only a single local hard drive, that drive is automatically selected for you.

Figure 2-11. *Installation Destination: Devices*

At the bottom of the screen, information is displayed about the selected disk (see Figure 2-12). The Full Disk Summary and Options link opens with information about the device, as well as buttons to remove the device and install the bootloader. You can use this dialog to choose not to install the bootloader. If you have several hard disks, you can choose which one to install the bootloader on (should this be an issue). Usually, you install the bootloader on the same device as Fedora.

Figure 2-12. *Installation Destination: Information and options*

A check box to the right lets you encrypt the device.

When you have selected the device you want, click the Continue button on the lower-right side of the screen. If the destination disk has enough space, the Installation Options dialog appears, telling you so and showing the partition type (see Figure 2-13). At this point, you can simply click the Continue button to let Fedora automatically configure and partition your hard disk and perform the installation.

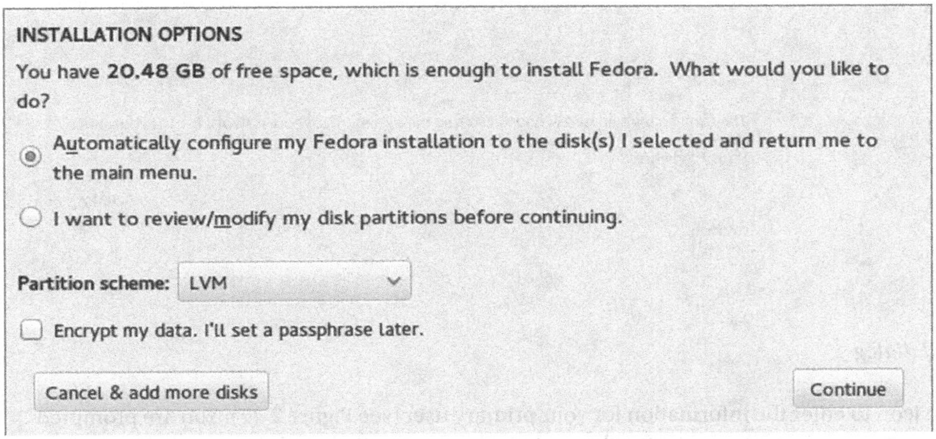

INSTALLATION OPTIONS

You have **20.48 GB** of free space, which is enough to install Fedora. What would you like to do?

◉ A̲utomatically configure my Fedora installation to the disk(s) I selected and return me to the main menu.

○ I want to review/m̲odify my disk partitions before continuing.

Partition scheme: LVM   ⌄

☐ Encrypt my data. I'll set a passphrase later.

[Cancel & add more disks]   [Continue]

Figure 2-13. Installation options

On the Installation Options screen, the LVM partition scheme is chosen by default. From the drop-down menu, you can choose a different scheme. The options are LVM, BTRFS (RAID), and Standard (ext4).

Upon pressing Continue from the Installation Options screen, your installation begins with a progress bar at the bottom of the screen (see Figure 2-14).

☼ Installing software 46%

Figure 2-14. Installation progress bar

At the same time, you're prompted to set the root password (see Figure 2-15). A warning emblem is displayed on the Root Password icon on the Configuration screen.

USER SETTINGS

ROOT PASSWORD
Root password is not set

USER CREATION
No user will be created

Figure 2-15. Configuration: Root Password

Click the Root Password icon to open the Root Password dialog. It has text boxes for entering the root user password (**administrator**). (See Figure 2-16.) Click the Done button at the upper left when you're finished. The warning emblem on the Root Password icon disappears.

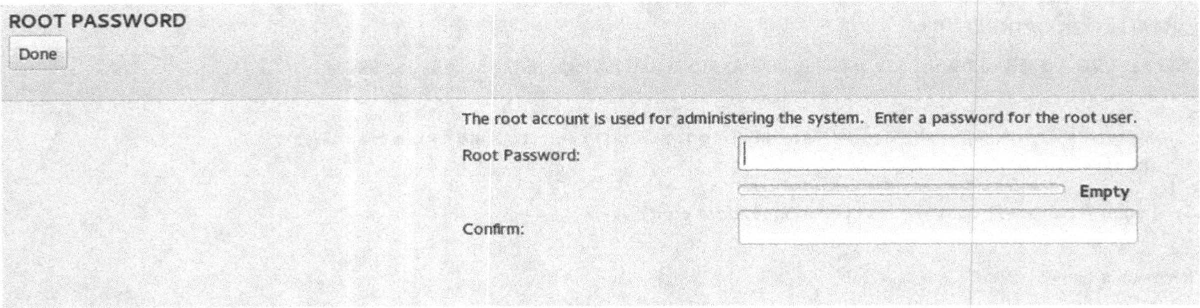

ROOT PASSWORD

Done

The root account is used for administering the system. Enter a password for the root user.

Root Password:

Empty

Confirm:

Figure 2-16. *Root Password dialog*

Click the User Creation icon to enter the information for your primary user (see Figure 2-17). You are prompted to enter the name, username, and password. You can also choose to make the user the administrator and to require a password for the user account. Click the Advanced button to open a dialog in which you can specify the home directory, user and group ids, and group memberships (see Figure 2-18). The home directory is already set up by default to be the name of the user in the /home directory. User and group ids are given automatically, but you can set them manually. You can also add groups for the user.

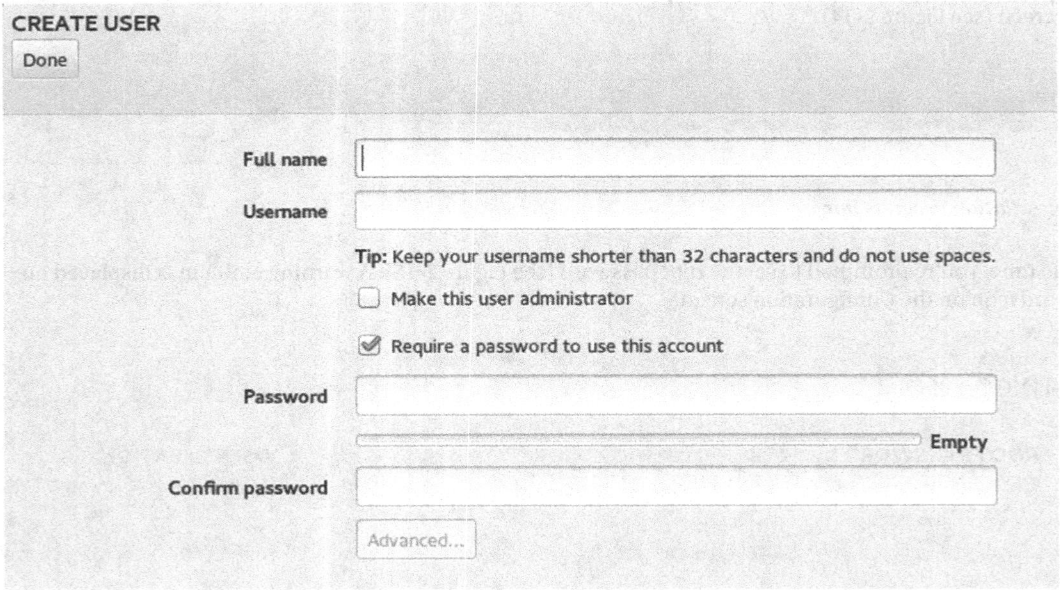

CREATE USER

Done

Full name

Username

Tip: Keep your username shorter than 32 characters and do not use spaces.

☐ Make this user administrator

☑ Require a password to use this account

Password

Empty

Confirm password

Advanced...

Figure 2-17. *Create User dialog*

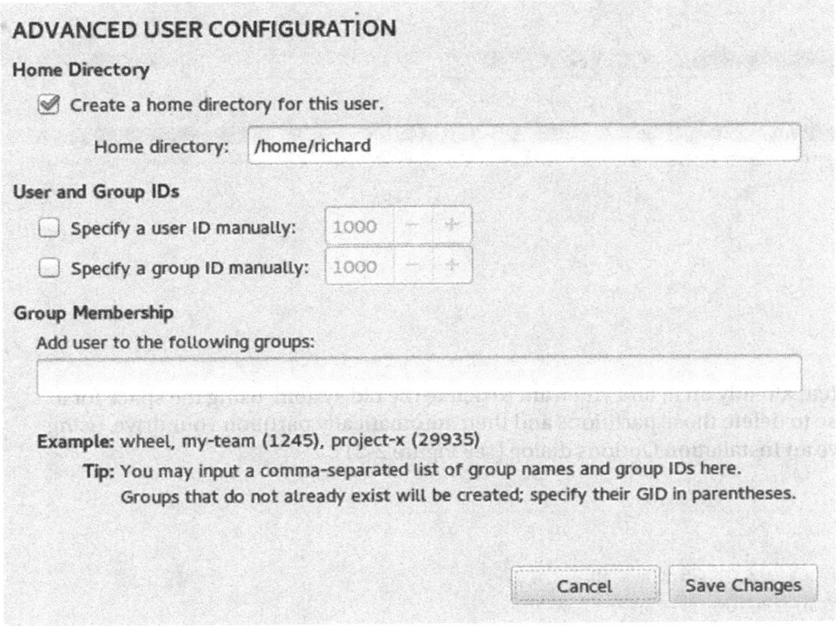

ADVANCED USER CONFIGURATION

Home Directory

☑ Create a home directory for this user.

Home directory: /home/richard

User and Group IDs

☐ Specify a user ID manually: 1000 − +

☐ Specify a group ID manually: 1000 − +

Group Membership

Add user to the following groups:

Example: wheel, my-team (1245), project-x (29935)

Tip: You may input a comma-separated list of group names and group IDs here.
Groups that do not already exist will be created; specify their GID in parentheses.

Cancel   Save Changes

Figure 2-18. *Advanced User Configuration*

Once you have finished creating the user, click the Done button to return to the Configuration screen. Both the Root Password and User Creation items show that you have completed those tasks (see Figure 2-19). The installation continues, as shown, on the progress bar at the bottom of the screen.

CONFIGURATION

USER SETTINGS

ROOT PASSWORD
Root password is set

USER CREATION
User richard will be created

Figure 2-19. *Configuration completed*

When installation finishes, a completion message is displayed at the bottom of the screen. The Fedora Live installation shows a Quit button that returns you to the Fedora Live Desktop (see Figure 2-20). The Install DVD shows a Reboot button.

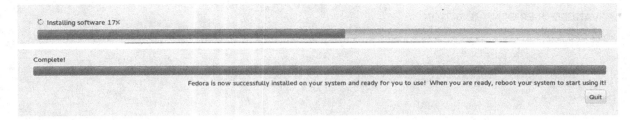

Figure 2-20. *Installation complete*

Automatic Partitioning

If you have a system with a Linux system already on it, and you want to delete the old system, using the space for a new Fedora 20 system, you can choose to delete those partitions and then automatically partition your drive, using the free space. You will initially receive an Installation Options dialog (see Figure 2-21).

> **INSTALLATION OPTIONS**
>
> Your current **Fedora** software selection requires **3.03 GB** of available space. The disks you've selected have the following amounts of free space:
>
> You don't have enough space available to install Fedora, but we can help you reclaim space by shrinking or removing existing partitions.
>
> **1.87 MB** Free space available for use.
>
> **7.93 GB** Free space unavailable but reclaimable from existing partitions.
>
> **16.38 GB** Space in selected disks reclaimable by deleting existing partitions.
>
> ⊞ Partition scheme configuration
>
> ☐ I don't need help; let me customize disk partitioning.
>
> [Cancel & add more disks]   [Modify software selection]   [Reclaim space]

Figure 2-21. *Installation options (full hard drive)*

Click the Reclaim Space button to open the Reclaim Disk Space dialog, which lists all your current partitions (see Figure 2-22). Should you also have a Windows system on your hard drive, it will have a partition type of ntfs. You should be careful to leave it alone. To free up space, click a partition entry, then click the Delete button located just below the list of partitions. If you make a mistake and mark the wrong partition for deletion, you can unmark the partition by clicking the partition again and then the Preserve button.

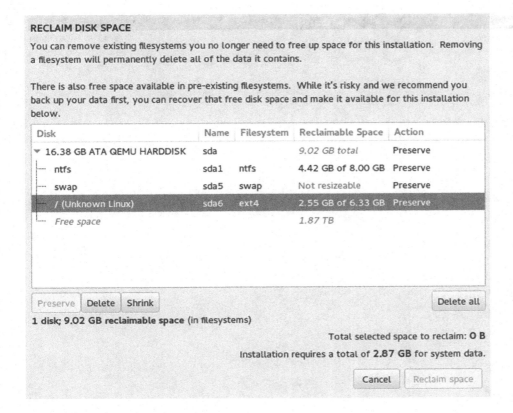

RECLAIM DISK SPACE

You can remove existing filesystems you no longer need to free up space for this installation. Removing a filesystem will permanently delete all of the data it contains.

There is also free space available in pre-existing filesystems. While it's risky and we recommend you back up your data first, you can recover that free disk space and make it available for this installation below.

Disk	Name	Filesystem	Reclaimable Space	Action
▼ 16.38 GB ATA QEMU HARDDISK	sda		*9.02 GB total*	Preserve
┊┈ ntfs	sda1	ntfs	4.42 GB of 8.00 GB	Preserve
┊┈ swap	sda5	swap	*Not resizeable*	Preserve
┊┈ / (Unknown Linux)	sda6	ext4	2.55 GB of 6.33 GB	Preserve
┊┈ *Free space*			*1.87 TB*	

Preserve | Delete | Shrink | Delete all

1 disk; 9.02 GB reclaimable space (in filesystems)

Total selected space to reclaim: **0 B**

Installation requires a total of **2.87 GB** for system data.

Cancel | Reclaim space

Figure 2-22. *Reclaim Disk Space dialog*

Once you have marked all the old partitions for deletion, you click the Reclaim Space button at the lower right. Your free space is automatically partitioned, and the Installation Summary screen shows automatic partitioning for the Installation Destination item.

Manual Partitioning: Partitions, BTRFS, RAID, and Logical Volumes

On the Installation Options screen, you are given the option of customizing the disk partitioning. Click the Let Me Customize the Partitioning of the Disks Instead check box, and then click the Continue button. This opens the Manual Partitioning screen (see Figure 2-23). The left-side scroll box lists the partitions as you create them. If your hard drive is blank, it will be empty. The button bar at the bottom of the scroll box has buttons for adding partitions, deleting them, displaying information, and for the Help dialog (right icon), as shown here.

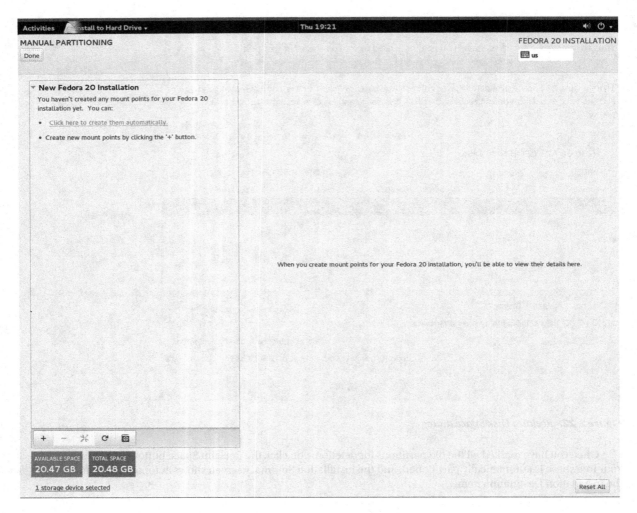

Figure 2-23. *Manual Partitioning dialog*

It is highly recommended that you read through the Help dialog, which provides a very detailed explanation of how to configure your partitions.

You are asked to designate the Linux partitions and hard disk configurations you want to use on your hard drives. Fedora provides automatic partitioning options if you just want to use available drives and free space for your Linux system. You can create specific partitions, configure RAID devices, or set up logical volumes (LVM).

No partitions will be changed or formatted until you leave the Manual Partitioning screen and, from the Installation Summary screen, you click the Continue button. You can opt out of the installation any time until that point, and your original partitions will remain untouched. A default layout sets up a swap partition, a boot partition of type ext4 (Linux native) for the kernel, and an LVM partition that will hold all your applications and files.

Initially, with no Linux partition set up and space available, you can click the Click Here to Create These Automatically link, to create a default set of Fedora partitions. These are a boot, root, and swap partition (see Figure 2-24). The root and swap partitions are LVM volumes. The boot partition is a standard ext4 partition. This is the default set of partitions used, should you skip manual partitioning.

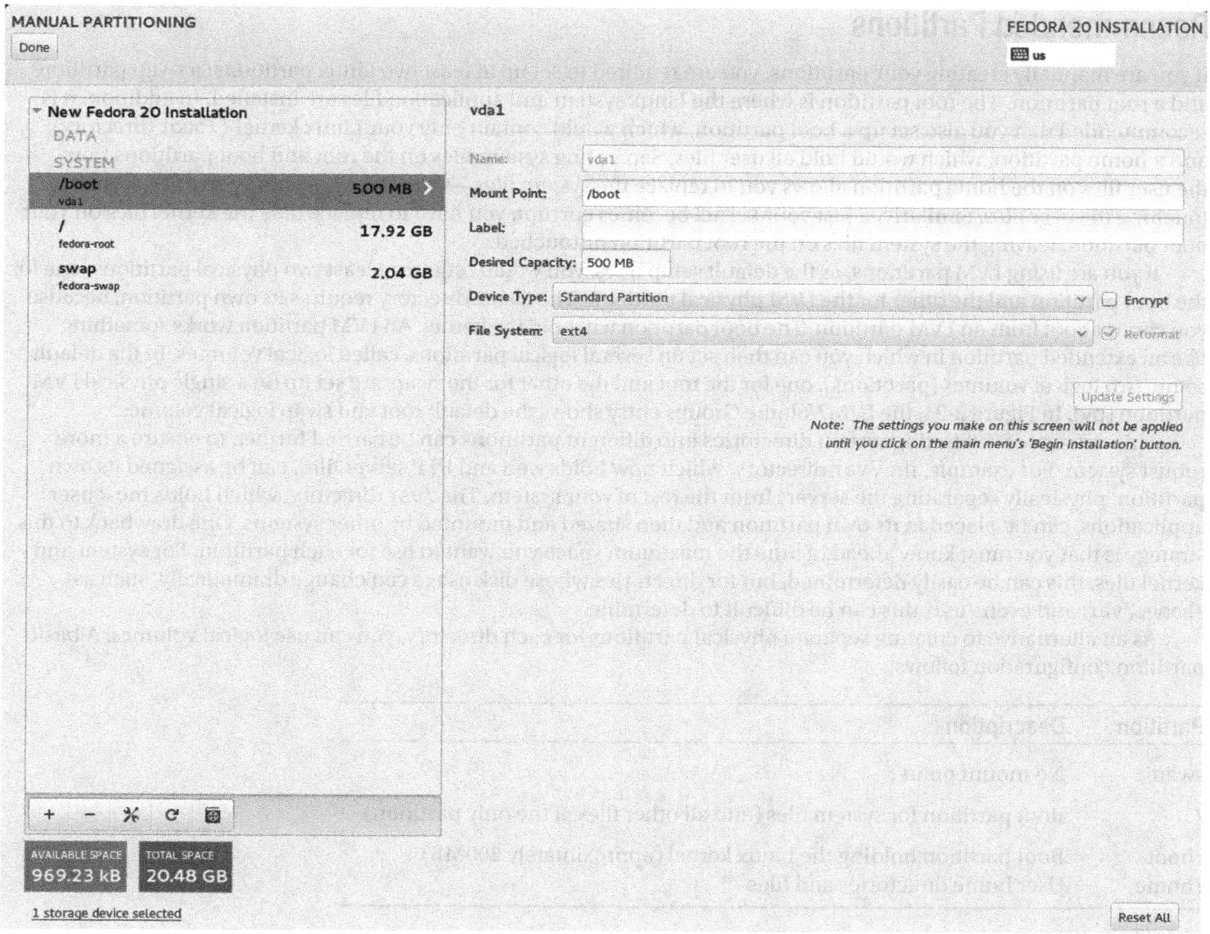

MANUAL PARTITIONING

FEDORA 20 INSTALLATION

⌨ us

Done

▾ New Fedora 20 Installation

DATA

SYSTEM

/boot vda1	**500 MB** ❯
/ fedora-root	**17.92 GB**
swap fedora-swap	**2.04 GB**

vda1

Name: | vda1

Mount Point: | /boot

Label: |

Desired Capacity: | 500 MB

Device Type: | Standard Partition ▾ | ☐ Encrypt

File System: | ext4 ▾ | ☑ Reformat

Update Settings

Note: The settings you make on this screen will not be applied until you click on the main menu's 'Begin installation' button.

+ − ✳ ⟳ ▣

AVAILABLE SPACE	TOTAL SPACE
969.23 kB	**20.48 GB**

1 storage device selected

Reset All

Figure 2-24. *Default partitions*

The side pane lists the partitions, showing the device name and size. The right pane shows the configuration for a selected partition. It displays the name, mount point, label, size, device type, file system, and encryption option. You can make changes to any of the entries and click the Apply Changes button, to change the configuration. (No changes are actually made to the hard disk until you begin the software installation.)

If you are reviewing after default partitioning, the hard disk partitions set up for you are displayed. The pane will show the specific partitions that will be created for your system. The default partitioning will set up an ext4 partition to be used as the boot partition. This is a small partition holding the Linux kernel and boot configuration information (/boot directory). An LVM physical volume will also be created, on which an LVM logical group and volumes will be set up. The LVM logical group will be listed at the top, under LVM Volume Groups. The volume group used for the default configuration will have a name such as fedora. You can edit these entries and change the names to ones you prefer, by clicking the Modify button.

Recommended Partitions

If you are manually creating your partitions, you are required to set up at least two Linux partitions: a swap partition and a root partition. The root partition is where the Linux system and application files are installed. In addition, it is recommended that you also set up a boot partition, which would contain only your Linux kernel (/boot directory), and a home partition, which would hold all user files. Separating system files on the root and boot partitions from the user files on the home partition allows you to replace the system files—should they become corrupt—without touching the user files. Similarly, if just your kernel becomes corrupt, you have to replace only the kernel files on your boot partition, leaving the system files on the root partition untouched.

If you are using LVM partitions, as the default setup does, you would require at least two physical partitions: one for the boot partition and the other for the LVM physical partition. The /boot directory requires its own partition, because you cannot boot from an LVM partition. The boot partition will hold the kernel. An LVM partition works something like an extended partition in which you can then set up several logical partitions, called logical volumes. In the default setup, two logical volumes (partitions), one for the root and the other for the swap, are set up on a single physical LVM partition (pv). In Figure 2-24, the LVM Volume Groups entry shows the default root and swap logical volumes.

This strategy of separating system directories into different partitions can be carried further, to ensure a more robust system. For example, the /var directory, which now holds web and FTP server files, can be assigned its own partition, physically separating the servers from the rest of your system. The /usr directory, which holds most user applications, can be placed in its own partition and then shared and mounted by other systems. One drawback to this strategy is that you must know ahead of time the maximum space you want to use for each partition. For system and kernel files, this can be easily determined, but for directories whose disk usage can change dramatically, such as /home, /var, and even /usr, this can be difficult to determine.

As an alternative to creating separate physical partitions for each directory, you can use logical volumes. A basic partition configuration follows:

Partition	Description
swap	No mount point
/	Root partition for system files (and all other files, if the only partition)
/boot	Boot partition holding the Linux kernel (approximately 200MB)
/home	User home directories and files

Except for the swap partition, when setting up a Linux partition, you must specify a mount point. A *mount point* is a directory in which the files on that partition are connected to the overall Linux file structure for your system. The mount point for your root partition is the root directory, represented by a single slash (/). The mount point for your boot partition is the path /boot. For a user's partition, it's /home.

The size of the swap partition should be the same as your RAM memory, with a recommended minimum size of 64MB. With 4GB of RAM, you should use a 4GB swap partition.

Creating Partitions

To create a new partition, click the Plus button to display the Add a New Mount Point dialog, where you can choose the mount point and the size. Mount points begin with a slash (/). If you enter a slash, a drop-down menu appears under the Mount Point text box. The common mount points for file systems are /, /boot, /home, /usr, and /var. If you have a root and boot system already configured, only the /home, /usr, and /var entries appear.

The new partition appears on the Manual Partitioning screen. Select it to configure the partition. You can set the size (in megabytes), the device type, and the file system type. For the device type, you have the choice of a Standard Partition, BTRFS, Software RAID, and LVM. For Software RAID, you can create RAID partitions and RAID devices, to which you can assign RAID partitions. For LVM, you can create Logical Volumes (logical partitions to which physical partitions are assigned) and a Volume Group (the group to which logical volumes are assigned). Physical volumes are set up for you.

There are several kinds of file systems supported during installation: ext2, ext3, ext4, swap, btrfs, xfs, and vfat. The ext2 and ext3 partitions are older forms of the Linux standard partition type, ext4.

To make configuration changes to any partition, select it, make the changes to its entries, and click the Apply Changes button.

Logical Volumes

Fedora supports Logical Volume Management (LVM), which enables you to create logical volumes that you can use instead of hard disk partitions directly. LVM provides a more flexible and powerful way of dealing with disk storage, organizing physical partitions into logical volumes in which memory can be managed easily. Disk storage for a logical volume is treated as one pool of memory, though the volume may in fact contain several hard disk partitions on different hard disks. There is one restriction. The boot partition cannot be a logical volume. You still have to create a separate hard disk partition as your boot partition with the /boot mount point in which your kernel will be installed.

If you selected default partitioning, the /boot partition will have already been set up for you, along with an LVM volume partition for the rest of the system. A logical group will be set up with volumes for both the swap and root partitions. The logical group will be labeled with a name such as fedora. You can change these names by editing the logical group and volumes during installation. Click the Modify button to the right of the volume group entry.

Creating logical volumes is now a simple process of specifying the LVM device type and the volume group. The physical LVM partitions that logical volumes are based on are generated automatically by Fedora. For a particular LVM partition (logical volume), you will have a Volume Group entry in which you can specify the volume group it belongs to.

RAID and BTRFS

You also have the option of creating RAID devices. Such devices are for use with the Linux software RAID service, and shouldn't be used for your motherboard RAID devices, as these are automatically detected. If you have already decided to use the motherboard RAID support, you do not require Software RAID. Linux supports both motherboard/computer RAID devices (DMRAID), as well as its own Linux Software RAID. The RAID option is visible only if you have selected two or more hard disks.

BTRFS is the new file system format, still under development. If operates much like RAID devices, providing RAID0 (stripe), RAID (mirrors), and RAID10 (optimization) levels of support. You create the BTRFS sub-volumes, and the installer creates the BTRFS volume for you.

Software Installation Configuration with the Fedora Install DVD/CDs

If you are installing from the Install DVD or the set of Install CDs, you have a more detailed and complex set of software package install options (see Figure 2-25). The Fedora Install DVD currently supports several preselection install environments, including the popular desktops, development workstation, web and infrastructure servers, and a minimal install. The desktop environments are GNOME, KDE, Xfce, LXDE, and Sugar. For each environment, there are different sets of add-ons that you can choose from. For GNOME, you can add the design suite, LibreOffice, and development tools. KDE includes KDE Office and KDE multimedia support. The Development and Creative Workstation has Design Suite, MySQL, and PostgreSQL databases, and programming tools such as Perl, Python, PHP, Ruby, and GCC. You can choose only one environment, but for any given environment, you can include as many add-ons as you wish.

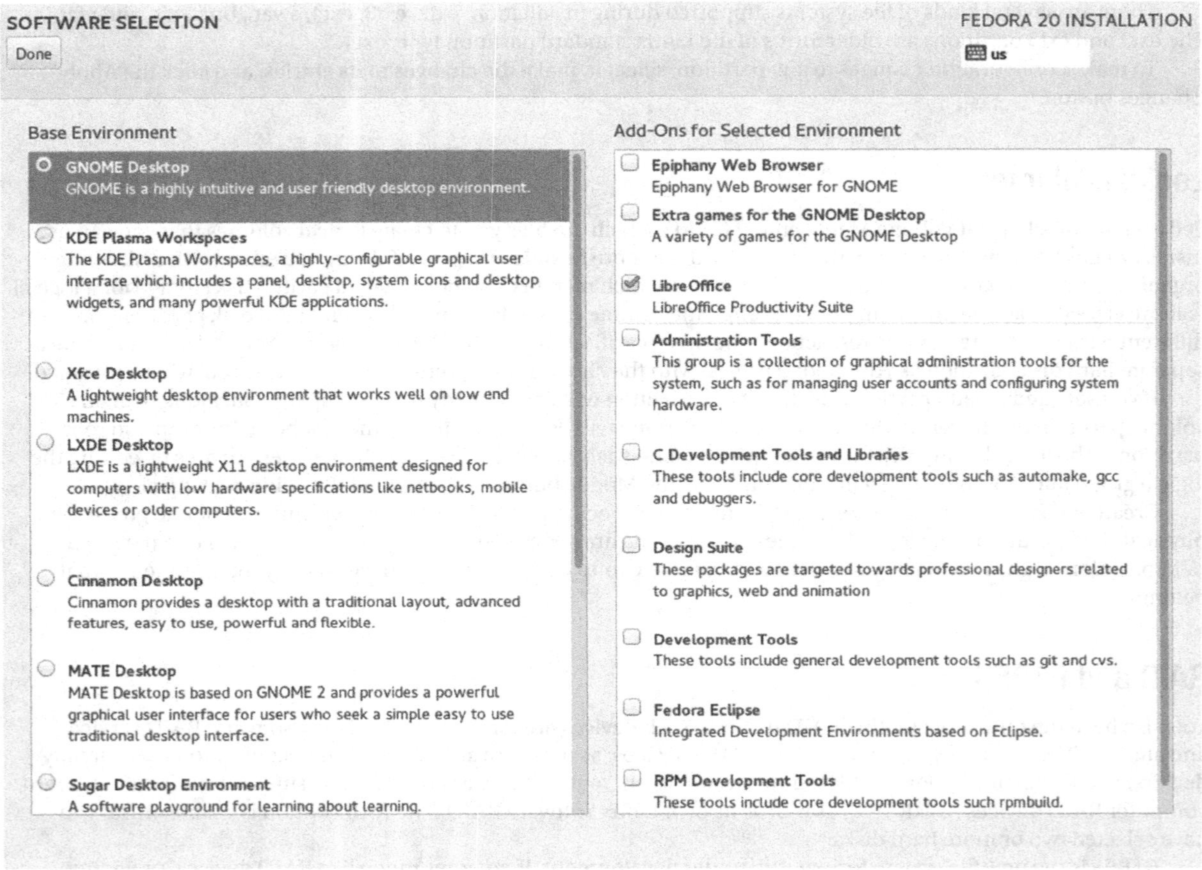

SOFTWARE SELECTION

Done

FEDORA 20 INSTALLATION

⌨ us

Base Environment

○ **GNOME Desktop**
GNOME is a highly intuitive and user friendly desktop environment.

○ **KDE Plasma Workspaces**
The KDE Plasma Workspaces, a highly-configurable graphical user interface which includes a panel, desktop, system icons and desktop widgets, and many powerful KDE applications.

○ **Xfce Desktop**
A lightweight desktop environment that works well on low end machines.

○ **LXDE Desktop**
LXDE is a lightweight X11 desktop environment designed for computers with low hardware specifications like netbooks, mobile devices or older computers.

○ **Cinnamon Desktop**
Cinnamon provides a desktop with a traditional layout, advanced features, easy to use, powerful and flexible.

○ **MATE Desktop**
MATE Desktop is based on GNOME 2 and provides a powerful graphical user interface for users who seek a simple easy to use traditional desktop interface.

○ **Sugar Desktop Environment**
A software playground for learning about learning.

Add-Ons for Selected Environment

☐ **Epiphany Web Browser**
Epiphany Web Browser for GNOME

☐ **Extra games for the GNOME Desktop**
A variety of games for the GNOME Desktop

☑ **LibreOffice**
LibreOffice Productivity Suite

☐ **Administration Tools**
This group is a collection of graphical administration tools for the system, such as for managing user accounts and configuring system hardware.

☐ **C Development Tools and Libraries**
These tools include core development tools such as automake, gcc and debuggers.

☐ **Design Suite**
These packages are targeted towards professional designers related to graphics, web and animation

☐ **Development Tools**
These tools include general development tools such as git and cvs.

☐ **Fedora Eclipse**
Integrated Development Environments based on Eclipse.

☐ **RPM Development Tools**
These tools include core development tools such rpmbuild.

Figure 2-25. *Software Selection dialog*

GRUB on Restart

When you reboot, a GRUB bootloader briefly displays a startup message indicating which operating system on your disk will be started. The default is usually your Linux system. If Fedora is the only operating system on your system, GRUB will skip the startup message and the GRUB menu access and start Fedora immediately. Fedora 20 uses GRUB2. You can find out more about GRUB2 at http://fedoraproject.org/wiki/GRUB_2.

If you have encrypted your hard disk partitions, you are then prompted to enter the LUKS passphrase for them. A standard installation will prompt for the same passphrase for your swap and root partitions on your LVM file system. The prompt will use the physical partition name used for the LVM group, in this example, /dev/sda2. There are two prompts: one for the LVM volume for the root file system, and one for the LVM volume swap file system.

The startup screen then shows the progress of your boot procedures. If your graphics card supports kernel mode settings, the Plymouth boot-up screen will be displayed; otherwise, a simple progress bar is shown. You can press the ESC key to see startup messages.

GNOME Initial Setup and GNOME Help

The first time you start up Fedora, the GNOME initial setup is run (see Figure 2-26), from which you confirm your choice of language and keyboard, choose a wireless connection, and configure a cloud connection.

Figure 2-26. *GNOME initial setup*

After completing the setup, the GNOME Help browser starts up at the Getting Started page (see Figure 2-27). The page displays icons for animations on basic tasks, such as starting applications using the dash, responding to messages using the message tray, and managing windows and workspaces.

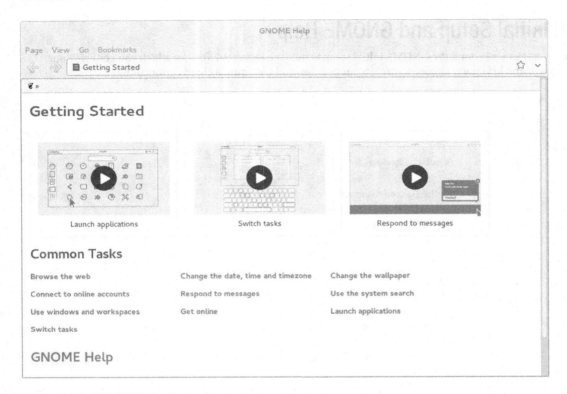

Figure 2-27. *GNOME Help: Getting Started animations*

Upgrading Fedora Linux

You can only upgrade an existing Fedora 19 system to Fedora 20. If you have Fedora 18, you first have to upgrade to Fedora 19. Be sure to back up your system, including the home, etc., and boot directories. The older methods of upgrading—preupgrade and the Install DVD—are no longer supported and do not work. Instead, you can use FedUp, which upgrades either from the repositories (such as preupgrade) or from a DVD (such as the Install DVD). You can find out more about FedUp at: `http://fedoraproject.org/wiki/FedUp`.

FedUp downloads all the packages for the new distribution in the background, allowing you to continue to use your system. The updated versions of these packages are downloaded, providing the most recent package versions. Be sure to first update the software on your current system. Fedora 19 software has to be updated to the most recent version, before it can be upgraded to Fedora 20. When you restart your system, the downloaded packages are installed.

On a Fedora 19 system, install the `fedup` package. This installs the FedUp client, via the `fedup-cli` command. You run this command from a terminal window as the root user. Open a terminal window; use the `su` command to log in as the root user; and then enter the `fedup-cli` command, specifying a network (`--network`), iso (`--iso`), or device (`--device`) source. The `--network` option downloads from the Fedora repository. You must specify only the version, such as 20 for Fedora 20. For `--iso`, you can use an ISO DVD image file instead. For `--device`, you reference a DVD-ROM containing a Fedora Install DVD. The `--network` option is recommended, as this provides you with the most recent updates from the Fedora repository.

For a --network update, enter the following commands:

```
su
fedup-cli --network  20
```

The repositories are located, then the packages are downloaded. You can interrupt the download at any time and restart it later. The download will start up from where it left off, after verifying that those packages already downloaded.

Should you use a device, specify its mount directory. This is usually the /var/run directory, the name of the user, and the name of the DVD, such as "Fedora 20 x86_64." The DVD mount directory name has spaces, so enclose the entire mount directory in quotes. The following upgrades are from a DVD mounted by the user Richard:

```
fedup-cli --device "/var/run/richard/Fedora 20 x86_64"
```

For a download ISO file, specify the full pathname of the ISO file. The full pathname for an ISO file in a user directory begins with /home and the name of the user. Include the full name of the ISO file. The following upgrades are from the Fedora DVD 64-bit ISO file located in the user Richard's Download directory.

```
fedup-cli --iso /home/richard/Download/Fedora-20-x86_64-DVD.iso
```

GRUB is not upgraded by the upgrade process. You have to reinstall and upgrade GRUB2 manually. See the following section on reinstalling the bootloader. Also, check the GRUB2 page (http://fedoraproject.org/wiki/GRUB_2), and for UEFI systems, see the FedUp page for instructions.

Creating Boot Disks

You can use mkbootdisk to create a boot CD-ROM. Use the --iso option and the --device option with the name of an ISO image file to create (install the mkbootdisk package). You then use CD-ROM-burning software to create the CD-ROM from the image file. The following example creates a CD-ROM image file called mybootcd.iso that can be used as a boot CD-ROM:

```
mkbootdisk --iso --device mybootcd.iso  3.7.4-204.fc20.x86_64
```

Booting in Rescue Mode

If you are not able to boot or access your system, it may be due to conflicting configurations, libraries, or applications. In this case, you can boot your Linux system in a rescue mode and then edit configuration files with a text editor, remove the suspect libraries, or reinstall damaged software with yum. To enter the rescue mode, run the Fedora DVD-ROM and then select Rescue a Fedora System from the Troubleshooting menu.

You will boot into the command-line mode with your system's files mounted at /mnt/sysimage. You will be notified that you can use the chroot command to set the / directory as the root. Issue the following command at the command-line prompt:

```
chroot /mnt/sysimage
```

Use the cd command to move between directories. Check /etc and /etc/sysconfig for your configuration files. You can use vi to edit your files and the less command to view them. To reinstall files, use the yum install command. When you are finished, use the exit command.

If you have a command-line system, enter the following at the boot prompt:

```
linux rescue
```

Reinstalling the Bootloader

If you have a dual-boot system, where you are running Windows and Linux on the same machine, you may run into a situation where you have to reinstall your GRUB bootloader. This problem occurs if you have installed a new version of Windows after installing Linux. Windows will automatically overwrite your bootloader (alternatively, you could install your bootloader on your Linux partition instead of the MBR). You will no longer be able to access your Linux system.

All you have to do is to reinstall your bootloader. First, boot from your Fedora Install DVD installation disk (not the Live DVD). From the Troubleshooting menu, select Rescue a Fedora System.

As noted in the preceding section, this boots your system in rescue mode. Then use grub2-install and the device name of your first partition to install the bootloader. At the prompt, enter

```
grub-install /dev/sda1
```

This will reinstall your current GRUB bootloader, assuming that Windows is included in the GRUB configuration. You can then reboot, and the GRUB bootloader will start up.

You then have to create a new configuration file (/boot/grub2/grub.cfg), using the grub2-mkconfig command, as follows:

```
grub2-mkconfig -o /boot/grub2/grub.cfg
```

If your Linux rescue disks are unable to access your system, you can use a Fedora Live DVD to start up Fedora and then manually mount your Fedora partitions. You will have to know your partition device names (use GParted). Once they are mounted, you can access the system files on the mounted partition and make any required changes.

■ ■ ■

## CHAPTER 3

Usage Basics: Login, Desktop, and Help

To start using Fedora, you must know how to access your Fedora system and, once you are on the system, how to use and configure the desktop. A set of desktop System Settings tools lets you easily configure such features as network access, desktop background, display resolution, and power usage. Access is supported through a graphical login. A simple screen appears with menus for selecting login options and your username.

User Accounts

User access to the system is provided through accounts. To gain access to the system, you must have a user account set up for you. A system administrator creates the account, assigning a username and password for it. You then use your account to log in to and use the system. You can create other new user accounts, by using special system administration tools like system-config-users or System Settings user accounts. You can access these tools from any user account, provided you supply the administrative password. You had to provide a root user password when you installed your system. This is the administrative password required to access any administrative tool, such as the one for managing user accounts.

GRUB Start Menu and Boot Problems

When you boot up, the GRUB screen is displayed for a few seconds before the boot procedure begins. Should you want to start a different operating system or add options to your startup, you have to display the GRUB startup menu (see Figure 3-1). Do this by pressing any key on your keyboard. The GRUB menu will be displayed and will list Linux and other operating systems you specified, such as Windows. Your Linux system should be selected by default. If not, use the arrow keys to move to the Linux entry, if it is not already highlighted, and press Enter.

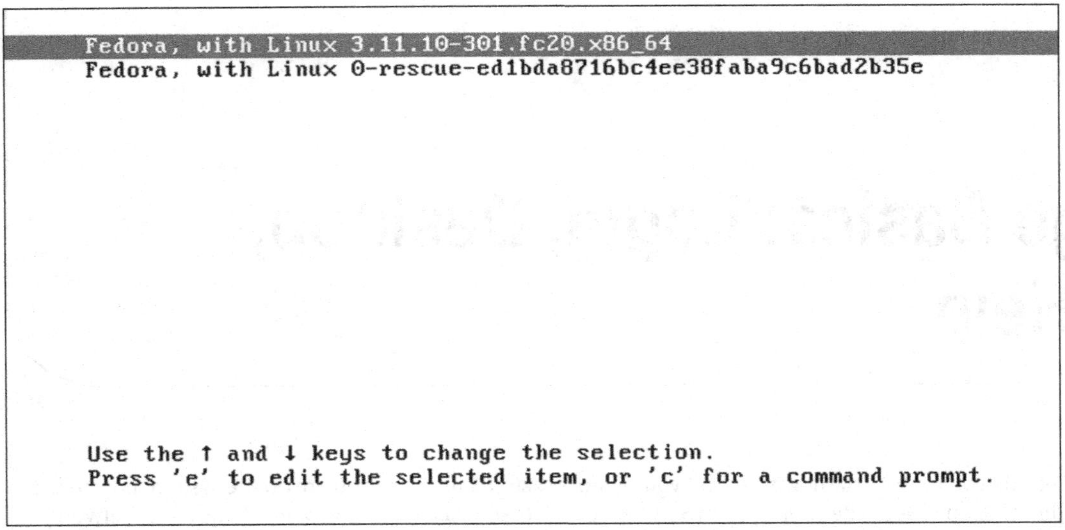

```
Fedora, with Linux 3.11.10-301.fc20.x86_64
Fedora, with Linux 0-rescue-ed1bda8716bc4ee38faba9c6bad2b35e




















   Use the ↑ and ↓ keys to change the selection.
   Press 'e' to edit the selected item, or 'c' for a command prompt.
```

Figure 3-1. *GRUB menu*

The Advanced Options for Fedora option opens another screen listing previously installed Fedora kernels. If you are having difficulty with your current kernel, you can use this screen to start up an older kernel.

To change a particular line, use the up/down arrow keys to move to the line. You can use the left/right arrow keys to move along the line. The Backspace key will delete characters and, simply by typing, will insert characters. The editing changes are temporary. Permanent changes can be made only by directly editing the GRUB configuration files. Fedora 20 uses GRUB2, which uses the configuration file /etc/default/grub. GRUB2 files are kept in the /etc/grub.d directory. Run as root the following grub2-mkconfig to apply changes made in /etc/default/grub:

```
grub2-mkconfig -o /boot/grub2/grub.cfg
```

See the GRUB2 page at http://fedoraproject.org/wiki/GRUB_2 for more information.

When your Fedora operating system starts up, a Fedora logo appears. You can press the ESC key to see the startup messages instead. Fedora uses Plymouth with its kernel-mode setting ability, to display a startup animation. The Plymouth Fedora logo theme is installed by default.

For graphical installations, some displays may have difficulty running the graphical startup display known as the Plymouth boot tool. This tool replaces the Red Hat Graphical Boot tool but still uses the command rhgb. If you have this problem, you can edit your Linux GRUB entry and remove the rhgb term from the Linux line. Press the e key to edit a Grub Linux entry (see Figure 3-2). Then move the cursor to the linux line and perform your edit. Use the Backspace key to delete. Then press Ctrl+x or the F10 key to boot the edited GRUB entry.

```
        insmod part_msdos                                              ↑
        insmod ext2
        set root='hd0,msdos1'
        if [ x$feature_platform_search_hint = xy ]; then
            search --no-floppy --fs-uuid --set=root --hint='hd0,msdos1'  20c8ae6\
3-a02a-47f4-9a56-73d62c25e5b3
        else
            search --no-floppy --fs-uuid --set=root 20c8ae63-a02a-47f4-9a56-73d6\
2c25e5b3
        fi
        linux        /vmlinuz-3.11.10-301.fc20.x86_64 root=/dev/mapper/fedora-\
root ro rd.lvm.lv=fedora/swap vconsole.font=latarcyrheb-sun16 rd.lvm.lv=fedora\
/root  rhgb quiet LANG=en_US.UTF-8
        initrd /initramfs-3.11.10-301.fc20.x86_64.img
  _

        Press Ctrl-x or F10 to start, Ctrl-c or F2 for a command prompt or
        Escape to discard edits and return to the menu. Pressing Tab lists
        possible completions.
```

Figure 3-2. *GRUB Edit window*

Your system will start up, initially using the text display for all the startup tasks, then shift to the graphical login.

Should you have difficulty displaying your graphical interface, you can instead choose to boot up the command-line interface. From the command-line interface, you can make any needed configuration changes. To boot to the command-line interface from GRUB, edit the linux line of the Linux GRUB entries, and add a 3 to the end of the line. The 3 indicates the command-line interface. In previous versions of Fedora, the 3 indicated a run level. Now it refers to a systemd target.

The Display Manager: GDM

The graphical login interface displays a login window with a box listing a menu of usernames. When you click a username, a login box replaces the listing of users, displaying the selected username and a text box in which you then enter your password. Upon clicking the Sign In button or pressing Enter, you log in to the selected account, and your desktop starts up.

Graphical logins are handled by the GNOME Display Manager (GDM). The GDM manages the login interface, in addition to authenticating a user password and username, and then starts up a selected desktop. From the GDM, you can shift to the command-line interface with Ctrl+Alt+F2, and then shift back to the GDM with Ctrl+Alt+F1 (from a desktop, you would use the same keys to shift to a command-line interface and to shift back). The keys F2 through F6 provide different command-line terminals, as in Ctrl+Alt+F3 for the third command-line terminal.

When the GDM starts up, it shows a listing of users (see Figure 3-3). A System Status Area at the top right of the screen displays icons indicating the status of the sound and battery. Clicking the icons displays the System Status Area menu, which shows the entries for sound adjustment, network wireless (if supported), and the battery status (if a laptop). A power button at the bottom will display a power off dialog with options to Power Off and Restart. To shut down your Fedora system, click the Power Off button on the dialog.

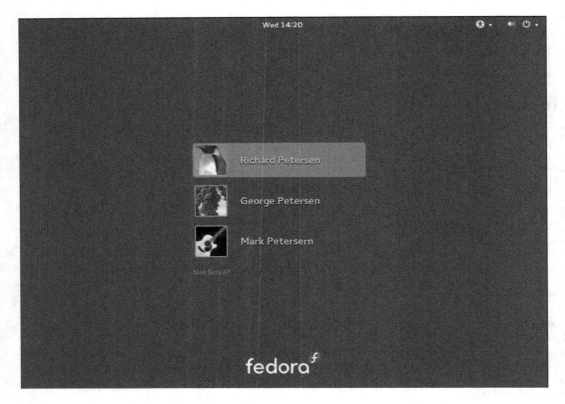

Figure 3-3. *The Fedora GDM user listing*

The date is displayed at the top center of the screen. Clicking the date displays a calendar.

Next to the System Status Area icons is a menu for accessibility, which displays a menu of switches that let you turn on accessibility tools and such features as the onscreen keyboard, enhanced contrast, and the screen magnifier.

To log in, click a username from the list of users. You are then prompted to enter the user's password (see Figure 3-4). A new dialog replaces the user list, showing the username you selected and a Password text box in which you can enter the user's password. Once you enter the password, click the Sign In button or press Enter. By default, the GNOME desktop starts up. If the name of a user you want to log in as is not listed, click the "Not Listed" entry at the end, to open a text box, which prompts you for a username, and then the password.

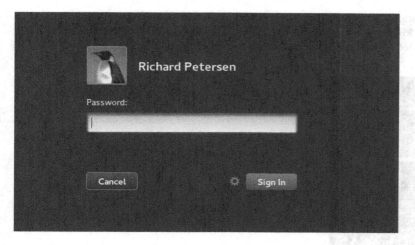

Figure 3-4. *GDM login*

Though GNOME is the primary desktop for Fedora, it is possible to install and use other desktosps, such as KDE, Cinnamon, and Mate. Should you have more than one desktop installed, such as both GNOME and KDE, when you click a username under which to log in, a Session button (gear icon) is displayed below the Password text box. Click that button to open a menu listing the installed desktops, then click the one you want to use (see Figure 3-5).

Figure 3-5. *GDM Session menu*

The System Status Area

Once logged in, the System Status Area is displayed on the right side of the top bar (see Figure 3-6). The area will include status icons for features such as sound and power. Clicking the button displays the System Status Area menu, with items for sound, brightness, wireless connections, the battery, the current user, in addition to buttons at the bottom for opening GNOME System Settings, activating the lock screen, and shutting down or rebooting the system. The sound and brightness items feature sliding bars with which you can adjust the volume and brightness. The Wi-Fi, Battery, and current user entries expand to submenus with added entries. The buttons at the bottom open separate dialogs.

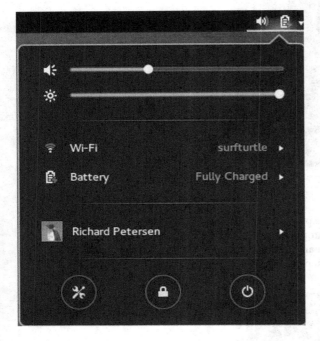

Figure 3-6. *System Status Area menu*

On systems that are not laptops, there will be no brightness slider or Battery entry on the System Status Area menu. If the system also has no wireless device, the Wi-Fi entry will also be missing. A system of this kind will only have a sound slider and, if more than one user is defined, a user entry.

To log out or switch to another user, you click the current user entry to expand the menu to show Switch User and Log Out entries. The Log Out entry returns you to the GDM login screen. If only one user is defined, there is no user entry, and, so, no Log Out entry, as there are no other users to log in.

Important Laptop Features

For working on a laptop, you will require two important operations: power management and support for multiple network connection, including wireless and LAN. Both are configured automatically.

For power management, Fedora uses System Settings Power. On a laptop, the Battery entry in the System Status Area (See Figure 3-7) will show how much power you have left, as well as when the battery becomes critical.

Figure 3-7. *System Status Area menu battery entry*

For network connections, Fedora uses Network Manager. Network Manager will detect available network connections automatically (see "Network Manager Wireless Connections," later in this chapter). Click the Wi-Fi entry in the System Status Area to expand the menu showing an entry for Select Network. Click this entry to display a dialog showing all possible wireless networks, as well as any wired networks. You can then choose the one you want to use. When you try to connect to an encrypted wireless network, you will be prompted for the security method and the password. Wireless networks that you successfully connect to will be added to your Network Manager configuration.

Desktops

Several alternative desktop interfaces, such as GNOME and the K Desktop (KDE), can be installed on Fedora. Each has its own style and appearance. It is important to keep in mind that, although the GNOME and KDE interfaces appear similar, they are really two very different desktop interfaces, with separate tools for selecting preferences.

KDE

The K Desktop Environment (KDE) displays a panel at the bottom of the screen that looks similar to one displayed on the top of the GNOME desktop. The file manager appears different but operates much the same way as the GNOME file manager. There is a System Settings entry in the main menu that opens the KDE System Settings window, from which you can configure every aspect of the KDE environment, such as desktop effects, workspace appearance, devices such as monitors and printers, and networking.

Xfce and LXDE

The Xfce and LXDE desktops are lightweight and designed to run fast without the kind of overhead seen in such full-featured desktops as KDE and GNOME. They use their own file manager and panel, but the emphasis is on modularity and simplicity. The desktop consists of a collection of modules, including the file manager, the panel, and the window manager. In keeping with its focus on simplicity, its small scale makes it appropriate for laptops or dedicated systems that have no need for the complex overhead found in other desktops.

Cinnamon and Mate

The Cinnamon and Mate desktops are designed to make use of more traditional desktop features, such as a main menu, panels, and applets. Mate has a traditional GNOME 2 design, with a top and bottom panel. Cinnamon is based on GNOME 3 and has workspace and windows overviews. It uses a bottom panel with a main menu and applets you can add. Cinnamon is designed and maintained by Mint Linux but is becoming popular on other distributions, including Fedora.

■ **Tip**   To restart the system from the login screen using the keyboard, you must first enter the command-line interface. Press Ctrl+Alt+F2 to enter the command-line interface, and then press Ctrl+Alt+Del to restart the system.

GNOME

The GNOME desktop provides easy-to-use overviews and menus, along with a flexible file manager and desktop. GNOME 3 is based on the gnome-shell, which is a compositing window manager. It replaces the GNOME 2 metacity window manager, gnome-panel, and a notification daemon.

The screen displays a top bar, through which you access your applications, windows, and system settings. Clicking the System Status Area button at the right side of the menu bar displays the status user area menu, from which you can access buttons at the bottom to display the system setting dialog, lock the screen, and shut down the system (see Figure 3-8).

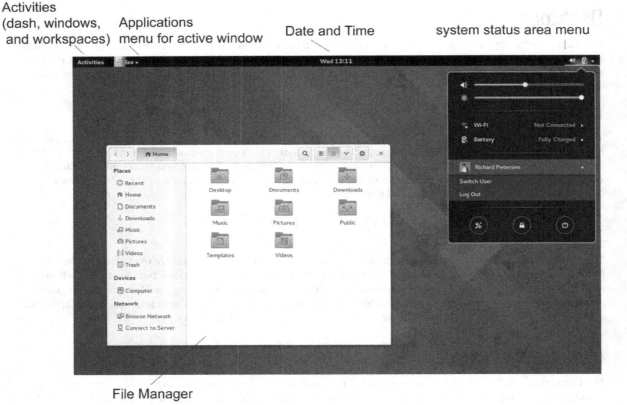

Figure 3-8. *The Fedora GNOME desktop*

To access applications and windows, use the Activities overview mode. Click the Activities button at the left side of the top bar (or move the mouse to the left corner, or press the Windows button). The overview mode consists of a dash listing your favorite and running applications, workspaces, and windows (see Figure 3-9). Large thumbnails of open windows are displayed on the windows overview (the desktop area). You can use the Search box at the top to locate an application quickly. Partially hidden thumbnails of your desktop workspaces are displayed on the right side. Initially there are two. Moving your mouse to the right side displays the workspace thumbnails.

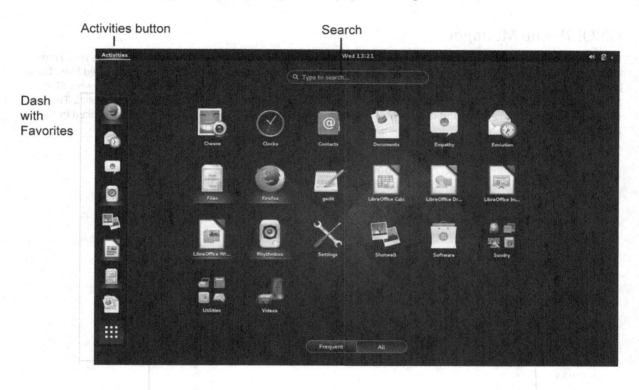

Figure 3-9. *GNOME 3 Activities overview mode for applications*

You can manually leave the overview at any time by pressing the ESC key or by clicking a window thumbnail.

The dash is a bar on the left side with icons for your favorite applications. Initially, there are icons for the Firefox web browser, mail (Thunderbird), sound (Rhythmbox), images (Shotwell), and files (the GNOME file manager), as depicted in Figure 3-9. The last icon opens an Applications overview that you can use to start other applications. To open an application from the dash, click its icon or right-click and choose New Window from the pop-up menu. You can also click and drag the icon to the windows overview or to a workspace thumbnail on the right side.

You can access windows from the windows overview, which is displayed initially when you start Activities. The windows overview displays thumbnails of all your open windows. When you pass your mouse over a window thumbnail, a close box appears, at the upper-right corner, with which you can close the window. You can also move the window on the desktop and to another workspace.

To move a window on the desktop, click and drag its title bar. To maximize a window, double-click its title bar or drag it to the top bar. To minimize, double-click the title bar again or drag it away from the top bar. To close a window, click its close box (upper right).

Two sub-overviews are available from the main overview: Utilities and Sundries. Utilities lists several tools, such as the text editor, and Sundries lists older administrative tools, such as `system-config-printer`. These sub-overviews function like a submenu, overlaying the main overview with a sub-overview.

GNOME File Manager

You can access your home folder from the Files icon on the dash. A file manager window opens, showing your Home folder (see Figure 3-10). Your Home folder will already have default directories created for commonly used files. These include Documents, Downloads, Music, Pictures, and Videos. Your office applications will automatically save files to the Documents folder by default. Image and photo applications place image files in the Pictures directory. The Desktop folder will hold all files and directories saved to your desktop. When you download a file, it is placed in the Downloads directory.

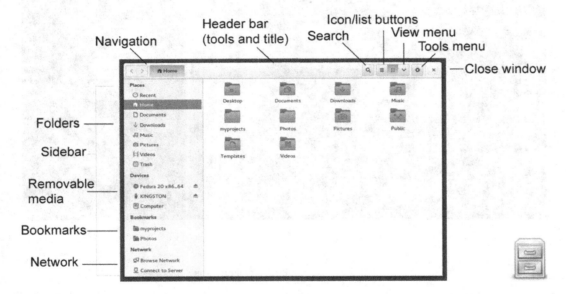

Figure 3-10. *File manager for the Home folder*

The file manager window displays several components, including a header bar, which combines the title bar and toolbar, and a sidebar. When you open a new directory, the same window is used to display it, and you can use the forward and back arrows to move through previously opened directories. The header bar displays navigation folder buttons that show your current folder and its parent folders. You can click a parent folder to move to it. The GNOME file manager also supports tabs. You can open several folders in the same file manager window.

GNOME Customization with Tweak Tool: Themes, Icons, Fonts, Startup Applications, and Extensions

You can perform common desktop customizations using the GNOME Tweak Tool. Areas to customize include the desktop icons, fonts, themes, startup applications, workspaces, window behavior, and the time display. You can access Tweak Tool from the Applications overview ➤ Utilities. The GNOME Tweak Tool has tabs for Appearance, Desktop, Extensions, Fonts, Keyboard and Mouse, Power, Startup Applications, Top Bar, Typing, Windows, and Workspaces (see Figure 3-11).

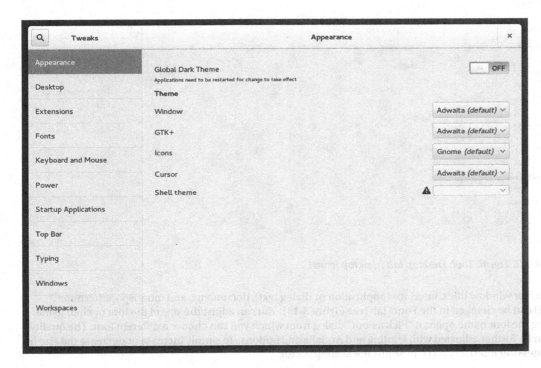

Figure 3-11. *GNOME Tweak Tool: Appearance tab (themes)*

The Appearance tab lets you set the theme for your windows, icons, and cursor. GNOME 3 uses the Adwaita Theme. This theme has a light and dark variant. The Global Light Theme is the default, but you can use the switch on the Appearance tab to enable the Global Dark Theme. The Global Dark Theme shades the background of windows to a dark gray, while text and button images appear in white.

As you add other desktops, such as Cinnamon, the themes available increase. There are many window themes to choose from, including Clearlooks, Mist, and Glider. For icons, you can choose among Oxygen (KDE), Mist (Cinnamon), and GNOME.

You may also want to display Home, Trash, and Mounted Volumes like USB drives, on the desktop, as other desktops do. Use the Desktop tab on Tweak Tool to display these icons (see Figure 3-12). Turn on the "Icons on Desktop" switch. Home, Trash, and Mounted Volumes are checked by default. Uncheck them in order not to display the icon. You can also a check a Network Servers option to display icons for remotely accessed folders.

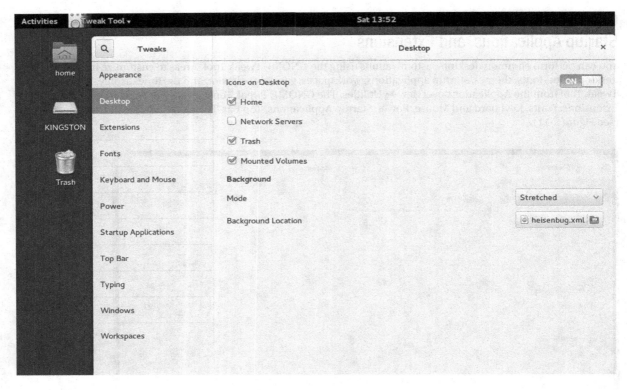

Figure 3-12. *GNOME Tweak Tool: Desktop tab (desktop icons)*

Desktop fonts for window titles, interface (application or dialog text), documents, and monospace (terminal windows or code) can be changed in the Fonts tab (see Figure 3-13). You can adjust the size of the font or change the font style. Clicking the font name opens a "Pick a Font" dialog from which you can choose a different font. The quality of text display can be further adjusted with Hinting and Antialiasing options. To simply increase or decrease the size of all fonts on your desktop interface, you can adjust the Scaling Factor.

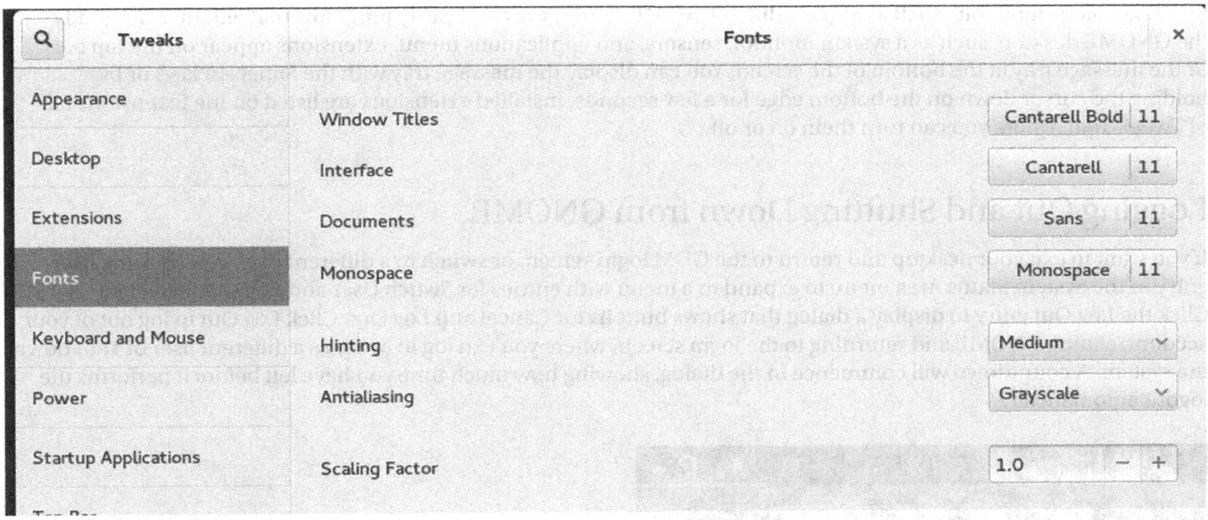

Figure 3-13. *GNOME Tweak Tool: Fonts tab*

At times, there may be certain applications that you want started up when you log in, such as the Gedit text editor, the Firefox web browser, or the Videos movie player. On the Startup Applications tab, you can choose the applications to start up (see Figure 3-14). Click the plus (+) button to open an applications dialog from which you can choose an application to start up. Once added, you can later remove the application by clicking its Remove button.

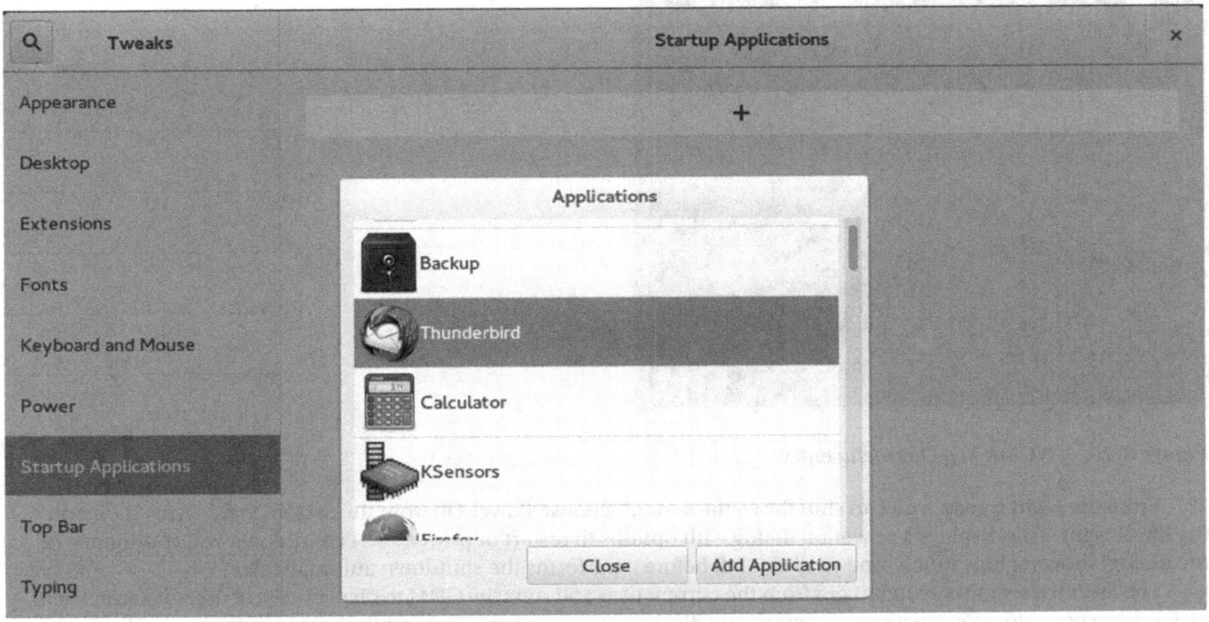

Figure 3-14. *GNOME Tweak Tool: Startup Applications tab*

Extensions function much as applets did in GNOME 2. They are third-party programs that enhance or modify the GNOME desktop, such as a system monitor, sensors, and applications menu. Extensions appear on the top bar or the message tray at the bottom of the screen. You can display the message tray with the Super+m keys or by holding the cursor down on the bottom edge for a few seconds. Installed extensions are listed on the Extensions tab of Tweak Tool, where you can turn them on or off.

Logging Out and Shutting Down from GNOME

If you want to exit your desktop and return to the GDM login screen, or switch to a different user, you click the user entry in the System Status Area menu to expand to a menu with entries for Switch User and Log Out (see Figure 3-15). Click the Log Out entry to display a dialog that shows buttons for Cancel and Log Out. Click Log Out to log out of your account, exiting GNOME and returning to the login screen, where you can log in again as a different user or shut down the system. A countdown will commence in the dialog, showing how much time you have left before it performs the logout automatically.

Figure 3-15. *GNOME Log Out menu entry*

From the login screen, you can shut down the system: choose Power Off from the System Status Area menu on the lower right. This displays a power off dialog with options to restart or power off. A countdown will commence in the dialog, showing how much time you have left before it performs the shutdown automatically.

The Switch User entry switches out from the current user and runs the GDM to display a list of users you can log in as. Click the name to open a password prompt and display a session menu. You can then log in as that user. The sessions of users already logged will continue with the same open windows and applications that were running when the user switched off. You can switch back and forth between logged-in users, with all users retaining their session from where they left off. When you switch off from a user, that user's running programs will continue in the background.

Network Connections

Network connections will be set up for you by Network Manager, which will detect your network connections automatically, both wired and wireless. Network Manager provides status information for your connection and allows you to switch easily from one configured connection to another, as needed. For initial configuration, it detects as much information as possible about the new connection.

Network Manager is user specific. Wired connections will be started automatically. For wireless connections, when a user logs in, Network Manager selects the connection preferred by that user. From a menu of detected wireless networks, the user can select a wireless connection to use.

Network Manager displays active network connections in the System Status Area. The Network Manager icon for this entry will vary according to the type of connection and your connection status. A wireless connection will display a staggered wave graph (see Figure 3-16). If no connection is active, an icon with the wave graph and an *x* mark is displayed.

Figure 3-16. *Network Manager: wireless*

Network Manager Wired Connections

For computers connected to a wired network, such as an Ethernet connection, Network Manager automatically detects and establishes the network connection. Most networks use DHCP to provide such network information as an IP address and DNS server. With this kind of connection, Network Manager can connect automatically to your network whenever you start your system. On wired systems that have no wireless devices, there is no network entry in the System Status Area menu.

Network Manager Wireless Connections

With multiple wireless access points for Internet connections, a system could have several network connections to choose from. This is particularly true for notebook computers that access different wireless connections at different locations. Instead of manually configuring a new connection each time one is encountered, the Network Manager tool can configure and select a connection to use automatically.

Network Manager will scan for wireless connections, checking for Extended Service Set Identifiers (ESSIDs). If an ESSID identifies a previously used connection, it is selected. If several are found, the recently used one is chosen. If only new connections are available, Network Manager waits for the user to choose one. A connection is selected only if the user is logged in.

Click the Wi-Fi entry in the System Status Area to expand the menu to show entries from which to select a network, turn off wireless networking, and open the GNOME network System Settings dialog. Click the Select Network item to open a dialog that shows a list of all available wireless connections (see Figure 3-17). Entries display the name of the wireless network and a wave graph showing the strength of its signal. To connect to a network, click its entry, then click the Connect button, to activate the connection. If this is the first time you are trying to connect to that network, you will be prompted to enter the password or encryption key (see Figure 3-18).

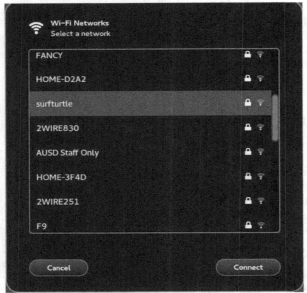

Figure 3-17. *Network Manager connections menu: wireless*

Figure 3-18. *Network Manager wireless authentication*

You can turn off wireless by clicking the Turn Off entry in the expanded Wi-Fi section of the System Status Area (see Figure 3-19). Airplane Mode is automatically activated, which you can then use to access a local network. You can, subsequently, turn off Airplane Mode to completely shut down your wireless connection. To reactivate your wireless connection, click the Turn On entry in the expanded Wi-Fi section of the System Status Area.

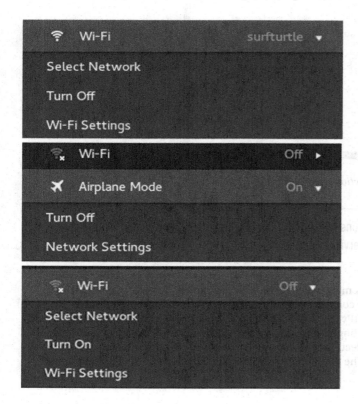

Figure 3-19. *Network Manager wireless on and off*

System Settings Network (GNOME and Proxies)

GNOME provides a network dialog for basic information and network connection management, including proxy settings. It is designed to work with Network Manager. Choose Network Settings from the expanded Wi-Fi entries in the System Status Area, or click the Network icon in the System Settings dialog, to open the Network dialog (see Figure 3-20). Tabs for network connections are listed to the right. There are entries for Wi-Fi, Wired, and Network proxy (Wi-Fi is displayed on computers with wireless connections). The Wired tab lets you turn the wired connection on or off. The Wi-Fi tab lets you choose a wireless network and then prompts you to enter a password or encryption key. The connection and security type is automatically detected. Instead of using a wireless network, you can choose an Airplane Mode wireless connection or use your connection as a hotspot. You can also connect to a local hidden network. A switch at the top right lets you turn the wireless connection on or off.

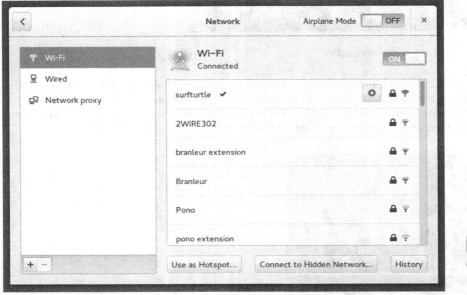

Figure 3-20. *System Settings Network wireless connections*

■ **Note**   You can still use the older Network Connections dialog to configure your network connection. Open Network Connection from the Sundries icon on the Activities overview.

Your current active connection will have a check mark next to it and a gear button to the right. Click the gear button to display a dialog with tabs for managing the connection. The Details tab provides information about the connection (see Figure 3-21). The Security, Identity, IPv4, and IPv6 tabs let you perform a detailed configuration of your connection, as described in Chapter 15. The settings are fixed to automatic by default. Should you make any changes, click the Apply button to have them take effect. To remove a network's connection information, open the Reset tab (Figure 3-22) and click the Forget button. The Reset button on the Reset tab lets you reset the settings.

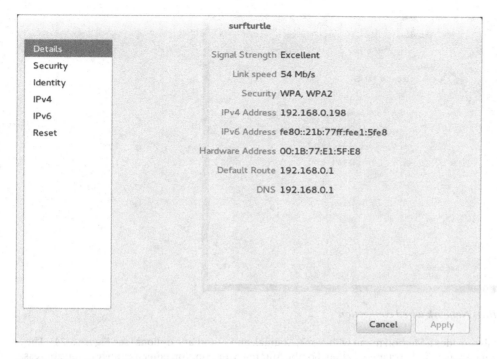

Figure 3-21. *System Settings Network wireless connection: Details tab*

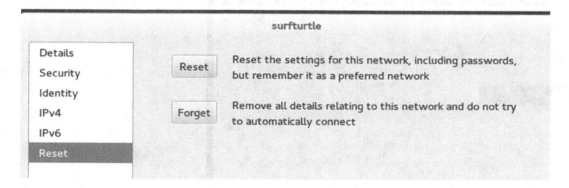

Figure 3-22. *System Settings Network wireless connection: Reset tab*

The Identity tab has options both for connecting automatically and for providing availability to other users. These are set by default. Should you not want to connect to the wireless network automatically, be sure to uncheck this option.

On the Network dialog, the Wired tab (Figure 3-23) shows basic information about the wired connection, including the IP addresses and DNS server. A switch at the top-right corner allows you to disconnect the wired connection, letting you effectively work offline. The gear button at the lower right opens a configuration dialog similar to the wireless configuration dialog, with tabs for Details, Security, Identity, IPv4, IPv6, and Reset. The Profile button to the left lets you add a different set of wired connection information (security, IPv protocols, and identity), should you connect to a different wired network.

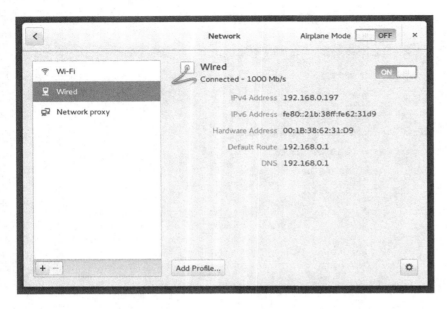

Figure 3-23. *System Settings Network wired connection*

The Network proxy tab provides a Method menu with None, Manual, and Automatic options (see Figure 3-24). The Manual option lets you enter address and port information. For the Automatic option, you enter a configuration address.

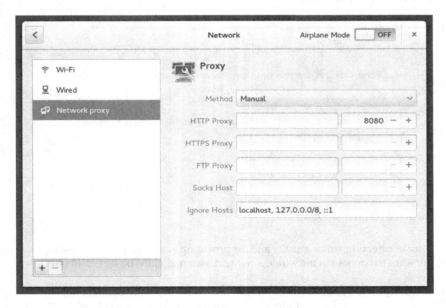

Figure 3-24. *Network proxy settings (System Settings Network)*

To add a new connection, such as a vpn or vlan connection, click the plus (✛) button below the network devices listing. You will be prompted to choose the interface types. Then the network configuration dialogs will start up, to let you enter configuration information.

System Settings

You can configure desktop settings and perform most administrative tasks using the GNOME configuration tools (see Table 3-1) listed in the GNOME System Settings dialog, accessible from the power menu. System settings organize tools into the Personal, Hardware, and System categories (see Figure 3-25). A few invoke the supported system tools available from previous releases, such as Sound (PulseAudio) and Displays (system-config-display). Most use the new GNOME 3 configuration and administrative tools such as Background, Privacy, Users, and Power (see Table 3-1).

Table 3-1. *System Settings*

Setting	Description
Personal	
Background	Sets desktop and screen lock backgrounds (wallpaper, color, and image)
Notifications	Turns on notifications for different applications
Online Accounts	Configures online accounts for use by e-mail and browser applications
Privacy	Turns on privacy features, such as screen lock and purging trash
Region & Language	Chooses a language, region (formats), and keyboard layout
Search	Specifies the resources and locations searched by the GNOME overview search box
Hardware	
Bluetooth	Sets Bluetooth detection and configuration
Color	Sets the color profile for a device
Displays	Changes your screen resolution, refresh rate, and screen orientation
Keyboard	Configures repeat key sensitivity and shortcut keys for special tasks, such as multimedia operations
Mouse & Touchpad	Sets mouse and touchpad configuration; selects hand orientation, speed, and accessibility
Network	Lets you turn wired and wireless networks on or off. Allows access to an available wireless network. Also specifies proxy configuration, if needed—manual or automatic
Power	Sets the power options for laptop inactivity
Printers	Turns printers on or off and accesses their print queues
Sound	Configures sound effects, output volume, sound device options, input volume, and sound application settings
Wacom Tablet	Provides tablet options
System	
Date & Time	Sets the date, time, time zone, and network time
Details	Sets the host name of your computer, displays hardware information, and assigns default applications for certain basic tasks
Sharing	Turns on sharing for media, remote login, and screen access
Users	Manages accounts
Universal Access	Enables features such as accessible login and keyboard screen

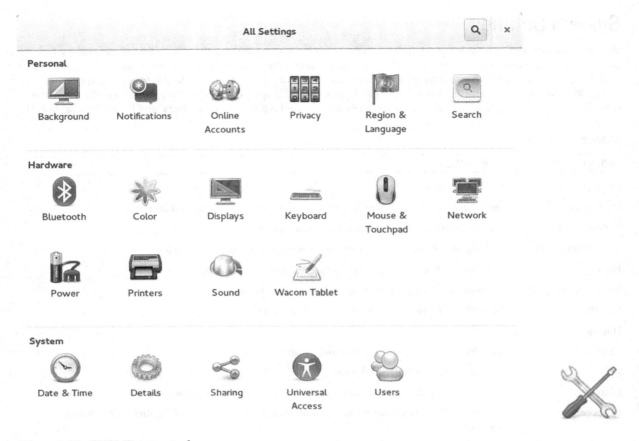

Figure 3-25. *GNOME system tools*

GNOME 3 tools will open with a back arrow button at the top, which you can click to return to the System Settings dialog.

Background

With the Background dialog you can set your background for both the desktop and screen lock backgrounds: wallpaper, picture, or color. You can access the Background dialog from Applications overview or from the System Settings dialog (see Figure 3-26). The current backgrounds are shown for the desktop and the screen lock. Click one to open the Select Background dialog, with buttons for Wallpapers, Pictures, and Colors (see Figure 3-27). The dialog is the same for both desktop and screen lock backgrounds. If you choose Wallpapers, the installed backgrounds are displayed. The Pictures button displays images in your Pictures folder, which you can scroll through to select one to use for your background. To add your own image, first add the image to your Pictures folder. Then click the Pictures button to display all the images in your Pictures folder. Once you make your selection, click the Select button at the lower right. You return to the main Background dialog, showing your new background. The background on your display is updated immediately.

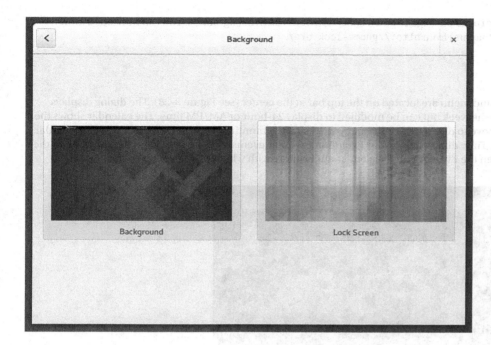

Figure 3-26. *Background*

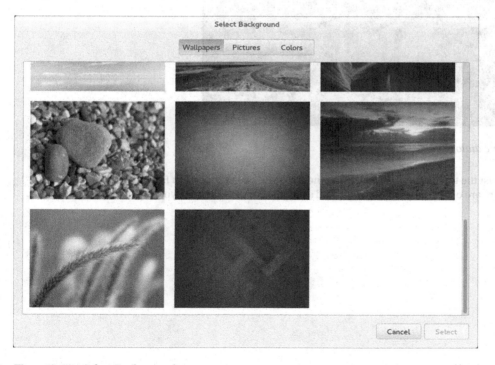

Figure 3-27. *Select Background*

Install the gnome-background package to add a collection of GNOME backgrounds. You can download more GNOME backgrounds (wallpapers) from http://gnome-look.org/.

Date & Time

The Date & Time calendar and menu are located on the top bar at the center (see Figure 3-28). The dialog displays the current time and day of the week but can be modified to display 24-hour or AM/PM time. The calendar shows the current date, but you can move to different months and years using the month scroll arrows at the top of the calendar. The right side of the Date & Time dialog shows your Evolution calendar events for the current and next days. Click the Open Calendar entry to open the Evolution mail calendar application, with which you can enter events.

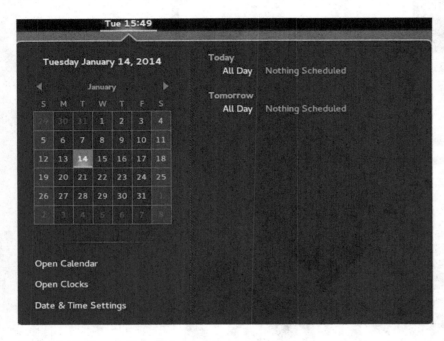

Figure 3-28. *Date & Time dialog*

You can further adjust the top bar time display using the GNOME Tweak Tool's Top Bar tab (see Figure 3-29). In the Clock section, there are options to show the date and seconds. For the Calendar, you can show week numbers.

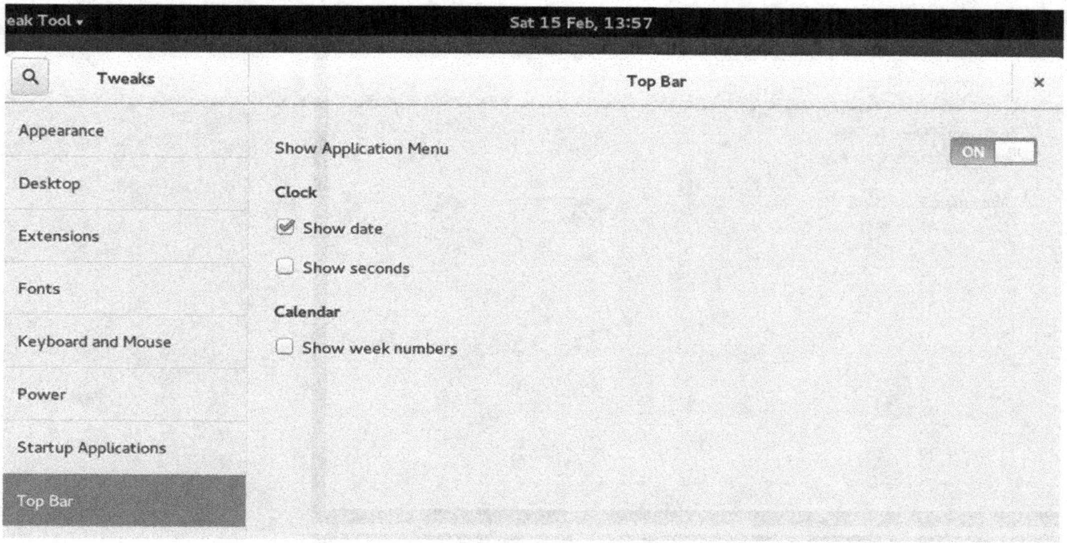

Figure 3-29. *GNOME Tweak Tool: Top Bar (clock options)*

Date & Time options are set using the Date & Time Settings dialog, which you can access from the System Setting dialog or from the Date & Time menu, using the "Date & Time Settings" link at the bottom-left side of the menu. The Date & Time Settings dialog lets you set the time zone and time. Both are configured for automatic settings using Internet time servers (see Figure 3-30). The time zone or the time and date can be set manually by turning off the Automatic switches. Once turned off, the Date & Time and the Time Zone links become active.

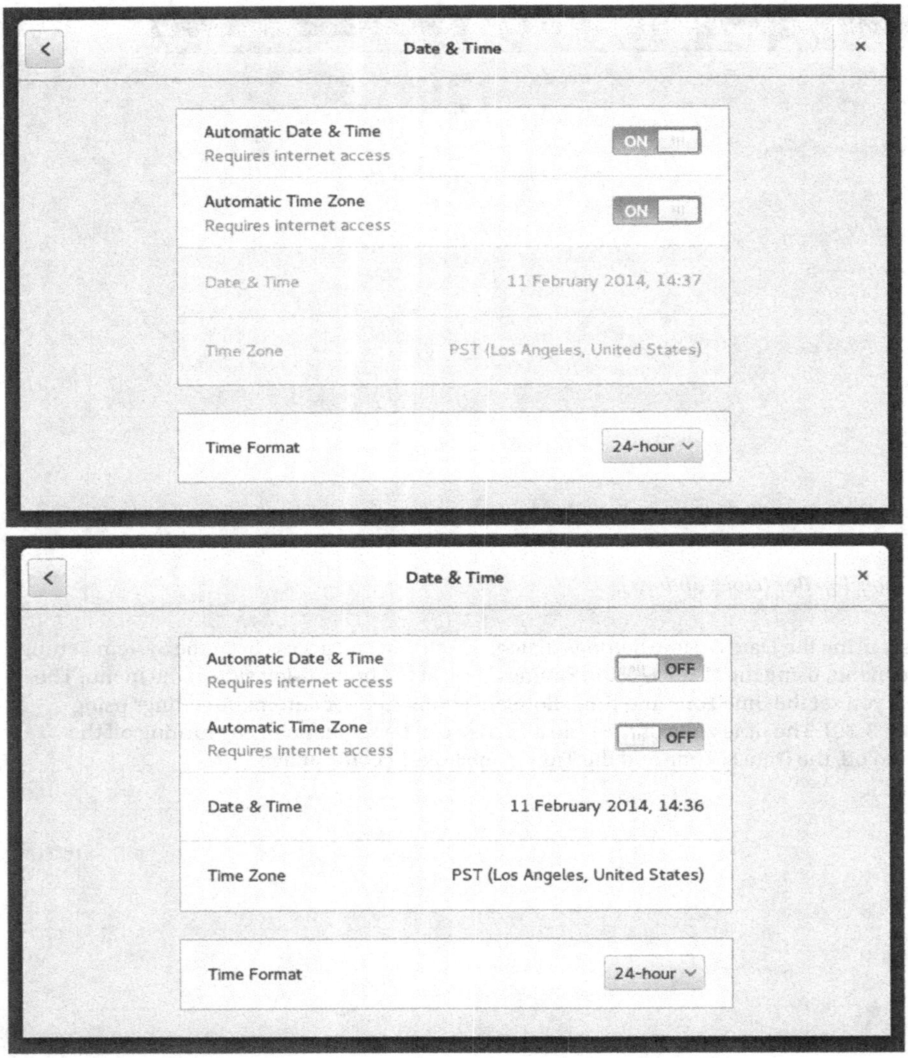

Figure 3-30. *Date & Time Settings dialog with automatic settings turned on (top) and off (bottom)*

The Date & Time link opens a dialog with settings for the hour, minutes, day, and year, with a menu for the month (see Figure 3-31). You can use the plus (+) and minus (-) buttons to sequentially change the values.

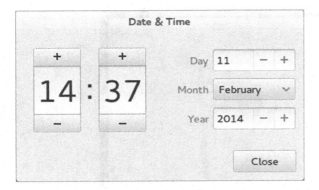

Figure 3-31. *Date & Time Settings dialog with automatic settings turned on and off*

The Time Zone link opens a dialog with a map of the time zones and the current one selected (see Figure 3-32). Click a new time zone to change the zone.

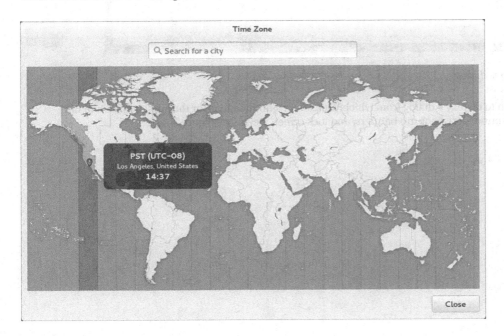

Figure 3-32. *Time Zone dialog*

Notifications

The Notifications dialog lets you configure notifications for different applications. You can also have the options show pop-up banners at the bottom of the screen or show notices on the lock screen. Both are turned on by default. A listing of supported applications for notifications is displayed (see Figure 3-33).

Figure 3-33. Notifications dialog

Click an application to display a dialog from which you can turn notifications for the application on or off, as well as set options—sound alerts, pop-up banners, and lock screen views (see Figure 3-34).

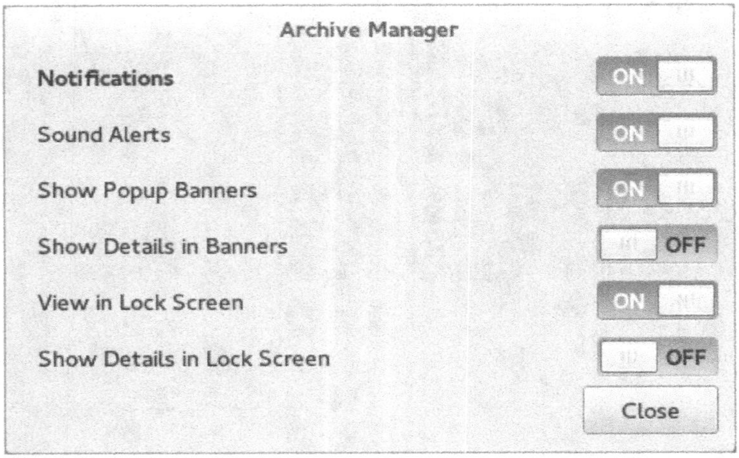

Figure 3-34. Notification settings for an application

Privacy

The Privacy dialog allows you to turn privacy features, such as the screen lock, usage and history logs, and the purging of trash and temporary files, on or off (see Figure 3-35). Screen Lock and Usage & History are turned on by default.

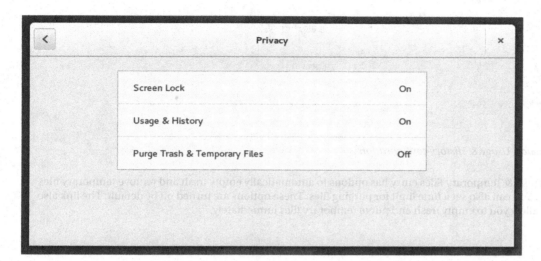

Figure 3-35. *Privacy*

Clicking the Screen Lock entry opens the Screen Lock configuration dialog, from which you can turn Screen Lock on or off or set it to turn on after a period of idle time and allow or deny notifications on the Screen Lock screen (see Figure 3-36).

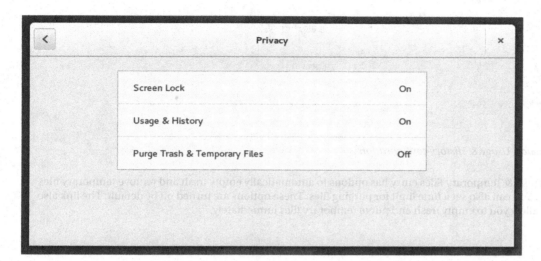

Figure 3-36. *Privacy: Screen Lock configuration*

Click the Usage & History entry to open a dialog from which you can turn usage history on or off and set how long to keep it. The entry also has a button that allows you to clear recent history (see Figure 3-37).

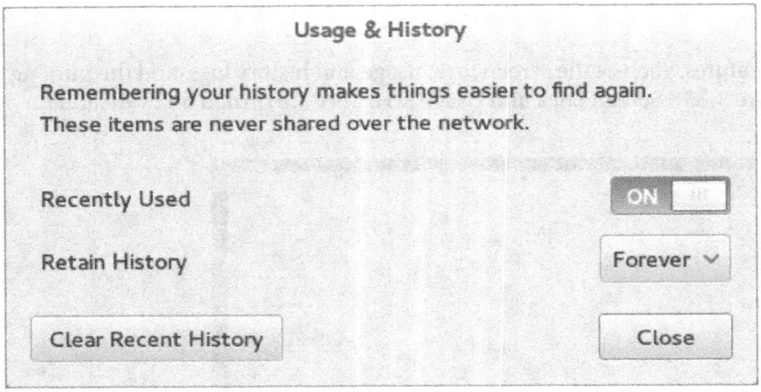

Figure 3-37. *Privacy: Usage & History configuration*

The Purge Trash & Temporary Files entry has options to automatically empty trash and remove temporary files (see Figure 3-38). You can also set a time limit for purging files. These options are turned off by default. The link also has buttons that allow you to empty trash and purge temporary files immediately.

Figure 3-38. *Privacy: Purge Trash & Temporary Files configuration*

Details (System Information)

The Details dialog shows system information, using the following three tabs: Overview, Default Applications, and Removable Media. The Overview tab shows your hardware specifications (memory, CPU, graphics card chip, and free disk space), in addition to the host name (Device name) and the OS type (64- or 32-bit system; see Figure 3-39). You can change the host name here if you wish. When you open the dialog, updates are checked, and, if found, an Install Update button is displayed, which opens Software Updates, allowing you to update your system (see Chapter 4).

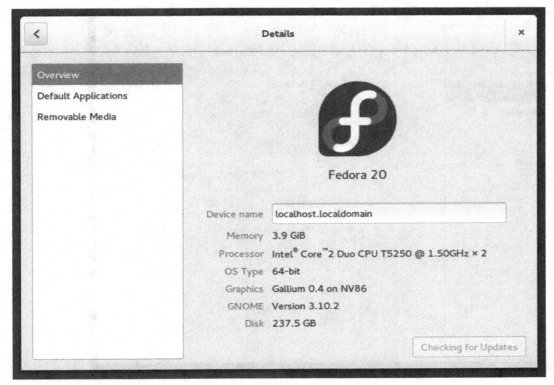

Figure 3-39. *Details: Overview*

The Default Applications tab lets you set default applications for basic types of files: Web, Mail, Calendar, Music, Video, and Photos (see Figure 3-40). Use the drop-down menus to choose installed alternatives, such as Thunderbird instead of Evolution for Mail or Image Viewer instead of Shotwell for Photos.

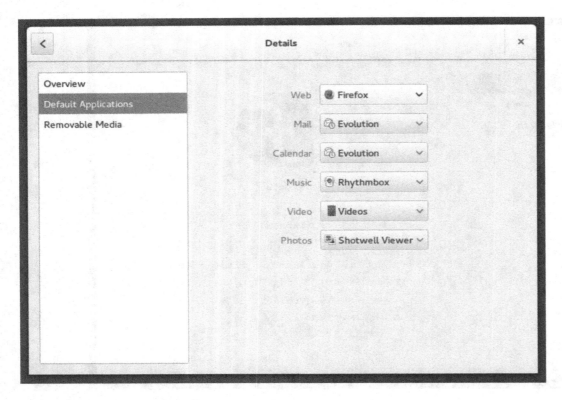

Figure 3-40. *Details: Default Applications*

Using Removable Devices and Media

Fedora supports removable devices and media, such as digital cameras, PDAs, card readers, and USB printers. These devices are handled automatically with device interfaces set up for them when needed. Removable media, such as CD and DVD discs, USB storage disks, digital cameras, and floppy disks, will be displayed as entries in the message tray Removable Devices menu. When you move your mouse to the lower-right corner of the screen, the Removable Devices button is displayed. Clicking this button displays a menu of all your removable devices, with an Eject button next to each entry. Click an entry to open the device in its associated applications, such as a file manager window for a USB drive. Be sure to always click the Eject button or entry before removing a drive, such as a USB drive, removable disk drive, or floppy disk. Removing the drive before clicking eject can result in incomplete write operations on the disk.

Removable media entries will also appear in the file manager Devices sidebar and on Favorites. For example, when you connect a USB drive to your system, it will be detected and displayed as a storage device with its own file system.

Removable media, such as USB drives and DVD/CD discs, can be ejected using Eject buttons in the Devices section of the file manager sidebar. The sidebar lists all your storage devices, including removable media. Removable media will have an Eject button to the right. Just click the Eject button, and the media is ejected or unmounted. You can right-click the Device entry and, from a pop-up menu, choose the Safely Remove Drive entry. You can also remove a device using the Eject button in the device's Removable Devices menu entry in the message tray.

The Details Removable Media tab lets you specify default actions for CD Audio, DVD Video, Music Player, Photos, and Software media (see Figure 3-41). You can select from drop-down menus the application to use for the different media These menus also include options for Ask What To Do, Do Nothing, and Open Folder. The Open Folder option will open a window displaying the files on the disc. A button labeled "Other Media" opens a dialog that lets you set up an association for less used media such as Blu-Ray discs and Audio DVD. Initially, the Ask What To Do option is set for all entries. Possible options are listed for the appropriate media, such as Rhythmbox Media Player for CD Audio discs and Videos (Totem) for DVD Video. Photos can be opened with the Shotwell photo manager.

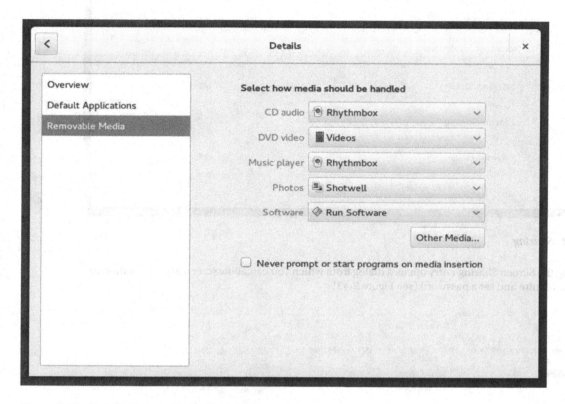

Figure 3-41. *Details: Removable Media defaults*

When you insert removable media, such as a CD audio disc, its associated application is automatically started, unless you change that preference. If you want to turn off this feature for a particular kind of media, you can select the Do Nothing entry from its application drop-down menu. If you want to be prompted for options, use the Ask What To Do entry. Then, when you insert a disc, a dialog with a drop-down menu for possible actions is displayed. From this menu, you can select another application or select the Do Nothing or Open Folder options.

You can turn the automatic startup off for all media by checking the box labeled "Never prompt or start programs on media insertion," at the bottom of the Removable Media tab.

Sharing

On the Sharing dialog, you can allow access to your account, your screen, and to media files in specified folders. A switch lets you turn all sharing on or off (see Figure 3-42).

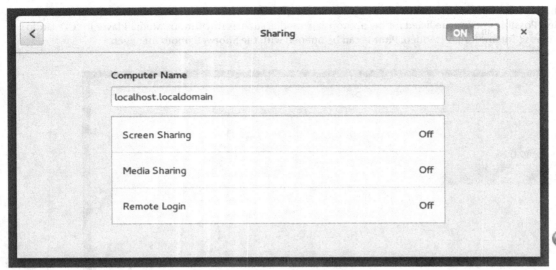

Figure 3-42. *Sharing*

Clicking the Screen Sharing entry opens a dialog from which you can allow screen access to other users. You can also require and set a password (see Figure 3-43).

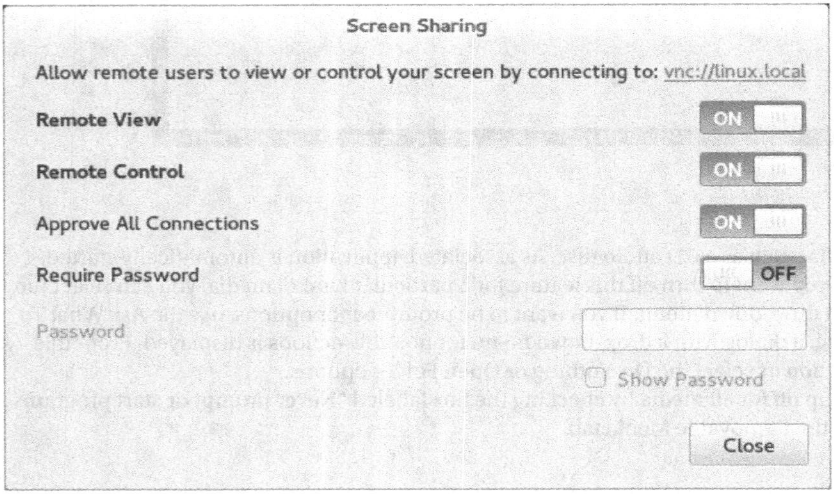

Figure 3-43. *Sharing: screen access to other users*

Power Management

For laptops and systems with remote battery devices such as mice, a power icon is displayed in the System Status Area (right side of top bar). The System Status Area menu shows the current strength of the battery (see Figure 3-44). The entry expands to show a Power Settings entry, which you can use to open the System Settings Power dialog.

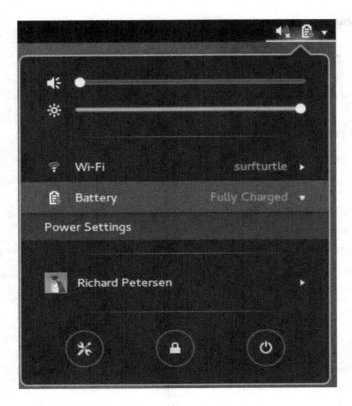

Figure 3-44. *GNOME Power Manager menu*

The GNOME Power manager is configured with the Power dialog, accessible as Power from System Settings (see Figure 3-45). The dialog is organized into four sections: Battery, Devices, Power Saving, and Suspend & Power Off. On laptops, the Battery section shows the battery charge. The Devices section shows the strength of any remote devices, such as a wireless mouse. In the Power Saving section, you can set power saving features for your monitor and wireless devices. When inactive for a period of time, you can choose to turn off the screen, as well as dim it whenever it is inactive. For laptops, you can also set the screen brightness. In the Suspend & Power Off section, you can turn on the automatic suspend for when a system remains inactive and, for laptops, hibernate, turn off, or suspend, when the batter is critically low.

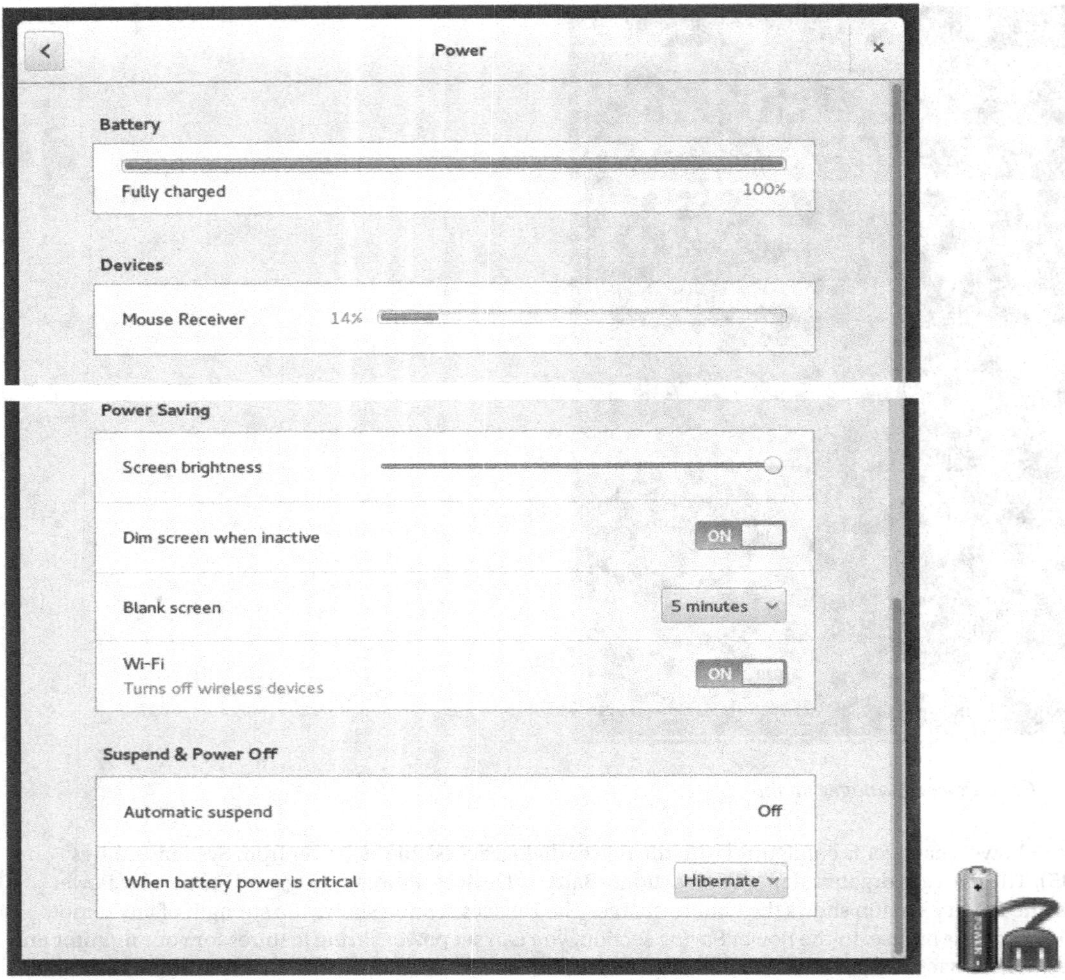

Figure 3-45. *GNOME Power manager*

Using the GNOME Tweak Tool's Power tab, you can further specify the action to take, such as suspend, shut down, or log out, when the Power button is pressed or the laptop lid is closed.

Mouse and Touchpad

The Mouse & Touchpad dialog is the primary tool for configuring your mouse and touchpad (see Figure 3-46). Mouse preferences allow you to choose the mouse's speed, hand orientation, and double-click times. A Test Your Settings button lets you check clicks, double-clicks, and scrolling. For laptops, you can configure your touchpad, enabling touchpad clicks and disabling them when typing. You can turn the touchpad on or off.

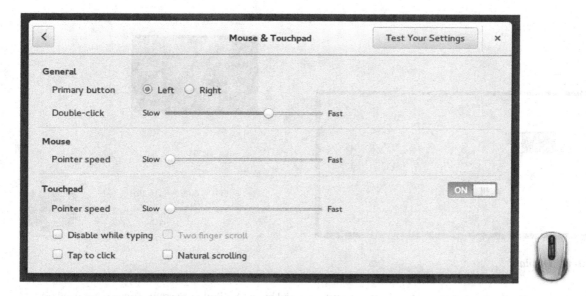

Figure 3-46. *GNOME system tools: mouse and touchpad*

The GNOME Tweak Tool's Keyboard and Mouse tab has options to enable a middle-click paste for the mouse and to show the location of the pointer on the screen.

Display (Resolution and Rotation)

The display drivers for Linux used on Fedora support user-level resolution and orientation changes. Any user can specify his or her own resolution or orientation, without affecting the settings of other users. The System Settings Displays dialog provides a simple interface for setting rotation, resolution, and selecting added monitors, allowing for cloned or extended displays across several connected monitors (see Figure 3-47). The dialog displays icons for connected montors. Click one to open a dialog, which shows the display's size, aspect ratio, and resolution. From the resolution menu, you can set the resolution. Use the arrow buttons below the display image to set the rotation. After you have made your changes, click Apply. The new resolution is displayed with a dialog with buttons that ask you whether to keep the new resolution or return to the previous one. With multiple displays, you can turn a monitor off or mirror displays.

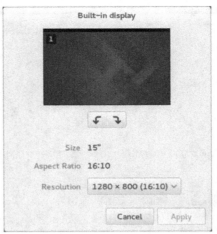

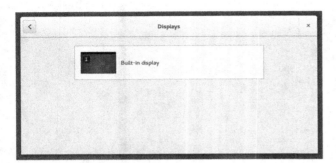

Figure 3-47. *Displays*

The graphics interface for your desktop display is implemented by the X Window System. The version used on Fedora is X.org (**x.org**). X.org provides its own drivers for various graphics cards and monitors. You can find out more about X.org at www.x.org.

X.org will automatically detect most hardware. The /etc/X11/xorg.conf file is no longer used for the open source drivers (nv and ati). It is still used to a limited extent by proprietary drivers, though mouse and keyboard entries are ignored. Information such as the monitor used is determined automatically. If you have an older monitor that is not correctly detected, you may have to specify monitor information by editing the /etc/X11/xorg.conf file.

Universal Access

The Universal Access dialog in System Settings lets you configure alternative access to your interface for your keyboard and mouse actions. Four sections set the display (Seeing), sound properties (Hearing), typing, and point-and-click features. Seeing lets you adjust the contrast and text size, and whether to allow zooming or use of screen reader (see Figure 3-48). Hearing uses visual cues for alert sounds. Typing displays a screen keyboard and adjusts key presses. Pointing and Clicking lets you use the keyboard for mouse operations.

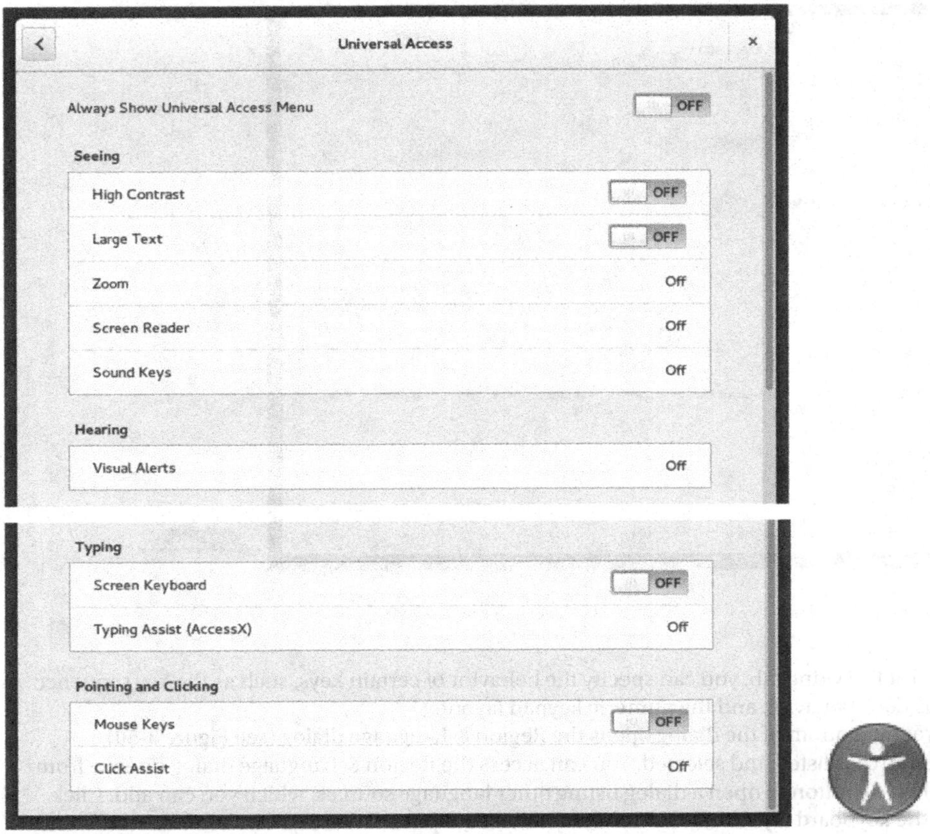

Figure 3-48. Universal Access

Keyboard and Language

The System Settings Keyboard dialog shows tabs for typing and shortcuts. The Typing tab adjusts repeat keys and cursor blinking (see Figure 3-49). The Shortcuts tab lets you assign keys to perform such tasks as starting the web browser.

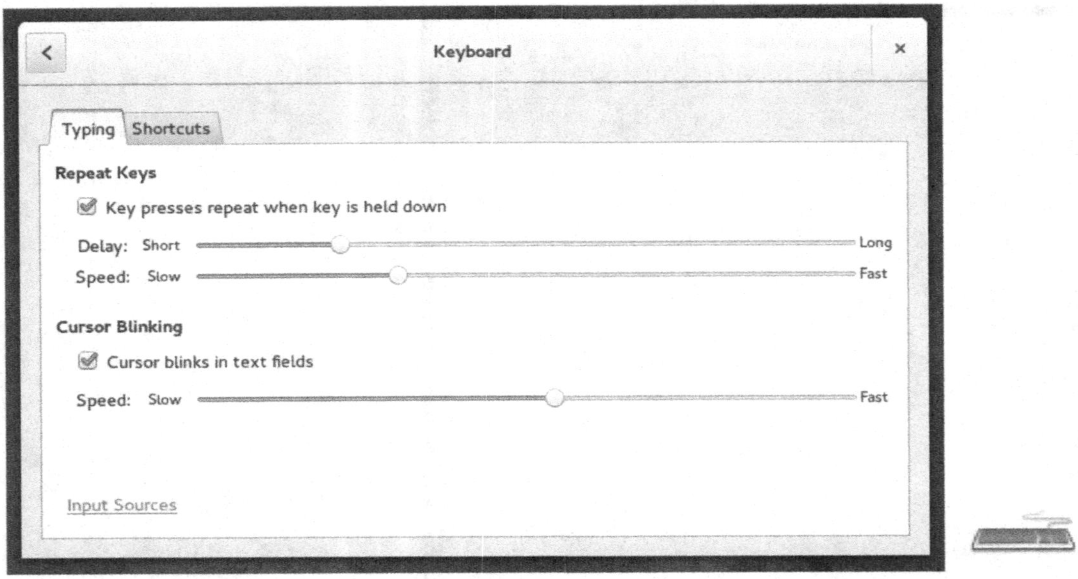

Figure 3-49. *Keyboard*

On the GNOME Tweak Tool's Typing tab, you can specify the behavior of certain keys, such as the key sequence to stop the X server, the Caps Lock behavior, and the numeric keypad layout.

The Input Sources link at the bottom of the dialog opens the Region & Language dialog (see Figure 3-50). The current input language source is listed and selected. You can access the Region & Language dialog directly from System Settings. Click the plus (+) button to open a dialog listing other language sources, which you can add. Click the Keyboard button to see the keyboard layout of your currently selected input source. You can also allow different language layouts for different windows.

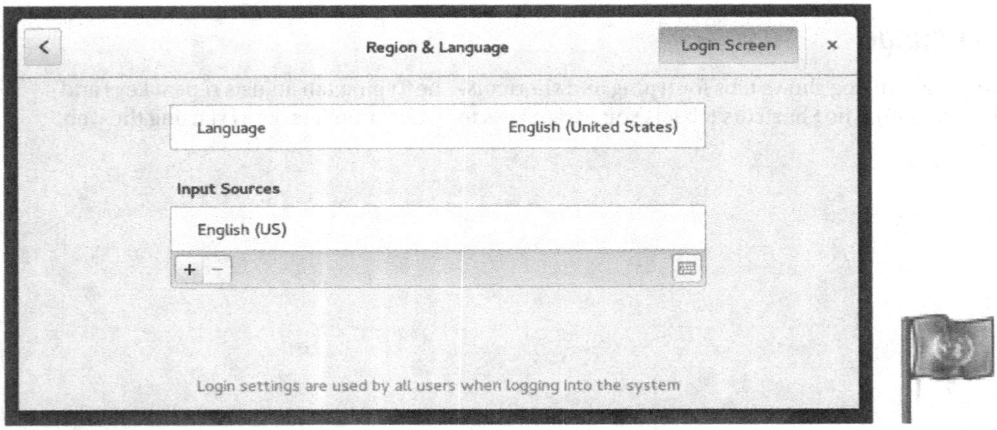

Figure 3-50. *Region & Language with Input Sources*

Color Profiles (GNOME Color Manager)

You can manage the color for different devices by using color profiles specified with the Color dialog accessible from System Settings. The Color dialog lists devices for which you can set color profiles. Click a device to display buttons at the bottom of the screen to Add profile and Calibrate. Your monitor will have a profile set up automatically. Click the Add Profile button to open a dialog with an Automatic Profiles menu from which you can choose a color profile. Click the Add button to add the profile. Available profiles include Adobe RGB, sRGB, and Kodak ProPhoto RGB. You can also import a profile from an ICC profile file of your own.

When you click on a device entry, its Profiles are listed (see Figure 3-51). Click on a profile to display buttons to Set for all users, Remove profile, and View details. Click the View details button for the color profile information.

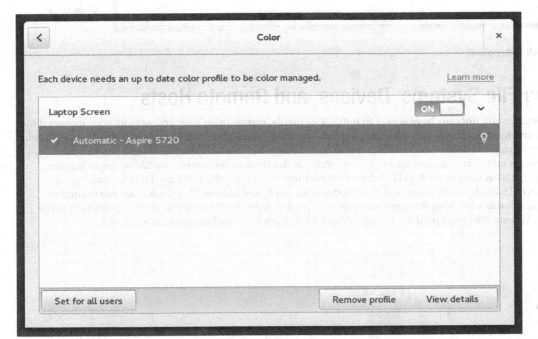

Figure 3-51. *Color management dialog*

Online Accounts

You can configure your online accounts using the Online Accounts dialog in System Settings. Instead of separately configuring mail and chat clients, you can set up access once, using online accounts. Click the plus (+) button at the lower left of the dialog to start the sign-in procedure. You are prompted to sign in using your e-mail and password. Access is provided to Gmail, Google Calendar, and Google Docs. Once access is granted, you will see an entry for Google and the different kinds of applications your Google resources can be used for: mail, calendar, contacts, chat, and documents (see Figure 3-52). Switches that you can use to turn access on and off are provided. Facebook provides Chat access.

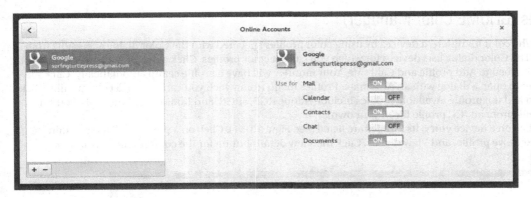

Figure 3-52. *Online Accounts*

Accessing File Systems, Devices, and Remote Hosts

From the file manager, you not only have access to removable media, but you also have access to all your mounted file systems, remote and local, including any Windows-shared directories accessible from Samba. You can browse all your file systems directly from GNOME.

Your file systems and removable media appear as entries in the Devices section of your file manager sidebar (see Figure 3-53). External devices such as USB drives are mounted automatically and have Eject buttons next to their entries. Internal hard drive partitions not mounted at boot, such as Windows file systems, are not mounted automatically. Double-click the hard drive partition entry to mount them. An Eject button then appears next to the hard drive entry. You are also prompted to open the drive's file system in a new file manager window.

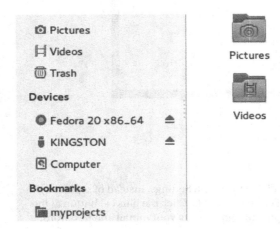

Figure 3-53. *Devices sidebar in the file manager window*

Once they're mounted, internal hard drives are listed, like removable media, in the Removable Devices message tray menu (lower-right corner of the screen; see Figure 3-54). Entries have an Eject button you can use to unmount the drive. Clicking the drive entry opens it in a new file manager window.

Figure 3-54. *Removable Devices message tray menu with hard drives mounted*

File systems on removable media will also appear automatically as entries directly on your desktop message tray. The message tray remains hidden, unless you access it manually by pressing the Super key with the m key on the keyboard (**Super+m**, Super is the Windows key), or by holding the mouse down at the bottom edge of the screen for a period of time. A DVD/CD-ROM is automatically mounted when you insert it into your DVD/CD-ROM drive, displaying a labeled icon for it. The same kind of access is also provided for card readers, digital cameras, USB drives, and external USB/ESATA hard drives (hot-plugged). When you attach an external USB/ESATA drive, it will be mounted automatically and opened in a file manager window. Be sure to unmount (Eject) the USB and external USB/ESATA drives before removing them, so that data will be written.

If you have already configured associated applications for video and audio DVD/CDs, or disks with images, sound, or video files, the disk will be opened with the appropriate application; such as Shotwell for images, Rhythmbox for audio, and Movie Player for DVD/video. If you have not yet configured these associations, you will be prompted to specify which application you want to open it with.

To see network resources, click the Browse Network entry in the Network section of a file manager sidebar. This network window will list your connected network computers. Opening these networks displays the shares they provide, such as shared directories that you can have access to. Drag-and-drop operations are supported for all shared directories, letting you copy files and folders between a shared directory on another computer with a directory on your system. You first must configure your firewall to accept Samba connections before you can browse Windows systems on GNOME. Opening a network resource may require you to login to access the resource.

Video Drivers

Due to open sourcing of much of both the Nvidia and ATI vendor drivers, the X.org and Nouveau open source versions are becoming almost as effective, especially for 2D display support. For normal usage, you may not require vendor driver support. When you installed your system, the correct driver was detected and configured for you automatically.

The name of the X.org ATI video driver is ati (the ATI vendor driver will have the name fglrx, when available). Fedora uses the Nouveau drivers (xorg-x11-drv-nouveau) for Nvidia, an open source project to provide accelerated drivers. These are the default drivers, although the older open source Nvidia drivers (xorg-x11-drv-nv.) are also available. The following are examples:

```
xorg-x11-drv-nouveau
xorg-x11-drv-ati
```

Alternatively, you can obtain the Nvidia and ATI vendor graphics drivers from the RPM Fusion nonfree repository (see Chapter 4 on how to configure access to RPM Fusion). You can download and install these with GNOME Software or the yum command. RPM Fusion, which now includes all the former Livna repository drivers, is the best repository for specialized kernel drivers and modules.

If RPM Fusion is configured for PackageKit, a search on nvidia displays Nvidia modules for each kernel version (fglrx for ATI, when available). The vendor graphic drivers use two packages, one for the supporting software and another for the kernel. The kernel modules are specific to the kernel you are using. Each time you update to a new kernel, you will need a new graphics kernel module created specifically for that kernel. This will be automatically downloaded and installed for you as a dependent package when you update your kernel (the RPM Fusion nonfree repository must be active). The driver package is named xorg-x11-drv-nvidia, and the kernel module is named kmod-nvidia, as in the following example:

```
xorg-x11-drv-nvidia
kmod-nvidia
```

Alternatively, you could use a yum command entered in a terminal window that references all the Nvidia packages, by using an asterisk (*), for example:

```
yum install nvidia*
```

If, once installed, your vendor driver fails (hangs or freezes), you must remove the vendor software packages. The easiest way to do this is to start up your system in the command-line mode. When the boot menu displays, edit the Fedora kernel line (press e) and add a 3 at the end of the linux line (see "GRUB Start Menu and Boot Problems," at the beginning of this chapter). You start up with the command-line interface. Log in as the root user and then use the yum command to remove the vendor driver, such as Nvidia. Use an asterisk (*) to select all the vendor packages. The following example will remove all the Nvidia vendor packages.

```
yum remove nvidia*
```

When you restart, your system reconfigures automatically to the originally installed drivers, such as nouveau for Nvidia cards.

Multimedia Support: MP3, DVD Video, and DivX

Due to licensing and other restrictions, the Fedora distribution does not include MP3, DVD video, or DivX media support. You cannot play MP3 files, DVD video disks, or DivX files after installing Fedora. RPM Fusion (http://rpmfusion.org) provides needed libraries and support files for these media formats. These are RPM packages that you can install with yum, after first downloading and installing their repository configuration files.

The commercial DVD-Video codec (DVDCSS) is available only from the Livna repository, not from RPM Fusion. See Chapter 4 for how to access the Livna repository. You can also download the libdvdcss package directly from http://rpm.livna.org. Also, www.fluendo.com will provide DVD video and MP3 codecs. The MP3 codec is free.

DivX support can be obtained using the open source version of DivX, called Xvid (xvid-core). It's available on the RPM Fusion repository and will play most DivX files.

Check http://fedoraproject.org/wiki/Multimedia for more information. There are many forbidden items that cannot be included with Fedora, due to licensing restrictions, including MP3 support, Adobe Reader, and Nvidia vendor-provided drivers. Check http://fedoraproject.org/wiki/ForbiddenItems for details.

Terminal Window

The terminal window allows you to enter Linux commands on a command line (Utilities ➤ Terminal). It also provides you with a shell interface for using shell commands instead of your desktop. The command line can be edited, allowing you to use the Backspace key to erase characters on the line. Pressing a key will insert that character. You can use the left and right arrow keys to move anywhere along the line, and then press keys to insert characters, or use Backspace to delete characters (see Figure 3-55). Folders, files, and executable files are color-coded—black for files, blue for folders, green for executable files, and aqua for links. Shared folders are displayed with a green background.

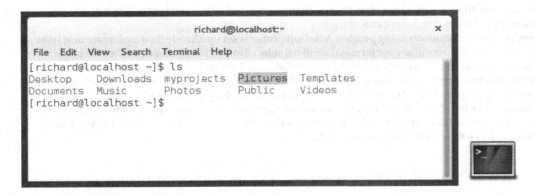

Figure 3-55. *Terminal window*

The terminal window will remember the previous commands you entered. Use the up and down arrows to display those commands in turn on the command line. Press the Enter key to re-execute the currently displayed command. You can even edit a previous command before running it, allowing you to execute a modified version of a previous command. This can be helpful if you need to re-execute a complex command with a different argument, or if you mistyped a complex command and want to correct it without having to retype the entire command. The terminal window will display all your previous interactions and commands for that session. Use the scrollbar to view any previous commands you ran and their displayed results.

You can open as many terminal windows as you want, each working in its own shell. Instead of opening a separate window for each new shell, you can open several shells in the same window, using tabs. Select Open Tab from the File menu to open a new tab (Shift+Ctrl+t). Each tab runs a separate shell, letting you enter different commands in each (see Figure 3-56). You can use the Tabs menu to move to different tabs, or just click on its tab to select it. The Tabs menu is displayed on the menu bar only if multiple tabs are open. For a single window, the Tabs menu is not shown (see Figure 3-41).

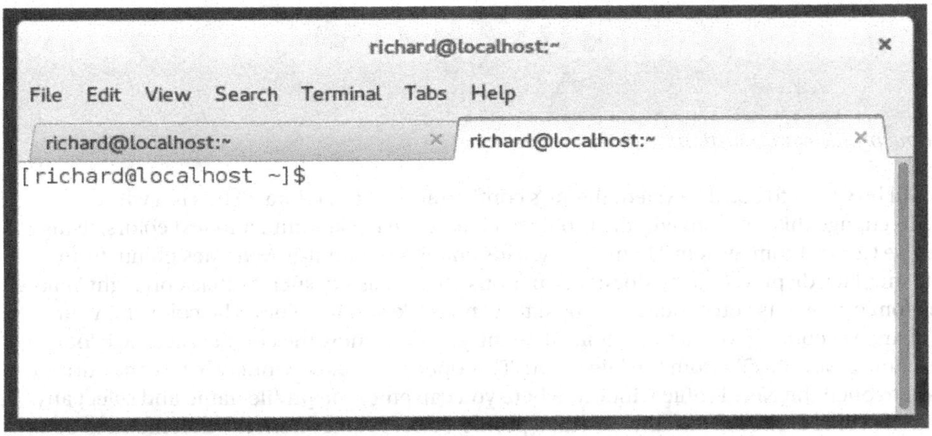

Figure 3-56. *Terminal window with tabs*

The terminal window also supports GNOME desktop cut/copy-and-paste operations. You can copy a line from a web page and then paste it to the terminal window. (You can use the Paste entry on the terminal window's Edit menu or press Shift+Ctrl+v.) The command will appear, and then you can press Enter to execute the command. This is useful for command-line operations displayed on an instructional web page. Instead of typing in a complex command yourself, just select and copy from the web page directly, and then paste to the terminal window. You can also perform any edits on the command, if necessary, before executing it.

You can customize terminal windows using profiles. A default profile is set up already. You can create new ones with customized preferences. To customize your terminal window, select Profile Preferences from the Edit menu. This opens a window for setting your profile options with tabs for General, Title and Command, Colors, Scrolling, and Compatibility. The window title lists your current profile. This will be the default profile, if you have not set one up and selected another profile (see Figure 3-57). On the General tab, you can select the default size of a terminal window in text rows and columns. The Scrolling tab specifies the number of command lines your terminal history will keep. These are the lines you can move back through and select to re-execute. You can set this to Unlimited to keep all the commands. You can also place the scrollbar on the right or left side.

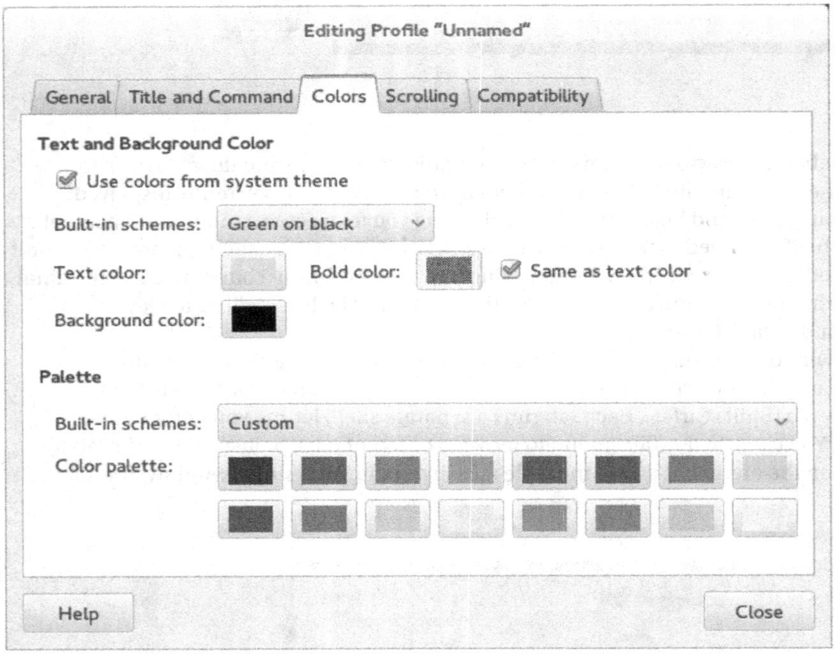

Figure 3-57. *Terminal window profile configuration*

Your terminal window will be set up to use the system theme's configuration. For Fedora 20 this is a white background with black text. To change this, you can edit the profile to change the background and text colors, using the Colors tab. Unselect the Use Colors From System Theme entry. This enables the Built-in Schemes menu, from which you can select a White on Black display. Other color combinations are also listed, such as Black on Light Yellow and Green on Black. The Custom option lets you choose your own text and background colors. The colors on your open terminal window will change according to your selection, allowing you to see how the color choices will look.

To create a new profile, choose New Profile from the File menu. This opens a Profiles window listing the current profiles. Click the New button to open the New Profile window, where you can enter the profile name and select any profile to base it on. The default profile is chosen initially. To edit a profile, select Profiles from the Edit menu to open the Profile window listing your profiles. Select the one you want to edit and then click the Edit button to open the Editing Profile window for that profile.

Command-Line Interface

The command-line interface displays a prompt at which you type a command. You then press the Enter key to run the command. From the desktop, you can open a terminal window (Utilities ➤ Terminal), which provides a command-line interface. Even when using a desktop, you sometimes have to execute commands on a command line.

Linux commands normally have various options and arguments, which must be placed in the correct order. The format for a Linux command is the command name, followed by options, and then arguments, as shown here:

```
$ command-name options arguments
```

An option is a single character preceded by ahyphen, or a word preceded by a double hypen, that determines the type of action the command takes. For example, the `ls` command can take the `-s` option; the `ls` command displays a listing of files in your directory; and the `-s` option adds the size of each file in blocks. You enter the command and its option on the command line, as follows:

```
$ ls -s
```

If you are uncertain as to which format and options a command uses, you can check the command syntax by displaying its man page. Most commands have a man page. Just enter the `man` command with the command name as an argument. See the Man Pages section the following Help section.

Arguments are usually file names or patterns that follow the options on the command line. For example, to display the contents of a file, you can use the `more` command with the file's name as its argument. The `less` and `more` commands, used with the file name `mydata`, would be entered on the command line as follows:

```
$ less mydata
```

The command line is a buffer of text you can edit. Before you press Enter to execute the command, you can edit the command on the command line. The editing capabilities provide a way to correct mistakes you make when typing a command and its options. The Backspace key lets you erase the character you just typed (the one to the left of the cursor) and the Del key lets you erase the character the cursor is on. With this character-erasing capability, you can Backspace over the entire line, if you want, erasing what you entered. Ctrl+u erases the entire command line and lets you start over again at the prompt.

You can use the up arrow to re-display your last executed command. You can then re-execute that command, or you can edit it and execute the modified command. This is helpful when you have to repeat certain operations, such as editing the same file. This is also helpful when you have already executed a command you entered incorrectly.

Running Windows Software on Linux: Wine

Wine is a Windows compatibility layer that allows you to run many Windows applications natively on Linux. The actual Windows operating system is not required. Windows applications will run as if they were Linux applications, and they can access the entire Linux file system and use Linux-connected devices. Applications that are heavily driver-dependent, such as graphic-intensive games, may not run. Others that do not rely on any specialized drivers may run very well, including Photoshop, Microsoft Office, and newsreaders like Newsbin. For some applications, you may also have to copy over specific Windows dynamic link libraries (DLLs) from a working Windows system to your Wine Windows System32 or System directory.

Once installed, Wine applications can be accessed from the Other overview. These applications include Wine configuration, the Wine software uninstaller, and the Wine file browser, as well as a Regedit registry editor, a notepad, and a Wine help tool.

To set up Wine, start the Wine Configuration tool. This opens a window with tabs for Applications, Libraries (DLL Selection), Audio (Sound Drivers), Drives, Desktop Integration, and Graphics. On the Applications tab, you can select the version of Windows an application is designed for. The Drives tab lists your detected partitions, as well as your Windows-emulated drives, such as drive C. The C drive is actually just a directory, .wine/drive_c, and not a partition of a fixed size. Your actual Linux file system will be listed as the Z drive.

Once configured, Wine will set up a .wine directory on the user's home directory. (The directory is hidden, so Show Hidden Files must be enabled in the file manager View menu to display it.) Within that directory will be the drive_c directory, which functions as the C drive that holds your Windows system files and program files in the Windows and Program File subdirectories. The System and System32 directories are located in the Windows directory. This is where you place any needed DLL files. The Program Files directory holds your installed Windows programs, just as they would be installed on a Windows Program Files directory.

To install a Windows application with Wine, double-click the application install icon in a file manager window, or right-click the application install icon and choose Open with Wine Windows Program Loader. Alternatively, you can open a terminal window and run the wine command with the Windows application as an argument. The following example installs the popular Newsbin program:

```
$ wine newsbin.exe
```

Icons for installed Windows software will appear on your Other overview. Just double-click an icon to start up the application. It will run normally within a Linux window, as would any Linux application.

Wine works on both .exe and .msi files installation files. You may have to make them executable by checking the file's Execute check box (from the Permissions tab on the Properties dialog).

■ **Tip** Alternatively, you can use Crossover Office, the commercial Windows compatibility layer. This is a commercial product tested to run certain applications such as Microsoft Office. Check www.codeweavers.com for more details. Crossover Office is based on Wine, which CodeWeavers supports directly.

Help Resources

A great deal of support documentation is already installed on your system, in addition to being accessible from online sources. Table 3-2 lists Help tools and resources accessible on your Fedora Linux system.

Table 3-2. *Fedora Linux Help Resources*

Resource	Description
KDE Help Center	KDE Help tool, desktop interface for documentation on KDE desktop and applications, man pages, and info documents
GNOME Help Browser	GNOME Help tool, desktop interface for accessing documentation for the GNOME desktop and applications
/usr/share/doc	Location of application documentation
man command	Linux man pages, detailed information on Linux commands, including syntax and options
info application	GNU info pages, documentation on GNU applications

(*continued*)

Table 3-2. (*continued*)

Resource	Description
http://fedoraproject.org	Fedora Project site, with numerous documentation, FAQ, and help resources and links, with links to forums, newsgroups, and community web sites
http://docs.fedoraproject.org	Online documentation, guides, HOWTOs, and FAQs for Fedora Linux
www.redhat.com	Red Hat Enterprise documentation, guides, HOWTOs, and FAQs; located under Support and Documentation; much of the Red Hat Linux documentation may be helpful
http://library.gnome.org	GNOME documentation site
http://fedoraforum.org	End-user discussion support forum, endorsed by the Fedora Project; includes FAQs and news links
http://fedorasolved.org	Solutions to common problems
http://ask.fedoraproject.org	Ask Fedora site, on which you can ask questions and search for previously answered questions

GNOME and KDE Help

Both the GNOME and KDE desktops feature Help systems that use a browser-like interface to display help files (Utilities ➤ Help). To start the GNOME Help browser, search for help on the Applications overview (see Figure 3-58). It opens with the GNOME desktop guide, showing links for desktop tasks and topics such as video, system settings, networking, and universal access. The Go menu's "All documents" entry lists links for manuals for different applications, such as the Archive Manager, Empathy, GEdit, and the Totem movie player. The GNOME Help browser and the KDE Help Center also incorporate browser capabilities, including bookmarks and history lists for documents you view.

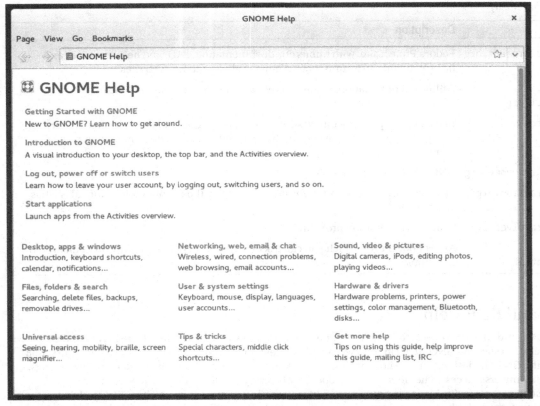

Figure 3-58. *GNOME Help browser*

Context-Sensitive Help

Both GNOME and KDE, in addition to other applications, provide context-sensitive help. Each KDE and GNOME application features detailed manuals that are displayed using their respective Help browsers. Also, system administrative tools feature detailed explanations for each task.

Application Documentation

On your system, the /usr/share/doc directory contains documentation files installed by each application. Within each directory, you can usually find HOWTO, README, and INSTALL documents for that application.

The Man Pages

Each Linux command usually has a corresponding man page that describes its syntax, options, and examples of its use. A man page is a screen of text displayed from the command line, which you can access from a terminal window. To display a man page, enter the man command with the name of the command you want information about. The following example asks for information about the ls command:

```
$ man ls
```

Use basic keyboard keys to navigate the page. Press the spacebar to display the next page. The b key moves you back a page. When you finish, press the q key to quit. To perform a search, press either the slash (/) or question mark (?). The / searches forward, and the ? searches backward. When you press the /, a line opens at the bottom of your screen on which you enter a word to search for. Press Enter to activate the search. You can repeat the same search by pressing the n key.

The Info Pages

Some applications also provide info page documentation. The info pages are similar to man pages but tend to be more detailed. You can also access this documentation by entering the info command, to display a listing of applications. The info interface has its own set of commands. You can learn more about it by entering info info. The m command lets you search for an application by using a search pattern.

Web Resources

You can obtain documentation on Fedora from the Fedora Project site at http://docs.fedoraproject.org and from the Fedora forum at http://fedoraforum.org. The Ask Fedora Project site at http://ask.fedoraproject.org displays answers to common questions and lets you ask your own.

Most Linux applications are covered by the Linux Documentation Project. It shows you how to use the desktop and takes you through a detailed explanation of Linux applications. The GNOME and KDE web sites also contain extensive documentation.

CHAPTER 4

■ ■ ■

Installing and Updating Software: YUM, GNOME Software, PackageKit, and RPM

Fedora software is distributed through an online Fedora software repository. Table 4-1 lists Fedora software information and site locations. Software is added to your system by accessing software repositories with the YUM (Yellowdog Update, Modified) software package manager. With the integration of YUM into your Fedora system, you can now think of that software as an easily installed extension of your current collection. The commonly used Fedora software repositories are listed in Table 4-2.

Table 4-1. *Fedora Software Information and Sites*

Internet Site	Description
http://fedoraproject.org/get-fedora-all	Fedora distribution disks, download links for all formats
http://rpmfusion.org	RPM Fusion repository for third-party multimedia and driver Fedora-compliant software (Fedora Project extension)
http://fedoraproject.org/wiki/ForbiddenItems	Packages not included in the main Fedora software repository
http://fedoraproject.org/wiki/Multimedia	Information on multimedia packages available for Fedora

Table 4-2. *Fedora and Fedora-Compliant Software Repositories*

Internet Site	Description
http://download.fedoraproject.org	Links are provided to the best available mirror.
http://rpmfusion.org/Configuration	Fedora applications not included with the distribution, due to licensing and other restrictions, are provided. Go to the Configuration page to download the YUM configuration files.
http://rpm.livna.org	This RPM Livna repository contains only the dvdcss package. Click the link for the YUM configuration file.
http://get.adobe.com/flashplayer/	The Adobe repository. Select the Linux for YUM to download the Adobe YUM configuration file. Select YUM for Linux from the drop-down menu.
www.google.com/linuxrepositories/	Provides Google repositories for accessing Google software.

Software applications, with all the needed programs, configuration files, and supporting library binaries, are combined into packages by the RPM Package Manager that will install all the componenets into the appropriate system folders. YUM manages all these RPM packages for your system, keep track of updates and what collection of packages belong to different systems and collections such as your desktop or office suite. It also keeps track of dependencies, such as what supporting software an application may need. Multimedia applications may need sound support. To easily manage YUM operations you cna use desktop front ends, such as GNOME Software and PackageKit. GNOME Software lets you manage software by topic, whereas PackageKit searches for particular RPM packages.

Fedora provides only open source applications in its own repository. For proprietary applications such as Nvidia's own graphics drivers, or multimedia applications that may have patent issues, you must use the third-party repository RPM Fusion. The list of forbidden items for the official Fedora repository can be found at `www.fedoraproject.org/wiki/ForbiddenItems`. The list includes such items as the Nvidia and ATI graphics drivers.

Software Repositories

For Fedora, you can add software to your system by accessing software repositories supporting YUM. In addition, many software applications, particularly multimedia ones, have potential licensing conflicts. By leaving such software in third-party repositories, Fedora avoids possible legal issues. Many of the popular multimedia applications, such as video and digital music support, can be obtained from third-party repositories using the same simple yum commands you use with Fedora-sponsored software. The commonly used Fedora software repositories are listed in Table 4-2.

Most software is now located on the Internet-connected repositories. With the integration of YUM into your Fedora system, you can now think of that software as an easily installed extension of your current collection. You can find out more about how YUM is used on "Fedora Software Management Guide, Chapter 4, Yum Configuration," which is located on the following Fedora documentation page:

`http://docs.fedoraproject.org/en-US/Fedora/14/html/Software_Management_Guide/Configuraci%C3%B3n_de_YUM.html`

You can also browse many of these repositories and download packages individually (see Table 4-3), although this is not recommended, as you would lose the automatic updating support provided by YUM.

***Table 4-3.** Fedora Repository Package Sites*

Menu Item	Description
`http://download.fedoraproject.org`	Fedora repository
`http://mirrors.fedoraproject.org`	Page listing Fedora mirrors
`http://rpmfusion.org`	Fedora applications not included with the distribution due to licensing and other restrictions. Select your Fedora version from the "Browse Available Packages" section
`http://rpm.livna.org/repo`	Livna repository site

Fedora Software Repositories

The Fedora Linux distribution provides a comprehensive selection of software, ranging from office and multimedia applications to Internet servers and administration services. The complete set is available on the Fedora repository. During installation, YUM is configured on your system, to access the Fedora repository. Some third-party applications with licensing issues are not included, though Fedora-compliant versions are provided on associated software repositories.

For Fedora, you can update to the latest software from the Fedora YUM repository using Software Update. Your Software Update tool is already configured to access the Fedora repositories.

RPM Fusion

Due to licensing restrictions, multimedia support for popular operations such as MP3, DVD, and DivX is not included with Fedora distributions. The Fedora Project associated site, RPM Fusion (`http://rpmfusion.org`), does provide support for these functions. Here, you can download support for MP3, DVD, and DivX software. This repository integrates support previously provided by Livna, Freshrpms, and Dribble. Fedora does include the generic X.org Nvidia and ATI drivers, which will provide all the capabilities most people need. You do not have to use the Nvidia or ATI vendor drivers.

■ **Note**   You can download the free licensed MP3 GStreamer plug-in from `www.fluendo.com`. You can also purchase a DVD video codec.

The Fedora-compliant repositories, such as RPM Fusion, will have Fedora-compliant YUM configuration files that you can download and install as an RPM package. You can then use the GNOME Software, PackageKit, or the yum command to select, download, and install software from the associated repository directly.

Adobe and Livna

Two smaller additional third-party repositories are often configured for desktop users: the Adobe repository and the Livna repository (see Chapter 6). The Adobe repository holds packages for the Linux version of the Adobe Flash software. (Two alternative Flash-compatible open source versions are already available, swfdec and gnash, and it is recommended that you use those instead.) The Livna repository provides the commercial DVD video codec, libdvdcss. The repository contains only this one package. If you want to play commercial DVD video disks, you have to configure access to this repository.

Third-Party Linux Software Archives

Though almost all applications should be included in the Fedora software repository or its associated repositories, such as `http://rpmfusion.org`, you could download and install software from third-party software archives. Always check to see if the software you want is already in the Fedora or Fedora-associated repositories. If it is not available, you can download it from a third-party online site.

Several third-party repositories make it easy to locate and find information about an application. Of particular note are `www.sourceforge.net`, `www.rpmfind.net`, `http://gnomefiles.org`, and `http://kde-apps.org`. Sites for Linux software are listed in Table 4-4, along with several specialized sites, such as those for commercial and game software. When downloading software packages, always check to see if the versions are packaged as RPM packages and if they are already available on the Fedora and RPM Fusion repositories.

Table 4-4. *Third-Party Linux Software Archives*

URL	Internet Site
http://sourceforge.net	SourceForge, open source software development site for Linux applications
http://gnomefiles.org	GNOME applications
http://kde-apps.org	KDE software repository
www.rpmfind.net	RPM package repository
www.gnu.org	GNU archive
www.linuxgames.com	Linux games
www.fluendo.com	Licensed multimedia codecs for Linux, including free MP3 code

Updating Fedora: GNOME Software and Software Update

New updates are continually being prepared for particular software packages. These are posted as updates that you can download from software repositories and install on your system. They include new versions of applications, servers, and even the kernel. Such updates may range from single software packages to whole components.

Updating your Linux system has become a very simple procedure, using the automatic update tools. For Fedora, you can update your system by accessing software repositories supporting the YUM update methods. YUM uses RPM headers to determine which packages have to be updated. To update your packages, you use Software Update (GNOME Software), labeled as Software Update. Software Update is a graphical update interface for YUM, which performs all updates from the desktop. From a command line, you can perform updates using the yum update command.

If updates are detected, GNOME Software will display an update message in the message tray (see Figure 4-1). Clicking the View button opens GNOME Software to the Updates tab, from which you can then perform the update. Clicking the Restart & Install button immediately shuts down your system, then restarts, and, as part of the startup process, downloads and installs updates.

Figure 4-1. *Update notification message and icon*

On Fedora, you can use either GNOME Software to perform updates (the default), or you can use the older Software Update. Software Update is part of the PackageKit software manager and is installed with PackageKit. PackageKit is not installed by default. The name used for PackageKit on GNOME Software is simply *Packages*.

Updating Fedora with GNOME Software Update

GNOME Software is the primary update tool for Fedora. You can view updates by using the Updates tab on GNOME Software (see Figure 4-2). The tab will display the number of updates. Clicking an update opens a dialog showing information about the update. Some entries, such as OS Updates, will have several packages that have to be updated (see Figure 4-3). When you are ready, click the Restart & Install button on the header bar to shut down your system and install the updates as it restarts.

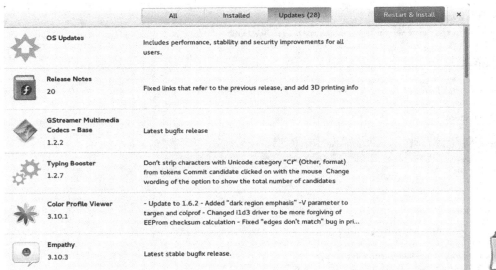

Figure 4-2. *GNOME Software: Updates tab*

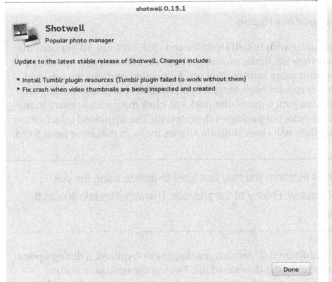

Figure 4-3. *GNOME Software: Update information dialog*

99

Updating Fedora with Software Update (PackageKit)

If you install PackageKit (Packages), the Software Update package will also have been installed. You can, if you wish, use it to update your system, instead of using GNOME Software. You can open Software Updates from the Applications overview. Software Update displays the Software Update dialog showing your updates (see Figure 4-4).

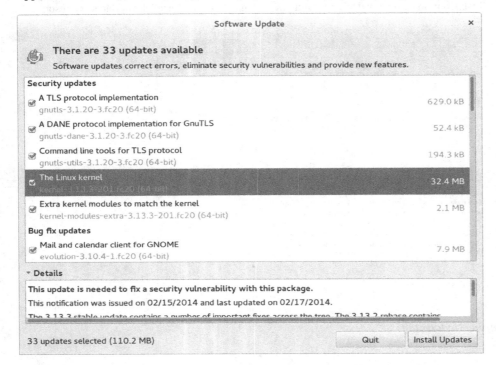

Figure 4-4. *Software Update: selected package with displayed description*

The number of updates is shown on the lower right, along with Install Updates and Quit buttons. To perform the updates, click the Install Updates button. If you want to review the updates, and perhaps deselect certain updates, you scroll through the list of updates, selecting the ones you want more information on. All needed updates are selected automatically when Software Update starts up. The check boxes for each entry let you deselect particular packages you may not want to update. Should you want to see details about a particular package, click the package entry in the package listing. The lower pane of the window displays the selected package's description. The displayed information includes features such as the version and repository. Bug fixes will show Bugzilla entries for bugs that have been fixed.

■ **Tip**   After a new install, if Software Update fails to run or function, you may first have to update using the yum command. Enter the yum update command in a terminal window. Enter y at the prompts. This initial update should fix problems with Software Update, which should then function.

Click the Install Updates button to start updating. If additional dependent packages are required, a dialog opens and lists them. Click the Continue button to add the packages to the download list. During the update, a status message is displayed at the bottom of the Software Update dialog for the different update stages, beginning with dependency checks, then download, followed by testing, and ending with installation and cleanup (see Figure 4-5). You can click the Quit button during dependency and downloading to cancel the update.

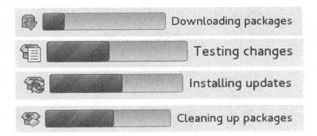

Figure 4-5. *Update progress messages*

If, during the update, PackageKit has to access a new repository for the first time, you will be prompted to accept the repository's key. Click the Yes button to approve access to that repository. You will then be prompted to authenticate the action by entering the root user (administrative) password.

If a new kernel is installed, you will be prompted to restart your system. If updates to GNOME have been installed, you may have to log out and log back in.

Should a new kernel be installed, when you boot, you will then be using the new kernel. Your old kernel will remain as a GRUB option, should you have difficulties with the new kernel. To choose the old kernel, you must select it from the GRUB boot screen. To make the old kernel the default, you can set the default option in the /etc/default/grub file to 1 (the new kernel will be 0).

You can also manually perform updates, instead of waiting for a notification icon. Start PackageKit from the Software icon on the System Tools overview. Then, from the PackageKit Software menu (located on the GNOME top bar), choose Check for Updates. This opens the Software Update dialog with a notice showing how many updates are available (see Figure 4-4). First, a check for updates is performed. Updates are then displayed, with a description of the selected one in the lower pane of the window. You can deselect those you do not want updated. To perform your package updates, you can just click the Install Updates button.

You can also start up Software Update by clicking the Check Now button on the Software Update Preferences dialog, accessible from the Software GNOME applications menu as Software Sources.

If there are no updates, a message is displayed, notifying you that no updates are available, and then the Software Update dialog closes.

Update Preferences

You can configure when checks are made for updating, as well as whether to perform the updates automatically. Use the Software Update Preferences dialog to set your update options. The dialog is accessible from the Software applications (PackageKit). From the Software application's GNOME applications menu, choose Software Sources, to open the Software Update Preferences dialog at the Update Settings tab. Here, you can set the intervals for checking for updates and major upgrades (see Figure 4-6). For wireless and laptop systems, you have the option to perform updates using mobile broadband and battery power.

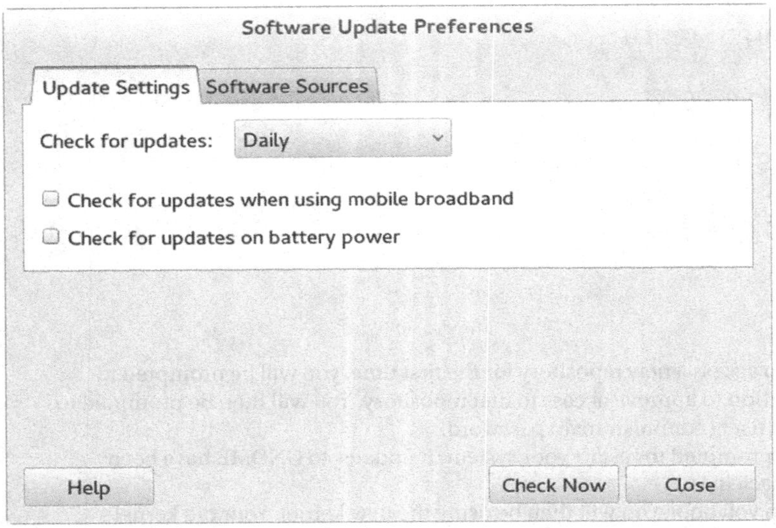

Software Update Preferences

Update Settings | Software Sources

Check for updates: Daily ∨

☐ Check for updates when using mobile broadband
☐ Check for updates on battery power

Help   Check Now   Close

Figure 4-6. *Software Update Preferences dialog*

Initially, updates are checked daily, and no action is taken. The user must apply the updates. On the Check for Updates pop-up menu, you can select hourly, daily, weekly, or never. Daily is the default and the option normally used. The Never option would require that the user manually check for updates. The check for major upgrades can be done weekly or not at all.

On the Software Sources tab, you can choose which software repositories to update from.

Clicking the Check Now button opens the Software Update dialog, which lets you check for updates immediately.

Update with the yum Command

Alternatively, you can update using the yum command and the update option. The following would update an already installed Gnumeric package.

```
yum update  gnumeric
```

You can use the check-update option to see which packages need to be updated.

```
yum check-update
```

To perform a complete update of all your installed packages, you just use the update option. This would have the same effect of updating with Software Update.

```
yum update
```

In some cases, when you first install a new system from your DVD/CD, there may be incompatibilities or bugs that prevent you from using Software Update to update to the latest system fixes on the Fedora repository. In such cases, you can open a terminal window (Utilities ➤ Terminal) and update directly with the yum command.

```
yum update
```

This can also occur if your display fails and you cannot access your desktop due to bugs in the initial release, which may be fixed with updates. You could then boot into the command-line interface (runlevel 3) and, after logging in, enter the yum update command.

A manual update may also become necessary if you have broken dependencies. If, among a set of packages to be updated, just one or more have broken dependencies, the entire set will not be updated by GNOME Software. GNOME Software does not always inform you of the packages causing trouble. Otherwise, you could just deselect them from the package listing in Software Update. To exclude such broken dependencies, you can open a terminal window and run yum update with the --skip-broken option.

```
yum update --skip-broken
```

To exclude a particular package or set of packages, you can run yum update with the --exclude option. To select several packages with the same prefix, add an asterisk (*) file-matching operator to the package name. You can add as many exclude options as you want. The following updates all packages except Perl packages:

```
yum update --exclude=perl*
```

Automatic YUM Update with cron

The yum-cron package installs a cron configuration file for YUM. These include yum.cron files in the /etc/cron.daily and /etc/cron.weekly directories, which will automatically update your system. The cron entry will first update the YUM software, if needed, and then proceed to download and install any updates for your installed packages. It runs yum with the update option.

The automatic update will run only if it detects a YUM lock file in the /var/lock/subsys directory. By default, this is missing. You can add it using the yum-cron service script. The start option creates the lock file, enabling the cron-supported updates, and the stop option removes the file, disabling the automatic update. Be sure to first log in as the root user (su).

```
su
service yum-cron start
```

Presto: Efficient Updating with DeltaRPM Packages

Presto updates packages by downloading only those parts of a package that have been modified, instead of the entire package, significantly reducing downloads. The Presto plug-in for YUM (the yum-presto package, installed by default) updates packages using DeltaRPM packages, instead of full-replacement packages. The DeltaRPM packages are much smaller, containing only changed data that is used to generate an updated package version on your system, which is then used to update your system. Only the changed data for an updated package needs to be downloaded.

Installing Software Packages

Installing software is an administrative function performed by a user with administrative access. Unless you chose to install all your packages during your installation, only some of the many applications and utilities available to Linux users were installed on your system. On Fedora, you can install or remove software from your system with either the GNOME Software software manager or the yum install command. Alternatively, you can install software as individual packages, with the rpm command or by downloading and compiling its source code. The procedure for installing software using its source code has been simplified to just a few commands, though you have a great deal of flexibility in tailoring an application to your specific system.

An RPM software package operates like its own installation program for a software application. A Linux software application often consists of several files that must be installed in different directories. The program is most likely placed in a directory called /usr/bin; online manual files go in another directory; and library files go in yet another directory. In addition, the installation may require modification of certain configuration files on your system. The RPM software packages perform all these tasks for you. Also, if you later decide you don't want a specific application, you can uninstall packages to remove all the files and configuration information from your system.

The software packages on your install disk, as extensive as they are, represent only some of the software packages available for Fedora Linux. Most reside on the Fedora Software repository, a repository whose packages are available for automatic download using the GNOME Software application. Many additional multimedia applications and support libraries can be found at the RPM Fusion repository (http://rpmfusion.org) and, once configured, downloaded directly with YUM and GNOME Software. Table 4-2 lists several Fedora software repositories. Fedora and RPM Fusion are YUM-supported, meaning that a simple YUM configuration enables you to directly download and install software from those sites using the yum command or the PackageKit software manager. Fedora repository configuration was performed during the installation of your Fedora system. RPM Fusion provides its own YUM configuration file that you install manually.

Installing with YUM

Downloading Fedora software or software from any configured Fedora YUM repository is a simple matter of using Software (GNOME Software), which provides a desktop interface for YUM. YUM, by default, stops the entire install process if there is any configuration or dependency problem with any one repository or package. Check http://fedoraproject.org/wiki/Tools/yum for tips on using YUM.

Alternatively, in a terminal window, you can enter the yum command with the install option and the name of the package. YUM will detect the software and any dependencies, and it will prompt you to download and install it. For example, the following command will install Abiword:

```
yum install abiword
```

YUM provides several plug-ins you can use to add update and install features, such as download-only (allows only to download packages), fastmirror (chooses the fastest mirror), and security (restricts to security updates) plug-ins. The YUM plug-in package names begin with the prefix yum-plugin. Additional information on YUM plug-ins is available at http://fedoraproject.org/wiki/Docs/Drafts/SoftwareManagementGuide/CustomizingYum.

Installing Individual Packages with Your Browser

You can use your browser to download an individual package from a site directly. You should use this method only for packages not already available from YUM-supported repositories. This is true for certain packages, such as the RPM Fusion YUM configuration packages you need to install before you can access the RPM Fusion repository. You also have to install any needed dependent packages manually, as well as check system compatibility. Your Fedora web browsers will let you perform both a download and install in one simple operation. A dialog opens that prompts you to open with the package installer, which invokes PackageKit (see Figure 4-7, left). The package is downloaded, and you are asked if you want to install the file (see Figure 4-7, right). Subsequent dialogs show the installation progress.

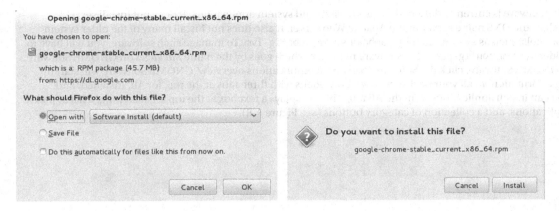

Figure 4-7. *Web browser package install*

On a GNOME desktop, packages that have already been downloaded can be installed with a simple right-click, then choose the install selection from the menu invoking GNOME Software, to perform the installation (gpk-install-file). As with the browser download, you are prompted to install the package.

GNOME Software (Software)

GNOME Software is the software management front end for YUM. The GNOME Software software manager is Internet-based, installing from online repositories, using YUM to download and install. It is designed to be a cross-distribution package manager that can be used on any YUM-supported Linux distribution. See http://fedoraproject.org/wiki/Changes/AppInstaller for more information.

GNOME Software performs a variety of different software tasks, including installation, removal, updating, and install of an individual RPM file (see Table 4-5). The GNOME Software application is gnome-software, accessible from the Applications overview as Software.

Table 4-5. *PackageKit Applications*

Application	Description
gpk-application	Software
gpk-update-viewer	Updates your system with Software Update
gpk-prefs	Configures update preferences
gpk-log	Views history of updates
gpk-install-local-file	Installs local software packages

GNOME Software is currently designed to install client and system applications. It does not install server software, such as the DNS name server or the Apache Web server. It also does not install many of the older system configuration tools, such as `system-config-samba` or `system-config-lvm`. To manage such software, you will have to install the older `system-config-packages` software manager, which goes by the name *Packages* on GNOME Software.

To use GNOME Software, click the Software icon on the Applications overview. GNOME Software will start up by gathering information on all your packages. A window opens with three tabs at the top, for All, Installed, and Updates. You can install applications from the All tab, which displays a text box at the top for searching, a list of picks, featured applications, and a collection of category buttons (see Figure 4-8).

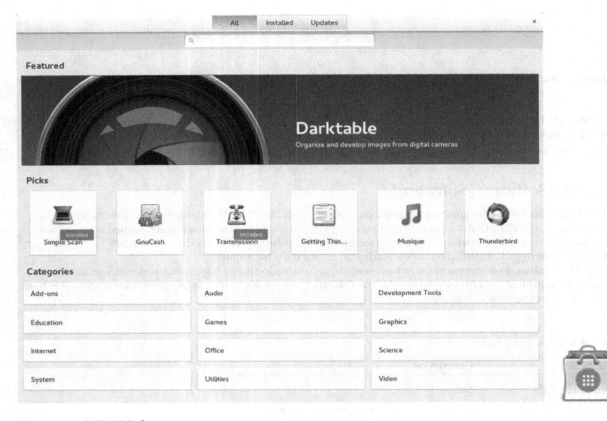

Figure 4-8. *GNOME Software*

Click any category tab to open a dialog with subcategories. The Graphics category has subcategories such as Vector Graphics, Publishing, and Photography (see Figure 4-9). To the right, the software in each category is listed as icons. Packages already installed are labeled as such.

Figure 4-9. *GNOME Software: Graphics category*

Click a software icon to open a page, which provides a brief description of the software and a link to its related web site (see Figure 4-10). Uninstalled software displays an Install button, on the header bar to the right, and installed software shows a Remove button. The History button displays a dialog showing when it was installed and any updates.

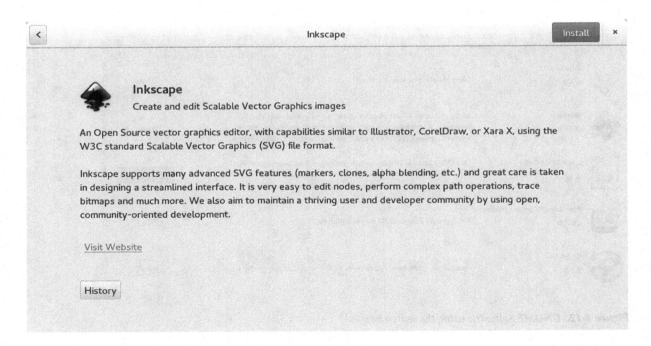

Figure 4-10. *GNOME Software: software descriptor page*

Click the Install button to install the software. As the software is installed, a label appears on the button (see Figure 4-11). When complete, the button displays a red Remove button, which you can use to uninstall the software, if you wish.

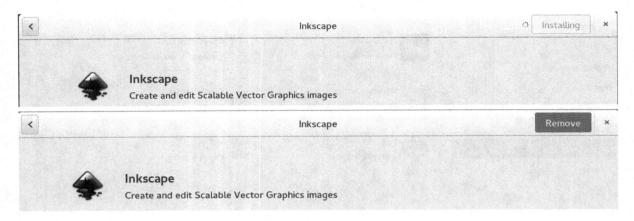

Figure 4-11. *GNOME Software: installing software*

You can also search for a package using the search box on the All tab. Enter part of the name or a term to describe the package (see Figure 4-12). Results are listed, showing an icon, name, version number, description, and an action button. An Install button is displayed for uninstalled software, and a Remove button for installed software. Click the button to perform the task. Clicking the software icon opens its descriptor page.

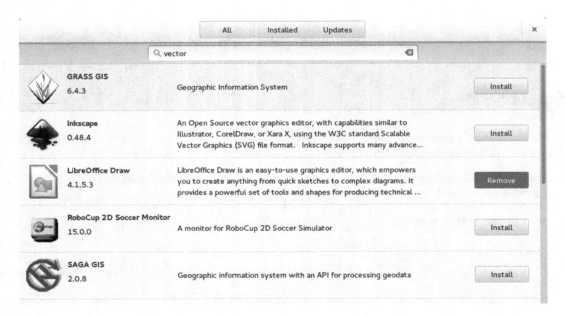

Figure 4-12. *GNOME Software: using the search box*

The Installed tab lists your installed software (see Figure 4-13). To remove software, click its Remove button.

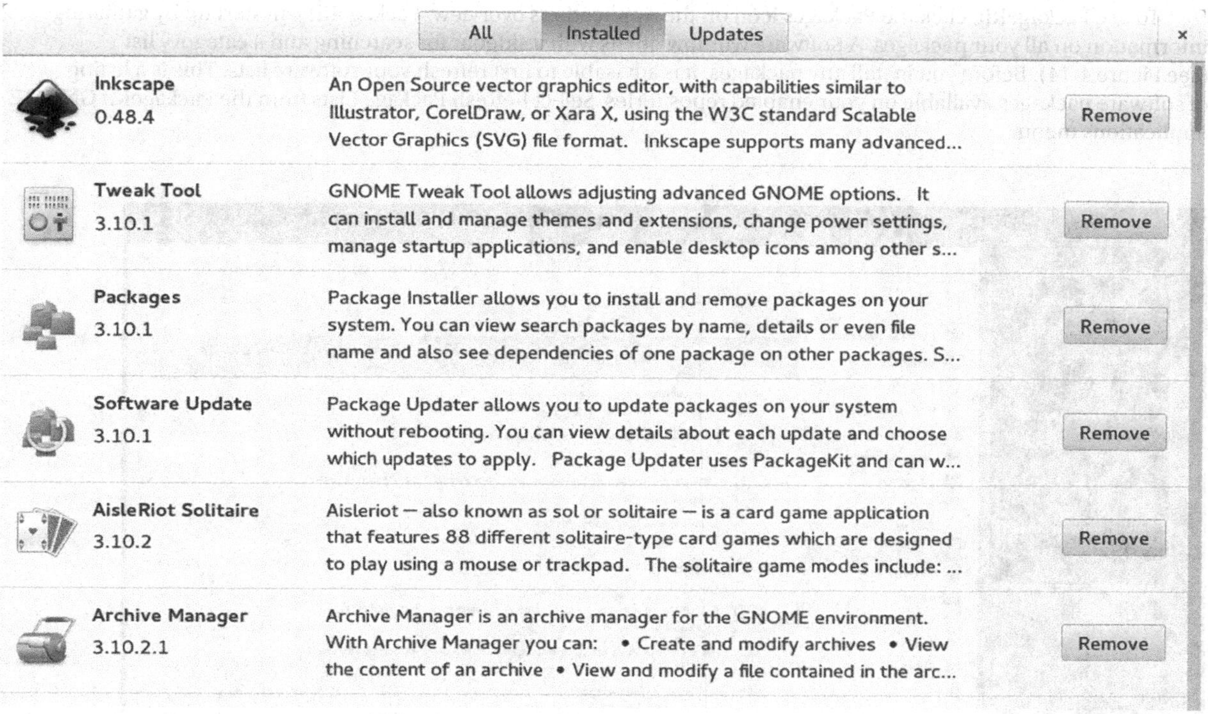

	All	Installed	Updates		×
Inkscape 0.48.4	An Open Source vector graphics editor, with capabilities similar to Illustrator, CorelDraw, or Xara X, using the W3C standard Scalable Vector Graphics (SVG) file format. Inkscape supports many advanced...			Remove	
Tweak Tool 3.10.1	GNOME Tweak Tool allows adjusting advanced GNOME options. It can install and manage themes and extensions, change power settings, manage startup applications, and enable desktop icons among other s...			Remove	
Packages 3.10.1	Package Installer allows you to install and remove packages on your system. You can view search packages by name, details or even file name and also see dependencies of one package on other packages. S...			Remove	
Software Update 3.10.1	Package Updater allows you to update packages on your system without rebooting. You can view details about each update and choose which updates to apply. Package Updater uses PackageKit and can w...			Remove	
AisleRiot Solitaire 3.10.2	Aisleriot — also known as sol or solitaire — is a card game application that features 88 different solitaire-type card games which are designed to play using a mouse or trackpad. The solitaire game modes include: ...			Remove	
Archive Manager 3.10.2.1	Archive Manager is an archive manager for the GNOME environment. With Archive Manager you can: • Create and modify archives • View the content of an archive • View and modify a file contained in the arc...			Remove	

Figure 4-13. *GNOME Software: Installed tab*

PackageKit (Packages)

PackageKit is the software management front end for YUM. The PackageKit Package Manager is Internet-based, which means it installs from online repositories, using YUM to download and install. It is designed to be a cross-distribution package manager that can be used on any YUM-supported Linux distribution. See www.packagekit.org for more information.

PackageKit provides a variety of applications for different software tasks, including installation, removal, updates, repository management, logs, and install of an individual RPM file (see Table 4-5). The primary PackageKit application is gpk-application, accessible as Packages. The gpk-update-viewer (Software Update) lets you examine and select updates. The gpk-log displays a list of all your previous install, removal, and update operations, including major updates and individual package installs (accessible on PackageKit from the Applications menu [top bar], as the "Software Log" menu item). The PackageKit gpk-install-local-file application is used to install an RPM package file that you downloaded separately.

To use PackageKit, click the Packages icon on the Applications overview. PackageKit will start up by gathering information on all your packages. A Software window opens with a sidebar for searching and a category list (see Figure 4-14). Before you install any packages, it is advisable to first refresh your software lists. This is a listing of software packages available on your enabled repositories. Select Refresh Package Lists from the PackageKit GNOME applications menu.

Figure 4-14. *PackageKit: Software*

PackageKit Browsing

You can find packages by category by selecting a category on the sidebar. All the packages in that category are listed. Uninstalled packages have faded package icons with an empty check box, and installed packages have a solid color with a check mark in the check box. Categories let you browse through your software, seeing what is available for different kinds of tasks or features, such as multimedia applications or applications designed for the GNOME desktop. Figure 4-15 shows the packages for the GNOME desktop category.

Figure 4-15. *Package information*

PackageKit Software Installation

To install a package, first click its check box (see Figure 4-15). The box is checked, and a plus sign (+) appears on the package icon, as in the following illustration:

111

You can click several packages to select them for installation. Once you are ready to install, click the Apply Changes button (upper right). The status bar at the bottom will show the tasks being performed, starting with downloading, then installing, and finally, finishing.

A progress bar will show the install task's progress. The PackageKit task messages are displayed at the top-right corner. At the download phase, a Cancel button becomes active, letting you cancel the install. Once the package is installed, the package icon color will change from faded to a solid color, and a check mark will be displayed in its check box.

If dependent or additional packages are required by the software you want to install, these are listed, and you are prompted to confirm their installation. Click Continue.

Each time you click Apply Changes to install packages, you are prompted to enter the root user password to authorize the installation.

After the installation, if the packages contain applications that can be run, a window opens, listing the applications and asking you if you want to run one now. Click the application entry and click Run.

If you choose to remove an installed package, click its check box. The check box becomes empty, and a wastebasket image is displayed on the package icon, as shown in the illustration following. Then click Apply Changes to uninstall. Once the package is removed, the package icon color becomes faded.

PackageKit Selected Package Actions and Information

To access information about a particular package, select it. A pane then opens at the bottom and displays a description of the software and a button bar to the right, with buttons for the software's web site, a list of installed files, required packages, and dependent packages (see Figure 4-16). The Visit Project Website button opens your browser to the package home page where you can find more detailed information about it.

Figure 4-16. *Package information*

You can also install or remove a selected package using the button bar. Click the package and then, from the button bar to the right of the description, choose Install Package or Remove Package. For an uninstalled package, clicking the Install Package button will place a check mark on the selected package's check box. To actually perform the install, you then click the Apply Changes button. An installed package allows only removal, and an uninstalled package allows only installation. For installed packages, clicking the Remove Package button will uncheck the package's check box. Clicking Apply Changes will then remove the package. Before you click Apply Changes, you can always change your selections, checking or unchecking a package's check box, as you wish.

The Files, Dependent Packages, and Required Packages buttons open a separate window listing those files and packages. The Files entry opens a window that lists all the files the package can install or has installed. This can be helpful for tracking down the command names and location of the configuration files. The Dependent Packages and Required Packages buttons open windows that show the package's dependencies—those that depend on it, as well as those it depends on.

PackageKit Searching

Instead of tracking down a package through categories, you can search for it using its package name. Enter a pattern to search for in the Search box, located at the top of the category sidebar, and press Enter, or click the Find button. If you enter a complete package name, like Wine, that package is selected and displayed.

PackageKit Filtering

Instead of showing all your available packages, both installed and uninstalled, you can filter the package listing. Two filter options are available from the PackageKit GNOME applications menu. You can filter by newest versions and native packages. Native packages are those for your system architecture, such as 64-bit (x86_64) or 32-bit (i686).

Managing Repositories

YUM is the primary package-management tool. When you install a package, YUM is invoked and automatically selects and downloads the package from the appropriate repository. After having installed your system, when you then want to install additional packages, PackageKit will use YUM to install from a repository. This will include all active YUM online repositories you have configured, such as sites like http://rpmfusion.org, not just the Fedora and update repositories configured during installation. You can also install from the Fedora Install DVD, if you have it.

You can enable or disable your configured YUM repositories using the Software Sources tab on the Software Update Preferences dialog. From the Software GNOME application's menu, select Software Sources. Click the Software Sources tab to see a listing of your configured repositories (see Figure 4-17).

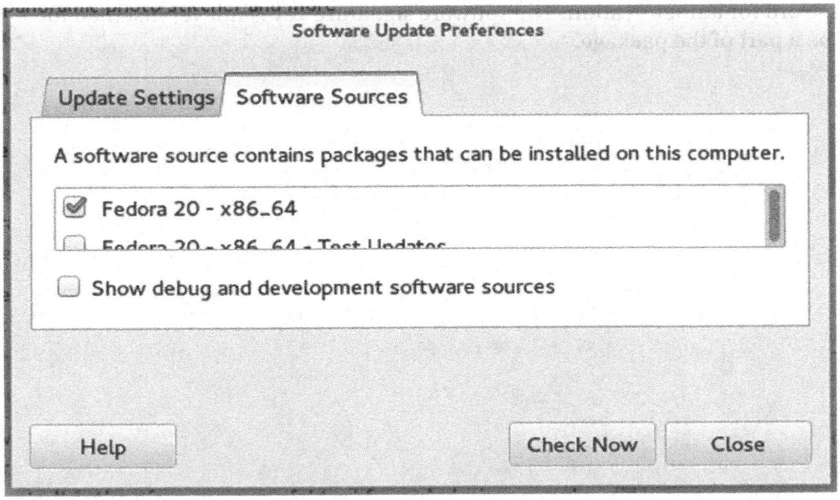

Figure 4-17. *Software Sources tab: configured software repositories*

These are repositories that have YUM configuration files in the /etc/yum.repos.d directory, holding information such as URLs, GPG keys, and descriptions. Enabled repositories are checked. You can disable a repository by unchecking it. The Fedora repository names include the release number and the platform, such as x86_64 for the 64-bit version. Fedora and Fedora Update repositories will be enabled.

Software lists the packages available from all the active repositories. If you want to see the package from just one repository, you can deactivate the others. For example, if you wanted to see only the RPM Fusion repository, you could deactivate all others, including Fedora. You can reactivate the other repositories later.

Repositories also have specialized repositories for development, debugging, and source code files. Here you find applications under development that may be useful, as well as the latest revisions. Some will have testing repositories for applications not yet completely validated for the current release. These applications might not work well. Source, Test, and Debug repositories will normally be disabled. Test is the development repository for a future release currently under development. The source repositories hold source code packages. To display the Source, Test, and Debug repositories, check the Show Debug and Development Software Sources check box at the bottom of the Software Sources menu.

Using the RPM Fusion Repository with PackageKit

The RPM Fusion repository (http://rpmfusion.org) holds popular third-party drivers and codecs. These include the vendor graphics drivers for Linux, when they become available, such as those provided by Nvidia and ATI/AMD. Also included are multimedia codecs with licensing issues, such as MP3, AC3, and MPEG2 codecs, as well as MPEG4 and DivX (Xvid).

To access the RPM Fusion repository, you first must download and install both its YUM configuration file and its GPG authentication key. These are both included in RPM Fusion's rpmfusion-free package. Simply download and install this package using your web browser. The package is located at http://wrpmfusion.org (see Figure 4-18). Click the Configuration link at the top of the page to go to the Configuration page. There are free and non-free packages, with links for each. Be sure to install the free package first. The non-free package is optional. On the section titled "Graphical Setup via Firefox Web Browser," click the link labeled "RPM Fusion Free for Fedora 20" to download the rpmfusion-free configuration package. When you click the link, Fedora detects that it is a software package and opens a dialog with the option to install it directly. During the installation, you are notified that the package is untrusted and are prompted to confirm installation, further requiring you to enter your root password for authentication. The software signature key is not yet installed for the RPM Fusion repository but will be a part of the package.

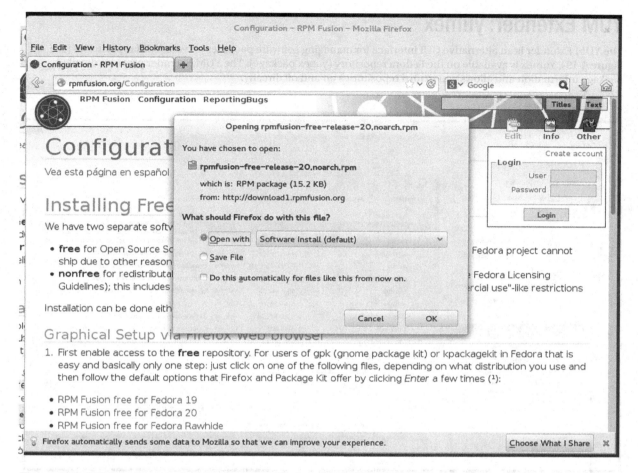

Figure 4-18. *RPM Fusion repository configuration file downloaded from* http://rpmfusion.org

After installing the free package, you can install the non-free package if you wish. Click the link labeled RPM Fusion Nonfree for Fedora 20, listed under the second paragraph in the Graphical Setup section, then proceed with the install.

The page also tells you how to perform an installation of both free and non-free RPM Fusion YUM configuration packages from the command line using the rpm command. The command is extensive and, instead of typing it on a command line in a terminal window, you can copy and paste the entire command from the web page to a terminal window. Click and drag the command on the web page to select it, then press Ctrl+c to copy it to the clipboard. Open a terminal window and press Ctrl+Shift+v to paste the command to the current command line. Then press Enter to run the command.

Once the repository is installed, you can open Software Sources to check that the RPM Fusion repository is enabled—Software Sources on the PackageKit Applications menu (top bar).

With the RPM Fusion repository now enabled, you can use PackageKit to search, select, and install any packages on its repository. Both RPM Fusion and the Fedora repositories have their packages intertwined on the GNOME Software and PackageKit software listings. When you first install the repository configuration, be sure to update your PackageKit package lists so that the new repository packages will be listed. From the PackageKit Applications menu, select Refresh Package Lists (top bar).

YUM Extender: yumex

The YUM Extender is an alternative GUI interface for managing software packages on your YUM repositories (see Figure 4-19). Yumex is available on the Fedora repository (yumex package). The YUM Extender provides detailed package information and allows you to turn repositories on and off directly.

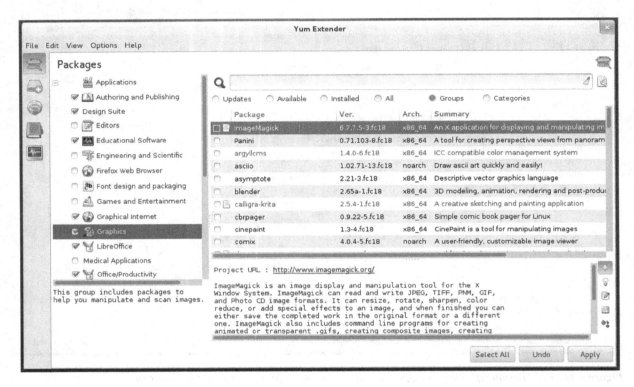

Figure 4-19. *YUM Extender: group view*

The YUM Extender screen has five tabs, each accessed by view icons on the left column, as shown in Figure 4-19. The buttons are Packages, Pending Actions, Repositories, YUM History, and Output Details. You can view packages using the Packages button. The updates are shown in red and installed packages are shown in green. A search text box lets you search for packages.

The Package tab features ways to narrow your displayed packages using radio buttons. You can choose to display updates (Updates), installed packages (Installed), uninstalled packages (Available), or all the packages (All). Clicking on Categories lets you specify a category, such as repositories, displaying only packages from a certain repository, or packages size. Clicking Groups opens a group sidebar with software groups. They are organized into an expandable tree, such as Applications with sub-groupings such as Office/Productivity and Sound and Video.

Clicking a package displays detailed information about it, where you can select the description, files included with the package, and the change log, if available.

To install a package, just check the one you want to install. Once selected, the package is added to the Pending Actions tab. Once you have added packages to the Pending Actions tab, click the Pending Actions icon to see the list of packages you want to install. From this panel, you can choose to remove items. To perform the installation, click the Apply button. All dependent packages will also be displayed. The install process is shown on the Watch Output Details tab.

The Repos tab operates as a repository manager, listing all your configured repositories. From this tab, you can enable or disable any repositories. For example, if you have to temporarily enable the RPM Fusion repository, you can select it on this panel and then install software from that repository. Once you're finished, you can then disable the repository.

Installing Packages with the yum Command

You can use the yum command, in a terminal window or command-line interface, to access Fedora repositories and install new software. To use the yum command, enter the yum command with the `install` option on a command line. The package will be detected, along with any dependent software, and you will be asked to confirm installation. The download and installation is automatic. The following command installs Gnumeric:

```
yum install gnumeric
```

You can also remove packages, as well as search for packages and list packages by different criteria, such as those for update, those on the repository not yet installed, and those already installed. The following example lists all installed packages:

```
yum list installed
```

The available option shows uninstalled packages.

```
yum list available
```

To search for a particular package, you can use the `search` option.

```
yum search wine-core
```

▦ **Tip** You can use third-party Fedora YUM software repositories such as `http://rpmfusion.org` to download additional software. Their configuration files will be installed in `/etc/yum.repos.d`.

Recovering Packages with the yum Command

Always be sure to check the dependency list, and make sure that a larger number of packages is not being marked for removal. In some cases, the entire GNOME desktop, along with the GDM and PackageKit (Software), could be selected and accidently removed. If this is the case, you should reinstall GNOME, GDM, and PackageKit with yum commands in a terminal window or using the command-line interface. You might also have to reinstall graphics drivers. You can use `groupinstall` to install the entire GNOME desktop. The `grouplist` command displays groups.

```
yum groupinstall gnome-desktop
yum install gdm
yum install PackageKit
```

Installing Some Popular Third-Party Software

For most third-party multimedia packages, you first install the YUM configuration file for a repository that carries them. Once configured, installation is a simple matter of using Software to search for and install packages. YUM downloads the package and performs the installation. It will also be careful to select the package for your architecture, such as x86_64 for 64-bit or i686 for 32-bit. YUM will ask for confirmation before installing, listing any dependent packages that will also have to be installed.

In addition, there are certain third-party applications that are not provided by a repository. Some of these can be installed easily using Autoten, a front end for installing popular applications such as RealPlayer and dropbox.

■ **Tip**   During both installation and removal, make sure that a large number of unrelated packages are not being removed. This can happen—possibly removing all of GNOME, in addition to PackageKit. If you find an extensive set of unrelated packages marked for removal as dependencies, you might want to cancel the installation. To do so, click the Cancel button on the Dependencies dialog.

Multimedia Packages

For your third-party packages, you can use RPM Fusion, which carries collections of multimedia packages, including GStreamer and MPlayer. DVD/MPEG video players you might want include Xine, MPlayer, and VideoLAN. All support DVD, DVB, HDTV, H264, and MP3, provided the needed codecs are installed.

■ **Tip**   For information on multimedia applications available for Fedora, go to http://fedoraproject.org/wiki/Multimedia.

Many of the following packages are automatically selected and installed for you as dependents when you install MPlayer. It may be simpler to just install one of these, rather than try to install all the added packages separately.

For audio, you may want HDTV audio, DVD/MPEG2 audio support, DTS, and MP3. Search for the following RPM Fusion packages using Software.

---

a52dec	HDTV audio (ATSC A/52, AC3)
faad2	MPEG2/4 AAC audio decoding, high quality
faac	MPEG2/4 AAC sound encoding and decoding
libdca	DTS Coherent Acoustics playback capability
lame	MPEG1 and MPEG2 audio decoding

For video, you may want DVD video capability, MPEG and MPEG2 playback, DVB/HDTV playback, and H264 (HD media) decoding capability.

libdvbpsi	MPEG TS stream (DVB and PSI) decoding and encoding
vlc	DVD video playback capability, VideoLAN project
libdvdnav	DVD video menu navigation
libdvdcss	DVD video commercial decoding, Livna repo (http://rpm.livna.org)
x264	H264/AVC decoding and encoding (high-definition media)

For all GStreamer supported applications, you will want the bad and ugly packages.

gstreamer-plugins-bad	Not fully reliable codecs and tools for GStreamer, some with possible licensing issues
gstreamer-plugins-ugly	Reliable video and audio codecs for GStreamer that may have licensing issues

The Win32 codecs are not available on the Fedora repositories. Keep in mind that wmv files and Win32 codecs are already supported by the ffmpeg Linux codecs and will play on Totem and Dragon Player. You can download the Win32 codecs separately from the MPlayer web site (www.mplayerhq.hu/MPlayer/releases).

Vendor Video Driver Support

You can obtain the Nvidia and ATI vendor graphics drivers from RPM Fusion (the nonfree repository). You can download and install them with YUM. RPM Fusion, which now includes all the former Livna repository drivers, is the best repository for specialized kernel drivers and modules. Keep in mind, however, that due to recent open sourcing of both the Nvidia and ATI vendor drivers, the X.org and Nouveau open source versions are becoming almost as effective, especially for 2D display support. For normal usage, you might not need vendor driver support.

If RPM Fusion is configured for PackageKit, a search on nvidia (or fglrx for ATI, when available) displays Nvidia modules for each kernel version. The vendor graphic drivers use two packages, one for the supporting software and another for the kernel. The kernel modules are specific to the kernel you are using. Each time you update to a new kernel, you will require a new graphics kernel module created specifically for that kernel. This will be automatically downloaded and installed for you as a dependent package when you update your kernel (the RPM Fusion non-free repository must be active). The driver package is named xorg-x11-drv-nvidia, and the kernel module is named kmod-nvidia.

```
xorg-x11-drv-nvidia
kmod-nvidia
```

You can use a yum command entered in a terminal window with nvidia* to reference all Nvidia packages.

```
yum install nvidia*
```

Installing Popular Third-Party Non-Fedora Applications

Certain applications are not yet supported by the Fedora and RPM Fusion repositories. Some have their own repositories, like Skype, which you can manually configure and then access with PackageKit. Others must be downloaded and installed separately. There are several third-party package managers that can install these packages using a simple desktop dialog. These include easyLife, Fedorautils, and PostinstallerF (see Table 4-6). You can also use the older Autoten. PostinstallerF and Fedorautils also allow you to tweak your system. You can download and install them using your browser. You can start them from the System Tools overview.

Table 4-6. *Post Install Third-Party Non-Fedora Package Managers*

Application	Description
`http://sourceforge.net/projects/postinstaller/`	PostinstallerF
`http://sourceforge.net/projects/easylife-linux`	easyLife
`http://autoten.co.uk`	Autoten
`http://sourceforge.net/projects/fedorautils/`	Fedorautils

easyLife and Fedorautils work much like the older Autoten and Autoplus. They use a dialog started from the terminal window. When you install an application, the dialog disappears, and you will see install operations taking place in the terminal window. When the installation finishes, the dialog reappears, except in the case of easyLife, which simply ends.

Fedorautils starts with a dialog that lets you choose to tweak your system, add software, or manage repositories. Choose the Add Software entry to open a dialog listing applications you can install (see Figure 4-20). Fedorautils notes what software is already installed. To install, click the check box for an application, then click the Select button. Fedorautils then installs the application, checking for dependent packages and setting up repositories, as available. A notice in the terminal window lets you know if the install failed. An installed application can be removed the same way.

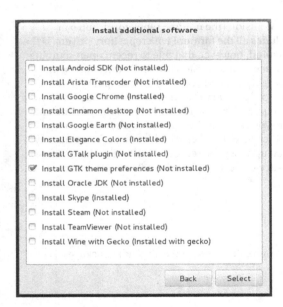

Figure 4-20. *Fedorautils dialog for installing third-party software*

easyLife works much like the older Autoten, but it conflicts with Autoten. You cannot have both installed. The easyLife dialog lists applications you can install or uninstall (see Figure 4-21). To install an application, just click its check box, located to the left of the application name, and click the OK button. easyLife then installs the application, checking for dependent packages and setting up repositories, as available. An installed application can be removed the same way.

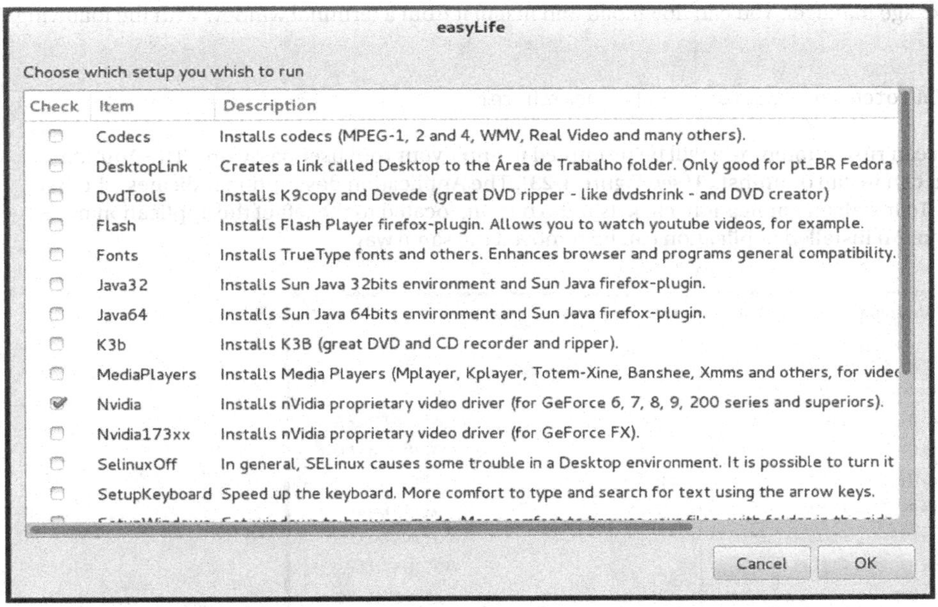

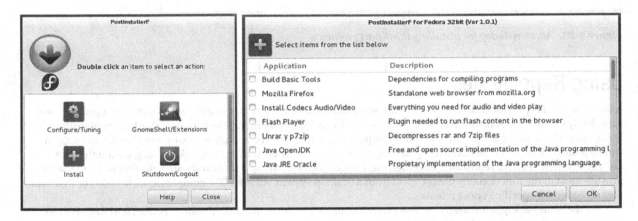

Figure 4-21. *The easyLife dialog for installing third-party software*

PostinstallerF first asks for your root user password. An initial dialog lets you choose to tweak your system or install software. The install software dialog lists popular applications, though many are available from the Fedora repositories directly using PackageKit (see Figure 4-22). Click the check box for the application you want to install, then click OK.

Figure 4-22. *PostinstallerF dialog for installing third-party software*

Autoten is an older package manager. You can download and install it from a terminal window with the following commands:

```
su -c "rpm -Uvh http://autoten.co.uk/autoten-1.4-7.noarch.rpm"
```

Once it's installed, you can run Autoten. You will be prompted to enter your root user password. The Autoten dialog lists applications you can install or uninstall (see Figure 4-23). The Application description indicates whether the application is installed. To install an application, click its radio button, located to the left of the application name, and then click the OK button. An installed application can be removed the same way.

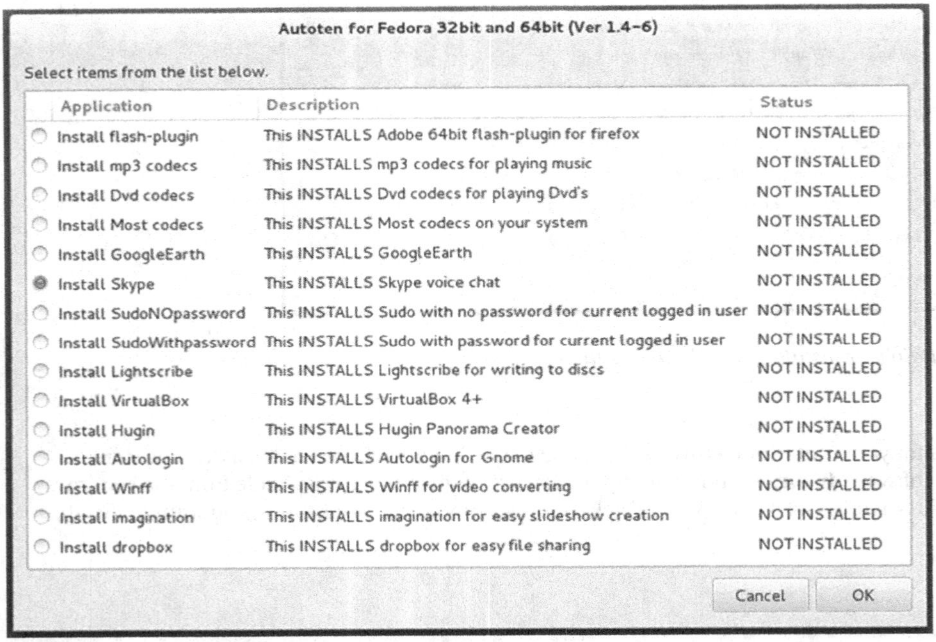

Autoten for Fedora 32bit and 64bit (Ver 1.4-6)

Select items from the list below.

Application	Description	Status
○ Install flash-plugin	This INSTALLS Adobe 64bit flash-plugin for firefox	NOT INSTALLED
○ Install mp3 codecs	This INSTALLS mp3 codecs for playing music	NOT INSTALLED
○ Install Dvd codecs	This INSTALLS Dvd codecs for playing Dvd's	NOT INSTALLED
○ Install Most codecs	This INSTALLS Most codecs on your system	NOT INSTALLED
○ Install GoogleEarth	This INSTALLS GoogleEarth	NOT INSTALLED
● Install Skype	This INSTALLS Skype voice chat	NOT INSTALLED
○ Install SudoNOpassword	This INSTALLS Sudo with no password for current logged in user	NOT INSTALLED
○ Install SudoWithpassword	This INSTALLS Sudo with password for current logged in user	NOT INSTALLED
○ Install Lightscribe	This INSTALLS Lightscribe for writing to discs	NOT INSTALLED
○ Install VirtualBox	This INSTALLS VirtualBox 4+	NOT INSTALLED
○ Install Hugin	This INSTALLS Hugin Panorama Creator	NOT INSTALLED
○ Install Autologin	This INSTALLS Autologin for Gnome	NOT INSTALLED
○ Install Winff	This INSTALLS Winff for video converting	NOT INSTALLED
○ Install imagination	This INSTALLS imagination for easy slideshow creation	NOT INSTALLED
○ Install dropbox	This INSTALLS dropbox for easy file sharing	NOT INSTALLED

Cancel   OK

Figure 4-23. *Autoten dialog for installing third-party software*

Using Repositories

A few repositories provide much of the software you will normally require. The main Fedora software repository will most likely contain the software you want. Always check this repository first, before trying a third-party repository. Some specialized applications, such as vendor-supplied graphics drivers, as well as third-party multimedia support, can be located at http://rpmfusion.org. Java applications are located at http://jpackage.org, although some are already in the Fedora repository. Together, these repositories make up a set of software sites that you can use to provide most of the functionality users expect from a desktop system. All are YUM-compliant, with YUM configuration files designed for specific Fedora releases.

To see what packages are available, you can use your web browser to access the sites. Fedora and RPM Fusion provide repodata directories for detailed listings.

To use YUM on a software repository, YUM has to be configured to access them. This is a simple matter of listing the site's URL, both its web address and directory location. Configurations for repositories are placed in repo files located in the /etc/yum.repos.d directory on your Linux system. The repo files for Fedora are already installed. You must add repo files for RPM Fusion before you can access them with YUM. RPM Fusion provides RPM packages, free and non-free collections, named `rpmfusion-free-release-stable.noarch.rpm` and `rpmfusion-nonfree-release-stable.noarch.rpm`, on their web site. When these are installed, they automatically set up the YUM configuration files. For RPM Fusion, these are `rpmfusion-free.repo` and `rpmfusion-nonfree.repo`, with corresponding update and development repo files.

The repository sites and their repo files are:

`http://download.fedoraproject.org`	The Fedora Repository, mirror link: Fedora-compliant software, `fedora.repo`
`http://download1.rpmfusion.org`	RPM Fusion: Repository for driver, multimedia, and other RPM packages, `rpmfusion-free.repo` and `rpmfusion-nonfree.repo`

Repository Repo Package Files

When you are installing packages, PackageKit, Yumex, and the yum command automatically use the repo files to check your enabled repositories. One important exception to this rule is the initial install of the repository configuration files from third-party repositories. These configuration files (repo files) are usually contained in their own RPM packages. You download and install a repo package directly from the repository web site, using your web browser. For example, the repo package for the RPM Fusion third-party Fedora YUM repository is `rpmfusion-free-release-stable.noarch.rpm`. You download and install this package directly, using a web browser. Repository configuration files are located in the `/etc/yum.repos.d` directory and have the extension `.repo`.

Fedora Repository

The Fedora repository is already configured for use by YUM. To download any Fedora package, simply use the PackageKit, or enter the yum command with the `install` option on a command line. The package will be detected, along with any dependent software, and you will be asked to confirm installation. The download and installation will be automatic. The first time you install a package from the Fedora repository, you are prompted to install the Fedora GPG key, used to authenticate the packages. Just click Yes to install the key.

A section of the following Fedora repo file (`/etc/yum.repos.d/fedora.repo`) lists several repository options. The name is Fedora, with `releasever` and `basearch` used to determine the release and architecture parts of the name. The `mirrorlist` option is used instead of `baseurl`, which is commented out (`mirrorlist` provides mirror access, selecting the fastest available mirror). Again, the `releasever` is used to specify the release. The gpgkey used, `RPM-GPG-KEY-fedora`, is already installed in the `/etc/pki/rpm-gpg` directory.

```
[fedora]
name=Fedora $releasever - $basearch
failovermethod=priority
#baseurl=http://download.fedoraproject.org/pub/fedora/linux/releases/$releasever/Everything/
basearch/os/
mirrorlist=http://mirrors.fedoraproject.org/metalink?repo=fedora-$releasever&arch=$basearch
enabled=1
#metadata expire=7d
gpgcheck=1
gpgkey=file:///etc/pki/rpm-gpg/RPM-GPG-KEY-fedora-$basearch
```

RPM Fusion

The http://rpmfusion.org site provides access to popular software for many software applications, including multimedia applications such as MPlayer, as well as those not included with Fedora, due to licensing issues. Several of the more popular packages include the vendor ATI and Nvidia graphics drivers (when available). RPM Fusion specializes in configuring sometimes difficult drivers for compatibility with Fedora. For example, you can download the Nvidia Linux driver directly from the Nvidia web site and try to install it on your Fedora system. But there can be complications, and the driver could require additional configuration. As an alternative, RPM Fusion provides a version of the driver that has already been configured for Fedora.

To configure YUM on your system to access http://rpmfusion.org, just install the rpmfusion-free-release and rpmfusion-nonfree-release packages. These will install the rpmfusion-free.repo and rpmfusion-nonfree.repo configuration files in the /etc/yum.repos.d directory, as well as download the RPM Fusion GPG key. You can install the GPG manually or just wait until you install a package from RPM Fusion, in which case, YUM will install it for you, after prompting for approval. Check the RPM Fusion configuration page at http://rpmfusion.org for details. The name of the package will be something like rpmfusion-free-release.

You can download and install the package directly with the rpm command from within a terminal window. Log in as root with su first. The RPM Fusion site's configuration page provides a detailed example.

The GPG keys are in included in the packages and installed automatically in the /etc/pki/rpm-gpg directory. They are named: RPM-GPG-Key-rpmfusion-free-fedora and RPM-GPG-Key-rpmfusion-nonfree-fedora.

To see which packages are available on RPM Fusion, use your web browser to go to http://download1.rpmfusion.org. Here, you will find a listing of directories for each supported release. After selecting your release directory, you then choose your architecture, such as i386 (32-bit) or x86_64 (64-bit). Here, you will see a simple file listing of all available packages. Alternatively, on PackageKit, you could deselect all software sources except RPM Fusion, so that only the RPM Fusion packages are listed in the Software window.

Part of the rpmfusion-free.repo configuration file installed by the rpmfusion-free-release package is shown following. The configuration specifies the mirror list located at http://mirrors.rpmfusion.org.

```
[rpmfusion-free]
name=RPM Fusion for Fedora $releasever - Free
#baseurl=http://download1.rpmfusion.org/free/fedora/releases/$releasever/Everything/$basearch/os/
mirrorlist=http://mirrors.rpmfusion.org/mirrorlist?repo=free-fedora-
$releasever&arch=$basearch
enabled=1
metadata expire=7d
gpgcheck=1
gpgkey=file:///etc/pki/rpm-gpg/RPM-GPG-KEY-rpmfusion-free-fedora-$releasever-$basearch
```

The corresponding part of the rpmfusion-nonfree.repo configuration file installed by the rpmfusion-nonfree-release package is shown following:

```
[rpmfusion-nonfree]
name=RPM Fusion for Fedora $releasever - Nonfree
#baseurl=http://download1.rpmfusion.org/nonfree/fedora/releases/$releasever/Everything/$basearch/os/
mirrorlist=http://mirrors.rpmfusion.org/mirrorlist?repo=nonfree-fedora-
$releasever&arch=$basearch
enabled=1
metadata expire=7d
gpgcheck=1
gpgkey=file:///etc/pki/rpm-gpg/RPM-GPG-KEY-rpmfusion-nonfree-fedora-$releasever-$basearch
```

Livna (dvdcss)

The Livna repository (http://rpm.livna.org) provides access to one package, the commercial DVD video codec, called libdvdcss. Install the livna-release.rpm package. It contains the repository file, livna.repo.

```
[livna]
name=rpm.livna.org for $releasever - $basearch
#baseurl=http://rpm.livna.org/repo/$releasever/$basearch/ http://ftp-stud.fht-esslingen.de/pub/
Mirrors/rpm.livna.org/repo/$releasever/$basearch/
mirrorlist=http://rpm.livna.org/mirrorlist
failovermethod=roundrobin
enabled=1
gpgcheck=1
gpgkey=file:///etc/pki/rpm-gpg/RPM-GPG-KEY-livna
```

Adobe (Flash)

The Adobe repository provides access to the Adobe proprietary version of the Adobe Flash player for Linux. Adobe provides 32- and 64-bit software. The Fedora project Flash wiki explains the procedure in detail (see http://fedoraproject.org/wiki/Flash).

First, download the RPM package for the repository configuration. Select YUM for Linux.

```
http://get.adobe.com/flashplayer/
```

Then install the repository configuration package, called adobe-release. You can do this directly from the web browser by choosing to install and then clicking Yes, when prompted, to install the unsigned software, as the package key is not yet installed (it is included in the repository package). You could also first download the package, then install it with the following rpm command in a terminal window for the 64-bit version:

```
su -c 'rpm -vhi adobe-release-x86_64-1.0-1.noarch.rpm'
```

This installs the /etc/yum.repos.d/adobe-linux-x86_64.repo file, shown here:

```
[adobe-linux-x86_64]
name=Adobe Systems Incorporated
baseurl=http://linuxdownload.adobe.com/linux/x86_64/
enabled=1
gpgcheck=1
gpgkey=file:///etc/pki/rpm-gpg/RPM-GPG-KEY-adobe-linux
```

Software Sources will list the repository as Adobe Systems Incorporated. You can then use PackageKit to search for Flash and select the Flash package for installation. The Flash plug-in package is flash-plugin and has the title "Adobe Flash Player 11.2."

The first time you install any package from the Adobe repository, you will be prompted to install its package key. A dialog will be displayed with the message "Do You Trust the Source of the Packages?" Click Yes to install the Adobe repository package key.

Alternatively, you can manually install the Adobe repository package key with the following command:

```
su -c 'rpm --import /etc/pki/rpm-gpg/RPM-GPG-KEY-adobe-linux'
```

Restart Firefox to enable your Flash plug-in. On the Tools ➤ Add-ons Plug-ins tab, you will find an entry for Flash.

Google

For Linux-compatible Google applications, you should configure access to the Google repository, which allows you to install applications such as Picasa from PackageKit. Google installs a separate repository file for each major application. Google Chrome has a google-chrome.repo file, and Google Earth has a google-earth.repo file. The signing key is installed manually. Follow the instructions for the RPM at: www.google.com/linuxrepositories/.

Installation is performed using a terminal window. Click and drag to select the wget command on the browser.

```
wget https://dl-ssl.google.com/linux/linux_signing_key.pub
```

Then open a terminal window and press Ctrl+Shift+v to copy the command to that window. The signing key is then installed. Next, import the key with the following rpm command. (If you do not have sudo enabled, use su for first login as the root user.)

```
sudo rpm --import linux_signing_key.pub
```

If you do not have sudo enabled, use su to first login as the root user.

```
su
rpm --import linux_signing_key.pub
```

A copy of the google-chrome.repo file follows:

```
[google-chrome]
name=Google - x86_64
baseurl=http://dl.google.com/linux/chrome/rpm/stable/x86_64
enabled=1
gpgcheck=1
```

YUM Configuration

YUM options are configured in the /etc/yum.conf file, and the /etc/yum.repos.d directory holds repository (repo) files that list accessible YUM repositories. The repository files have the extension .repo. Check the yum.conf man page for a listing of the different YUM options, along with entry formats. The yum.conf file consists of different segments separated by bracket-encased headers, the first of which is always the main segment. Segments for different YUM server repositories can follow, beginning with the repository label encased in brackets. On Fedora, however, these are currently placed in separate repository files in the /etc/yum.repos.d directory.

In addition to yum.conf, YUM also supports a /etc/yum directory that can hold additional configuration information. On Fedora, this directory has a pluginconf.d subdirectory with configuration for YUM plug-ins. These include blacklist, whiteout, presto, and refresh-packagekit. The blacklist and whiteout plug-ins are disabled, but presto and refresh-packagekit are enabled.

/etc/yum.conf

The yum.conf file contains the main segment with settings for YUM options, as shown here:

```
[main]
cachedir=/var/cache/yum/$basearch/$releasever
keepcache=0
debuglevel=2
logfile=/var/log/yum.log
```

```
exactarch=1
obsoletes=1
gpgcheck=1
plugins=1
installonly_limit=3

# PUT YOUR REPOS HERE OR IN separate files named file.repo
# in /etc/yum.repos.d
```

There are general YUM options, such as logfile, which lists the location of YUM logs, and plugins, which enables the use of YUM plug-ins like presto. Packages are downloaded to the directory specified with the cachdir option, in this case, /var/cache/yum. You can elect to keep the downloaded packages or have them removed after they are installed. The tolerant option allows for package-install errors, and the retries option specifies the number of times to try to access a package. Both exactarch and obsoletes apply to YUM updating procedures, invoked with the YUM update command. The obsoletes option is used for distribution-level updates, and exactarch will only update packages in your specific architecture, such as i386 instead of i686. gpgcheck is a repository option that is set globally for the repo files. It checks for GPG software signatures.

Repository Files: /etc/yum.repos.d

The repository entries in the repo files begin with a bracket-enclosed server ID, a single-word unique name. Repository-specific options govern the access of software repositories. These include gpgcheck, which checks for GPG software signatures; gpgkey, which specifies the location of the signature; metalink, which references fast links from a mirror list; and mirrorlist, which references a URL holding mirror sites. The repository-specific name option provides a name for the repository. The URL reference is then assigned to the baseurl option. There should be only one baseurl option, but you can list several URLs for it, each on its own line. With the mirrorlist option, you can just list a URL for a list of mirrors, instead of listing each mirror separately in the baseurl option. The URL entries often make use of special variables, releasever and basearch. The releasever obtains the release information from the distroverpkg option set in the main segment. The basearch variable specifies the architecture you are using, as determined by YUM, such as i386. The enabled option actually turns on access to the repository. By setting it to 0, you choose not to access a specific repository. The gpgcheck option specifies that you should perform a GPG authentication check to make sure the download is intact. The enabled option will enable a repository, allowing YUM to use it. You can set the enable bit to 0 or 1 to turn off or on access to the repository.

The gpgkey option provides an authentication check on the package to make sure you have downloaded the appropriate version. Downloads can sometimes be intercepted and viruses inserted. The GPG key check protects against such attacks. It can also check to make sure the download is not corrupt or incomplete. The Fedora public GPG key may already be installed on your system. If you have already used YUM, you have already downloaded it. The Fedora GPG key allows you to access Fedora packages. The RPM Fusion free and non-free repositories use their own public keys, referenced with the gpgkey option in their repos files. The keys for all these repositories will be installed in the /etc/pki/rpmgpg directory.

Creating Local YUM Repositories

For local networks where you may have several Fedora systems, each of which may have to update using YUM, you can set up a local repository, instead of having each system update from Internet sites directly. In cases where local systems share a single Internet connection, this may significantly reduce download speeds. You can also control which packages can be installed. In effect, you download those packages on the YUM repository you want and then create from those packages a local repository on one of your local systems. Your local systems then use the local repository to install and update packages. You must manually keep the local repository updated. Use the createrepo command to create a repository from a directory holding the packages you want in it. Then it is a simple matter of providing a configuration file for it and specifying its location.

Managing YUM Caches

With the keepcache option enabled, YUM will keep its downloaded packages in the /var/cache/yum directory. Should you want to save or copy any particular packages, you can locate them there. Caching lets you easily uninstall and reinstall packages without having to download them again. The package is retained in the cache. If caching is disabled, the packages are automatically deleted after they are installed.

Your cache can increase rapidly, so you may want to clean it out on occasion. If you just want to delete these packages, as they are already installed, you can use the clean packages option.

```
yum clean packages
```

YUM also maintains a list of package headers with information on all packages downloaded. The headers are used to update your system, showing what has already been installed. You can opt to remove the headers with the clean headers option.

If you want YUM to access only the packages in the cache, you use the -C option. The following lists only packages in the cache:

```
yum -C list
```

Manually Installing Packages with rpm

You can use the rpm command to install individual RPM packages that are not part of a YUM repository. Keep in mind that most software resides on YUM-supported, Fedora-compliant repositories. For such software, you would use the yum command or the PackageKit (Software) front end. YUM has the advantage of automatically installing any dependent packages, whereas the rpm command, although it will detect needed packages, will not install them. Using only the rpm command, you would have to separately install any dependent packages in the correct order.

The rpm command is useful for packages that are not part of any YUM-supported repository, such as custom-made packages, and that have few or no dependent packages. You can also use the rpm command to bypass YUM, forcing installation of a particular package, instead of from YUM repositories (YUM's localinstall option will achieve the same purpose).

The rpm command performs installation, removal, and verification of software packages. An RPM package is an archive of software files. Each archive has a name that ends with .rpm, indicating it is a software package that can be installed by the Red Hat Package Manager.

The rpm command uses a set of options to determine what action to take. The -i option installs the specified software package, and the -U option updates a package. With an -e option, rpm uninstalls the package. A q placed before an i (-qi) queries the system to see if a software package is already installed and displays information about the software (-qpi queries an uninstalled package file). The rpm command with no options provides a complete list of rpm options. A set of commonly used options is shown in Table 4-7.

Table 4-7. *rpm Command Options*

Option	Action
-U	Updates a package
-i	Installs a package
-e	Removes a package
-qi	Displays information for an installed package
-ql	Displays file list for an installed package
-qpi	Displays information from an RPM package file (used for uninstalled packages)
-qpl	Displays the file list from an RPM package file (used for uninstalled packages)
-K	Authenticates and performs integrity check on a package

The software package name includes information about the version and release date. In the next example, the user installs the xvidcore package using the rpm command. Notice that the full file name is entered. In most cases, you would install packages with the -U option, for update. If the package is not already installed, -U will install it. The following examples use the DivX xvidcore RPM packages downloaded from http://rpmfusion.org.

```
$ rpm -Uvh xvidcore--1.3.2-3.fc17.x86_64.rpm
```

To list the full name, you can use the ls command with the first few characters and an asterisk (*), as follows:

```
ls xvid*
```

You can also use the * to match the remainder of the name, as in the following:

```
ls xvidccore-1*.rpm
```

When RPM performs an installation, it first checks for any dependent packages. These are other software packages with programs the application you are installing has to use. If other dependent packages must be installed first, RPM cancels the installation and lists those packages. You can install those packages and then repeat the installation of the application. To determine if a package is already installed, use the -qi option with rpm. The -q stands for query. To obtain a list of all the files the package has installed, as well as the directories it installed to, use the -ql option. To query package files, add the p option. The -qpi option displays information about a package, and -qpl lists the files in it. The following example lists all the files in the xvidcore package:

```
$ rpm -qpl xvidcore-1.3.2-3.fc17.x86_64.rpm
```

To remove a software package from your system, first use rpm -qi to make sure it is actually installed, then use the -e option to uninstall it. As with the -qi and -e options, you needn't use the full name of the installed file. You only need the name of the application. In the following example, the user removes the DivX xvidcore package from the system:

```
$ rpm -e xvidcore
```

Package Security Check

YUM automatically performs integrity and authentication checks on all software downloaded from Fedora-compliant repositories, confirming that the package was obtained from a valid source, and that it has not been modified. Each repository configuration file in the /etc/yum.repos.d directory will have its gpgcheck option set to 1. Should you want to turn off this check for a particular repository, you can set its gpgcheck option to 0.

For packages not downloaded from a YUM repository, you may want to manually check their integrity and authentication. To authenticate a package, you check its digital signature. Packages are signed with encrypted digital keys that can be decrypted using the public key provided by the author of the package. This public key has to be downloaded and installed on the encryption tool used on your system. Fedora, along with most Linux distributions, uses the GNU Privacy Guard (GPG) encryption tool. To use a public key to authenticate an RPM package, you first must install it in the RPM key database. For all RPM packages that are part of the Fedora distribution, you can use the Fedora public key, placed during installation in the /etc/pki/rpm-gpg/ directory. Here, you will find the RPM GPG keys for all your configured repositories, including RPM Fusion. The Fedora key is RPM-GPG-KEY-fedora-20-primary. Several keys are links to this key, such as RPM-GPG-KEY-20-fedora and RPM-GPG-KEY-fedora-20-x86_64. The RPM Fusion keys will have the same structure, with a primary key, such as RPM-GPG-KEY-rpmfusion-free-fedora-20-primary, and links to it, such as RPM-GPG-KEY-rpmfusion-free-fedora-20-x86_64.

You must import the key to the RPM database before you can check Fedora RPM packages. The first time you use PackageKit to install a package, you will be prompted to import the GPG key. Once imported, you need not import it again. Alternatively, you can manually import the key, as follows:

```
rpm --import /etc/pki/rpm-gpg/RPM-GPG-KEY-fedora
```

If you have downloaded an RPM package from another site, you can also download and install its public key, with which you can authenticate that package. For example, there are public keys for both the RPM Fusion free and non-free Fedora YUM repositories. These are included in the RPM Fusion YUM configuration files, which you can download and install, such as rpmfusion-free-release-stable.noarch.rpm for RPM Fusion repositories. The keys will be automatically installed with the configuration.

Once the public key is installed, you can check the package authentication using the rpm command with the -K option.

```
$ rpm -K xvidcore-1.3.2-3.fc17.x86_64.rpm
```

To see a list of all the keys you have imported, you can use the -qa option and match the gpg-pubkey* pattern. Using rpm with the -qi option and the public key, you can display detailed information about the key. The following example shows the Fedora public key:

```
$ rpm -qa gpg-pubkey*
gpg-pubkey-4f2a6fd2-3f9d9d3b
gpg-pubkey-db42a60e-37ea5438
```

You can manually check a package's integrity with the rpm command with the -K and the --nosignature options. A value called the MD5 digest measures the contents of a package. If the value is incorrect, the package has been tampered with. Some packages provide just digest values, allowing only integrity checks. In the next example, the user checks whether the xvidcore package has been tampered with. The --nosignature option says not to perform authentication, performing the integrity check only.

```
$ rpm -K --nosignature xvidcore-1.3.2-3.fc17.x86_64.rpm
```

Installing Source Code Applications

Some applications are available for Linux in source code format. These programs are stored in a compressed archive that you have to decompress and then extract. The resulting source code can then be configured, compiled, and installed on your system. Always check the README and INSTALL files that come with the source code to check the appropriate method for creating and installing that software. Be sure that you have installed all development packages onto your system. Development packages contain the key components, such as the compiler, GNOME and KDE headers and libraries, and preprocessors. You cannot compile the source code software without them.

Extracting the Archive: Archive Manager (File Roller)

From the desktop, you can extract compressed archives with the Archive Manager. Archive Manager is the fileroller application. Archive Manager displays the top-level contents of the archive, which you can browse if you want, even reading such text files as README and INSTALL files. You also can see which files will be installed. To extract the archive, click Extract.

Alternatively, on a command line (terminal window), you can use the tar command to extract archives. On the command line, enter the tar command with the xvjf options (j for bz2 and z for gz), as in the following:

```
tar xvjf freeciv-2.3.4.tar.bz2
```

Configure, Compile, and Install

Extracting the archive creates a directory with the name of the software, in this case, freeciv-2.3.4. Once it is extracted, you must configure, compile, and install the software, using command-line commands (terminal window).

Change to the software directory with the cd command.

```
cd freeciv-2.3.4
```

Run the command ./configure to generate a compiler configuration for your particular system (creates a custom makefile used to compile the source code).

```
./configure
```

Compile the software with the make command.

```
make
```

Then install the program with the make install command.

```
make install
```

CHAPTER 5

■ ■ ■

Office Applications and Editors

Several office suites are now available for Fedora (see Table 5-1). These include professional-level word processors, presentation managers, drawing tools, and spreadsheets. The freely available versions are described in this chapter. LibreOffice is currently the primary office suite supported by Fedora. Calligra is an office suite designed for use with KDE. The GNOME Office suite integrates GNOME applications into a productivity suite. CodeWeavers CrossOver Office provides reliable support for running Microsoft Office Windows applications directly on Linux, integrating them with KDE and GNOME. You can also download the Apache OpenOffice suite (originally, Oracle/StarOffice). For desktop publishing, especially PDF generation, you can use Scribus, a cross-platform tool available from the Fedora repository.

Table 5-1. *Linux Office Suites*

Web Site	Description
www.libreoffice.org	LibreOffice open source office suite
www.calligra.org	Calligra suite, for KDE
https://wiki.gnome.org/action/show/Apps/GnomeOffice	GNOME Office, for GNOME
www.openoffice.org	Apache OpenOffice
www.codeweavers.com	CrossOver Office (Microsoft Office support)
www.scribus.net	Scribus desktop publishing tool

Linux provides many text editors that range from simple text editors to those with complex features such as spell-checking, buffers, or complex searches. All generate character text files and can be used to edit Linux text files.

Fedora also provides a wide range of electronic mail applications, including desktop e-mail applications featuring calendars and address books. Evolution and Thunderbird are the primary applications, both of which support GNOME Contacts. Newsreaders are also supported.

Fedora also supports several e-book readers, such as Calibre and FBReader, which run natively on Linux.

Fedora includes MySQL and PostgreSQL open source databases in its distribution, which can support smaller databases. Several database management systems are also available for Linux. The various database management systems that run under Linux are listed in Table 5-11, later in this chapter.

LibreOffice

LibreOffice is a fully integrated suite of office applications developed as an open source project and freely distributed to all. It is the primary office suite for Fedora, accessible from the Applications overview. LibreOffice is the open source and freely available office suite derived originally from OpenOffice. LibreOffice is supported by the Document

Foundation, which was established after Oracle's acquisition of Sun, the main developer for OpenOffice. LibreOffice is now the primary open source office software for Linux. Oracle retains control of all the original OpenOffice software and does not cooperate with any LibreOffice development. LibreOffice has replaced OpenOffice as the default office software for most Linux distributions.

LibreOffice includes word processing, spreadsheet, presentation, and drawing applications (see Table 5-2). Versions of LibreOffice exist for Linux, Windows, and Mac OS. You can obtain information such as online manuals and FAQs, as well as current versions, from the LibreOffice web site at `www.libreoffice.org`.

Table 5-2. *LibreOffice.org Applications*

Application	Description
Calc	LibreOffice spreadsheet
Draw	LibreOffice drawing application
Writer	LibreOffice word processor
Math	LibreOffice mathematical formula composer
Impress	LibreOffice presentation manager
Base	Database front end for accessing and managing a variety of different databases

LibreOffice is an integrated suite of applications. You can open the writer, spreadsheet, or presentation application directly from the Applications overview. The word processing, spreadsheet, and presentations applications are also accessible from the Launcher: Writer, Calc, and Impress. You can also open existing office documents (Open button) and manage document templates. Buttons at the bottom of the dialog let you download new features and templates and access the LibreOffice web site.

The LibreOffice Writer word processor supports standard word processing features, such as cut-and-paste, spell-checking, and text formatting, as well as paragraph styles (see Figure 5-1). Context menus let you format text easily. Wizards (Letter, Web Page, Fax, and Agenda) let you generate different kinds of documents quickly. You can embed objects within documents, such as using Draw to create figures that you can then drag and drop to the Writer document. LibreOffice Writer is compatible with earlier versions of Microsoft Word. It will read and convert Word 2003 and earlier documents to a LibreOffice Writer document, preserving most features, including contents, tables, and indexes. Writer documents also can be saved as Word documents.

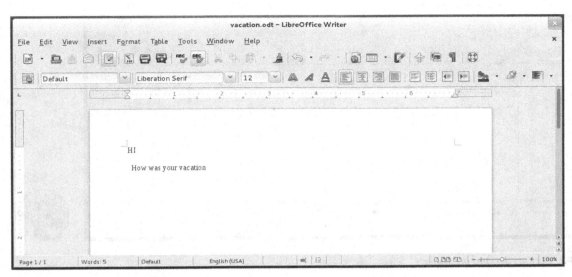

Figure 5-1. *LibreOffice.org Writer word processor*

LibreOffice provides access to many database files. File types supported include ODBC (Open Database Connectivity), JDBC (Java), MySQL, PostgreSQL, and MDB (Microsoft Access) database files. You can also create your own simple databases. Check the LibreOffice Features ➤ Base page at `www.libreoffice.org/discover/base` for detailed information on drivers and supported databases.

LibreOffice Calc is a professional-level spreadsheet. With LibreOffice Math (LibreOffice Formula), you can create formulas that you can embed in a text document. With the presentation manager (LibreOffice Impress), you can create images for presentations, such as circles, rectangles, and connecting elements like arrows, as well as vector-based illustrations. Impress supports advanced features, such as morphing objects, grouping objects, and defining gradients. Draw is a sophisticated drawing tool that includes 3D modeling tools (LibreOffice Drawing). You can create simple or complex images, including animation text aligned on curves. LibreOffice also includes a printer setup tool with which you can select printers, fonts, paper sizes, and page formats.

Also for use on GNOME is Scribus, the desktop publishing tool (see Figure 5-2), available at `www.scribus.net`.

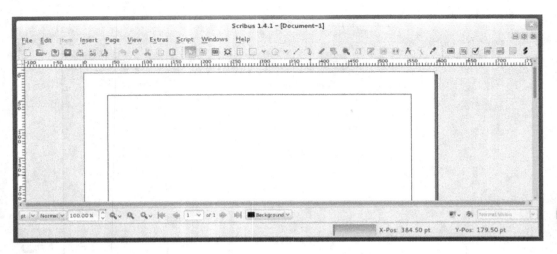

Figure 5-2. *Scribus desktop publisher*

▪ **Note**   The former Oracle OpenOffice suite is now Apache OpenOffice. It is a fully integrated and Microsoft Office–compatible suite of office applications developed and supported originally by Sun Microsystems under the name StarOffice. It is now developed and supported by Apache; see `www.openoffice.org`. You can download and install directly from the web site. It is not yet available on the Fedora repositories.

Calligra

Calligra is an integrated office suite for the K Desktop Environment (KDE), consisting of several office applications, including a word processor, a spreadsheet, and graphics applications (`calligra` package). Calligra is the new version of KOffice, integrating many of the older applications provided by KOffice. Calligra allows components from any one application to be used in another, allowing you to embed a spreadsheet from Calligra Sheets or diagrams from Karbon in a Calligra Words document. It also uses the open document format (ODF) for its files, providing cross-application standardization. There is also a Windows version available. You can obtain more information about Calligra from `www.calligra.org`.

Currently, Calligra includes Calligra Sheets, Calligra Flow, Calligra Words, Karbon, Krita, Plan, Calligra Stage, Braindump, and Kexi (accessible from Office and Graphics; see Table 5-3). The contact application, Kontact, has been spun off as a separate project. Kontact is an integrated contact application including Kmail, Korganizer, Kaddressbook, and Knotes. Calligra Sheets is a spreadsheet; Calligra Stage is a presentation application; Karbon is a vector graphics program; and Calligra Words is a publisher-like word processor. Krita is a paint and image editor. Kexi provides database integration with Calligra applications, currently supporting PostgreSQL and MySQL.

Table 5-3. *Calligra Applications*

Application	Description
Braindump	Whiteboards for notes, images, and charts
Calligra Flow	Flowchart applications
Calligra Stage	Presentation application
Calligra Words	Word processor (desktop publisher)
Calligra Sheets	Spreadsheet
Karbon	Vector graphics program
Kexi	Database integration
Plan	Project management and planning
Krita	Paint and image-manipulation program
Kontact (separate project)	Contact application including mail, address book, and organizer

Calligra Sheets is the spreadsheet application, and it incorporates the basic operations found in most spreadsheets, with formulas similar to those used in MS Excel. You can also embed charts, pictures, or formulas using Krita and Karbon. With Calligra Stage, you can create presentations consisting of text and graphics modeled using different fonts, orientations, and attributes, such as colors. Karbon is a vector-based graphics program, much like Adobe Illustrator and LibreOffice Draw. It supports the standard graphic operations, such as rotating, scaling, and aligning objects. Calligra Words can best be described as a desktop publisher, with many of the features found in publishing applications. Although it is a fully functional word processor, Calligra Words sets up text in frames that are placed on the page like objects. Frames, like objects in a drawing program, can be moved, resized, and reoriented. You can organize frames into a frame set, having text flow from one to the other.

GNOME Office Applications

There are several GNOME Office applications available, including AbiWord, Gnumeric, Evince, and Evolution. GNOME Office applications are part of Fedora and can be downloaded with PackageKit. You can find out more from the GNOME Office applications at `http://live.gnome.org/GnomeOffice`. A current listing for common GNOME Office applications is shown in Table 5-4. All applications implement the support for embedding components, ensuring drag-and-drop capability throughout the GNOME interface.

Table 5-4. *GNOME Office and Other Office Applications for GNOME*

Application	Description
AbiWord	Cross-platform word processor
Gnumeric	Spreadsheet
Evince	Document viewer
Evolution	Integrated e-mail, calendar, and personal organizer
Dia	Diagram and flowchart editor

(continued)

Table 5-4. (*continued*)

Application	Description
GnuCash	Personal finance manager
Glom	Database front end for PostgreSQL database
glabels	Label designer
Inkscape	Vector graphics and presentation creation
Ease	Presentation manager

AbiWord is an open source word processor that aims to be a complete cross-platform solution, running on Mac, UNIX, and Windows, as well as Linux. It is part of a set of desktop productivity applications being developed by the AbiSource project (www.abisource.com).

Gnumeric is a professional-level GNOME spreadsheet meant to replace commercial spreadsheets. Gnumeric supports standard desktop spreadsheet features, including auto filling and cell formatting, and an extensive number of formats. Gnumeric also supports plug-ins, making it possible to extend and customize its capabilities easily.

Dia is a drawing program designed to create diagrams, such as database, circuit object, flowchart, and network diagrams. You can create elements along with lines and arcs with different types of endpoints, such as arrows or diamonds. Data can be saved in XML format, making it transportable to other applications.

GnuCash (www.gnucash.org) is a personal finance application for managing accounts, stocks, and expenses.

The GNOME Ease presentation manager lets you create simple presentations.

Running Microsoft Office on Linux: Wine and CrossOver

One of the concerns that new Linux users have relates to the kind of access they will have to their Microsoft Office files, particularly Word files. The major Linux Office suites, including Calligra, LibreOffice, and Oracle OpenOffice, all read and manage Microsoft Office files.

Wine (Windows Compatibility Layer) allows you to run many Windows applications directly, using a supporting virtual windows API. See the Wine web site for a list of supported applications; see also www.winehq.org, the AppDB tab. Well-written applications may run directly from Wine, like the Newsbin newsreader. Each user can install a version of Wine with its own simulated C partition on which Windows applications are installed. The simulated drive is installed as drive_c in the .wine directory. The .wine directory is a hidden directory. It is not normally displayed with the ls command or the GNOME file manager (View ➤ Show Hidden Files). You can also use any of your Linux directories for your Windows application data files instead of the simulated C drive. These are referenced by Windows applications as the z: drive.

It is possible to install Microsoft Office on Fedora using Wine. Although there may be difficulties with the latest Microsoft Office versions, earlier versions, such as 2002, should work fine for the most part (see www.winehq.org, AppDB tab, search on Word). Applications are rated platinum, gold, silver, bronze, and garbage. Although effective, Wine support is not as stable as CrossOver.

CrossOver Office is a commercial product that lets you install and run most Microsoft Office applications (it has a silver rating). CrossOver Office was developed by CodeWeavers, which also supports Windows web browser plug-ins as well as several popular Windows applications, such as Adobe Photoshop. CrossOver features both standard and professional versions, providing reliable application support. You can find out more about CrossOver Office at www.codeweavers.com.

CrossOver can be installed either for private multiuser mode or managed multiuser mode. In private multiuser mode, each user installs Windows software, such as full versions of Office. In managed multiuser mode, the Windows software is installed once, and all the users share it. Once the software is installed, you will see a Windows Applications menu on the main menu, from which you can start your installed Windows software. The applications will run within a Linux window, but they will appear just as if they were running in Windows.

With VMware, you can run Windows under Linux, allowing you to run Windows applications, including Microsoft Office, on your Linux system. For more information, check the VMware web site at www.vmware.com.

Another option, for users with high-powered computers that support virtualization, is to install the Windows OS on a virtual machine, using the Boxes virtual machine manager. You could then install and run Windows on the virtual machine and install Microsoft Office on it.

GNOME Documents

You can use the GNOME Documents application to access and search for local and cloud-based documents. Documents can be text (word processing), spreadsheets, presentations, or PDF files. Currently, both Google docs and Microsoft SkyDrive documents are supported. You have to enable access from the Online Accounts dialog on System Settings.

GNOME Documents is accessible from the Applications overview. The Documents dialog lists your local and cloud-based documents (see Figure 5-3). The Documents GNOME applications menu lets you view the documents in a grid (icons) or as a list. You can also access help and quit. Click the Search button to open a search box with a menu that lets you search for source (local or cloud), type, and search target (title or author).

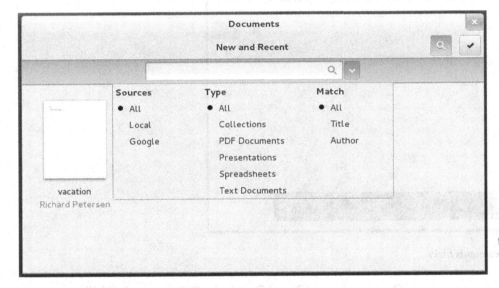

Figure 5-3. *GNOME Documents, with search*

Click the check mark button at the top right to open a taskbar, which lets you open the document or print it (see Figure 5-4). In the list view, click the check box to the left of the document you want to perform the task on. In the grid view, a check box is displayed at the lower right of each icon. When you click a check box, the taskbar is displayed. A properties button displays information about the document. When you click the Done button.

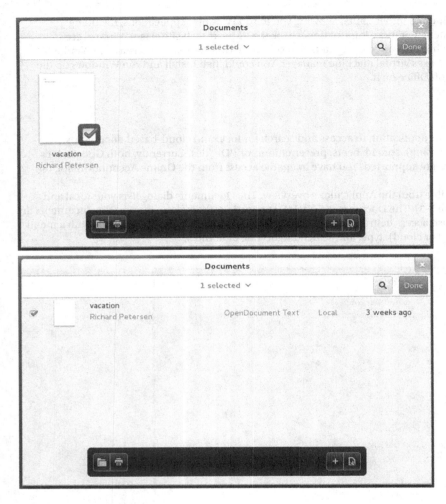

Figure 5-4. *GNOME Documents tasks*

Document Viewers and Scanning (PostScript, PDF, and DVI)

Although technically considered graphics applications, PostScript, PDF, DVI, and viewers are more commonly used with Office applications (see Table 5-5). Evince and Okular can display both PostScript (`.ps`) and PDF (`.pdf`) files. Evince is the default document viewer for GNOME. It is started automatically whenever you double-click a PDF file on the GNOME desktop. Okular is the default document viewer for KDE, with its overview icon as Okular.

Table 5-5. *PostScript, PDF, and DVI Viewers*

Viewer	Description
Evince	Document viewer for PostScript, DVI, and PDF files
Okular	KDE tool for displaying PDF, DVI, and PostScript files (replaces KPDF, Kghostview, and Kdvi)
Xpdf	X Window System tool for displaying PDF files only
Acrobat Reader for Linux	Adobe PDF viewer and e-book reader (`http://get.adobe.com/flashplayer/`)
Scribus	Desktop publisher for generating PDF documents
Simple Scan	GNOME Scanner interface for scanners (Graphics ➤ Simple Scan)
cuneiform and Yagf	OCR text conversion supporting multiple languages

Okular, Evince, and Xpdf are PDF viewers. They include many of the standard Adobe Reader features, such as zoom, two-page display, and full-screen mode. Alternatively, you can use Acrobat Reader from Adobe to display PDF files. You can install it with PackageKit (Software) once you have enabled the Adobe repository (`http://get.adobe.com/flashplayer/` as `YUM for Linux`). The package name is `AdobeReader`.

All these viewers can also print documents. To generate PDF documents, you can use LibreOffice Writer or the Scribus desktop publisher (`www.scribus.net`), and to edit PDF documents, you can use `pdfedit`.

Linux also features a professional-level typesetting tool, called TeX, commonly used to compose complex mathematical formulas. TeX generates a DVI document that can be displayed by DVI viewers, several of which are available for Linux. DVI files generated by the TeX document application can be viewed by Evince, Okular, and LibreOffice.

To scan documents directly, you can use Simple Scan, which you can save as JPEG, PNG, or PDF files. For OCR tasks, you can use cuneiform. Yagf provides a desktop front end for cuneiform, allowing you to scan and convert text. You can choose from several languages.

E-book Readers: FBReader and Calibre

On Fedora, you can use the Linux versions of Calibre and FBReader for e-books (see Table 5-6). FBReader is an open source reader that can read non-DRM e-books, including Mobipocket, HTML, Palmdoc, chm, EPUB, text, and RTF (install the `fbreader-gtk` package). The toolbar holds operations that move you through the text and configure your reader, adding books and setting interface preferences (see Figure 5-5). To see your selection of books, click the Library Tree icon on the left. You can organize text by author or tag. On the Options window, the Library tab lets you choose where your books are stored. You also can search for public domain books on `http://feedbook.com`.

Table 5-6. *E-book Readers*

Reader	Description
Calibre	E-book reader and library, also converts various inputs to EPUB e-books
E-book reader	FBReader e-book reader

Figure 5-5. FBReader e-book reader

Calibre reads PDF, EPUB, Lit (Microsoft), and Mobipocket e-books (see Figure 5-6). Calibre functions as a library for accessing and managing your e-books. Calibre can convert many document files and e-books to the EPUB format, the new open source standard used by Apple (iPad) and Barnes & Noble (Nook). It can take as conversion input text, HTML, TRF, and ODT (LibreOffice), as well as e-books.

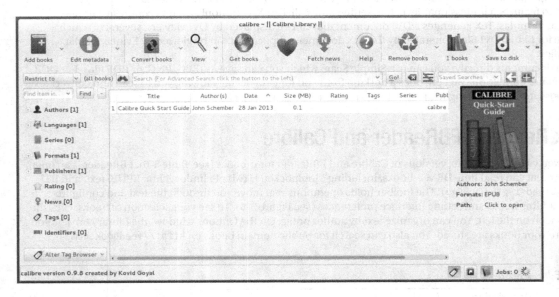

Figure 5-6. Calibre e-book reader and converter

■ **Note**   For older PDAs, you can use the pilot tools to access your handheld device, transferring information between it and your system. You can use the J-Pilot, KPilot, and GnomePilot applications to access your PDA from your desktop. The `pilot-link` package holds tools you can use to access your PDA. Check `www.pilot-link.org` for detailed documentation and useful links.

GNOME Notes

The GNOME Notes application lets you create and organize simple notes on your desktop. The Notes window lists your new and recent notes, showing the note title and the first few lines of text (see Figure 5-7). In the header bar, the search button opens a search box that lets you search for notes. The list button lets you switch between icon and list views. The check button adds a check box to each note icon, letting you delete them or add them to a collection.

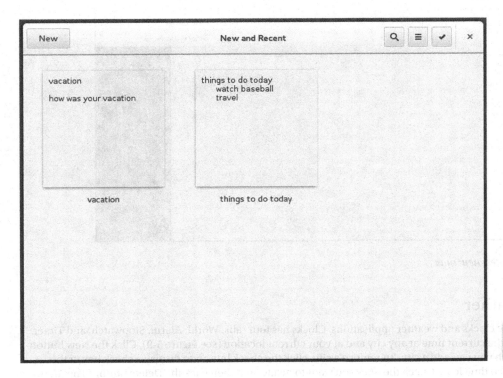

Figure 5-7. *GNOME Notes*

To create a new note, click the New button on the header bar to open a new text. The first line is the title of your note. Press the Enter key to move to the next line (see Figure 5-8). The task menu (gear button) provides undo/redo functions and list formatting (bullets and numbered). You can also delete the note or add it to a collection. The share button lets you share the note with other users.

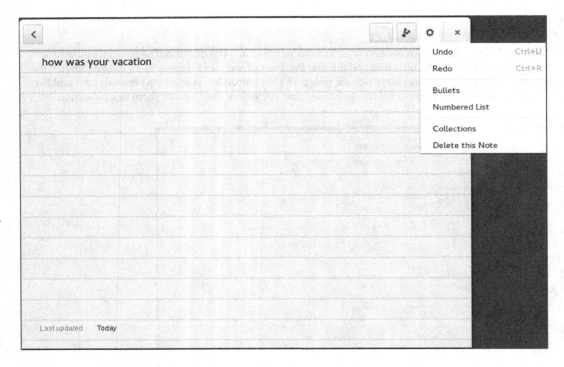

Figure 5-8. *GNOME Notes: new note*

Clocks and Weather

Two helpful tools are the clocks and weather applications. Clocks has four tabs: World, Alarm, Stopwatch, and Timer. The World tab displays the current time at any city and at your current location (see Figure 5-9). Click the New button to open a dialog in which you can add a city. To remove a city, click the check button to display a check box in the lower-right corner of each time icon. Check the ones you want to delete, and then click the Delete button. The Alarm tab works as an alarm clock. The Stopwatch tab operates a stopwatch, letting you mark laps. The timer counts down in time. You set the start amount.

Figure 5-9. *GNOME Clocks, World tab*

The weather tool lets you display the weather at any city. It operates much the same as the Clocks World tab (see Figure 5-10). Click the New button to open a dialog in which you can enter the name of a city. A partial entry is matched, giving you a listing of possible cities. An icon appears for the city with an image indicating the weather, along with a description. . Clicking on a city displays a full image of the weather for that city, with the temperature and forecast for the next 24 hours, and a sidebar with the forecast, date, and data source (see Figure 5-11). Click on the arrow button to remove the right sidebar. To remove a city, click the check mark at the top right to display check boxes at the lower right of each icon (see Figure 5-12). Check the ones you want to delete and click the Delete button. The top center of the header bar is also a button for a menu with entries to select all the icons or to de-select them all.

Figure 5-10. *GNOME Weather*

Figure 5-11. *GNOME Weather: city with forcast*

Figure 5-12. *GNOME Weather: deleting cities*

Editors

The Fedora desktops (GNOME and KDE) support powerful text editors with full mouse support, scrollbars, and menus. These include basic text editors, such as Gedit and Kate, as well as word processors, such as LibreOffice Word, AbiWord, and KWord. Fedora also provides the cursor-based editors Nano, Vim, Emacs, and Leafpad. Nano is a cursor-based editor with an easy-to-use interface supporting menus and mouse selection (if run from a terminal window). Vim is an enhanced version of the vi text editor used on UNIX. These editors use simple, cursor-based operations to give you a full-screen format. Table 5-7 lists several desktop editors for Linux. Vim and Emacs have powerful editing features that have been refined over the years. Emacs, in particular, is extensible to a full-development environment for programming new applications. Later versions of Emacs and Vim—such as GNU Emacs, XEmacs, and Gvim—provide support for mouse, menu, and window operations.

Table 5-7. *Desktop Editors*

Application	Description
Desktop	
KEdit	Text editor
Kate	Text and program editor
Words	Desktop publisher, part of Calligra
Gedit	Text editor
AbiWord	Word processor
GNU Emacs	Emacs editor with X Window System support
XEmacs	X Window System version of Emacs editor

(continued)

Table 5-7. (*continued*)

Application	Description
gvim	Vim version with X Window System support
OpenWriter	LibreOffice word processor that can edit text files
Command-Line Interface	
Vim	Vim version of vi
Emacs	Emacs command-line editor
Nano	Screen-based command-line interface editor
Leafpad	Screen-based command-line interface editor with mouse support when run from a terminal window on desktop

Text editors are often used in system administration tasks to change or add entries in Linux configuration files found in the /etc directory or in the user's initialization or application configuration files located in a user's home directory (dot files). You can use any text editor to work on source code files for any of the programming languages or shell program scripts.

GNOME Text Editor: Gedit

The Gedit editor is the basic text editor for the GNOME desktop. It provides full mouse support, implementing standard desktop operations, such as cut-and-paste to move text, and click-and-drag to select and move/copy text. It supports standard text-editing operations such as Find and Replace. You can use Gedit to create and modify your text files, including configuration files. Gedit also provides more advanced features, such as Print Preview and configurable levels of undo/redo operations, and it can read data from pipes. It features a plug-in menu that provides added functionality, and it includes plug-ins for spell-checking, encryption, e-mail, and text-based web page display.

KDE Editor: Kate (KWrite)

The KDE editor Kate provides full mouse support, implementing standard desktop operations, such as cut-and-paste to move text, and click-and-drag to select and move/copy text. The editor is accessible from the Applications ➤ Utilities menu on the KDE desktop, and as KWrite on GNOME. Kate is an advanced editor, with such features as spell-checking, font selection, and highlighting. Most commands can be selected by using menus. A toolbar of icons for common operations is displayed across the top of the Kate window. A sidebar displays panels for a file selector and a file list. With the file selector, you can navigate through the file system, selecting files to access. Kate also supports multiple views of a document, letting you display segments in their own windows, vertically or horizontally. You can also open several documents at the same time, moving among them with the file list. Kate is designed to be a program editor for editing software programming/development-related source code files. Kate can format the syntax for different programming languages, such as C, Perl, Java, and XML.

Leafpad

Leafpad is a very simple text editor that provides basic mouse support, letting you edit a file easily (install the leafpad package). It uses an interface similar to Windows Notepad, displaying a menu bar with the File, Edit, Search, and Options menu items. Features are limited to basic operations such as open, save, print, cut, copy, paste, find, and replace.

Nano

Several simple keyboard-based editors are available for Fedora that work on the command-line interface, such as nano and joe. The Nano editor is a simple screen-based editor that lets you visually edit your file, using arrow and page keys to move around the file (install the nano package). You use control keys to perform actions. Ctrl+x will exit and prompt you to save the file; Ctrl+o will save it. You start Nano with the nano command.

```
nano myreport
```

To edit a configuration file, you need administrative access, so you first have to log in as the root user, su. Figure 5-13 shows the Nano editor being used to edit the GRUB configuration file, /etc/default/grub.

```
su
nano /etc/default/grub
```

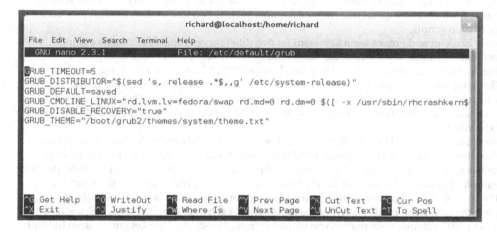

Figure 5-13. Editing with Nano

The Emacs Editor

The Emacs editor is tailored for program development, enabling you to format source code according to the programming language you use. The versions usually included with Linux distributions are GNU Emacs and XEmacs. GNU Emacs is desktop-capable, with features such as menus, scrollbars, and mouse-based editing operations. You can find more information about Emacs at www.emacs.org and about XEmacs at its web site at www.xemacs.org.

The Emacs editor operates much like a standard word processor. The keys on your keyboard represent input characters. Commands are implemented with special keys, such as control (Ctrl) and alternate (Alt) keys. There is no special input mode, as in vi. You type in your text, and if you have to execute an editing command, such as moving the cursor or saving text, you use a Ctrl key. Such an organization makes the Emacs editor easy to use. You invoke the Emacs editor with the command emacs. You can enter the name of the file you want to edit, and if the file does not exist, it is created. In the following example, the user prepares to edit the file mydata with Emacs:

```
emacs mydata
```

The GNU Emacs editor supports basic desktop-editing operations such as selection of text with click-and-drag mouse operations, cut/copy/paste, and a scrollbar for moving through text. The Mode line and Echo areas are displayed at the bottom of the window, where you can enter keyboard commands.

■ **Note**   XEmacs is the complete Emacs editor with a graphical user interface and Internet applications, including a web browser, a mail utility, and a newsreader. XEmacs is available on the Fedora repository.

The Vi Editor: Vim and Gvim

The Vim editor included with most Linux distributions is an enhanced version of the vi editor. It includes all the commands and features of the vi editor. *Vi*, which stands for "visual," remains one of the most widely used editors in Linux. There are two versions of Vim available, vim-minimal, which is installed by default and provides vi editing capabilities, and vim-enhanced, which provides more advanced features such as Perl and Python interpreters, useful if you use vi to create Perl or Python scripts.

Keyboard-based editors like Vim and Emacs use a keyboard for two different operations: to specify editing commands and to receive character input. Used for editing commands, certain keys perform deletions, some execute changes, and others perform cursor movement. Used for character input, keys represent characters that can be entered into the file being edited. Usually, these two different functions are divided among different keys on the keyboard. Alphabetic keys are reserved for character input, while function keys and control keys specify editing commands, such as deleting text or moving the cursor. Such editors can rely on the existence of an extended keyboard that includes function and control keys.

Editors in UNIX, however, were designed to assume a minimal keyboard with alphanumeric characters and some control characters, as well as the ESC and Enter keys. Instead of dividing the command and input functions among different keys, the vi editor has three separate modes of operation for the keyboard: the command and input modes and a line-editing mode. In command mode, all the keys on the keyboard become editing commands; in the input mode, the keys on the keyboard become input characters. Some of the editing commands, such as a and i, enter the input mode. On typing i, you leave the command mode and enter the input mode. Each key now represents a character to be input to the text. Pressing ESC automatically returns you to the command mode, and the keys once again become editor commands. As you edit text, you are constantly moving from the command mode to the input mode and back again. With Vim, you can use the Ctrl+o command to jump quickly to the command mode and enter a command, and then automatically return to the input mode. Table 5-8 lists a basic set of vi commands to get you started.

Table 5-8. Editor Commands

Command	Description
h	Moves the cursor left one character.
l	Moves the cursor right one character.
k	Moves the cursor up one line.
j	Moves the cursor down one line.
Ctrl+f	Moves forward by a screen of text; the next screen of text is displayed.
Ctrl+b	Moves backward by a screen of text; the previous screen of text is displayed.
Input	*(All input commands place the user in input; the user leaves input with esc.)*
a	Enters input after the cursor.

(*continued*)

Table 5-8. (*continued*)

Command	Description
i	Enters input before the cursor.
o	Enters input below the line the cursor is on; inserts a new empty line below the one the cursor is currently on.
Text Selection (Vim)	
v	Visual mode; move the cursor to expand selected text by character. Once selected, press key to execute action: c change, d delete, y copy, : line-editing command, J join lines, U uppercase, u lowercase.
V	Visual mode; move cursor to expand selected text by line
Delete	
x	Deletes the character the cursor is on
dd	Deletes the line the cursor is on
Change	Except for the replace command, r, all change commands place the user into input after deleting text.
cw	Deletes the word the cursor is on and places the user into the input mode
r	Replaces the character the cursor is on. After pressing r, the user enters the replacement character. The change is made without entering input; the user remains in the Vi command mode.
R	First places into input mode, and then overwrites character by character. Appears as an overwrite mode on the screen but actually is in input mode.
Move	Moves text by first deleting it, moving the cursor to desired place of insertion, and then pressing the p command. (When text is deleted, it is automatically held in a special buffer.)
p	Inserts deleted or copied text after the character or line the cursor is on
P	Inserts deleted or copied text before the character or line the cursor is on
dw p	Deletes a word, and then moves it to the place you indicate with the cursor (press p to insert the word after the word the cursor is on)
yy or Y p	Copies the line the cursor is on
Search	*The two search commands open a line at the bottom of the screen and enable the user to enter a pattern to be searched for; press Enter after typing in the pattern.*
/pattern	Searches forward in the text for a pattern
?pattern	Searches backward in the text for a pattern
n	Repeats the previous search, whether it was forward or backward
Line-Editing Commands	*Effect*
w	Saves the file
q	Quits the editor; q! quits without saving

Although you can create, save, close, and quit files with the vi editor, the commands for each are not very similar. Saving and quitting a file involves the use of special line-editing commands, whereas closing a file is a vi editing command. Creation of a file is usually specified on the same shell command line that invokes the vi editor. To edit a file, type vi or vim and the name of a file on the shell command line. If a file by that name does not exist, the system creates it. In effect, entering the name of a file that does not yet exist instructs the vi editor to create that file. The following command invokes the vi editor, working on the file booklist. If booklist does not yet exist, the vi editor creates it.

```
$ vim booklist
```

After executing the vim command, you enter vi's command mode. Each key becomes a vi editing command, and the screen becomes a window onto the text file. Text is displayed screen by screen. The first screen of text is displayed, and the cursor is positioned in the upper-left corner. With a newly created file, there is no text to display. When you first enter the vi editor, you are in the command mode. To enter text, you must enter the input mode. In the command mode, a is the editor command for appending text. Pressing this key places you in the input mode. Now the keyboard operates like a typewriter, and you can input text to the file. If you press Enter, you merely start a new line of text. With Vim, you can use the arrow keys to move from one part of the entered text to another and work on different parts of the text. After entering text, you can leave the input mode and return to the command mode by pressing ESC. Once you've finished with the editing session, you exit vi by typing two capital Zs, ZZ. Hold down the Shift key and press Z twice. This sequence first saves the file and then exits the vi editor, returning you to the Linux shell. To save a file while editing, you use the line-editing command w, which writes a file to the disk. w is equivalent to the Save command found in other word processors. You first type a colon to access the line-editing mode, and then type w and press Enter, :w.

You can use the :q command to quit an editing session. Unlike the ZZ command, the :q command does not perform a save operation before it quits. In this respect, it has one major constraint. If any modifications have been made to your file since the last save operation, the :q command will fail, and you will not leave the editor. However, you can override this restriction by placing a ! qualifier after the :q command. The command :q! will quit the vi editor without saving any modifications made to the file during that session (the combination :wq is the same as ZZ).

To obtain online help, enter the :help command. This is a line-editing command. Type a colon, enter the word help on the line that opens at the bottom of the screen, and then press Enter. You can add the name of a specific command after the word help. Pressing the F1 key also brings up online help.

As an alternative to using Vim in a command-line interface, you can use gvim, which provides X Window System–based menus for basic file, editing, and window operations.

The package vim is called the vim-X11 package, which includes several links to Gvim, such as evim, gview, and gex (open Ex editor line). To use Gvim, you can enter the gvim command at a terminal prompt. The standard vi interface is shown, but with several menu buttons displayed across the top, along with a toolbar with buttons for common commands like search and file saves. All the standard vi commands work as described previously; however, you can use your mouse to select items on these menus. You can open and close a file, or open several files, using split windows or different windows. The editing menu enables you to cut, copy, and paste text as well as undo or redo operations. In the editing mode, you can select text with your mouse with a click-and-drag operation or use the Editing menu to cut or copy and then paste the selected text. Text entry, however, is still performed using the a, i, or o commands to enter the input mode. Searches and replacements are supported through a dialog window. There are also buttons on the toolbar for finding next and previous instances. You can also split the view into different windows to display parts of the same file or different files. Use the :split command to open a window, and use :hide to close the current one. Use Ctrl+w with the up and down arrow keys to move between them. On Gvim, you use entries in the Windows menu to manage windows. Configuration preferences can be placed in the user's .vimrc file.

Mail (E-mail) and News

Electronic mail utilities perform the same basic tasks of receiving and sending messages. Some mail clients operate on a desktop, such as KDE or GNOME. Others are designed to use a screen-based interface and can be run only from the command line (the terminal window). For web-based Internet mail services, such as Gmail and Yahoo, you can use a web browser instead of a mail client to access mail accounts provided by those services. Table 5-9 lists several popular Linux mail clients. Mail is sent to and from destinations using mail transport agents, such as Sendmail, Exim, and Smail.

Table 5-9. *Linux Mail Clients*

Mail Client	Description
Kontact (KMail, KAddressBook, KOrganizer)	Includes the K Desktop mail client, KMail; integrated mail, address book, and scheduler
Contacts	GNOME contact database synced with Online Accounts (currently supports only Google contacts)
Documents	GNOME documents for locating local and cloud-based documents; synced with Online Accounts (Google Docs and Microsoft SkyDrive)
Evolution	E-mail client
Thunderbird	Mozilla group standalone mail client and newsreader
Sylpheed	Gtk mail and news client
Claws Mail	Extended version of the Sylpheed e-mail client
GNU Emacs and XEmacs	Emacs mail clients
Mutt	Screen-based mail client
Mail	Original UNIX-based command-line mail client
Squirrel Mail	Web-based mail client

Evolution

Evolution is the primary mail client for the GNOME desktop. Although it's designed for GNOME, it works equally well on other desktops. Evolution provides a mail client, calendar, and address book. The mailer supports several protocols (SMTP, POP, and IMAP), multiple mail accounts, and encryption. It also supports Pretty Good Privacy (PGP) and GNU Privacy Guard (GPG) encryption. Messages are indexed for easy searching. Junk mail filtering is provided. See the Evolution web site (http://projects.gnome.org/evolution/) for a complete description of its features.

You can access Evolution from the Applications overview. The Evolution mailer provides a simple desktop interface, with a toolbar for commonly used commands and a sidebar for shortcuts. A set of buttons on the lower left allows you to access other operations, such as the calendar and contacts. The mail screen is divided into two panes, one for listing the mail headers and the other for displaying the currently selected message (see Figure 5-14). You can click any header title to sort your headers by that category. Evolution also supports the use of virtual folders created by the user to hold mail that meets specified criteria. Incoming mail can be automatically distributed to a particular virtual folder.

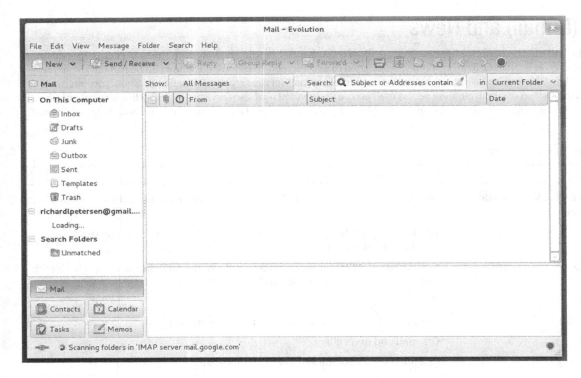

Figure 5-14. *Evolution e-mail client*

To configure Evolution, select Preferences from the Edit menu (Edit ➤ Preferences). On the Evolution Preferences window, a sidebar shows icons for mail accounts, contacts, mail preferences, composer preference, network preferences, calendar and tasks, and certificates. The main accounts entry displays a list of current accounts. An Add button lets you add new accounts, and the Edit button allows you to change current accounts.

Numerous plug-ins are available to extend Evolution's capabilities. Most are installed and enabled for you automatically, including the SpamAssassin plug-in for handling junk mail. To manage your plug-ins, select the Plugins entry in the Edit menu (Edit ➤ Plugin) to open the Plugin Manager. The plug-ins are listed in a left scroll window, and the configuration tabs for a selected plug-in are on the right.

Evolution also supports contact operations such as calendars, contact lists, and memos. On the left-side pane, the bottom section displays buttons for these different functions: Mail, Contacts, Calendars, Tasks, and Memos. To see and manage your contacts, click the Contacts button on the left sidebar. The Calendar displays a browseable calendar on the left pane to move easily to a specific date. The right pane shows a daily calendar page by the hour, with sections for tasks and memos. You can set up several calendars, which you can access at the top of the right pane. A personal calendar is set up for you already. To add a new calendar, select Calendar from the New menu. This opens a New Calendar dialog, from which you can choose the type and name.

Thunderbird

Thunderbird is a full-featured standalone e-mail client provided by the Mozilla project (www.mozilla.org). It is designed to be easy to use, highly customizable, and heavily secure. It features advanced intelligent spam filtering, as well as security features such as encryption, digital signatures, and S/MIME. To protect against viruses, e-mail attachments can be examined without being run. Thunderbird supports both the Internet Message Access

Protocol (IMAP) and the Post Office Protocol (POP). It also functions as a newsreader and features a built-in RSS reader. Thunderbird also supports the use of the Lightweight Directory Access Protocol (LDAP) for address books. Thunderbird is an extensible application, allowing customized modules to be added to enhance its capabilities. You can download extensions such as dictionary search and contact sidebars from the web site. GPG encryption can be supported with the Enigmail extension.

Thunderbird provides integration with popular online mail services like Gmail, saved searches, and customized tags for selected messages. You can access Thunderbird from the Applications overview.

The Thunderbird interface uses a standard three-pane format, with a side pane for listing mail accounts and their mailboxes (see Figure 5-15). The top pane is the message list pane, and the bottom pane shows a selected message's text. Commands can be run using the toolbar, the tool menu (button at the right of the toolbar), or keyboard shortcuts. You can even change the appearance using different themes. Thunderbird also supports HTML mail, displaying web components such as URLs in mail messages.

Figure 5-15. *Thunderbird e-mail client*

To edit an e-mail account, select the Edit ➤ Account Settings menu entry. In the Account Settings window, you will see an entry for your mail account, with tabs for Server Settings, Copies & Folders, Composition & Addressing, Offline & Disk Space, Return Receipt, and Security. The Server Settings tab has entries for your server name, port, username, and connection and task configurations such as downloading new messages automatically. The Security tab opens the Certificate Manager, from which you can select security certificates to use to digitally sign or encrypt messages.

Thunderbird provides an address book in which you can enter complete contact information, including e-mail addresses, street addresses, phone numbers, and notes. Select Address Book from the Tools menu to open the Address Book window (Tools ➤ Address Book).

GNOME Contacts

If you have enabled contacts for Online Accounts, you can use the GNOME Contacts application to manage and access your contacts. Contacts are downloaded from an online account. Currently, only Google is supported. You can then access and edit your contacts with the Contacts application, which is accessible from the Applications overview. First be sure to switch on Contacts in System Setting's Online Accounts (see Figure 5-16).

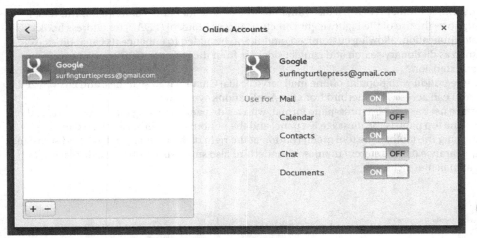

Figure 5-16. *Online Accounts contacts switch*

Contacts displays a sidebar listing your contacts. A search box lets you search for contacts. To add a contact manually, click the plus button (+) above the search box (see Figure 5-17). The selected contact shows the name, icon used, and the e-mail address. The e-mail entry is a mail button, which you can click to open your mailer to compose a message to be sent to that address.

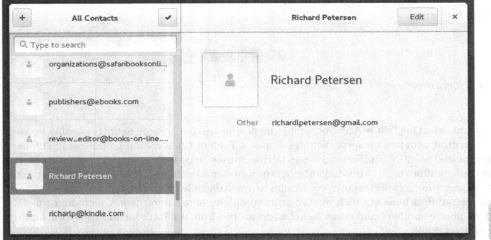

Figure 5-17. *GNOME Contacts*

To edit the contact information, click the Edit button at the top-right corner. From the New Detail menu, you can provide additional information, such as the address, phone, links, web site, birthday, and notes (see Figure 5-18). For each entry, you can classify whether it is work, home, or other. To remove a contact, edit the contact and click the Remove Contact button at the lower right.

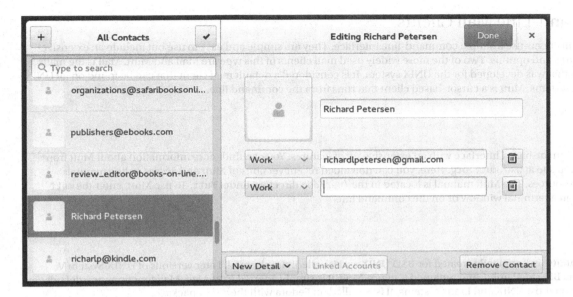

Figure 5-18. *GNOME Contacts edit*

The KDE Mail Client: KMail

The KDE mail client, KMail, provides a full-featured desktop interface for composing, sending, and receiving e-mail messages. KMail is part of the KDE Personal Information Management suite (KDE-PIM), which also includes an address book (KAddressBook), an organizer and scheduler (KOrganizer), and a note writer (KNotes). All these components are directly integrated on the desktop into Kontact. You can start up KMail directly or as part of the Kontact applications (Mail). KMail, along with Kontact, KOrganizer, and KAddressBook, is accessible from the KDE Desktop Office and Internet menus. On GNOME, you can access it from Applications overview. You can access Kontact in the Office filter. KMail is installed as part of the KDE desktop, but you can install it separately.

To quickly set up a new e-mail account, you can use the Account Wizard (Tools ➤ Account Wizard). A series of dialogs will prompt you to enter the account type, the account name and address, a login name and password, and the incoming and outgoing servers. For more detailed configuration, select the Configure Kmail entry in the Settings menu (Settings ➤ Configure Kmail).

Emacs Mail

The GNU version of Emacs includes a mail client, in addition to other components, such as a newsreader and editor. GNU Emacs is included on Fedora distributions. Check the Emacs web site at www.gnu.org/software/emacs for more information. When you start GNU Emacs, menu buttons are displayed across the top of the screen. If you are running Emacs in an X Window System environment, you have full desktop capabilities and can select menus using your mouse. To access the Emacs mail client, select from the mail entries in the Tools menu. To compose and send messages, just select the Send Mail item in the Tools menu.

Command-Line Mail Clients

Several mail clients use a simple command-line interface. They are simple and easy to use but include an extensive set of features and options. Two of the more widely used mail clients of this type are Mail and Mutt. Mail is the mailx mail client that was developed for the UNIX system. It is considered a default mail client that can be found on all UNIX and Linux systems. Mutt is a cursor-based client that runs from the command line.

Mutt

Mutt has a cursor-based interface with an extensive set of features. You can find more information about Mutt from the Mutt web site at www.mutt.org. Here, you can download recent versions of Mutt and access online manuals and help resources. The Mutt manual is located in the /usr/doc directory under Mutt. To use Mutt, enter the mutt command in a terminal window or on the command line.

Mail

The Mail utility was originally created for BSD UNIX and is called, simply, mail. Later versions of UNIX System V adopted the BSD mail utility and renamed it *mailx*. Now, it is simply referred to as Mail. Mail functions as a default mail client on most UNIX and Linux systems. It is installed on Fedora with the mailx package.

To send a message with Mail, type mail on the command line, in addition to the address of the person to whom you are sending the message. Press Enter, and you are prompted for a subject. Enter the subject of the message and press Enter again. At this point, you are placed in input mode. Anything you type is considered the contents of the message. Pressing Enter adds a new line to the text. When you finish typing your message, press Ctrl+d on a line of its own to end the message. You will then be prompted to enter a user to whom to send a carbon copy (cc) of the message. If you do not want to send a carbon copy, just press Enter. You will then see EOT (end of transmission) displayed after you press Ctrl+d.

You can send a message to several users at the same time by listing those users' addresses as arguments on the command line following the mail command. In the following example, the user sends the same message to chris and aleina:

```
$ mail chris aleina
```

To receive mail, you first enter the mail command and press Enter. This invokes a Mail shell with its own prompt and mail commands. A list of message headers is displayed. Header information is arranged into fields, beginning with the status of the message and the message number. The status of a message is indicated by a single uppercase letter, usually N for "new" or U for "unread." A message number, used for easy reference to your messages, follows the status field. The next field is the address of the sender, followed by the date and time the message was received, and then the number of lines and characters in the message. The last field contains the subject the sender gave to the message. After the headers, the Mail shell displays its prompt, an ampersand (&). At the Mail prompt, you enter commands that operate on the messages. An example of a Mail header and prompt follows:

```
$ mail
Mail version 8.2 01/15/2001. Type ? for help.
"/var/spool/mail/larisa": 3 messages 1 new 2 unread
 1 chris@turtle.mytrek. Thu Jun 7 14:17 22/554 "trip"
>U 2 aleina@turtle.mytrek Thu Jun 7 14:18 22/525 "party"
 U 3 dylan@turtle.mytrek. Thu Jun 7 14:18 22/528 "newsletter"
& q
```

Mail references messages either through a message list or through the current message marker (>). The greater-than sign (>) is placed before the current message. The current message is referenced by default when no message number is included with a Mail command. You can also reference messages using a message list consisting of several message numbers.

Use the R and r commands to reply to a message you have received. The R command entered with a message number generates a header for sending a message and then places you into input mode to type the message. The q command quits Mail. When you quit, messages you have already read are placed in a file called mbox in your home directory. Instead of saving messages in the mbox file, you can use the s command to save a message explicitly to a file of your choice. Mail has its own initialization file, called .mailrc, which is executed each time Mail is invoked, for sending or receiving messages. Within it, you can define Mail options and create Mail aliases.

Accessing Mail on Remote Mail Servers

Most new mail clients are equipped to access mail accounts on remote servers. Mail clients, such as Evolution, KMail, Sylpheed, and Thunderbird, enable you to set up a mailbox for such an account and access a mail server to check for and download received mail. You must specify what protocol a mail server uses. This is usually either the Post Office Protocol (POP) or the IMAP protocol (IMAP). Using a mail server address, you can access your account with your username and password.

For e-mail clients, such as Mail and Mutt, that do not provide mail server access, you can use Fetchmail to have mail from those accounts sent directly to the inbox of your Linux account. All your mail, whether from other users on your Linux system or from remote mail accounts, will appear in your local inbox. Fetchmail checks for mail on remote mail servers and downloads it to your local inbox, where it appears as newly received mail. Enter fetchmail on the command line with the mail server address and any needed options. The mail protocol is indicated with the -p option and the mail server type, usually POP3. If your e-mail username is different from your Linux login name, you use the -u option and the e-mail name. Once you execute the fetchmail command, you are prompted for a password. The syntax for the fetchmail command for a POP3 mail server follows:

```
fetchmail -p POP3 -u username mail-server
```

You will see messages telling you if you have mail and how many messages are being downloaded. You can then use a mail client to read the messages from your inbox. You can run Fetchmail in daemon mode to have it check automatically for mail. You must include an option specifying the interval in seconds, for checking mail.

```
fetchmail -d 1200
```

To have fetchmail run automatically, you can set the START DAEMON option to yes in the /etc/default/fetchmail file. Edit the file with the gksu gedit command.

You can specify options, such as the server type, username, and password, in a .fetchmailrc file in your home directory. You can also include entries for other mail servers and accounts. Once Fetchmail is configured, you can enter fetchmail with no arguments; it will read entries from your .fetchmailrc file. You can also make entries directly in the .fetchmailrc file. An entry in the .fetchmailrc file for a particular mail account consists of several fields and their values—poll, protocol, username, and password. The poll field refers to the mail server name. You can also specify your password, instead of having to enter it each time Fetchmail accesses the mail server.

Mailing Lists

Users on mailing lists automatically receive messages and articles sent to the lists. Mailing lists work much like a mail alias, broadcasting messages to all users on the list. Mailing lists were designed to serve specialized groups of people. Numerous mailing lists, as well as other subjects, are available for Linux. By convention, to subscribe to a list, you send a request to the mailing list address with a -request term added to its username. For example, to subscribe to gnome-list@gnome.org, you send a request to gnome-list-request@gnome.org.

You can use the Mailman and Majordomo programs to manage your mailing lists automatically. Mailman is the GNU mailing list manager that is included with Fedora (`www.list.org`). You can find out more about Majordomo at `www.greatcircle.com/majordomo` and about Mailman at `http://sourceforge.net`.

Usenet News

Usenet is an open mail system on which users post messages that include news, discussions, and opinions. It operates like a mailbox to which any user on your Linux system can read or send messages. Users' messages are incorporated into Usenet files, which are distributed to any system signed up to receive them. Each system that receives Usenet files is referred to as a *site*. Certain sites perform organizational and distribution operations for Usenet, receiving messages from other sites and organizing them into Usenet files, which are then broadcast to many other sites. Such sites are called backbone sites, and they operate like publishers, receiving articles and organizing them into different groups.

To access Usenet news, you require access to a news server. A news server receives the daily Usenet newsfeeds and makes them accessible to other systems. Your network may have a system that operates as a news server. If you are using an Internet service provider (ISP), a news server is probably maintained by your ISP for your use. To read Usenet articles, you use a *newsreader*, a client program that connects to a news server and accesses the articles. On the Internet and in TCP/IP networks, news servers communicate with newsreaders using the Network News Transfer Protocol (NNTP) and are often referred to as NNTP news servers. You can also create your own news server on your Linux system to run a local Usenet news service or to download and maintain the full set of Usenet articles. Several Linux programs, called news transport agents, can be used to create such a server.

You read Usenet articles with a newsreader, such as KNode, Pan, Thunderbird, or tin, which enables you to select a specific newsgroup and then read the articles in it. A newsreader operates like a user interface, letting you browse through and select available articles for reading, saving, or printing. Most newsreaders employ a retrieval feature called *threads,* which pulls together articles on the same discussion or topic. Several popular newsreaders are listed in Table 5-10.

Table 5-10. *Linux Newsreaders*

Newsreader	Description
Pan	GNOME desktop newsreader
KNode	KDE desktop newsreader
Thunderbird	Mail client with newsreader capabilities (X-based)
Sylpheed	GNOME Windows-like newsreader
slrn	Newsreader (cursor-based)
Emacs	Emacs editor, mail client, and newsreader (cursor-based)
tin	Newsreader (command-line interface)
Newsbin	Newsreader (Windows version; works under Wine)
kwooty	Binary only NZB-based news grabber

Most newsreaders can read Usenet news provided on remote news servers that use the NNTP. Desktop newsreaders, such as KNode and Pan, have you specify the Internet address for the remote news server in their own configuration settings. Shell-based newsreaders such as tin obtain the news server's Internet address from the NNTPSERVER shell variable, configured in the .profile file.

```
NNTPSERVER=news.domain.com
export NNTPSERVER
```

Binary Newsreaders and Grabbers

There are few binary-based newsreaders for Linux—that can convert text messages to binary equivalents—like those found in alt.binaries newsgroups. There are some news *grabbers*, which are applications designed only to download binaries. The binaries are normally encoded with RAR compression, which can be decoded by Fedora. Binaries normally consist of several rar archive files, some of which may be incomplete. To repair them, you can use par2. Install the par2 and gpar2 packages. A binary should have its own set of par2 files also listed on the new server that you can download and use to repair any incomplete rar files. The principle works much the same as RAID arrays using parity information to reconstruct damaged data. You can use the gpar2 application to manually repair rar archive files; chooseGPar2 (install the gpar2 package). An alternative solution is to use the Windows version of the Newsbin newsreader running under Wine (Windows compatibility layer for Linux). You will have to install Wine first.

The slrn newsreader is cursor-based. Commands are displayed across the top of the screen and can be executed using the listed keys. Different types of screens exist for the newsgroup list, article list, and article content, each with its own set of commands. An initial screen lists your subscribed newsgroups with commands for posting, listing, and subscribing to your newsgroups. When you start slrn for the first time, you may have to create a .jnewsrc file in your home directory. Use the following command: slrn -f .jnewsrc -create. Also, you must set the NNTPSERVER variable and make sure it is exported. The slrn newsreader features a utility called slrn-pull that you can use to download articles in specified newsgroups automatically.

Database Management Systems

Several database systems are provided for Fedora, including LibreOffice Base, MariaDB, Derby, and PostgreSQL. MariaDB is derived from MySQL but is fully open sourced. It is the default MySQL type database for Fedora. MariaDB is supported and developed by the original MySQL developers. The original MySQL is owned by Oracle and features commercial versions. You can still install the older noncommercial version of MySQL, if you wish. In addition, commercial SQL database software is also compatible with Fedora. Table 5-11 lists database management systems currently available for Linux.

Table 5-11. *Database Management Systems for Linux*

System	Site
LibreOffice Base	LibreOffice.org database: www.libreoffice.org
PostgreSQL	The PostgreSQL database: www.postgresql.org
MariaDB	Advanced and fully open source version of MySQL (Fedora default)
Derby	Apache JAVA-based database
MongoDB	Document-based database
Hadoop	Apache distributed database for very large data sets
sqlite	Simple SQL database

Derby is a JAVA-based database developed by Apache. SQLite is a simple and fast database server requiring no configuration and implementing the database on a single-disk file. For small embedded databases, you can use Berkeley DB (db4).

In addition, Fedora also supports document-based non-SQL databases such as MongoDB and Hadoop. MongoDB is a document-based database that can be quickly searched. Hadoop is an Apache project for accessing very large data sets distributed across a network.

SQL Databases (RDBMS)

SQL databases are relational database management systems (RDBMSs) designed for extensive database management tasks. Many of the major SQL databases now have Linux versions, including Oracle, Informix, Sybase, and IBM. These are commercial and professional database management systems. Linux has proved itself capable of supporting complex and demanding database management tasks. In addition, many free SQL databases are available for Linux that offer much the same functionality. Most commercial databases also provide free personal versions.

LibreOffice.org Base

LibreOffice provides a basic database application, called LibreOffice Base, which can access many database files. You can set up and operate a simple database as well as access and manage files from other database applications. When you start up LibreOffice Base, you will be prompted either to start a new database or connect to an existing one. File types supported include ODBC (Open Database Connectivity), JDBC (Java), Adabas D, MySQL, PostgreSQL, and MDB (Microsoft Access) database files (install the unixodbc and java-libmysql packages). You can also create your own simple databases. Check the LibreOffice Base page at www.libreoffice.org/features/base/ for detailed information on drivers and supported databases.

MariaDB

MariaDB, included with Fedora, is a true multiuser, multithreaded SQL database server. MySQL is an open source product available free of charge under the GPL license. It is the default MySQL type database for Fedora. MariaDB is supported and developed by the original MySQL developers. MariaDB is designed to be fully compatible with MySQL. The original MySQL is owned by Oracle and features commercial versions. You can obtain current information on MariaDB from its web site at https://mariadb.org. You can use the MySQL documentation for MariaDB that is available at http://dev.mysql.com/doc/.

PostgreSQL

PostgreSQL is based on the POSTURES database management system, although it uses SQL as its query language. PostgreSQL is a next-generation research prototype developed at the University of California, Berkeley. Linux versions of PostgreSQL are included in most distributions, including Red Hat, Fedora, Debian, and Ubuntu. You can find more information about it from the PostgreSQL web site at www.postgresql.org. PostgreSQL is an open source project developed under the GPL license.

CHAPTER 6

■ ■ ■

Graphics and Multimedia

The Fedora repositories provide an extensive variety of graphic and multimedia applications, including image viewers like Eye of GNOME, advanced image-manipulation programs like GIMP, music and CD players like Rhythmbox, and video players like Totem and VLC. Graphics tools available for use under Linux are listed in Table 6-2. Additionally, there is strong support for multimedia tasks from video and DVD to sound and music editing (see Tables 6-5 and 6-6).

Support for many popular multimedia codecs, specifically MP3, DVD, MKV, and DivX, are not included with the Fedora distribution, because of licensing and other restrictions. To play MP3, DVD, MKV, or DivX files, you must download and install support packages manually. Precompiled RPM binary packages for many popular media applications and libraries, such as MPlayer and Xvid, are available on the RPM Fusion repository (see `http://rpmfusion.org`). RPM Fusion is an official Fedora repository that provides RPM Fedora–compatible packages for many multimedia and other applications that cannot be included with the Fedora distribution. These include MP3 support and DVD and DivX codecs. Current multimedia sites are listed in Table 6-1.

Table 6-1. *Linux Multimedia Sites*

Project and Site	Description
Fedora repository `http://fedoraproject.org`	Fedora repository, which includes most GNU licensed multimedia applications
RPM Fusion `http://rpmfusion.org`	Repository for drivers and multimedia applications and libraries that are not included with Fedora. This is an official extension of the Fedora Project.
Fedora Design Suite `http://spins.fedoraproject.org/design/`	Fedora spin, featuring graphics applications
Korora Project `https://kororaproject.org`	Fedora spin that includes most multimedia codecs and applications
PulseAudio `www.pulseaudio.org`	PulseAudio sound interface, now the default for Fedora
Sound & MIDI Software for Linux `http://linux-sound.org`	Lists a wide range of multimedia and sound software
Advanced Linux Sound Architecture (ALSA) `www.alsa-project.org`	The Advanced Linux Sound Architecture (ALSA) project for current sound drivers
Open Sound System `www.opensound.com`	Open Sound System, drives for older devices

For those who wish to work primarily with graphics applications (see Table 6-2), you can install the Fedora Design Suite, a Fedora spin that installs available Fedora image applications such as Inkscape (vector graphics), Blender (3D modeling), and Dia (charts); see `http://spins.fedoraproject.org/design/`.

Table 6-2. *Graphics Applications for Linux*

Tool	Description
Shotwell	GNOME digital camera application and image library manager (`www.yorba.org/shotwell`)
F-Spot	GNOME digital camera application and image library manager (`http://f-spot.org`)
Cheese	GNOME web cam application for taking pictures and videos
Photos	GNOME photo viewer and organizer
digiKam	Digital photo-management tool; works with GNOME and KDE
KDE	
Gwenview	Image browser and viewer (default for KDE)
ShowFoto	Simple image viewer; works with digiKam (`www.digikam.org`)
KSnapshot	Screen grabber
KolourPaint	Paint program
Krita	Image editor (`www.calligra.org/krita`)
GNOME	
Eye of GNOME	GNOME image viewer
GIMP	GNU image-manipulation program (`www.gimp.org`)
Inkscape	GNOME vector graphics application (`www.inkscape.org`)
gpaint	GNOME paint program
Blender	3D modeling, rendering, and animation program
Synfig Studio	2D modeling, rendering, and animation program
CinePaint	Paint and image retouching for high-resolution images
Entangle	Camera and computer-linked photographic system
Agave	Generates color schemes
RawTherapee	Digital processing and raw image converter
LibreOffice Draw	LibreOffice Draw program
X Window System	
XPaint	Paint program
Xfig	Drawing program
ImageMagick	Image format conversion and editing tool

For the commercial DVD video codec, you still have to use the http://rpm.livna.org repository. Here you will find only one package, the libdvdcss package, for playing DVD video. Enable the Livna repository (livna-release.rpm) and then use PackageKit to install the libdvdcss package. You can also download it directly from http://rpm.livna.org/repo/20/.

For those who want to install a multimedia system, such as for an HTPC, you can use the Korora Project spin (https://kororaproject.org). It includes Fedora as well as many free and non-free multimedia codecs and applications available from the RPM Fusion repository.

Graphics Applications

The GNOME and KDE desktops support an impressive number of graphics applications, including image viewers, screen grabbers, image editors, and paint tools. These tools can be found in the Applications overview.

Photo Management: Shotwell, F-Spot, Cheese, and Photos

The Shotwell photo manager provides an easy and powerful way to manage, display, import, and publish your photos and images (www.yorba.org/shotwell). It is the default photo manager for Fedora 20. See the Shotwell user manual for full details (Help ➤ User Manual, http://yorba.org/shotwell/help). You can open the Shotwell Photo Manager as Shotwell, using either the Applications overview or the Shotwell icon on the Activities sidebar.

You can import folders from cameras, folders, or from F-Spot (see Figure 6-1). Photo thumbnails are displayed in the main right pane. The View menu lets you control the thumbnail display, allowing you to sort photos, zoom, show photo filenames (Titles), or select by rating. You can adjust the size of the displayed thumbnails using a slider bar in the toolbar located at the bottom right of the Shotwell window. The small figure button to the left of the slider reduces thumbnails to their smallest size, and the large figure button to the right of the slider expands them to the largest size. To see a full-screen slideshow of the photos, choose the slideshow entry from the View menu (F5). The slideshow starts automatically. Moving your mouse to the bottom middle of the screen displays slideshow controls for pausing and stepping through photos. The Settings button opens a dialog in which you can set the display time. To end the slideshow and return to the desktop, click the Full Screen button. The slideshow buttons are shown here.

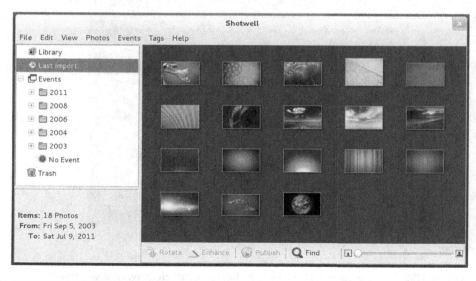

Figure 6-1. *Shotwell photo management*

165

Photos are organized automatically according to the time they were taken. Dates are listed under the Events entry in the left sidebar, arranged by year, month, and date. To name a photo, right-click it and choose Edit Title. This opens a dialog in which you can enter the name. You can also tag photos by placing them in groups, making them easier to access. To tag a photo, right-click it and choose Add Tags to open a dialog in which you can enter a tag name. The tag will show up as a label for the photo. You can access photos by tags by using the Tags entries in the left sidebar. For each photo, you can also set a rating indicated by five stars or fewer. You can also mark a photo as rejected. To rate a photo, right-click it and choose Set Rating, which then lists rating options in a submenu. Use the Show Photos button in the bottom toolbar to display photos by rating. You can select several photos at once by using click-and-drag, Ctrl-click, or Shift-click (as you do for files in a file manager window), then right-click to give them the same rating (Set Rating) or same tag (Add Tags).

When you select a photo or a group of photos, the Rotate, Enhance, and Publish buttons in the bottom toolbar become active. The Publish button lets you publish the photo on a web service: Facebook, Flickr, or Picasa. The Rotate button rotates the photo (from the Photos menu, you can also flip the photo horizontally or vertically). The Enhance button adjusts the photo automatically.

To perform more complex edits, select the photo and then choose View ➤ Fullscreen (F11) to open the photo in the Shotwell photo editor (see Figure 6-2). Move your mouse to the bottom of the screen to display the editing toolbar, which includes the Rotate, Crop, Red-eye, Adjust, and Enhance buttons. You can also enlarge or reduce the photo display by using the slider bar. The Crop button opens an adjustable border, with a menu for choosing the display proportions, such as HD video or postcard. The Adjust button opens a dialog for refined changes, such as exposure, saturation, tint, temperature, and shadows. The toolbar will keep disappearing. Click the Pin button to have it displayed permanently. Edits are stored in a Shotwell database; they are not made to the original photo. To revert to the original photo, right-click and choose Revert to Original or choose that entry from the Photos menu.

Figure 6-2. *Shotwell photo editing*

The Shotwell Preferences dialog (Edit ➤ Preferences) lets you set the background intensity, choose a photo library folder, and select a photo editor. To open a photo with an external photo editor, right-click the photo thumbnail and select Open with External Editor. Photos are stored in your Pictures directory under the Events subfolders, by year and then month. To open a photos folder, right-click and select Show in File Manager.

The F-Spot photo manager also manages photos (http://f-spot.org). Photos can be organized by different categories, such as events, people, and places (see Figure 6-3). You can perform standard display operations such as rotation or full-screen viewing, in addition to slideshows. Image-editing support is provided. F-Spot includes a photo editor that provides basic adjustments and changes such as rotation, red-eye correction, and standard color settings, including temperature and saturation. You can tag photos by placing them in groups, making them easier to access. With a tag, you can label a collection of photos. Then use the tag to access them instantly. The tag itself can be a user-selected icon, including one that the user can create with the included Tag icon editor.

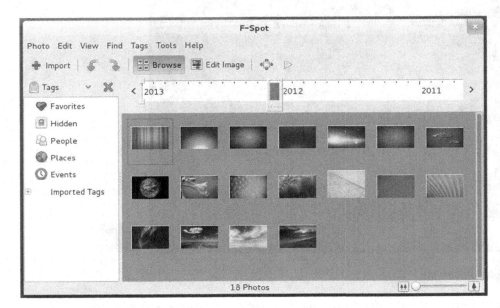

Figure 6-3. *F-Spot photo management*

digiKam (www.digikam.org) is a KDE photo manager with many of the same features as F-Spot. A side panel allows easy access by album, date, tags, or previous searches. The program also provides image-editing capabilities, with numerous effects. The digiKam configuration (Settings menu) provides extensive options, including image editing, digital camera support, and interface configuration.

■ **Tip** The Windows version of Photoshop is supported by Wine. You can use Wine to install Photoshop CS on Fedora. Once started, Photoshop will operate like any Linux desktop application.

Cheese is a web cam picture-taking and video-recording tool (www.gnome.org/projects/cheese). You can snap pictures from your web cam and apply simple effects. You can open it from the Applications overview. Click the Photo button to manage photos and the Video button to record video. Icons of photos and video appear on the bottom panel, letting you select ones for effects or removal. The Effects pane shows effects that can be turned on or off for the current image. To save a photo, right-click its icon on the lower panel and select Save from the pop-up menu.

GNOME Photos is a simple image viewer and organizer for the images in your Pictures folder. GNOME Photos has three tabs: Albums, Photos, and Favorites (see Figure 6-4). It opens to the Photos tab. You can click a photo to open it, and then use arrow buttons to display the next or previous ones (see Figure 6-5). A task menu at the top right (gear button) lets you open the photo with Shotwell, print it, set it as the background of your desktop, or display it on another device. The Properties dialog displays detailed information about the image and lets you give it a name.

Click the back arrow to return to the main dialog. To choose several photos to work on, click the check mark button at the top right. Check boxes appear on the lower-right corner of each image (see Figure 6-6). A menu at the top center lets you choose all or de-select all images. When you check a single image, a toolbar appears at the bottom that lets you print the image, check its properties, add it to an album, or tag it as a favorite. If you have F-Spot installed, you can also open the photo in F-Spot. If you check several photos, you can add them to an album or mark them as favorites.

Figure 6-4. *GNOME Photos: Photos tab*

Figure 6-5. *GNOME Photos: image display*

Figure 6-6. GNOME Photos: selection

When you open a photo, you can also tag it as a favorite by clicking the heart button at the lower-right corner. On the Photos tab, favorite images show a heart emblem in the lower-right corner of the image. To remove an image from favorites, click its heart.

Photos can be organized into albums. The albums are also displayed on the Photos dialog. When you add a photo to an album, you are prompted to choose an existing album or to create a new one.

GNOME Graphics Tools

Many powerful and easy-to-use graphic applications are available for use on GNOME. The Eye of GNOME is the GNOME image viewer accessible as Image Viewer. It lets you display images and provides rotation capability and zooming. You can display images in a slideshow. An image gallery toolbar lets you quickly choose an image.

GIMP is the GNU image-manipulation program, much like Adobe Photoshop. You can use GIMP for such tasks as photo retouching, image composition, and image authoring. It supports features such as layers, channels, blends, and gradients. GIMP makes effective use of the GTK+ widget set. You can find out more about GIMP and download the newest versions from its web site at www.gimp.org. GIMP is freely distributed under the GNU Public License.

■ **Note**   The gPhoto project provides software for accessing digital cameras (www.gphoto.org). Several front-end interfaces are provided for a core library, called libgphoto2, consisting of drivers and tools that can access numerous digital cameras.

Inkscape is a GNOME-based vector graphics application for SVG (Scalable Vector Graphics) images (see Figure 6-7). It has capabilities similar to professional-level vector graphics applications such as Adobe Illustrator. The SVG format allows easy generation of images for web use as well as complex art. Though its native format is SVG, it can also export to the Portable Network Graphics (PNG) format. It features layers and easy object creation, including stars and spirals. A color bar lets you quickly change color fills.

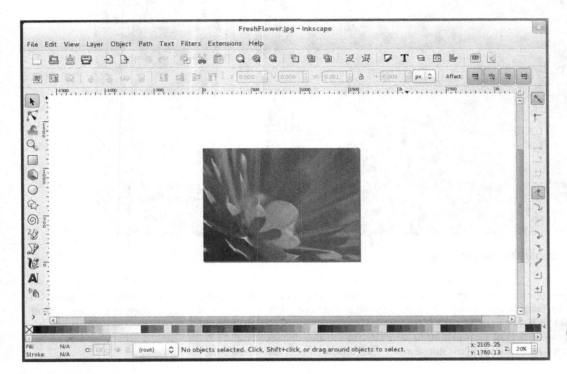

Figure 6-7. *Inkscape*

KDE Graphics Tools

The KDE desktop features the same variety of graphics tools found on the GNOME desktop. Many are available from the Fedora main repository. Most do not require a full installation of the KDE desktop. The KSnapshot program is a simple screen grabber for KDE. Gwenview is an easy-to-use image browser and viewer supporting slideshows and numerous image formats. It is the default viewer for KDE. KolourPaint is a basic paint program with brushes, shapes, and color effects; it supports numerous image formats. Krita is the Calligra professional image paint and editing application, with a wide range of features, such as the ability to create web images and modify photographs (formerly known as Krayon and KImageShop).

X Window System Graphic Programs

X Window System–based applications run directly on the underlying X Window System. These applications tend to be simpler, lacking the desktop functionality found in GNOME or KDE applications. Most are available on the Fedora repository. XPaint is a simple paint program that allows you to load graphics or photographs and then create shapes, add text and colors, and use brush tools with various sizes and colors. Xfig is a drawing program. ImageMagick lets you convert images from one format to another; you can, for instance, change a TIFF to a JPEG image. Table 6-2 (preceding) lists some popular graphics tools for Linux.

Multimedia

Many applications are available for both video and sound, including sound editors, MP3 players, and video players (see Tables 6-5 and 6-6). Linux sound applications include mixers, digital audio tools, CD audio writers, MP3 players, and network audio support.

■ **Note**   Linux has become a platform of choice for many professional-level multimedia tasks, such as generating computer-generated images (CGI), using such demanding software as Maya and Softimage. Linux graphic libraries include those for OpenGL, MESA, and SGI.

Information about many applications designed specifically for the GNOME or KDE user interface can be found at their respective software sites (`www.gnomefiles.org` and `www.kde-apps.org`). Precompiled binary RPM packages for most applications are at the Fedora or RPM Fusion repositories.

Codec Support with PackageKit

PackageKit is designed to work with GStreamer to detect and install needed codecs. Whenever you try to run a media file using a GStreamer-supported application such as the Totem movie player, and the codec is missing, PackageKit is run to check for supporting codec packages and lets you install them (see Figure 6-8). A dialog lists the required packages (including any required additional plug-ins), and you are prompted to install them.

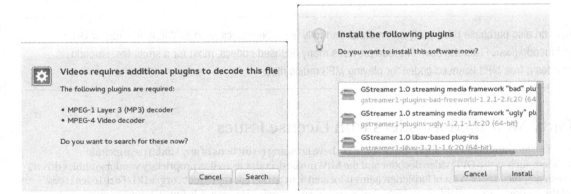

Figure 6-8. *Detecting and installing needed multimedia codecs*

If you have RPM Fusion support installed for YUM, PackageKit will find and install multimedia codecs not included with the official Fedora release. For MP3, you can download the MP3 codec directly. There are also several multimedia codecs, such as MPEG2 (DVD video), MPEG4 (DivX), Dolby AC3 audio, and MPEG video playback.

For the commercial DVD video codec, you still must use the `http://rpm.livna.org` repository. Here, you will find only one package, the `libdvdcss` package, for playing DVD video. You can install repository support for `rpm.livna.org` by installing the `livna-release` package, which you can download from `http://rpm.fusion.org`. You can also download directly from `http://rpm.livna.org/repo/20/`. Figure 6-9 shows the DVD codecs available from both the `libdvdcss` package and the Livna repositories, as well as other supporting DVD packages from the RPM Fusion repository.

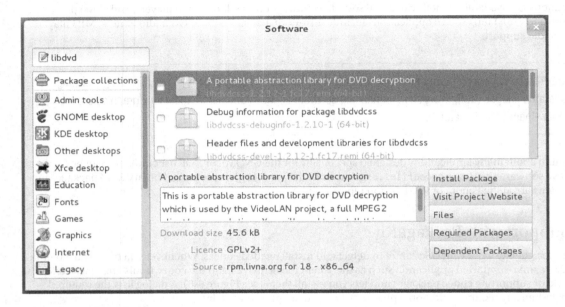

Figure 6-9. *DVD codec and support*

■ **Note**   You can also purchase third-party commercial and fully licensed codecs such as Window media or Dolby codecs from Fluendo (`www.fluendo.com`). Fluendo provides many licensed codecs, most for a small fee. Fluendo currently provides a free MP3 licensed codec for playing MP3 music files.

Third-Party Multimedia Codecs with License Issues

Fedora does not include any codecs or applications that may have licensing restrictions of any kind. These include multimedia codecs such as the DVD video decoder and the MP3 music decoder, as well as proprietary vendor graphics drivers like Nvidia's own graphics driver. A list of forbidden items is located at `http://fedoraproject.org/wiki/ForbiddenItems`.

Many of these codecs are available from RPM Fusion; see `http://rpmfusion.org`. A listing of popular multimedia codecs available at these sites is shown in Table 6-3. Of particular interest may be the `a52dec`, `faad2`, and `lame` codecs for sound decoding, as well as the `xvidcore`, `x264`, and `libdvbpsi` for video decoding. For GStreamer-supported applications such as the Totem movie player, you need a special set of packages called `gstreamer-plugins-bad` and `gstreamer-plugins-ugly`. The packages labeled `freeworld` provide open source solutions for added capability, such as DVD support for Xine and MP3 support for Audacious. For extensive video and DVD support, you can install VLC media player (`vlc` package). The commercial DVD video codec `dvdcss` is available only from the Livna repository, `http://rpm.livna.org`, directly, not from RPM Fusion. The `libdvdcss` package is the only package on Livna; all the others have been moved to RPM Fusion.

Table 6-3. Multimedia Third-Party Codecs

Package	Description
a52dec	HDTV audio (ATSC A/52 and AC3)
faad2	MPEG2/4 AAC audio decoding, high quality
ffmpeg, ffmpeg-libs	Play, record, convert, stream audio and video. Includes digital streaming server, conversion tool, and media player
gstreamer-ffmpeg	ffmpeg plug-in for GStreamer
gstreamer-plugins-bad	Not fully reliable codecs and tools for GStreamer, some with possible licensing issues
gstreamer-plugins-ugly	Reliable video and audio codecs for GStreamer that may have licensing issues
audacious-plugins-freeworld-mp3, -aac, -wma, -alac	MP3, AAC, WMA, ALAC plug-in packages for Audacious, among others
lame	MP3 playback capability, not an official MP3 decoder
libdca	DTS Coherent Acoustics playback capability
libdvbpsi	MPEG TS stream (DVB and PSI) decoding and encoding capability, VideoLAN project
libdvdnav	DVD video menu navigation
libfame	Fast Assembly MPEG video encoding
libmad	MPEG1 and MPEG2 audio decoding
libmpeg3	MPEG video audio decoding (MPEG1/2 audio and video, AC3, IFO, and VOB)
libquicktime	QuickTime playback
mpeg2dec	MPEG2 and MPEG1 playback
twolame	MPEG audio layer 2, MP2 encoding
x264	H264/AVC decoding and encoding (high-definition media)
xvidcore	OpenDivx codec (DivX and Xvid playback)
swftools	*Adobe FLASH Utilities for SWF Files*
swfdec	Flash animation decoding
vlc	DVD video playback capability, VideoLAN project
libdvdcss	DVD video codec for commercial DVDs; available only from Livna site at http://rpm.livna.org.

Obtaining the DVDCSS DVD Video Codec from Livna

The dvdcss decryption coded used to play back commercial DVD video disks is not included in the RPM Fusion repositories, free or non-free. Due to licensing issues, the dvdcss codec could not be included in the RPM Fusion repository. Instead, this codec remains the only software package still available on the Livna repositories. All other packages from Livna have been transferred to RPM Fusion and are no longer available on the Livna repository (beginning with Fedora 10). In effect these repositories currently have only one package, the dvdcss DVD video decryption package. The package is same in either repository. You only need to access one or the other.

To obtain the dvdcss decryption package, either download it directly from Livna and install it, or install the Livna repository YUM configuration package, and then use PackageKit to install the dvdcss package from Livna. The Livna web site is located at http://rpm.livna.org.

You can install repository support for rpm.livna.org by installing the livna-release package, which you can download from http://rpm.fusion.org. You can install directly from the web site by using your web browser or run an rpm install command in a terminal window. The "How to Use rpm.livna.org" section on the web site provides a link to download the livna-release package, as well as the following command-line alternative. Clicking the link, you will be prompted to open the package with the package installer. You will then be prompted to install the file. As with the RPM Fusion YUM configuration package, the Missing Security Signature dialog will be displayed. Click the Force Install button. You will be prompted to enter your root user password.

The rpm install command is shown here. The su command logs in as the root user, and the -c option indicates a command to run. The command to run is an rpm command to install (ivh) the livna-release.rpm package, which will be downloaded by rpm from http://rpm.livna.org.

```
su -c "rpm -ivh http://rpm.livna.org/livna-release.rpm"
```

Once installed, you can search for the libdvdcss package on PackageKit, which will then install the correct version for your system (see Figure 6-9). The first time you install a package from Livna, you will be prompted to install its package key, asking if you trust packages from this repository. Click Yes to install the key.

The actual Livna libdvdcss package is located at: http://rpm.livna.org/repo/20/. There are x86_64 and i386 directories.

GStreamer

Many of the GNOME-based applications make use of GStreamer. GStreamer is a streaming media framework based on graphs and filters. Using a plug-in structure, GStreamer applications can accommodate a wide variety of media types (http://gstreamer.freedesktop.org). Fedora includes several GStreamer applications, such as the Totem video player, which uses GStreamer to play DVDs, VCDs, and MPEG media. Rhythmbox provides integrated music management. Sound Juicer is an audio CD ripper.

GStreamer can be configured to use different input and output sound and video drivers and servers. You can make these selections using the GStreamer properties tool (install the gnome-media-apps package). Enter gstreamer-properties in a terminal window. The properties window displays two tabbed panels: one for audio and the other for video. The output drivers and servers are labeled Default Output, and the input drivers are labeled Default Input. There are pop-up menus for each, listing the available sound or video drivers or servers. For output, the AutoDetect option for a driver will use the default. You can change this to a specific device, such as using ALSA or OSS instead of PulseAudio.

GStreamer Plug-ins: The Good, the Bad, and the Ugly

Many GNOME multimedia applications such as Totem use GStreamer to provide multimedia support. To use such features as DVD video and MP3, you must install additional GStreamer plug-ins. You can find out more information about GStreamer and its supporting packages at http://gstreamer.freedesktop.org.

For version 1.0 and above, GStreamer establishes four support packages: the base, the good, the bad, and the ugly. The base package is a set of useful and reliable plug-ins. These are in the Fedora repository. The good package is a set of supported and tested plug-ins that meets all licensing requirements. This is also part of the Fedora repository.

The bad is a set of unsupported plug-ins whose performance is not guaranteed and may crash but still meets licensing requirements. The ugly package contains plug-ins that work fine but may not meet licensing requirements, such as DVD support. The bad and uglycan be obtained from the RPM Fusion repositories:

The base Reliable, commonly used plug-ins

The good Reliable, additional and useful plug-ins

The ugly Reliable, but not fully licensed, plug-ins (DVD/MP3 support)

The bad Possibly unreliable but useful plug-ins (possible crashes)

Another plug-in for GStreamer that you may want to include is ffmpeg, gstreamer-ffmpeg (RPM Fusion repositories). ffmpeg provides several popular codecs, including ogg and 264. For Pulse (sound server) and Farsight (video conferencing) support, use their respective GStreamer plug-ins on the Fedora repository.

PackageKit will automatically detect the codec you will need to use for your GStreamer application. For commercial codecs such as MP3 or AAC, PackageKit will select the appropriate RPM Fusion package (with RPM Fusion enabled). This capability is provided by the PackageKit-gstreamer-plugin, installed during installation. For commercial DVD video, you can install the libdvdcss package from the Livna repository (http://rpm.livna.org).

To download and install the GStreamer plug-in packages, just search for gstreamer on PackageKit. If you have enabled RPM Fusion or repository, you will also see entries for the ugly and bad packages. Alternatively, you could use the following yum command to install all plug-ins at once. Be sure to include the asterisk (*) to match all the plug-in packages. Your architecture (i586, i686, or x86_64) will be detected automatically.

```
yum install gstreamer-plugins*
```

GStreamer MP3 Compatibility

To play MP3 and iPod song files and to configure other MP3 devices to work with GNOME applications such as Rhythmbox, you have to install MP3 support for GStreamer. MP3 support is not included with Fedora distributions because of licensing issues. Install the GStreamer gstreamer-plugins-ugly package, which contains most multimedia support codecs and applications that are not included with the distribution. This is a RPM Fusion package. Be sure that the RPM Fusion repository is configured for your system. The package will then appear in PackageKit, which you can then use to install it.

iPod

To play songs from your iPod, Fedora provides the libgpod library for GNOME. It allows player applications such as Rhythmbox, Banshee, and Amarok to use your iPod Touch and iPhone. GStreamer MP3 support is provided by the gstreamer-plugins-ugly package. To sync, import, or extract from your iPod, you can also use gtkpod.

Music Applications

Many music applications are currently available for GNOME, including sound editors, MP3 players, and audio players (see Table 6-4). You can use Rhythmbox, Banshee, GNOME Music, and Clementine to play music from different sources and the GNOME Sound Recorder to record sound sources. Several applications are also available for KDE, including the media player Amarok, a mixer (KMix), and a CD player (Kscd). Rhythmbox, Banshee, and Amarok provide access to the iPod iTouch and iPhone. For sound and music editing, you can use Audacity.

Table 6-4. *Music Players, Editors, and Rippers*

Application	Description
Rhythmbox	Music management (GStreamer); default CD player with iPod support
Sound Juicer	GNOME CD audio ripper (GStreamer)
Amarok	KDE4 multimedia audio player
Banshee	Multimedia player
Audacious	Multimedia player
Kscd	Music CD player
JuK	KDE4 music player (jukebox) for managing music collections
GNOME Music	GNOME Music player
GNOME CD Player	CD player
GNOME Sound Recorder	Sound recorder
XMMS	CD player
Clementine	Clementine music player (based on Rhythmbox)
Radio Tray	The RadioTray radio streaming player, works from the panel like an applet
Xnoise	The Xnoise music player uses a music track orientation
Audacity	Professional multitrack audio editor
Ardour	Digital Audio Workstation (DAW) and Hard Disk Recorder (HDR)
Rosegarden	Audio/MIDI multitrack sequencer and score editor
FluidSynth	Software synthesizer
Qtractor	Audio/MIDI multitrack sequencer base on Qt toolkit

GNOME includes sound applications such as the GNOME CD player, Sound Juicer (Audio CD Extractor), GNOME Music, and Rhythmbox. Rhythmbox is the default sound multimedia player, supporting music files, radio streams, and podcasts (see Figure 6-10). In addition, you can use the Banshee and Clementine music players (similar to Rhythmbox), Xnoise music player (tracklist-oriented interface), and the RadioTray radio streaming player (simple message tray access).

Figure 6-10. *Rhythmbox GNOME multimedia player*

GNOME Music is the new GNOME Music player with tabs for Albums, Artists, and Songs (see Figure 6-11). GNOME Music accesses sound files in your Music folder. On the Songs tab, you can click on a file to play it. A toolbar opens at the bottom with buttons to control the playback. The button to the right opens a menu with shuffle and repeat options. At the top, click the Search button to search the list of sound files. To add files to the playlist, click the check button to display the check box next to each sound file, which you can check and then click the Add to Playlist button.

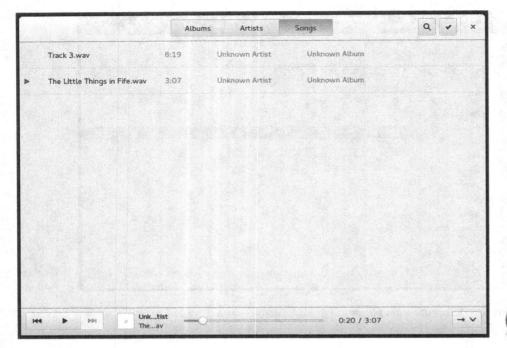

Figure 6-11. *GNOME Music*

KDE music applications include Amarok and JuK. Amarok is the primary multimedia player for KDE4 but will play on the GNOME desktop (see Figure 6-12). It includes access to Internet sources, local music files, and local devices such as Audio CDs. JuK (Music Jukebox) is the KDE4 music player for managing music collections.

Figure 6-12. *Amarok KDE multimedia player*

Due to licensing and patent issues, Fedora does not install MP3 support by default. MP3 playback capability has been removed from multimedia players such as Rhythmbox and Banshee. The Fedora codec wizard will prompt you to install MP3 support when you first try to play an MP3 file, usually the GStreamer package and the free Fluendo MP3 codec. As an alternative to MP3, you can use Ogg Vorbis compression for music files (http://www.vorbis.com).

Musicians should check the Fedora Musicians Guide for details on using Fedora applications for music development. Applications covered include Audacity (multitrack audio editor), Ardour (Digital Audio Workstation), Qtractor (multitrack sequencer), Rosegarden (audio and MIDI sequencer), FluidSynth (software synthesizer), LilyPond (music notation engraving), and GNU Solfege (music education).

http://docs.fedoraproject.org/en-US/Fedora/20/html/Musicians_Guide/index.html

Several DVD/CD ripper and writer programs can be used for CD music and MP3 writing (burners and rippers). These include Sound Juicer, Brasero (see Chapter 3), and K3b (see Table 6-5). GNOME features the CD audio ripper Sound Juicer. For burning DVD/CD music and data disks, you can use the Brasero DVD/CD burner. The Brasero DVD/CD burner is integrated into the GNOME file manager, the default file manager for the GNOME desktop. For KDE, you can use K3b.

Table 6-5. *DVD/CD Burners*

Application	Description
Brasero	Full-service DVD/CD burner for music, video, and data disks
Sound Juicer (audio CD extractor)	GNOME music player and CD burner and ripper (sound-juicer package)
ogmrip	DVD ripping and encoding with DivX support
K3b	KDE CD-writing interface
dvdauthor	Tools for creating DVDs
Qdvdauthor	KDE front end for dvdauthor (`www.kde-apps.org`)

Brasero, K3b, and dvdauthor can all be used to create DVD video disks. All use the `mkisofs`, `cdrecord`, and `cdda2wav` DVD/CD-writing programs installed as part of your desktop. OGMrip can rip and encode DVD video. DVD video and CD music rippers may require additional codecs, for which the codec wizard will prompt you.

Burning DVD/CDs with GNOME (Brasero)

GNOME performs disk-burning operations using the Brasero Disc Burner application. Brasero is integrated into GNOME. The DVD/CD disk's GNOME desktop menu (right-click the DVD/CD disk's desktop icon) displays DVD/CD disk operations, such as burning data using a GNOME file manager window, copying disks, erasing them, and checking a disk.

Using the GNOME file manager to burn data to a DVD or CD is a matter of dragging files to an open blank CD or DVD and clicking the Write To Disk button. When you insert a blank DVD/CD, a window will open labeled CD/DVD Creator. To burn files, just drag them to that window. Click the Write To Disc button when you're ready to burn a DVD/CD. A Brasero Disc Burning Setup dialog will open, which will perform the actual write operation. You can also click the Properties button to open a dialog with burning options such as the burn speed.

The GNOME desktop also supports burning ISO images using Brasero. Just double-click the ISO image file or right-click the file and select Open with Brasero. This opens the Image Burning Setup dialog, which prompts you to burn the image. Be sure first to insert a blank DVD or CD into your DVD/CD burner.

You have the option of writing an ISO image to another disk. For the ISO image file, the Properties dialog lets you choose the folder to save the file. For copying to another disk, the Properties dialog lets you choose the burning speed and such options as using burnproof or performing a simulation first. Check Disc will check the integrity of the disk, with the option of using the disk's MD5 file, if available. The menu for DVD/CD RW disks will also display a Blank Disc entry, which will erase a disk.

For more complex DVD/CD burning options, you can use the Brasero DVD/CD burner application interface, called Brasero Disc Burner. Brasero supports drag-and-drop operations for creating audio CDs. In particular, it can handle DVD/CD read/write disks and can erase disks. It also supports multi-session burns, which add data to DVD/CD disks. Initially, Brasero displays a dialog with buttons for the type of project you want to create. You can create a data or audio project, create a DVD video disk, copy a DVD/CD, or burn a DVD/CD image file.

For a data project, the toolbar displays an Add button, which you use to select files and directories to be burned to your disk. You also can drag-and-drop files and folders to your data listing (right pane). You can choose to display a side panel (View menu), which will let you select files and directories.

Video Applications

Several projects provide TV, video, DivX, DVD, and DTV support for Linux. Most applications are already available from the RPM Fusion repository (http://rpmfusion.org). Be sure that the RPM Fusion YUM repository is configured for your system, and then use PackageKit (Software) to install the applications. Aside from GStreamer applications, there are also several third-party multimedia applications you may want. All are available on the Fedora and RPM Fusion repositories.

Video and DVD Players

Several popular video and DVD players are listed in Table 6-6.

Table 6-6. *Video Players*

Video Player	Description
Dragon Player	KDE multimedia player installed with KDE desktop but plays on the GNOME desktop (see Figure 6-13); Dragon Player
Kaffeine	KDE multimedia player (video and dvb) (kaffeine package, Kaffeine—see Figure 6-14)
MPlayer	Popular and capable multimedia/DVD players in use (RPM Fusion free repository). It is a cross-platform open source alternative to RealPlayer and Windows Media Player (www.mplayerhq.hu). MPlayer uses an extensive set of supporting libraries and applications such as lirc, lame, lzo, and aalib, which are also available on the RPM Fusion repository. If you have trouble displaying video, be sure to check the preferences for different video devices and select the one that works best.
Totem	GNOME movie player that uses GStreamer (see Figure 6-15) Movie Player. To expand Totem capabilities, you have to install added GStreamer plug-ins. The codec wizard will prompt you to install any needed media codecs and plug-ins.
VLC	The VideoLAN project (http://www.videolan.org) offers network streaming support for most media formats, including MPEG4 and MPEG2. It includes a multimedia player, VLC, which can work on any kind of system (vlc package). VLC supports high-def hardware decoding (see Figure 6-16).
Xine	Multipurpose video engine, also for Linux/UNIX systems, that can play video, DVD, and audio disks. Many applications, such as Totem and Kaffeine; uses Xine support to play back DVD video. See http://xinehq.de for more information. For the Xine user interface, install the xine-ui package.

Figure 6-13. KDE4 Dragon Player

Figure 6-14. Kaffeine

Figure 6-15. *Totem movie player*

Figure 6-16. *VLC video player (VideoLAN)*

Totem Plug-ins

The Totem movie player uses plug-ins to add capabilities such as Internet video streaming. Select the menu item Edit ➤ Plugins to open the Configure Plugins window (see Figure 6-17). Select the plug-ins you want. For added support, install the totem plug-in packages.

```
totem-youtube
totem-lirc
```

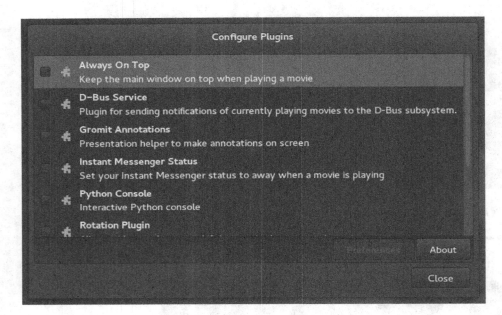

Figure 6-17. *Totem movie player plug-ins*

The lirc package gives infrared remote control support.

PiTiVi Video Editor

The PiTiVi video editor is an open source application that lets you edit your videos. It is accessible from the Applications overview as PiTiVi video editor. Check the PiTiVi web site for more details (www.pitivi.org). You can download a quick-start manual from the Documentation page. PiTiVi is a GStreamer application and can work with any video file supported by an installed GStreamer plug-in, including the ugly and bad plug-ins.

The PiTiVi window shows a Clip Library pane on the left and video playback for a selected video clip on the right (see Figure 6-18). To run a video clip, right-click its icon and select Play Clip. To add a video file to the library, click the Import clips button on the toolbar. You can also drag-and-drop files directly to the Clip Library. The time line at the bottom of the window displays the video and audio streams for the video clip you are editing, using a rule to show your position. To edit a video, drag its icon from the Clip Library to the time line. To trim a video, you pass the mouse over the time line video and audio streams. Trimming handles will appear that you can use to shorten the video. PiTiVi features ripple editing and rolling editing, splitting, and transitions.

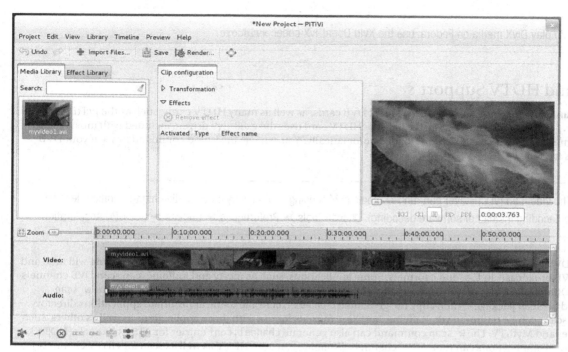

Figure 6-18. *PiTiVi video editor*

TV Players

The TV players that are provided on Fedora repositories are listed in Table 6-7.

Table 6-7. *TV Players*

TV Player	Description
Totem	Movie player that can access DVB stations using gnome-dvb. Choose Watch TV from the Movie menu. The Digital Television Assistant configures access to your DVB card. ATSC cards are not yet supported.
tvtime	TV player that works with many common video-capture cards, relying on drivers developed for TV tuner chips on those cards, such as the Conexant chips. It can only display a TV image. It has no recording or file playback capabilities. Check http://tvtime.sourceforge.net for more information.
Dragon Player	These are KDE multimedia players that will also play TV.
Kaffeine	KDE video recording and playback application on Linux systems. It can also play ATSC over-the-air digital broadcasts.
MythTV	Popular video recording and playback application on Linux systems. MythTV is available from the RPM Fusion free repository.

■ **Note**   To play DivX media on Fedora, use the Xvid OpenDivX codec xvidcore.

DVB and HDTV Support

For DVB and HDTV reception, you can use most DVB cards, as well as many HDTV cards, such as the pcHDTV video card (www.pdhdtv.com). For example, the latest pcHDTV card uses the cx88-dvb drivers included with most recent Linux kernels. The DVB kernel driver is loaded automatically. You can use the lsmod command to see if your DVB module is loaded.

■ **Tip**   The VideoLan (VLC) player can run HD media (x264) using your display card's native high-definition decoder (hardware decoding instead of software decoding). Choose Tools ➤ Preferences ➤ Codecs ➤ Use GPU Acceleration.

For DVB broadcasts, many DVB-capable players and tools such as VLC and Kaffeine, as well as vdr, will tune and record DVB broadcasts in t, s, and c formats. Some applications, such as me-tv and Kaffeine, can scan DVB channels directly. Others, like Klear, require that you first generate a channels.conf file. You can do this with the w_scan command (w-scan package). Then copy the generated channels.conf file to the appropriate applications directory. Channel scans can be output in vdr, Kaffeine, and Xine formats for use with those applications as well as others, such as MPlayer and MythTV. The w_scan command can also generate channel.conf entries for ATSC channels (HDTV), though not all applications can tune ATSC channels. (Kaffeine can tune HDTV as well as scan for HDTV channels.) You can also use the dvbscan tool (dvb-apps package) for scanning your channels and the azap tool for accessing the signal directly. This tool makes use of channel frequencies kept in the /usr/share/dvb directory. There are files for ATSC broadcast as well as for cable.

The DVB applications can also be used to record DVB broadcasts to files that can then be viewed with a DVB capable viewer, such as MPlayer or Videolan VLC media player. You can use Kaffeine, MythTV, kvdr, and vdr (video disk recorder) to view and record. Check the MythTV site for details (www.mythtv.org).

You can use Kaffeine to both tune and record both DVB and ATSC HDTV channels. Kaffeine records an HDTV file as an m2t HDV MPEG2 file, the High Definition Video (HDV) format used for high-definition camcorders. The m2t files that Kaffeine generates can be played back by most video players, including Totem, Dragon Player, and VLC.

The raw transport stream (.ts or .tp) files generated by HDTV cards like PCHDTV can be viewed with any HDTV capable viewer, such as Kaffeine and VideoLan VLC media player. One solution for recording raw HDTV is to use the dvb-atsc-tools provided by the PCHDTV web site. The pcHDTV card and related cards using the Conexant c88 chips and the c88x DVB kernel module will automatically be detected and loaded. You can then use the PCHDTV atsc tools to access and record programs. From the PCHDTV site, download the dvb-atsc-tools package (www.pchdtv.com/downloads/dvb-atsc-tools-1.0.7.tgz). These are source code programs you will have to compile. Unzip the archive file to a directory. You can use either the tar command or Archive Manager.

```
tar xvzf dvb-atsc-tools-1.0.7.tgz
```

In a terminal window, change to that directory issue the make and make install commands. Be sure you have already downloaded and installed the kernel development packages.

```
make
make install
```

You can then use the dtvsignal and getatsc commands to check and record HDTV receptions. The following records a channel to a file. The -dvb 0 option is the DVB device number, usually 0, and the following number is the channel, in this case channel 12. The output is directed by the > operator to a file called my.ts.

```
getatsc -dvb 0 12 > my.ts
```

This is an open ended process that will continue until you kill the process. To stop the recording, you could do the following, which uses the ps command to obtain the process id (pid) for the getatsc process. These getatsc and kill operations can be set up as scheduled tasks (GNOME Schedule) to implement automatic recording like a DVR or VCR.

```
kill `ps -C getatsc -o pid=`
```

You could then use any application, such as the VLC media player, Kaffeine, or an HDTV-capable MPlayer to play back the file.

Xvid (DivX) and Matroska (mkv) on Linux

MPEG4 compressed files provide DVD-quality video with relatively small file sizes. They have become popular for distributing high-quality video files over the Internet. When you first try to play an MPEG4, the codec wizard will prompt you to install the needed codec packages to play it. Many multimedia applications such as VLC already support MPEG4 files.

MPEG4 files using the Matroska wrapper, also known by their file extension, mkv, can be played on most video players, including the VideoLan VLC player, Totem, Dragon Player, and Kaffeine. You will need HDTV codecs, such as MPEG4 AAC sound codec, installed to play the high-definition mkv file files. If needed, the codec wizard will prompt you to install them. To manage and create mkv files you can install the mkvtoolnix packages and use the mkvmerge application.

You use the open source version of DivX, known as Xvid, to play DivX video (libxvidcore package). Most DivX files can be run using Xvid. Xvid is an entirely independent open source project, but it is compatible with DivX files. You can also download the XviD source code from http://xvid.org.

To convert DVD-Video files to an MPEG4/DivX format you can use transcode or the ffmpeg libraries. Many DVD burners can use these to convert DVD video files to DivX/Xvid files.

Sound Settings

Your sound cards are detected automatically for you when you start up your system by ALSA, which is invoked by udev when your system starts up. Removable devices, such as USB sound devices, are also detected. See Table 6-8 for a listing of sound device and interface tools.

Table 6-8. *Sound Devices and Interface Tools*

Sound Tool	Description
KMix	KDE sound connection configuration and volume tool
alsamixer	ALSA sound connection configuration and volume tool
amixer	ALSA command for sound connection configuration
Sound	GNOME Sound Settings, used to select and configure your sound interface (System Settings ➤ Sound)
PulseAudio	PulseAudio sound interface, the default sound interface for Fedora. www.pulseaudio.org
PulseAudio Volume Control	PulseAudio Volume Control, controls stream input, output, and playback, pavucontrol package
PulseAudio Volume Meter	Volume Meter, displays active sound levels
PulseAudio Manager	Manager for information and managing PulseAudio, pman package
PulseAudio Device Chooser	PulseAudio Device selection
PulseAudio Preferences	Options for network access and virtual output.

In addition to hardware drivers, sound systems also use sound interfaces to direct encoded sound streams from an application to the hardware drivers and devices. Fedora uses the PulseAudio server for its sound interface. PulseAudio aims to combine and consolidate all sound interfaces into a simple, flexible, and powerful server. The ALSA hardware drivers are still used, but the application interface is handled by PulseAudio. PulseAudio is installed as the default set up for Fedora for both GNOME and KDE.

PulseAudio provides packages for interfacing with Gstreamer, VLC, and xmms, replacing those sound interfaces with PulseAudio. It is also compatible with KDE.

PulseAudio is a cross-platform sound server allowing you to modify the sound level for different audio streams separately. See www.pulseaudio.org for documentation and help. PulseAudio offers complete control over all your sound streams, letting you combine sound devices and direct the stream anywhere on your network. PulseAudio is not confined to a single system. It is network capable, letting you direct sound from one PC to another.

As an alternative, you can use the command-line ALSA control tool alsamixer. This will display all connections and allow you to use keyboard commands to select (arrow keys), mute (m key), or set sound levels (Page Up and Down). Press the ESC key to exit. The amixer command lets you perform the same tasks for different sound connections from the command line. To actually play and record from the command line, you can use the play and rec commands.

Volume Control

GNOME volume control is managed using a slider bar on the system status area menu. A speaker icon on the system status area on the top bar shows the status of your sound device (see Figure 6-19).

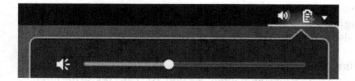

Figure 6-19. *Volume control*

To perform volume control for specific devices like a microphone, you use Sound Settings, which you can access from System Settings ➤ Sound.

Sound: PulseAudio

You configure sound devices and set volume for sound effects, input and output, and applications using the GNOME sound settings. On GNOME, open the System Settings dialog and choose Sound. This opens the Sound window, which has four tabs: Output, Input, Sound Effects, and Applications (see Figure 6-20). Corresponding sound preferences are available on KDE, which also uses PulseAudio.

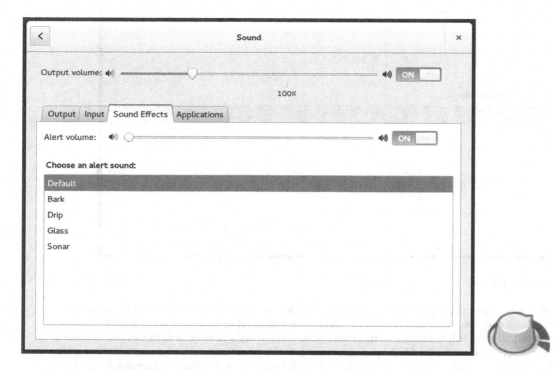

Figure 6-20. *Sound: System Settings*

A sliding bar at the top of the window, above the tabs, lets you set the output volume. The On/Off switch lets you mute the sound. The former Hardware tab for devices has been integrated into the Input and Output tabs.

The Sound Effects tab lets you select an installed sound theme. Sound themes can be selected from the drop-down menu by the Sound Theme label. A sliding bar allows you to set the volume for your sound alerts or to turn them off by checking the on/off switch. You can also choose other sound alerts from the "Choose an alert sound" list, such as Drip or Sonar.

On the Input tab, you set the input volume and turn the input device on or off. When speaking or recording, the input level is displayed (see Figure 6-21). In the "Choose a device for sound input" section, you can choose the input interface with which to set the volume, such as a particular microphone or the Line-In connection. Most laptops will have only an "Internal Microphone—Built-in Audio" device.

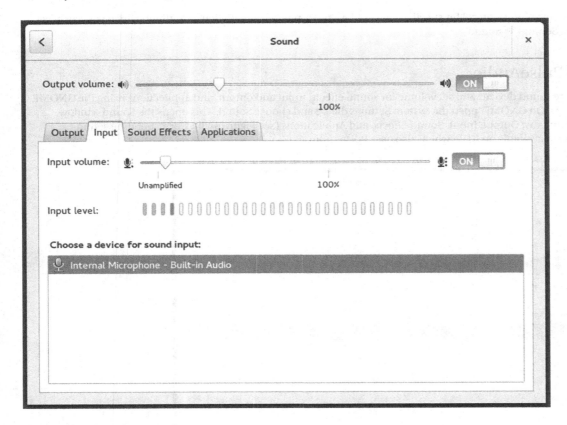

Figure 6-21. *Sound: Input tab*

On the Output tab, you can configure settings for a selected device. The "Choose a device for sound output" section lists your audio devices. The available settings will change according to the device selected. For a simple Analog Stereo Output, there is only a Balance setting (see Figure 6-22). Once you select a device in the "Choose a device for sound output" section, the Profile drop-down menu lists the different input and output interfaces that device supports. A laptop may support only a simple internal audio device with interfaces for Analog Stereo Input, Output, and Duplex. Computers with more powerful sound devices have many more options. To test your speakers, click the Test Speakers button to open the Speakers Testing dialog with test buttons for each speaker.

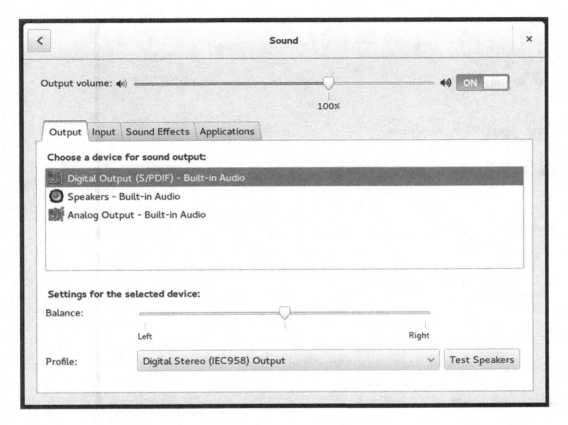

Figure 6-22. *Sound: Output tab*

The Applications tab will show applications currently using sound devices. You can set the sound volume for each (see Figure 6-23).

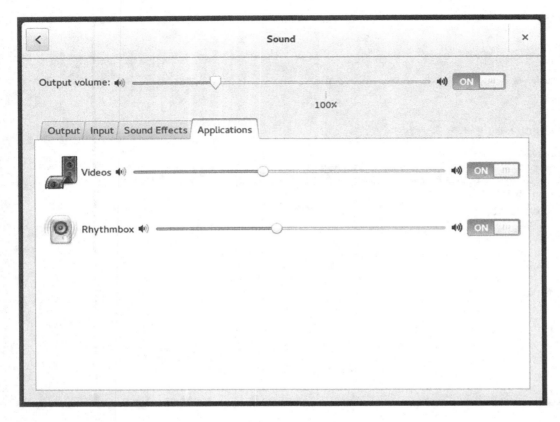

Figure 6-23. *Sound: Applications tab*

Sound devices that support multiple interfaces, such as analog surround sound 7.1 or digital SPDIF output, may have an extensive list of interface combinations in the Profile menu. Configuring digital output for SPDIF (digital) connectors is a simple matter of selecting the digital output in the "Choose a device for sound output" section of the Output or Input tabs. The SPDIF entries will include the device name, such as S/PDIF.

Installed with PulseAudio are the PulseAudio utilities (pulseaudio-utils package). These are command-line utilities for managing PulseAudio and playing sound files (see Table 6-9). The paplay and pacat will play sound files; pactl will let you control the sound server; and pacmd lets you reconfigure it. Check the man pages for each for more details. If you change your sound preferences frequently, you could use these commands in a shell script to make the changes, instead of having to use the preferences dialog each time. Some of these commands, such as parec and paplay, are links to the pacat command, which performs the actual tasks.

Table 6-9. *PulseAudio Commands (Command Line)*

Sound Tool	Description
pabrowse	List PulseAudio sound servers
pacat	Play, record, and configure a raw audio stream
pacmd	Generates a shell for entering configuration commands
pactl	Control a PulseAudio server, changing input and output sources and providing information about the server.
padsp	PulseAudio wrapper for OSS sound applications
pamon	Link to pacat
paplay	Playback audio. The -d option specifies the output device, the -s option specifies the server, and the --volume option sets the volume (link to pacat)
parec	Record and audio stream (link to pacat)
parecord	Record and audio stream (link to pacat)
pasuspender	Suspend a PulseAudio server
pax11publish	Access PulseAudio server credentials

PulseAudio applications

For additional configuration abilities, you can also install the PulseAudio applications. Most begin with the prefix pa in the package name. PulseAudio tools are accessible from the Applications overview. The PulseAudio Manager and PulseAudio Volume Meter menu entries are not listed by default. The PulseAudio tools and their command names are shown in Table 6-9. You can also use the PulseAudio Device Chooser applet (padevchooser) to run them.

The PulseAudio Device Chooser provides a message tray device menu for accessing PulseAudio applications directly. To run the PulseAudio Device Chooser, select its entry in the Applications overview. The PulseAudio Device Chooser will appear in the message tray (lower-right corner of screen). Clicking it displays a pop-up menu with entries for Manager (PulseAudio Manager), Volume Control, Volume Meter (Playback and Recording), and Configure Local Sound Server (PulseAudio Preferences, papref). You can also use the Device Chooser to select the default server, sink (output device), and source (input device), should there be more than one. PulseAudio could be running on different hosts and configured by different users on a given host. You can choose which one to use.

> PulseAudio Device Chooser, padevchooser
>
> PulseAudio Volume Control, pavucontrol
>
> PulseAudio Volume Meter, pavumeter
>
> PulseAudio Manager, paman
>
> PulseAudio Preferences, papref

You can use the PulseAudio Volume Control tool to set the sound levels for different playback applications and sound devices (choose PulseAudio Volume Control on the Applications overview).

The PulseAudio Volume Control applications will show five tabs: Playback, Recording, Output Devices, Input Devices, and Configuration (see Figure 6-24). The Playback tab shows all the applications currently using PulseAudio. You can adjust the volume for each application separately.

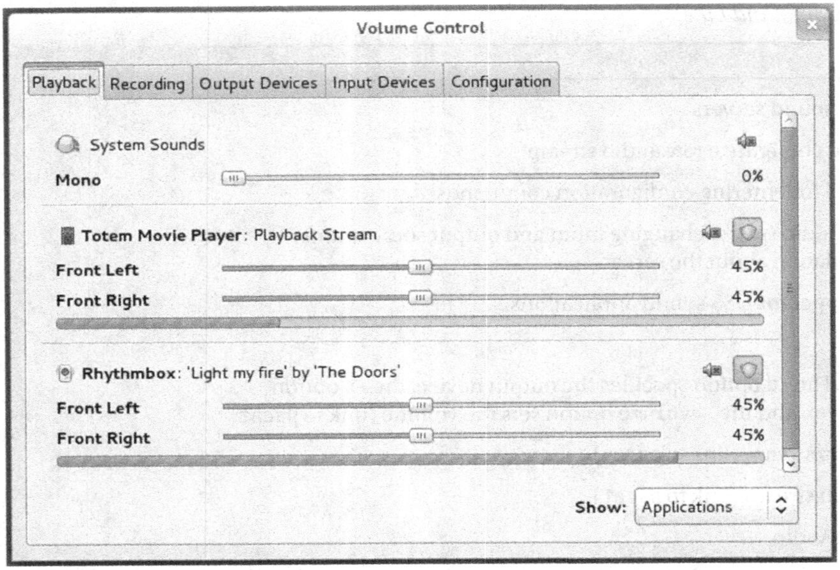

Figure 6-24. *PulseAudio Volume Control: Playback tab*

You can use the Output tab panel to set the volume control at the source and select different output devices, such as Headphones (see Figure 6-25). The volume for input and recording devices are set on the Recording and Input Devices tabs. The Configuration tab lets you choose different device profiles, such as selecting Digital output or Surround Sound 5.1.

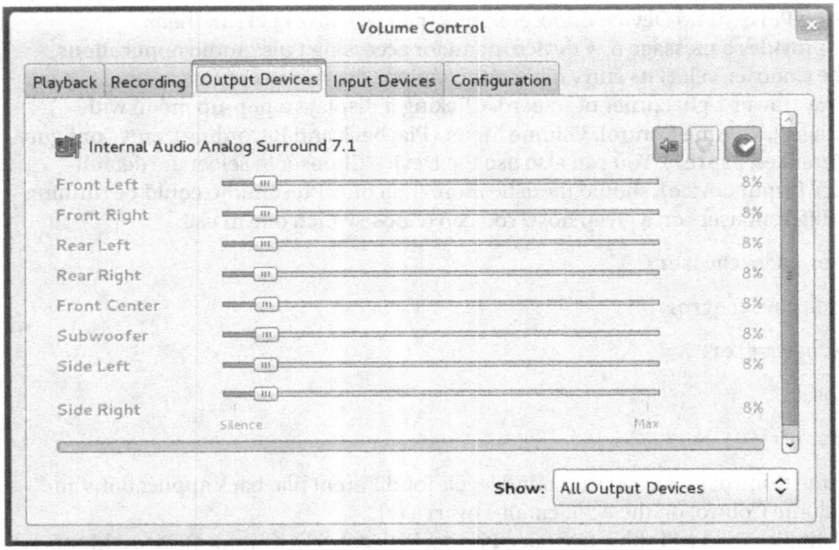

Figure 6-25. *PulseAudio Volume Control: Output Devices tab*

You can also use the PulseAudio Volume control to direct different applications (streams) to different outputs (devices). For example, you could have two sound sources running—one for video and another for music. The video could be directed through one device to headphones, and the music through another device to speakers, or even to another PC. To redirect an application to a different device, right-click its name in the Playback tab. A pop-up menu will list the available devices and let you select the one you want to use.

The PulseAudio Volume Meter tool will show the actual volume of your devices.

The PulseAudio Manager will show information about your PulseAudio configuration, accessible from the Applications overview. The Devices tab shows the currently active sinks (outputs or directed receivers) and sources (see Figure 6-26). The Clients tab shows all the applications currently using PulseAudio for sound.

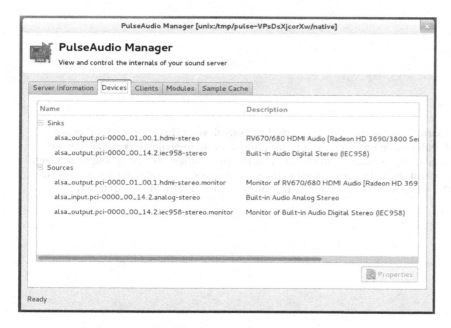

Figure 6-26. *PulseAudio Manager: Devices tab*

To configure network access, you use the PulseAudio Configuration tool, accessible from the Applications overview. Here you can permit network access, configure the PulseAudio network server (see Figure 6-27), and enable multicast and simultaneous output. If you are connected to a network with Linux systems also running PulseAudio that have allowed network access to their sound devices, their shared sound devices will be listed in the Sound Preferences Output tab, allowing you to access them.

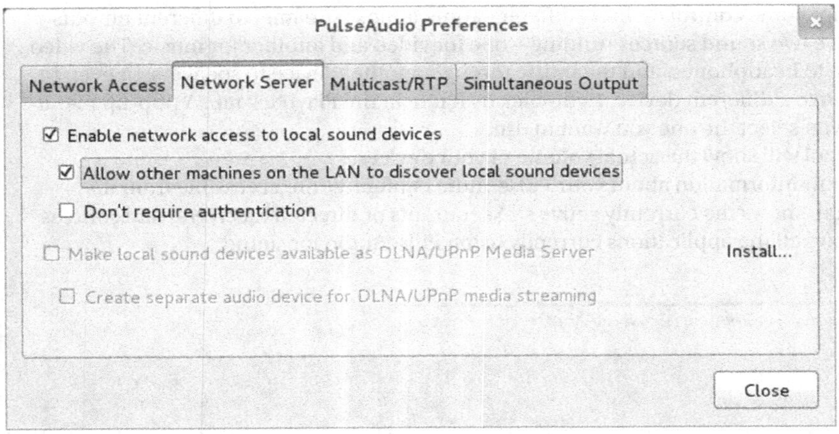

Figure 6-27. *PulseAudio Preferences*

Simultaneous output creates a virtual output device to the same hardware device. This lets you channel two sources onto the same output. With PulseAudio Volume Control, you could then channel playback streams to the same output device, but using a virtual device as the output for one. This lets you change the output volume for each stream independently. You could have music and voice directed to the same hardware device, using a virtual device for music and the standard device for voice. You can then reduce the music stream or raise the voice stream.

CHAPTER 7

■ ■ ■

Internet Applications: Web and FTP

Fedora provides powerful web and FTP clients for accessing the Internet. Many are installed automatically and are ready to use when you first start up your Linux system. Linux also includes full Java development support, letting you run and construct Java applets. This chapter covers some of the more popular web, Java, and FTP clients available on Linux. Web and FTP clients connect to sites that run servers, using web pages and FTP files to provide services to users.

Web browsers and FTP clients are commonly used to conduct secure transactions, such as logging in to remote sites, ordering items, or transferring files. Such operations are currently secured by encryption methods provided by the Secure Sockets Layer (SSL). If you use a browser for secure transactions, it should be SSL-enabled. Most browsers, such as Mozilla and ELinks, include SSL support. For FTP operations, you can use the SSH version of ftp, sftp, or the Kerberos 5 version. Linux distributions include SSL as part of a standard installation.

Web Browsers

Most web browsers are designed to access several different kinds of information. Web browsers can access a web page on a remote web site or a file on your own system. Some browsers can also access a remote news server or an FTP site. The type of information for a site is specified by the keyword **http** for web sites, **nntp** for news servers, **ftp** for FTP sites, or **file** for files on your own system.

Popular browsers for Fedora include Firefox (Mozilla), Konqueror, Rekonq, Epiphany, Chrome (Google), and Lynx (see Table 7-1). Firefox is the default web browser used on most Linux distributions, including Fedora. Rekonq is the KDE web browser, accessible from the KDE desktop, and Epiphany is the GNOME web browser. Chrome is the Google web browser. Lynx and ELinks are command-line-based browsers with no graphics capabilities, but in every other respect they are fully functional web browsers.

Table 7-1. Web Browsers

Web Site	Description
Firefox	The Mozilla project Firefox web browser; Fedora desktop default browser www.mozilla.org
Konqueror	KDE desktop web browser www.konqueror.org
Rekonq	KDE desktop web browser http://rekonq.kde.org
Epiphany	GNOME web browser http://projects.gnome.org/epiphany
Chrome	Google Chrome web browser www.google.com/chrome
Lynx	Text-based command-line web browser http://lynx.isc.org
ELinks	Text-based command-line web browser http://elinks.or.cz

The Firefox Web Browser

Firefox is based on the Netscape core source code known as Mozilla (see Figure 7-1). In current releases, Fedora uses Firefox as its primary browser. The Mozilla project is an open source project based on the original Netscape browser code that provides a development framework for web-based applications, primarily the web browser and e-mail client. The Mozilla project site is `www.mozilla.org`, and the site commonly used for plug-in and extension development is `www.mozdev.org`.

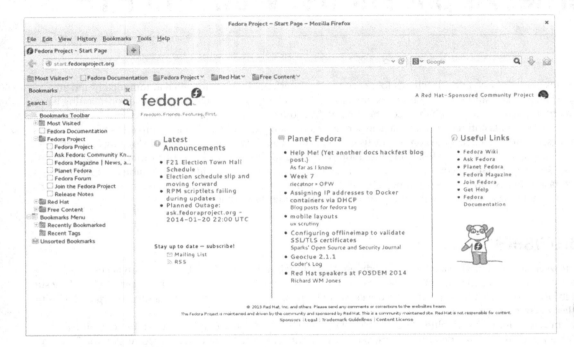

Figure 7-1. *Firefox web browser*

Firefox is installed by default with icons on the Applications overview. When opened, Firefox displays a navigation toolbar at the top of the screen below the title bar and tabs, with a text box for entering a URL address and a series of navigation buttons for accessing web pages. On the left side are the Next and Previous buttons for paging through previously accessed web pages. A Home button at the far-right side of the navigation bar moves you to your home page. To the right of the URL text box is a Refresh button for re-accessing a page. When you enter a web page name in the text box, Firefox performs a dynamic search on previously accessed pages and displays the pages in a drop-down menu, which you can choose from. Click the drop-down menu button at the right side of the text box to display a list of previously accessed pages. Menus on the top menu bar provide access to such Firefox features as View, History, Bookmarks, and Tools. A status bar at the bottom shows the state of the current page.

To the right of the URL box is a search box where you can use different search engines for searching the Web, selected sites, or particular items. A pop-up menu lets you select a search engine. Currently included are Google, Yahoo, Amazon, and eBay. Firefox also features button links and tabbed pages. You can drag the URL from the URL box to the button link bar to create a button with which to quickly access the site. Use this button for frequently accessed sites.

For easy browsing, Firefox features tabs for displaying web pages. To open an empty tab, press Ctrl+t or select New Tab from the File menu. To display a page in that tab, drag its URL from the URL box or from the bookmark list to the panel. You can have several tabs open at once, moving from one page to the next by clicking their tabs. You can elect to open all your link buttons as tabs by right-clicking the link bar and selecting Open In Tabs.

To search a current page for certain text, enter Ctrl+f. This opens a search toolbar at the bottom of Firefox from which you can enter a search term. You have search options to highlight found entries or to match character case. The Next and Previous buttons let you move to the next found pattern.

When you download a file using Firefox, the download is managed by the Download Manager. You can download several files at once. Progress is displayed in the Download Manager window, accessible from the Tools menu. You can cancel a download at any time or just pause a download, resuming it later. Right-clicking a download entry will display the site it was downloaded from as well as the directory you saved it in. To remove an entry, click Remove from the toolbar. To clear out the entire list, click Clean Up.

Firefox Bookmarks and History

The Bookmarks menu enables you to add your favorite web pages. You can also press Ctrl+d to add a bookmark. You can then view a list of your bookmarks and select one to view. You can also edit your list, adding new ones or removing old ones. When adding a bookmark, an Add Bookmark window opens with a pop-up menu for folders and tags. The Folder menu is set to the Bookmarks folder by default. You can also select the Bookmarks Toolbar or use unfilled bookmarks.

History is a list of previous URLs you have accessed. The URL box also features a pop-up menu listing your previous history sites. Bookmarks and History can be viewed as sidebars, selectable from the View menu.

Firefox also features a Bookmark toolbar that you use for frequently accessed sites. The Bookmark toolbar is displayed just above the web page. You can drag the site address from the URL box to the Bookmark toolbar to create a button for quick access to a site. Buttons can also be folders, containing button links for several pages. Clicking a folder button will display the button links in a pop-up menu. You can also right-click the Bookmark toolbar to open a pop-up menu with options to add entries: New Bookmark, New Folder, and New Separator. The New Bookmark entry opens a New Bookmark dialog in which you can enter the bookmark name and URL address. The New Folder entry lets you create a bookmark folder in which you can place bookmarks of your choosing, allowing you to organize your bookmarks into folders. From the Bookmark toolbar pop-up menu, you can also sort your bookmark buttons by name. To delete a Bookmark toolbar button, right-click it and choose Delete. You can also use the cut, copy, and paste options in the menu to move or copy a bookmark from the Bookmark sidebar to the Bookmark toolbar and vice versa. You can also use these options to copy or move a bookmark to a folder on the Bookmark toolbar.

To manage your bookmarks, click the Organize Bookmarks entry in the Bookmarks menu. This opens the Library window with bookmark folders displayed in a sidebar. Bookmarks in a folder are shown in the upper-right pane, and properties for a selected bookmark in that list are displayed in the lower-right pane. The Organize menu has an option to create a new folder. The View menu lets you sort your bookmarks. The Import and Backup menu has options to save backups of your bookmark, as well as export your bookmark for use on other systems using Firefox. You can also import exported Firefox bookmarks from other systems. Bookmarks also maintain Most Visited, Recently Bookmarked, and Recent Tags folders. This lets you easily find sites you visit most often or ones you consider important.

Firefox supports live bookmarks, which connect to sites that provide a live RSS feed. This page is constantly being updated, like a news site. Live bookmarks are indicated by a live bookmark icon to the right of its address. Click this icon or select Subscribe to This Page from the Bookmark menu, to subscribe to the site (Bookmarks ➤ Subscribe to This Page). A pop-up menu is displayed in the main window with the prompt "Subscribe to This Feed Using." Live Bookmarks is selected by default, but you can also choose My Yahoo!, Bloglines, or Google. You can also choose to Always Use Live Bookmarks for Feeds. You can then click Subscribe Now to set up the live bookmark. This opens a dialog from which you can choose to place the live bookmark in the Bookmark menu or on the Bookmark toolbar. In the Bookmark toolbar, the live bookmark becomes a pop-up menu listing the active pages, with an entry at the end for the main site.

Firefox Configuration

The Preferences menu (Edit ➤ Preferences) in Firefox enables you to set several different options. There are preference buttons for General, Tabs, Content, Applications, Privacy, Security, Sync, and Advanced (see Figure 7-2). On the General page, you can set your home page, download options, and access add-on management. Tabs control tab opening and closing behavior. Content lets you set the font and font size, as well as color and language to use. You can also block pop-ups and enable Java. Applications associate content with the applications to run it, such as video or MP3. Privacy controls history, cookies, and private data. Security is where you can remember passwords and set warning messages. The Sync tab lets you set up web browser syncing. Sync is a new feature that sets up the Firefox's sync service, letting you synchronize your history, bookmarks, passwords, and open tabs on all your devices. You are first prompted to create a new account, prompting you for your e-mail address, password, and a Firefox server. You are then provided with a Sync key, which you should save.

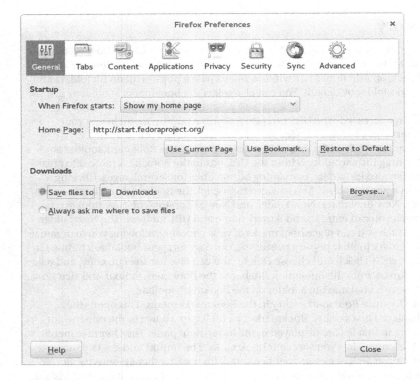

Figure 7-2. *Firefox Preferences*

The Advanced page has several tabs: General, Network, Update, and Encryption. The General tab provides features such as spell-checking and keyboard navigation. The Network tab has a Settings button for the Connection feature, from which you set up your network connections, such as the direct connection to the Internet or proxy settings. Here you can also set up offline storage size. The Update tab lets you configure how updates are performed. The Encryption tab is where you can manage certificates, setting up validation methods, viewing, and revocation.

If you are on a network that connects to the Internet through a firewall, you use the Connection Settings dialog to enter the address of your network's firewall gateway computer. The Connection Settings dialog is open from the Advanced tab's Network tab, on which you click the settings button titled "Configure How Firefox Connects to the Internet." Several types of firewalls exist. The most restrictive kinds of firewalls use programs called *proxies*, which receive Internet requests from users and then make those requests on their behalf. There is no direct connection to the Internet.

The Add-ons entry on the Tools menu opens the Add-ons window with tabs for Get Add-ons, Extensions, Appearance, Plugins, and Services (see Figure 7-3). Click the one you want to open a brief description and display the Add to Firefox button, which you click to open a download and install dialog. The Extensions tab lists installed Extensions with buttons for Preferences, Disable, and Uninstall for each. On the Plugins tab, you can disable or enable embedded applications, such as DivX, iTunes, QuickTime, and Skype. The Appearance tab lets you choose a theme.

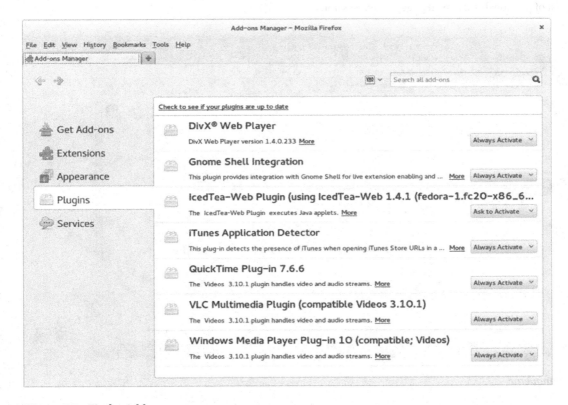

Figure 7-3. *Firefox Add-ons management*

Firefox also support profiles. You can set up different Firefox configurations, each with preferences and bookmarks. This is useful for computers like laptops that connect to different networks or are used for different purposes. You can select and create profiles by starting up the profile manager. Enter the firefox command in a terminal window with the -P option.

```
firefox -P
```

A default profile is already set up. You can create a new profile, which runs the profile wizard to prompt you for the profile name and directory to use. Select a profile to use and click Start Firefox. The last profile you used will be used again the next time you start Firefox. You have the option to prompt for the profile to use at startup, otherwise run the firefox -P command again to change your profile.

Konqueror: KDE Web and FTP Access

The KDE Konqueror is a full-featured web browser and an FTP client. It includes a box for entering either a pathname for a local file or a URL for a web page on the Internet or your intranet (see Figure 7-4). A navigation toolbar can be used to display previous web pages. The Home button will always return you to your home page. When accessing a web page, the page is displayed as on any web browser. With the navigation toolbar, you can move back and forth through the list of previously displayed pages in that session.

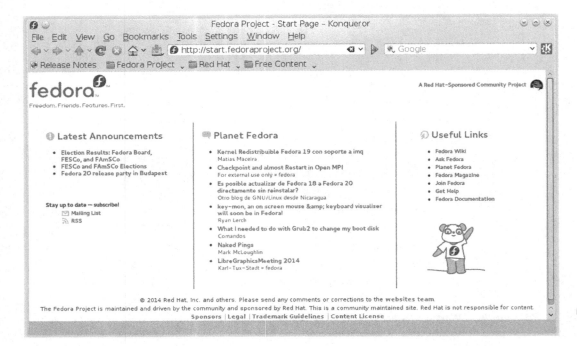

Figure 7-4. *Konqueror*

You can set the view mode (View ➤ View Mode menu) to use KHTML, WebKit, or Embedded Advanced Text Editor. The editor displays the web page source code and allows you to edit a copy of the page locally, or to the site, if you have permission.

Konqueror also operates as an FTP client. When you access an FTP site, you navigate the remote directories as you would your own. The operations to download a file are the same as copying a file on your local system. Just select the file's icon or entry in the file manager window and drag it to the local directory where you want it downloaded, then select the Copy entry from the pop-up menu that appears.

■ **Tip**   KDE features the KGet tool for Konqueror, which manages FTP downloads, letting you select, queue, suspend, and schedule downloads, while displaying status information on current downloads.

To configure Konqueror, select Configure Konqueror from a Konqueror window Settings menu. You can perform configuration tasks such as specifying proxies and web page displays, choosing fonts to use, managing cookies, and setting bookmarks. The History category lets you specify the number of history items and their expiration date. With the Plugins category, you can see a listing of current browser plug-ins as well as scan for new ones.

Konqueror supports split views as well as a navigation sidebar. You can select vertical or horizontal split views from the Window menu. Also, you can add split view icons to the toolbar by selecting Settings ➤ Toolbar ➤ Extra Toolbar (see Figure 7-5). With split views, you can display two different web sites at the same time in the same Konqueror window.

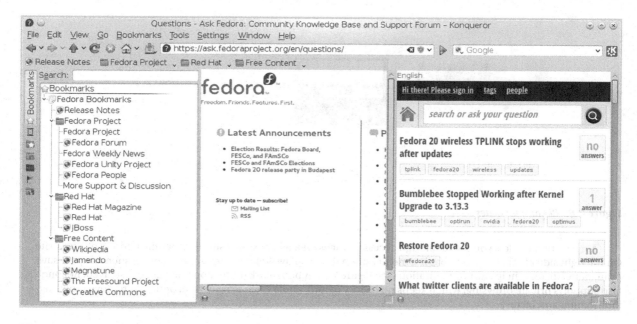

Figure 7-5. *Konqueror with split views and sidebar*

The Konqueror sidebar can display bookmarks, history, folders (home, places, root, and network), and services (applications, fonts, and DVD/CD browsing). To show the sidebar, choose Settings ➤ Show Sidebar or display the Extra toolbar and then click the Show Sidebar bar button. The sidebar displays buttons for bookmarks, history, home folder, places, root folder, services, and the network folder. In effect, Konqueror can be used as an alternative file manager to Dolphin.

Konqueror also supports tabbed displays. Instead of opening a folder or site in the same Konqueror window or a new one, you can open a new tab for it using the same Konqueror window. One tab can display the initial folder or site opened, and other tabs can be used for folders or sites opened later. You can then move from viewing one folder to another by simply clicking the latter folder's tab. This way, you can view multiple folders or sites with just one Konqueror window. To open a folder as a tab, right-click its icon and select Open Tab. To later close the folder, click the tab's red x button. You can also detach a tab, opening it up in its own file manager window (right-click the tab name and choose Detach Tab from the pop-up menu).

Konqueror can also operate as a file manager. To use Konqueror as a file manager, on the Konqueror window, choose Settings ➤ Load View Profile ➤ File Management. Konqueror will open to your home folder, and the sidebar will list your file system directories. You can also use split views on different folders, showing two or more open side by side. You can then move files directly between the displayed folders.

The KDE Rekonq Web Browser

Rekonq is the new web browser for KDE (see http://rekonq.kde.org for more details). Rekonq is based on the WebKit layout engine, like Chrome and Apple's Safari. It provides full integration with the KDE Desktop for tasks such as editing and file management (see Figure 7-6). Install Rekonq using PackageKit. You can then access it from the Applications ➤ Internet menu.

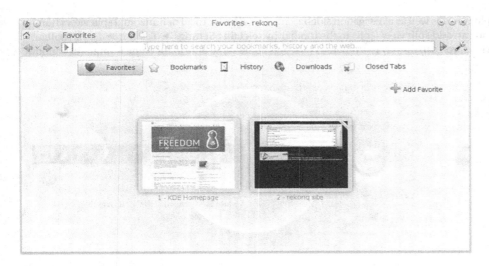

Figure 7-6. *Rekonq favorites*

A navigation bar lets you move through accessed pages on a tab, refresh a site, or enter the address of a new site. On the right side of the navigation bar is a menu button that displays Rekonq browser operations such as open, save, print, panel display, help, and configuration (see Figure 7-7). A bookmark navigation bar can be displayed. Rekonq also supports private browsing, which keeps no history record, and a Clear Private Data option to remove browsing information and history.

Figure 7-7. *Rekonq with panels, bookmarks, and menus*

Like Chrome, Rekonq is tab-based. Tabs can be reordered with a click-and-drag of their tab thumbnails. To close a tab, click its x button to the right of its name. You add new tabs by clicking the New Tab button to the right of an open tab. The new tab opens to the Favorites page. Should you ever want to return to the Favorites page, just open a new tab (see Figure 7-7).

The Favorites page shows a button bar across the top that lets you choose Favorites, Closed Tabs, Bookmarks, History, and Downloads. Favorites displays icons of your favorite sites, initially showing Google, KDE UserBase, and KDE Community Forums. Click the Add Favorite button to the right to add a favorite site of your own. A blank icon appears. Click it to display a button labeled "Set to This Page." The notice "Please open up the webpage you want to add as favorite" will appear. You then enter the site you want to use in the navigation bar and click the Set to This Page button to add that page as the favorite. On the Favorites page, the site is previewed in the new favorites icon you set up. To remove a favorite, move to that icon and click the red x that appears to the right of the favorite's name.

The History tab displays your previous history, with a Clear Private Data button to the right, which you can click to clear your history components, such as visited pages, downloads, cookies, and cached pages. To reopen closed tabs, use the Closed Tabs tab. Downloads lists your recent downloads.

You add a page as a bookmark by right-clicking it and choosing Add Bookmark or by pressing Ctrl+b. The bookmark appears on the Bookmark toolbar located above the tabs (see Figure 7-7). The Bookmarks tab, accessed from the Favorites page, also lists your bookmarks. Click the Edit Bookmarks button to open the Bookmark Editor, which lets you organize your bookmarks, setting up folders for them, deleting bookmarks, or importing bookmarks from other browsers. You can also add new bookmarks or change the names and icons of current ones.

To configure Rekonq, select Configure Rekonq from a Rekonq window Settings menu. The General tab specifies the page displayed on Rekonq at startup, the default being a new tab page. You can set it to your home page or to the last opened pages. Set your home page in the Home Page URL text box. The Tabs tab determines new tab behavior, such as displaying your Favorites page in a new tab or opening links in a new tab. Appearance is where you set the default font and font size. WebKit sets WebKit and Plugin settings, such as image loading, Java support, and storage use. Network controls your cache, cookies, and proxy settings. Ad Block, which is enabled by default, filters ads. Shortcuts sets up keyboard shortcuts for Rekonq tasks like those for navigation or tab operations. Web Shortcuts lets you specify your default search provider.

Web (Epiphany)

Web, formerly known as Epiphany, is a GNOME web browser, with a simple interface, designed to be fast (see Figure 7-8). You can find out more about Epiphany at https://wiki.gnome.org/Apps/Web. Web works well as a simple browser with a clean interface. It is also integrated with the desktop, featuring a download applet that will continue after closing Web. Web also supports tabbed panels for multiple web site access. Its GNOME applications menu lists options such as New Window, New Incognito Window, Bookmarks, History, Personal Data, and Preferences. For page-specific operations such as tabs, print, save, and find, click the tool button (gear icon) at the top right. You can install Web using the PackageKit package manager and searching under Epiphany or Web. Install the Epiphany package. Once installed, you can access it as Web.

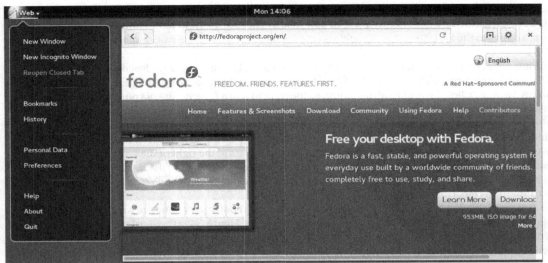

Figure 7-8. *Web (Epiphany) web browser*

Chrome

Google's Chrome web browser provides easy and very secure access to the Web with full Google integration (see Figure 7-9). You can download it from `www.google.com/chrome`. The download page detects that you are using Fedora and will select the Fedora RPM Chrome package for you to download. You can then install it directly from your browser. The installation will also download and configure the Chrome repository, `google-chrome.repo`, allowing you to use GNOME Software or PackageKit to remove, update, and reinstall Chrome (`google-chrome` package).

Figure 7-9. *Chrome web browser (Google)*

You can access Chrome from the Applications overview. You are first prompted to enter your Google account e-mail and password so that your online preferences and bookmarks can be used. Primacy is afforded to tabs. At the top of the Chrome window are your tabs for open web pages, with a square image button at the end of the tabs for opening a new tab. Chrome features a simple toolbar with navigation buttons and a bookmark button (start icon). To close a tab, click the x icon to the right of the tab title.

To the right of the URL box, a page button displays a drop-down menu for web page operations such as search, print, and zoom. The tool button (list icon) displays menu items for browser operations such as new tabs, zoom, history, bookmarks, and downloads. To configure Chrome, select Settings from this menu to open the Chrome Settings dialog. Here you can set your home page, default search service, and themes. Click the Show Advanced Settings dialog for password, font size, privacy options, and proxy settings.

When you open a new tab, a thumbnail listing of recently closed and most visited sites is displayed. Clicking a thumbnail moves you to that site. On a new tab, the bookmark toolbar is also displayed, which you can use to access a site.

Lynx and ELinks: Line-Mode Browsers

Lynx is a line-mode browser you can use without the X Window System. A web page is displayed as text only. A text page can contain links to other Internet resources but does not display any graphics, video, or sound. Except for the display limitations, Lynx is a fully functional web browser. You can also use Lynx to download files or access local pages. All information on the Web is still accessible to you. Because it does not require much of the overhead that graphics-based browsers need, Lynx can operate much faster, quickly displaying web page text. To start the Lynx browser, enter lynx on the command line and press Enter.

Another useful text-based browser shipped with most distributions is ELinks. ELinks is a powerful screen-based browser that includes features such as frame, form, and table support. It also supports SSL secure encryption. To start ELinks, enter the elinks command in a terminal window.

Enabling the Flash Plug-in

Fedora includes two free and open source versions of Flash: swfdec and gnash. It is preferable that you try these before attempting to use the version provided directly by Adobe. The swfdec version is newer. Both are available on the Fedora repository.

You can also download and install the Adobe Flash plug-in provided by Adobe for Linux. Adobe maintains a repository compatible with Fedora that contains the Flash plug-in.

The easiest way to download and install the Flash plug-in is to use a third-party package manager, such as easyLife and Fedorautils (see Chapter 4). Adobe provides both 32- and 64-bit versions of Flash for Linux.

Alternatively, you can manually configure access to the Adobe repository and then use PackageKit to download and install the Flash plug-ins (see Chapter 4). The Fedora project Flash wiki refers to an Ask Fedora page that explains the procedure in detail; see http://fedoraproject.org/wiki/Flash.

Once the repository is configured, you can then use PackageKit to search for Flash and select the Flash package for installation. The Flash plug-in package is flash-plugin.

The first time you install any package from the Adobe repository, you are prompted to install its package key. A dialog will be displayed with the message "Do You Trust the Source of the Packages?" Click Yes to install the Adobe repository package key.

Simply restart Firefox to enable your Flash plug-in. On the Tools ➤ Add-ons Plugins tab, you will find an entry for Flash.

Java for Linux

To develop Java applications, use Java tools, and run many Java products, you must install the Java Software Development Kit (SDK) and the Java Runtime Environment (JRE) on your system. The SDK is a superset of the JRE, adding development tools such as compilers and debuggers, along with other technologies, such as the Java API. Java packages and applications are listed in Table 7-2.

Table 7-2. *Java Packages and Java Web Applications*

Application	Description
Java Software Development Kit (SDK), OpenJDK	The open source Java development environment with a compiler, interpreters, debugger, and more; see http://openjdk.java.net. Part of the Java platform. Included as part of the Fedora 20 distribution as java-1.7.0-openjdk-devel.
Java Runtime Environment, OpenJRE	The open source Java runtime environment, including the Java virtual machine. Included as part of the Fedora 20 distribution as java-1.7.0-openjdk.
Java compatibility layer	The Java-like free and open Environment, consisting of the GNU Java runtime (libgcj), the Eclipse Java compiler (ecj), and supporting wrappers and links (java-1.5.0-gcj). Included with Fedora.
GNU Java Compiler	GNU Public Licensed Java Compiler (GJC) to compile Java programs; see http://gcc.gnu.org/java. Included with Fedora, libgjc.
Jakarta Project	Apache Software Foundation project for open source Java applications; see http://jakarta.apache.org.

Oracle continues to open source Java as the OpenJDK. Oracle supports and distributes Linux versions of this product. OpenJDK is directly supported by Fedora as packages on the main repository. You can install the recommended and required Java packages on Fedora with PackageKit by selecting the Java meta package (Package collections category). The Java set of packages is normally installed as part of a basic desktop installation. On Fedora, the java-1.7.0-openjdk package installs the Java runtime environment (JRE). The package is called OpenJDK Runtime Environment on PackageKit. To install the SDK, you use the java-1.7.0-openjdk-devel package, named OpenJDK Development Environment.

OpenJDK provides a Java development platform for entirely open source Java applications. Detailed descriptions of its features can be found in the SDK documentation on the Oracle Java web site.

jpackage, Sun, and Java-Like

Fedora includes numerous free Java applications and support, such as Jakarta. Go to http://fedoraproject.org/wiki/JavaFAQ for information on how Java is implemented on Fedora. You should use the Fedora versions of Java packages, as they have been specially modified for use on Fedora. The main Java Runtime Environment and SDK are now supported directly by the openjdk packages.

Fedora still includes a Java-like collection of support packages that enables the use of Java runtime operations. Keep in mind that the openjdk packages are now used for the JRE. There is no official name for this collection, although it is unofficially referred to as the Java Runtime Compatibility Layer. This collection provides a free and open source environment included with Fedora, consisting of three packages: GNU Java runtime (libgcj), the Eclipse Java compiler (ecj), and a set of wrappers and links (java). The java and libgcj packages are installed by default.

Java Applications

Numerous additional Java-based products and tools are currently adaptable for Linux. Tools include Java 3D, Java Media Framework (JEFF), and Java Advanced Imaging (JAI). Many of the products such as the Java web server run directly as provided by Sun. You can download several directly from the Sun Java web site at www.oracle.com/technetwork/java/index.html. The Jakarta project (http://jakarta.apache.org), part of the Apache Software Foundation, provides open source Java tools and applications, including libraries, server applications, and engines. Jakarta, along with other packages, is included with Fedora. These are derived from the JPackage Project at jpackage.org, which also includes some packages that are not in Fedora, which you can download and install. JPackage is a Fedora YUM–supported repository.

BitTorrent Clients (Transmission)

GNOME and KDE provide very effective BitTorrent clients. With BitTorrent, you can download very large files quickly in a shared distributed download operation where several users participate in downloading different parts of a file, sending their parts of the download to other participants, known as *peers*. Instead of everyone trying to access a few central servers, all peers participating in the BitTorrent operation become sources for the file being downloaded. Certain peers function as seeders—those who have already downloaded the file but continue to send parts to those who need them.

Fedora will install and use the GNOME BitTorrent client, Transmission. For KDE, you can use the KTorrent BitTorrent client. To perform a BitTorrent download, you need the BitTorrent file for the file you want to download. The BitTorrent file for the Fedora DVD ISO image is Fedora-20-x86_64-DVD.torrent. When you download the file from the http://fedoraproject.org/en/get-fedora-all site, you will be prompted to open it directly with Transmission or to save it to a file.

Transmission can handle several torrents at once. On the toolbar are buttons for starting, pausing, and removing a download. The Add button can be used to load a BitTorrent file (`.torrent`), thus setting up a download. You also can drag-and-drop a torrent file to the Transmission window. When you first open a torrent file, the Torrent Options window opens where you can specify the destination folder and the priority. The option to start the download automatically will be selected by default. Figure 7-10 shows Transmission with two BitTorrent operations set up. A progress bar shows how much of the file has been downloaded.

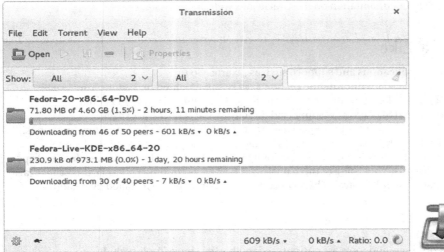

Figure 7-10. *Transmission BitTorrent client*

You could set up Transmission to manage several BitTorrent operations, of which only a few may be active, others paused, and still others complete but continuing to function as seeders. From the first drop-down menu, you can select All, Active, Downloading, Seeding, Paused, Finished, and Queued torrents. You can also choose those verifying and those that have errors. From the second menu, you can choose trackers, public or private torrents (privacy), and select by priority (high, normal, or low).

To remove a torrent, right-click it and select Remove. Choose Delete Files and Remove to remove what you have downloaded so far.

To see more information about a torrent, select it and then click the Properties button (see Figure 7-11). This opens a Properties window with tabs for Information, Peers, Trackers, Files, and Options. On the Information tab, the Activity section shows statistics such as the progress, times, and errors, and the Details section shows the origin, comment, and location of the download folder. Peers shows all the peers participating in the download. Trackers displays the location of the tracker, which is the server that manages the torrent operation. Files shows the progress of the file download (a torrent could download more than one file). The Options tab lets you set bandwidth and connection parameters, limiting the download or upload and the number of peers.

Figure 7-11. *Transmission BitTorrent client properties*

FTP Clients

With File Transfer Protocol (FTP) clients, you can connect to a corresponding FTP site and download files from it. These sites feature anonymous logins that let any user access his or her files. Basic FTP client capabilities are incorporated into the Dolphin (KDE) and Files (GNOME) file managers. You can use a file manager window to access an FTP site and drag files to local directories to download them. Effective FTP clients are also now incorporated into most web browsers, making web browsers the primary downloading tool. Firefox in particular has strong FTP download capabilities.

Although file managers and web browsers provide effective access to public (anonymous login) sites, to access private sites, you may need a standalone FTP client such as curl, wget, Filezilla, gFTP, lftp, or ftp. These clients let you enter usernames and passwords with which you can access a private FTP site. The standalone clients are also useful for large downloads from public FTP sites, especially those with little or no web display support. Popular Linux FTP clients are listed in Table 7-3.

Table 7-3. Linux FTP Clients

FTP Client	Description
Firefox	Mozilla web and FTP browser
Dolphin	KDE file manager
Files	GNOME file manager
gFTP	GNOME FTP client, `gftp-gtk`
ftp	Command-line FTP client
lftp	Command-line FTP client capable of multiple connections
curl	Internet transfer client (FTP and HTTP)
Filezilla	Linux version of the open source Filezilla FTP client

Network File Transfer: FTP

With File Transfer Protocol (FTP) clients, you can transfer extremely large files directly from one site to another. FTP can handle text and binary files. FTP performs a remote login to another account on another system connected to you on a network. Once logged in to that other system, you can transfer files to and from it. To log in, you must know the login name and password for the account on the remote system; however, many sites on the Internet allow public access using FTP. Such sites serve as depositories for large files that anyone can access and download. These sites are often referred to as FTP sites, and in many cases, their Internet addresses begin with the term `ftp`, such as `ftp.gnome.org`. These public sites allow anonymous FTP login from any user. For the login name, you use the word *anonymous*, and for the password, you use your e-mail address. You can then transfer files from that site to your own system.

Several FTP protocols are available for accessing sites that support them. The original FTP protocol is used for most anonymous sites. FTP transmissions can also be encrypted using SSH2, the SFTP protocol. More secure connections use FTPS for TLS/SSL encryption. Some sites support a simplified version of FTP called File Service Protocol, FSP. FTP clients may support different protocols, such asgFTP for FSP and Filezilla for TLS/SSL. Most clients support both FTP and SSH2.

Web Browser-Based FTP: Firefox

You can access an FTP site and download files from it with any web browser. Browsers are useful for locating individual files, although not for downloading a large set of files. A web browser is effective for checking out an FTP site to see what files are listed there. When you access an FTP site with a web browser, the entire list of files in a directory is listed as a web page. You can move to a subdirectory by clicking its entry. You can easily browse through an FTP site to download files. To download a file, click the download link. This will start the transfer operation, opening a dialog for selecting your local directory and the name for the file. The default name is the same as on the remote system. On many browsers, you can manage your downloads with a download manager, which will let you cancel a download operation in progress or remove other downloads requested. The manager will show the time remaining, the speed, and the amount transferred for the current download.

GNOME Desktop FTP: Connect to Server

The easiest way to download files is to use the built-in FTP capabilities of the GNOME file manager. On GNOME, the desktop file manager has a built-in FTP capability much like the KDE file manager. The FTP operation has been seamlessly integrated into standard desktop file operations. Downloading files from an FTP site is as simple as dragging files from one directory window to another, where one of the directories happens to be located on a remote FTP site. Use the GNOME file manager to access a remote FTP site, listing files in the remote directory, just as local files are. In a file manager's Location bar (Ctrl+l or Enter Location from the file manager GNOME applications menu), enter the FTP site's URL following the prefix `ftp://` and press Enter. A dialog opens, prompting you to specify how you want to connect. You can connect anonymously for a public FTP site or connect as a user, if you supply your username and password (private site). You can also choose to remember the password.

For more access options, such as a secure SSH connection, windows share, and secure web (HTTPS), you can use the Connect to Server dialog (see Figure 7-12). To open the Connect to Server dialog, choose the Connect to Server menu item on any file manager window's GNOME applications menu. Enter the server address. The address is added to the Recent Servers section. For an FTP login, a dialog opens, allowing you to specify an anonymous login or to enter a username and password. Click the Connect button to access the site.

Figure 7-12. *GNOME FTP access with the Connect to Server dialog*

The top directory of the remote FTP site will be displayed in a file manager window (see Figure 7-13). Use the file manager to progress through the remote FTP site's directory tree until you find the file you want. Then open another window for the local directory to which you want the remote files copied. In the window showing the FTP files, select those you want to download. Then click-and-drag those files to the window for the local directory. As files are downloaded, a dialog appears, showing the progress.

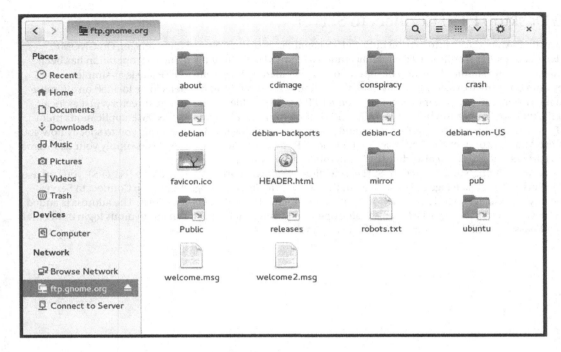

Figure 7-13. *GNOME FTP access on the file manager*

The file manager window's Network section on the sidebar will list an entry for the FTP site accessed. An eject button is shown to the right of the FTP site's name. To disconnect from the site, click this button. The FTP entry will disappear, along with the FTP site's icons and file listings.

The KDE File Managers: Konqueror and Dolphin

On the KDE Desktop, the desktop file managers (Konqueror and Dolphin) have built-in FTP capability. The FTP operation has been seamlessly integrated into standard desktop file operations. Downloading files from an FTP site is as simple as copying files by dragging them from one directory window to another, with one of the directories located on a remote FTP site. On KDE, you can use a file manager window to access a remote FTP site. Files in the remote directory are listed just as your local files are. To download files from an FTP site, you open a window to access that site, entering the URL for the FTP site in the window's location box. Use the ftp:// protocol for FTP access. Once connected, open the directory you want, and then open another window for the local directory to which you want the remote files copied. In the window showing the FTP files, select the ones you want to download. Then click-and-drag those files to the window for the local directory. A pop-up menu appears with choices for Copy, Link, or Move Select Copy. The selected files are then downloaded. Another window opens, showing the download progress and displaying the name of each file in turn, along with a bar indicating the percentage downloaded so far.

Filezilla

Filezilla is an open source FTP client originally implemented on Windows systems (www.filezilla.org). Use PackageKit to install it. Once installed, you can access it from the Applications overview. The interface displays a left and right pane for local and remote folders. You navigate through folder trees, with the files of a selected folder displayed below. To download a file, right-click a file in the Remote site pane (right) and select Download. To upload, right-click the file in the Local site pane (left) and select Upload. Text boxes at the top let you specify the host, username, password, and port. A Quick Connect drop-down menu will connect you to a preconfigured site.

To configure a remote-site connection, use the Site Manager (File ➤ Site Manager). In the Site Manager window, click the New Site button to create a new site connection. Four configuration tabs become active: General, Advanced, Transfer Settings, and Charset. On the General tab, you can specify the host, user, password, and account. The server type drop-down menu lets you specify a particular FTP protocol, such as SFTP for SSH encrypted transmissions or FTPS for TLS/SSL encryption.

gFTP

The gFTP program is a simpler GNOME FTP client designed to enable standard FTP file transfers. The package name for gFTP is gftp. You can access it from the Applications overview. The gFTP window consists of several panes. The top-left pane lists files in your local directory, and the top-right pane lists your remote directory. Subdirectories have folder icons preceding their names. The parent directory can be referenced by the double period entry (..) with an up arrow at the top of each list. Double-click a directory entry to access it. The pathnames for all directories are displayed in boxes above each pane. A drop-down menu to the far right lets you specify the FTP protocol to use, such as FTP for a standard transmission, SSH2 for SSH encrypted connections, and FSP for File Service Protocol transmissions.

Two buttons between the panes are used for transferring files. The left arrow button, <-, downloads selected files in the remote directory, and the right arrow button, ->, uploads files from the local directory. To download a file, click it in the right pane and then click the left arrow button, <-. When the file is downloaded, its name appears in the left pane, which is your local directory. Menus across the top of the window can be used to manage your transfers. A connection manager enables you to enter login information about a specific site. You can specify whether to perform an anonymous login or provide a username and password. Click Connect to connect to that site. A drop-down menu for sites lets you choose the site you want. Interrupted downloads can be restarted later.

wget

The wget tool lets you access web and FTP sites for particular directories and files. Directories can be recursively downloaded, letting you copy an entire web site. The wget command takes as its option the URL for the file or directory you want. Helpful options include -q for quiet, -r for recursive (directories), -b to download in the background, and -c to continue downloading an interrupted file. One of the drawbacks is that your URL reference can be very complex. You must know the URL already. You cannot interactively locate an item as you would with an FTP client. The following would download the Fedora Install DVD in the background:

```
wget -b http://download.fedoraproject.org/pub/fedora/linux/releases/20/Fedora/x86_64/iso/Fedora-20-
x86_64-DVD.iso
```

■ **Tip** With the GNOME wget tool (gwget package), you can run wget downloads using a GUI interface.

curl

The curl Internet client operates much like wget but with much more flexibility. With curl, you can specify multiple URLs on its command line. You can also use braces to specify multiple matching URLs, like different web sites with the same domain name. You can list the different web site hostnames within braces, followed by their domain name (or vice versa). You can also use brackets to specify a range of multiple items. This can be very useful for downloading archived files that have the same root name with varying extensions, such as different issues of the same magazine. curl can download using any protocol and will try to intelligently guess the protocol to use if none is provided. Check the curl man page for more information.

ftp

The ftp client uses a command-line interface, and it has an extensive set of commands and options you can use to manage your FTP transfers. It is the original FTP client used on UNIX and Linux systems. See the ftp man page for more details. Alternatively, you can use sftp for more secure access. The sftp client has the same commands as ftp, but provides SSH (Secure SHell) encryption. Also, if you installed the Kerberos clients (krb5-clients), a Kerberized version of FTP is set up, which provides for secure authentication from Kerberos servers. It has the same name as the FTP client (an ftp link to Kerberos FTP) and the same commands.

You start the ftp client by entering the command ftp at a shell prompt. If you want to connect to a specific site, you can include the name of that site on the command line after the ftp keyword. Otherwise, you have to connect to the remote system with the ftp command open. You are then prompted for the name of the remote system with the prompt "(to)." When you enter the remote system name, FTP connects you to the system and then prompts you for a login name. After entering the login name, you are prompted for the password. In the next example, the user connects to the remote system garnet and logs in to the robert account:

```
$ ftp
ftp> open
(to) garnet
Connected to garnet.berkeley.edu.
220 garnet.berkeley.edu FTP server ready.
Name (garnet.berkeley.edu:root): robert
password required
Password:
user robert logged in
ftp>
```

Once logged in, you can execute Linux commands on either the remote system or your local system. You execute a command on your local system in ftp by preceding the command with an exclamation point. Any Linux commands without an exclamation point are executed on the remote system. One exception exists to this rule. Whereas you can change directories on the remote system with the cd command, to change directories on your local system, you need to use a special ftp command called lcd (local cd). In the next example, the first command lists files in the remote system, while the second command lists files in the local system.

```
ftp> ls
ftp> !ls
```

The ftp program provides a basic set of commands for managing files and directories on your remote site, provided you have the permission to do so. You can use mkdir to create a remote directory and rmdir to remove one. Use the delete command to erase a remote file. With the rename command, you can change the names of files. You close your connection to a system with the close command. You can then open another connection if you want. To end the FTP session, use the quit or bye command.

```
ftp> close
ftp> bye
Good-bye
$
```

To transfer files to and from the remote system, use the get and put commands. The get command receives files from the remote system to your local system, and the put command sends files from your local system to the remote system. In a sense, your local system gets files from the remote and puts files to the remote. In the next example, the file weather is sent from the local system to the remote system using the put command.

```
ftp> put weather
PORT command successful.
ASCII data connection
ASCII Transfer complete.
ftp>
```

lftp

The lftp program is an enhanced FTP client with advanced features, such as the capabilities to download mirror sites and to run several FTP operations in the background at the same time.

It uses a command set similar to that for the ftp client. You use get and mget commands to download files, with the -o option to specify local locations for them. Use lcd and cd to change local and remote directories.

When you connect to a site, you can queue commands with the queue command, setting up a list of FTP operations to perform. With this feature, you could queue several download operations to a site. The queue can be reordered and entries deleted, if you wish. You can also connect to several sites and set up a queue for each one. The mirror command lets you maintain a local version of a mirror site. You can download an entire site or just update newer files, as well as remove files no longer present on the mirror.

You can tailor lftp with options set in the .lftprc file. System-wide settings are placed in the /etc/lftp.conf file. Here, you can set features such as the prompt to use and your anonymous password. The .lftp directory holds support files for command history, logs, bookmarks, and startup commands. The lftp program also supports the .netrc file, checking it for login information.

## CHAPTER 8

Social Networking: Microblogging, IM, VoIP, and Social Desktop

Fedora provides integrated social networking support for microblogging, IM (Instant Messenger), and VoIP (Voice over Internet Protocol). To access broadcast services such as Twitter and Facebook, you can use the Gwibber application, which enables you to broadcast short messages across the Internet. Instant messenger (IM) clients allow users on the same IM system to communicate anywhere across the Internet. With VoIP applications, you can speak over Internet connections, talking as if on a phone. The GNOME Maps application displays maps for cities, as well as your current location.

Microblogging: Gwibber

Fedora provides integrated support for social broadcasts (microblogging), based on the Gwibber project (install the gwibber package). You access broadcast accounts using Gwibber (Applications overview). The first time you use Gwibber, the Broadcast Accounts dialog is opened, letting you add a broadcast service. The Gwibber window will then open (see Figure 8-1). The toolbar lists icons for Home, Messages, Replies, Private Messages, Attachments, Searches, Users, and New Message. An arrow below the icon indicates the currently selected one. The Home icon lists postings from your authorized services as they arrive. Searches displays a search box. Users lets you search for and select users from Twitter.

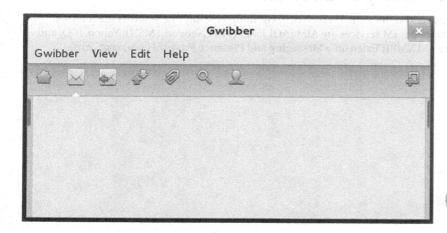

Figure 8-1. *Gwibber broadcast messages*

To send a message, click the New Message icon on the right side to open a text box in which you can enter the message. Icons for the available services are listed below the text box (see Figure 8-2). Click the service you want to send the message with. Clicking toggles a service on and off. As you type, the number of remaining available characters to the right will count down. When ready, click the Send button.

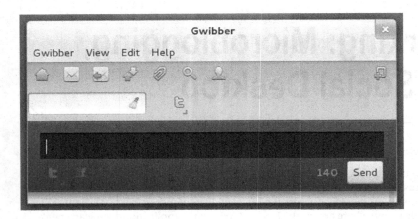

Figure 8-2. *Gwibber messaging*

To configure Gwibber, select Preferences from the Edit menu to display the Broadcast Messaging Preferences dialog with tabs for Options and Messages. There are options for notifications and update frequency. For messages, you can choose to show your real name or shorten pasted URLs.

If you have no accounts configured, Gwibber will open a Broadcast Accounts dialog. You can add or edit accounts later by selecting Account from the Edit menu (Edit ➤ Accounts). On the Broadcast Accounts dialog, from the drop-down menu, you can select the type of service you want, such as Flickr, Twitter, Digg, or Facebook. Click the Add button to display the configuration entries for your selection. Click the Advanced Expansion button to show account status options you can select and appearance features such as the message color.

Instant Messenger: Empathy and Pidgin

Instant messenger (IM) clients allow users on the same IM service to communicate anywhere across the Internet (see Table 8-1). Currently, some of the major IM services are AIM (AOL), Microsoft Network (MSN), Yahoo, ICQ, and Jabber. Some use an XML protocol called XMPP, Extensible Messaging and Presence Protocol (www.xmpp.org).

Table 8-1. *Talk and Messenger Clients*

Client	Description
Ekiga	VoIP application
Empathy	GNOME instant messenger client
KDE Empathy	KDE version of the Empathy instant messenger client
Pidgin	Older instant messenger client used in previous releases and still available
Jabber	Jabber IM client (XMPP)
psi	Jabber client using QT (KDE), XMPP
Finch	Command-line cursor-based IM client
naim	Command-line cursor-based AOL IM and IRC client
X-Chat	Internet Relay Chat (IRC) client, also has a GNOME version called gnome-xchat
Konversation	KDE IRC client

Empathy

Fedora uses Empathy as the default IM application. Empathy is the GNOME replacement for Pidgin. There is also a KDE version, called KDE Empathy, which is the default IM applications for the KDE desktop (it replaces Kopete; see Figure 8-8, later in this chapter). Empathy is based on the Telepathy framework, which is designed to provide IM support to any application that wants an IM capability. All major IM services are supported, including Google Talk, AIM, Bonjour, MSN Messenger, MySpaceIM, Jabber (XMPP), ICQ, and Yahoo.

Empathy is accessible from the Applications overview (see Figure 8-3). Messages can be sent and received using the Empathy dialog and the message bar at the bottom of the screen. Empathy is integrated into the GNOME desktop, with its applications menu on the top bar. From the menu, choose Accounts to open the Messaging and VoIP Accounts dialog. Here, you can edit and add new accounts. Accounts are listed to the left. Information for a selected account is shown on the right. Click the plus button on the lower left to open the Adding New Account dialog. From a menu, you can choose from supported chat services, such as Facebook Chat, Jabber, Yahoo, and MSN. You enter your ID and password.

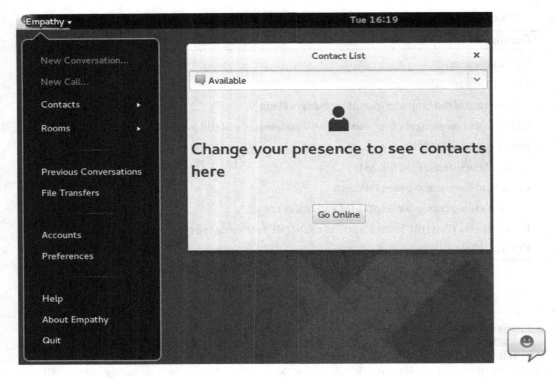

Figure 8-3. *Empathy IM client*

The login information will differ according to the chat service you choose. Facebook requires only a username and password. Others, such as MSN and AIM, have an advanced expansion set of entries from which you can specify the server and port (see Figure 8-4). A drop-down menu on the Contact List window lets you select your status, such as Available, Busy, Away, Invisible, or Offline. You can specify a custom message for a particular status.

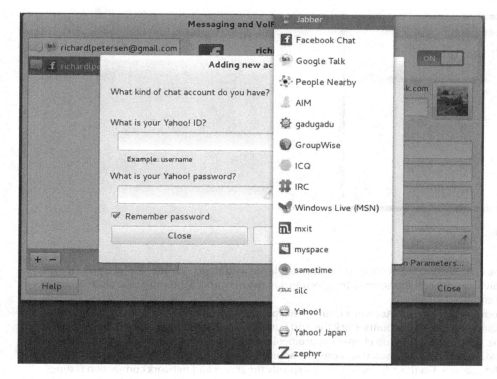

Figure 8-4. Empathy IM client account setup

You can edit your configuration by clicking the Edit Connection Parameters on the Messaging and VoIP Accounts dialog. This opens the Online Accounts dialog with the service selected. You can then turn the chat service off, if you wish.

Telepathy provides IM support with connection managers, making IM services easy to maintain and add. Current connection managers include telepathy-gabble for Jabber/XMPP, telepathy-idle for IRC, telepathy-butterfly for MSN, telepathy-salut for local network (link-local) XMPP connections, telepathy-sofiasip for SIP, and telepathy-haze for Pidgin's Yahoo, AIM, and other support (libpurple; see http://telepathy.freedesktop.org).

Pidgin

Pidgin is the older IM application used on previous Fedora releases. Pidgin is a multi-protocol IM client that works with most IM protocols, including AIM, MSN, Jabber, Google Talk, ICQ, IRC, Yahoo, MySpaceIM, and more. Pidgin is accessible from the Applications overview. Pidgin will open a Buddy List window with menus for Buddies, Accounts, Tools, and Help (see Figure 8-5). Use the Buddies menu to send a message or join a chat. The Accounts menu lets you configure and add accounts. The Tools menu provides configuration features, such as preferences, plug-in selection, privacy options, and sound.

Figure 8-5. *Pidgin's Buddy List*

The first time you start Pidgin, the Add Account window is displayed with Basic, Advanced, and Proxy tabs for setting up an account. Later you can edit the account by selecting it in the Accounts window (Accounts ➤ Manage) and clicking the Modify button.

To create a new account, select Manage Accounts from the Accounts menu (Accounts ➤ Manage). This opens the Accounts dialog, which lists your current accounts. Click the Add button to open the Add Account dialog with a Basic, Advanced, and Proxy tabs. On the Basic tab, you choose the protocol from a pop-up menu that shows items such as AIM, Bonjour, MySpaceIM, Yahoo!, and IRC, and then enter the appropriate account information. You can also select a buddy icon to use for the account. On the Advanced tab, you specify the server and network connection settings. Many protocols will have a server entered already. The configuration entries for both the Basic and Advanced tabs will change, depending on the protocol. On the Proxy tab, you can enter specific proxy server host and connection information, should your network use a proxy.

To edit an account, click its entry in the Accounts menu and select Edit Account to open a Modify Account dialog with the same Basic, Advanced, and Proxy tabs. Make your changes and click Save. You can also select Accounts ➤ Manage Accounts to open the Accounts dialog, from which you can select the accounts you want to modify.

To configure your setup, select Preferences from the Tools menu (Tools ➤ Preferences) to open the Preferences dialog, from which you can set options for logging, sounds, themes, and the interface display. You can find out more about Pidgin at http://pidgin.im. Pidgin is a GNOME front end that uses the libpurple library for its IM tasks (formerly libgaim). The libpurple library is used by many IM applications, including Finch.

Ekiga

Ekiga is GNOME's VoIP application. It provides Internet IP telephone and video conferencing support (see Figure 8-6); see www.ekiga.org. Ekiga supports the H.323 and SIP (Session Initiation Protocol) protocols. It is compatible with Microsoft's NetMeeting. H.323 is a comprehensive protocol that includes the digital broadcasting protocols, such as digital video broadcast (DVB) and H.261 for video streaming, as well as the supporting protocols such as the H.450 series for managing calls. You can access Ekiga from the Applications overview. Ekiga has panel status icons that display Online, Away, and Do Not Disturb.

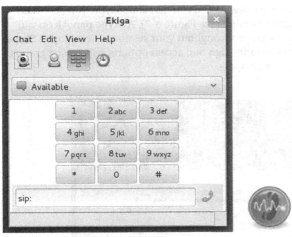

Figure 8-6. *Ekiga VoIP*

To use Ekiga, you will need an SIP address. You can obtain a free address from www.ekiga.org. You first have to subscribe to the service. When you start Ekiga, the Ekiga Configuration Assistant prompts you to configure your connection (SIP address, callout account—if you wish, connection type, and audio and video devices). Here, you can provide contact information, your connection method, sound driver, and video device. Use the address book to connect to another Ekiga user. A white pages directory lets you search for people who are also using Ekiga.

▦ **Note** Twinkle is a VoIP SIP-compatible softphone that uses SIP Witch Domain Telephony, which allows users to set up direct telephone connections without a service provider or central directory service. You can set up a direct computer connection or use an SIP server, such as a Fedora Talk, FreeWorld Dialup, or sipgate.co.uk.

Skype (VoIP)

Skype is one of the most popular VoIP applications. Skype provides a Fedora 16 i586 version that works on Fedora 20. You can install Skype directly from the Skype web site or install Skype using a third-party package manager script such as Autoten, easyLife, PostinstallerF, and Fedorautils (see Chapter 4). To install Skype from the Skype web site, go to the Skype Download page at www.skype.com/en/download-skype/skype-for-computer.

On Fedora, your browser will display the download page for Linux. From the menu of Linux versions, choose the Fedora 16 link. This is an i586 version that is meant to run only on 32-bit versions of Fedora, though it will work on the 64-bit, x86_64, version, provided that supporting packages are also installed.

```
skype-4.2.0.13-fedora.i586.rpm
```

To install the package, choose either the install option when you download the package from the Skype web site using your web browser or download the file and then double-click it. Both will use the software install tool to install the package. You will be prompted to enter your root user password. The package is untrusted, so you are asked to confirm installation. For Fedora x86_64 (64-bit), you will also have to install the 32-bit (i686) supporting libraries for sound and video. These are selected, downloaded, and installed for you automatically by Yum when you install the Skype package.

Once installed, you can access Skype from the Applications overview. When you first start Skype, you are asked to accept a user agreement. The interface is similar to the Windows version (see Figure 8-7). A Skype panel icon will appear on the panel once you start Skype. You can use it to access Skype throughout your session. Click to open Skype and right-click to display a menu from which you can change your status, sign out, access options, list contact groups, and start a conference call. The panel icon changes according to your status.

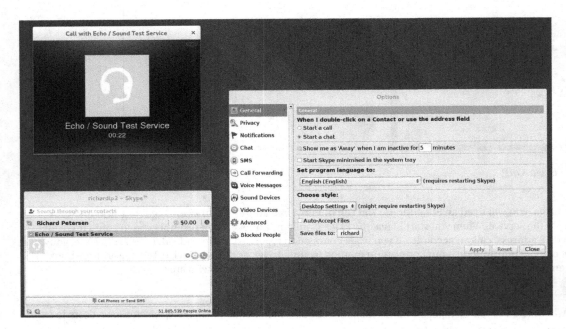

Figure 8-7. *Skype VoIP and panel icon*

KDE Social Desktop

KDE provides a set of Internet applications as part of the KDE Social Desktop initiative. The social desktop is based on a web API called the Open Collaboration Services (OCS) that allows applications to interface easily with Internet services like blogging and Twitter (http://freedesktop.org/wiki/Specifications/open-collaboration-services). KDE provides a data engine for Plasma widgets supporting social desktop features. In effect, it establishes an open source method for social networking. In addition, the Geolocation data engine allows plasmoids to detect and respond to users' geographic locations. Currently, the social desktop supports plasmoids for microblogging, knowledge bases, messaging, and social networking (see Figure 8-8).

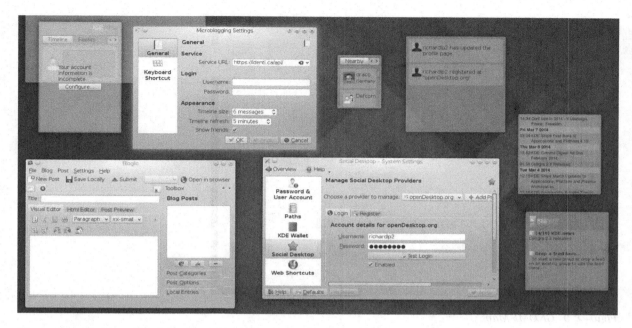

Figure 8-8. *KDE Social Desktop (microblogging, blogging, location detection, and news)*

When initially opened, the Microblogging plasmoid displays a Configure button, which you click to open the Microblogging Settings dialog. The KDE service is selected by default using the identi.ca microblogging site. You can configure access to Twitter by selecting the Twitter service instead, from the Service URL drop-down menu. Once configured, the Microblogging plasmoid will display an emblem for the service and a text box for entering messages. For regular blogging, you would use the Blogilo blogging client, which features a text editor.

You configure Social Desktop support using System Settings ➤ Account Details, Social Desktop tab (see Figure 8-8). Here, you select a provider (currently, there is only one, openDesktop.org). On the Login tab, enter your username and password. New users must use the Register tab to create an openDesktop.org account. You can then use openDesktop plasmoids, including Community, which lets you detect the location of friends, and Social News, which lists the latest news of social users. On the Community configuration dialog, you specify your location. The Geolocation engine will detect your system's location automatically. The Community plasmoid also detects the location of other KDE users near you, from the Nearby tab. You can choose to add one as a friend and send a message. Moving your mouse over a name displays a person icon. From that icon, you can add or remove the person as a friend. There is also a mail icon for sending a message. Clicking the name displays information about the user.

▓ **Note** For Facebook on KDE, add the Facebook plasmoid.

Maps

GNOME Maps is a GNOME map utility that provides both street and satellite maps. It can also detect your current location or close to it (see Figure 8-9). From the task menu, you can choose a street or satellite view. Use the plus and minus button to zoom in and out. To search for a location, enter the name in the search box, and options will be listed (see Figure 8-10). To see your current location, click the Geolocation button to the left (see Figure 8-11).

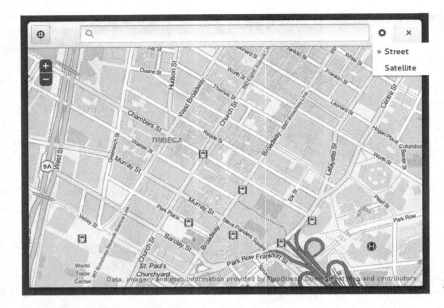

Figure 8-9. GNOME Maps

Figure 8-10. GNOME Maps: search

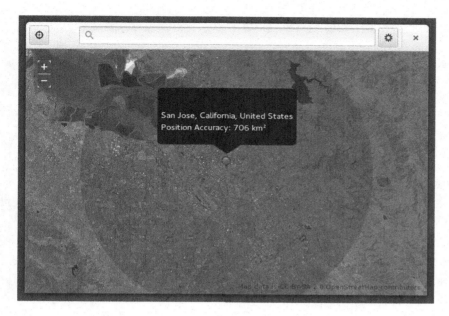

Figure 8-11. *GNOME Maps: current location*

CHAPTER 9

■ ■ ■

GNOME 3

The GNU Network Object Model Environment, also known as GNOME, is a powerful and versatile desktop. Currently, GNOME is supported by several distributions and is the primary desktop for Fedora. GNOME is free and released under the GNU Public License. Check www.gnome.org for a detailed description of GNOME features and enhancements, with screenshots and references.

The www.gnomefiles.org site provides a detailed software listing of current GNOME applications and projects. For detailed documentation, check the GNOME documentation site at http://library.gnome.org. Documentation is organized by users, administrators, and developers. "GNOME Help" provides a complete tutorial on desktop use. For administrators, the "GNOME Desktop System Administration Guide" details how administrators can manage user desktops. Table 9-1 offers a listing of useful GNOME sites.

Table 9-1. *GNOME Resources*

Web Site	Description
www.gnome.org	Official GNOME web site
http://library.gnome.org	GNOME documentation web site for users, administrators, and developers
http://art.gnome.org	Desktop themes and background art
www.gnomefiles.org	GNOME software applications, applets, and tools
http://live.gnome.org/GnomeOffice	GNOME office applications
http://developer.gnome.org	GNOME developer's site; see library.gnome.org for developer documentation

GNOME releases new versions on a frequent schedule. Fedora 20 uses GNOME 3.10, with many features included from GNOME 3.0. Key changes with GNOME 3.10 and GNOME 3.0 are described in detail at the following:

http://library.gnome.org/misc/release-notes/3.0/
http://library.gnome.org/misc/release-notes/3.10/

GTK+ is the widget set used for GNOME applications. The GTK+ widget set is entirely free under the Lesser General Public License (LGPL). The LGPL enables developers to use the widget set with proprietary software, as well as free software (the GPL restricts it to just free software).

The GNOME 3 Interface

GNOME 3 is based on the gnome-shell, which is a compositing window manager. It replaces the GNOME 2 metacity window manager, gnome-panel, and a notification daemon. The key components of the gnome-shell are a top bar, an Activities overview, and a notification/message tray feature. The top bar has menus for network access, the date and time, sound volume, power information, and user tasks such as accessing system settings and logging out. The Activities overview lets you quickly access favorite applications, locate applications, select windows, and change workspaces. The message tray and notification system lets you access removable devices and check messages.

As noted in Chapter 3, you can configure desktop settings and perform most administrative tasks using the GNOME configuration tools (see Table 3-1) listed in the GNOME System Settings dialog, accessible from the System Status Area menu. System Settings organizes tools into Personal, Hardware, and System categories (see Figure 3-25). A few invoke the supported system tools available from previous releases, such as Sound (PulseAudio) and Displays. Most use the new GNOME 3 configuration and administrative tools such as Background, Lock Screen, User Accounts, and Power.

Top Bar

The screen displays a top bar, through which you access your applications, windows, and such system properties as sound and networking. Clicking the System Status Area icons at the right of the top bar displays a menu with options to log out, switch users, activate notifications, and set your online status. There are also entries to access the system settings to configure your desktop (see Figure 9-1). The center of the top bar has a button to display your clock and calendar. To the left is the Applications menu, which is a menu for the currently selected open application, such as the Files menu for a file manager window (see Figure 9-11). Most applications have only a Quit entry; others list key tasks.

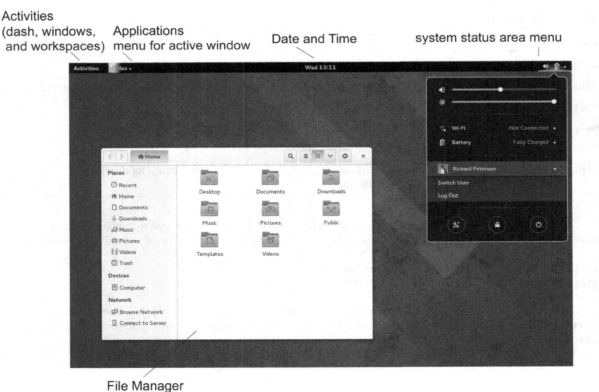

Activities
(dash, windows, and workspaces)   Applications menu for active window   Date and Time   system status area menu

File Manager

Figure 9-1. *GNOME 3 top bar*

Activities Overview

To access applications and windows, you use the Activities overview mode. Click the Activities button at the left side of the top bar (or move the mouse to the left corner, or press the Windows button). The Activities overview mode consists of a dash listing your favorite and running applications, thumbnails of open windows, and workspace thumbnails (see Figure 9-2). You can use the search box at the top center to locate applications and files. Partially hidden thumbnails of your desktop workspaces are displayed on the right side. Initially, there are two. Moving your mouse to the right side displays the workspace thumbnails.

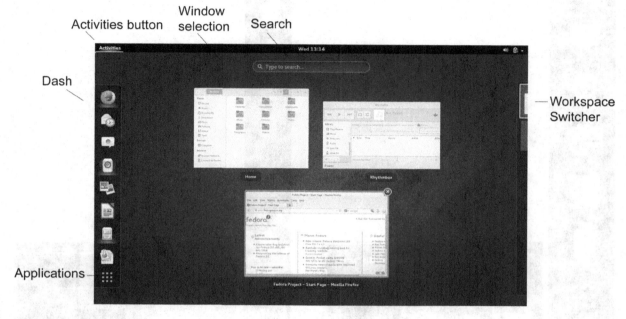

Figure 9-2. *GNOME 3 Activities overview mode*

You can manually leave the Activities overview mode at any time by pressing the ESC key.

Dash

The dash is a bar on the left side with icons for your favorite applications. Initially, there are icons for the Firefox web browser, mail (Evolution), sound (Rhythmbox), images (Shotwell), and files (the file manager); see Figure 9-3. To open an application from the dash, click its icon, or right-click and choose New Window from the pop-up menu. You can also click-and-drag the icon to the Windows tab or to a workspace thumbnail on the right side.

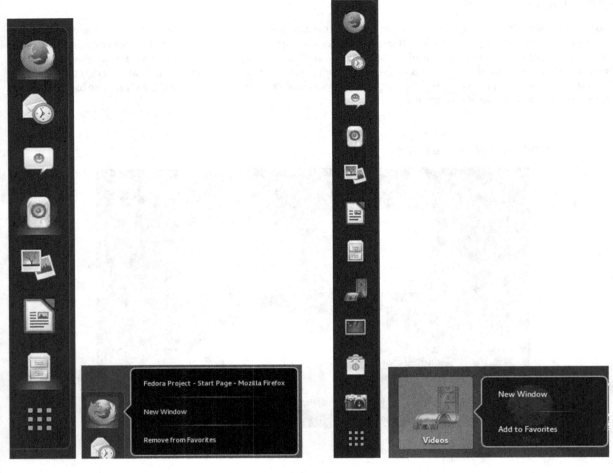

Figure 9-3. *Overview dash with favorites and running applications*

Favorites are always displayed on the dash. When you run other applications, they are also placed on the dash during the time they are running. To add a running application to the dash, right-click the icon and choose Add to Favorites. You can later remove an application as a favorite by choosing Remove from Favorites. You can also add any application to the dash from the Applications overview, by clicking-and-dragging its icon to the dash, or by right-clicking the icon and choosing Add to Favorites from the menu, as shown here.

Window Thumbnails

You access windows using the window thumbnails on the Activities overview. Thumbnails are displayed of all your open windows (see Figure 9-4). You can use the scroll button on your mouse to enlarge a thumbnail. To select a window, move your mouse over the window's thumbnail. The selected window also shows an x (close) button at the top right of the window's thumbnail, which you can use to close the window directly. To access the window, move your mouse over it and click. This displays the window, exiting the overview and returning to the desktop.

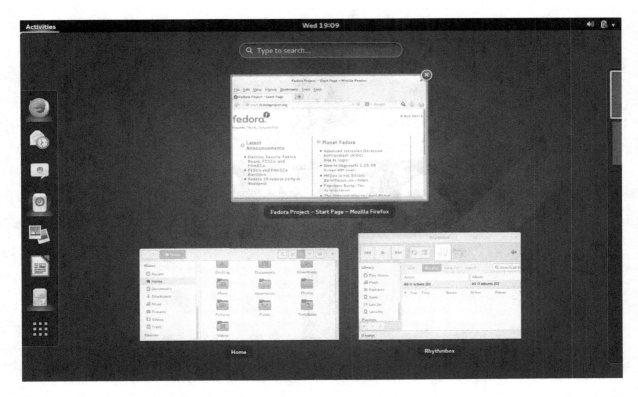

Figure 9-4. *Window thumbnails*

You can use the Window Switcher to quickly search open windows. Press the Alt+Tab keys to display an icon bar of open windows on the current workspace (see Figure 9-5). While holding down the Alt key, press the Tab key to move through the list of windows. Use the Shift key to move backward. Windows are grouped by application. Instead of the Tab and Shift keys, you can use the forward and back arrow keys. For applications with multiple open windows, press the tilde (~) key (above the Tab key) to move through a list of the open windows.

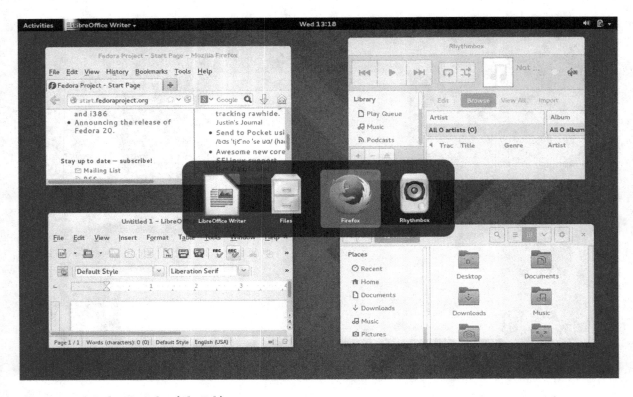

Figure 9-5. *Window Switcher (Alt+Tab)*

Moving your mouse to the right side of the screen displays the workspace thumbnails, with the current workspace highlighted (see Figure 9-6). You can switch to another workspace by clicking its thumbnail. You can also move windows or applications directly to a workspace. If your mouse has a scroll wheel, you can press the Ctrl key and use the scroll whell to move through workspaces, forward or backward.

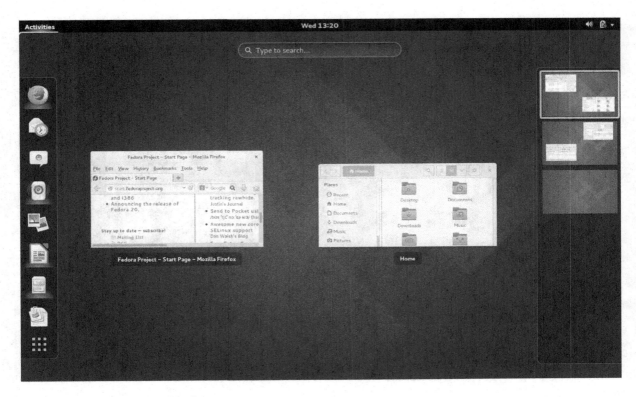

Figure 9-6. *Workspace thumbnails*

Applications Overview

Clicking the Applications icon (last icon, grid button) on the dash opens the Applications overview, from which you can locate and open applications. Icons for installed applications are displayed (see Figure 9-7). The Frequent button at the bottom of the overview lets you see only your most frequently used applications. Click the All button to see them all. A pager consisting of buttons, on the right side, lets you move quickly through the list of applications. You can move anywhere to a page in the list using the buttons. There are two special subsections: Utilities and Sundry. Clicking those icons opens another, smaller overview, showing applications in those categories, such as terminal and help in the Utilities overview. Click an application icon to open it and exit the overview. Should you return to the overview mode, you will see its window in the overview. The windows key with the a key (windows+a) will switch automatically from the desktop to the Applications overview. Continuing to press it, switches between the applications overview and the window thumbnails.

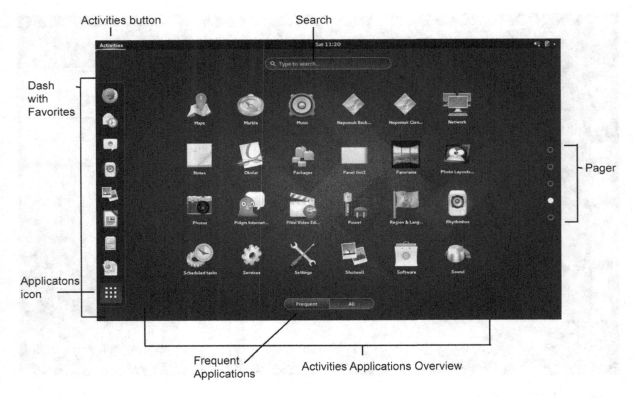

Figure 9-7. *Applications overview*

You can also open an application by dragging its icon to a workspace thumbnail on the right side, starting it in that workspace.

Also, to add an application as a favorite on the dash, you can simply drag its icon from the Applications overview to the dash directly.

Activities Search

The Activities search will search applications and files. Should you know the name of the application you want, you can simply start typing, and the matching results are displayed (see Figure 9-8). Your search term is entered in the search box as you type. The results dynamically narrow the more you type. The first application is selected automatically. If this is the one you want, just press Enter to start it. Results will also show Settings tools and recently accessed files.

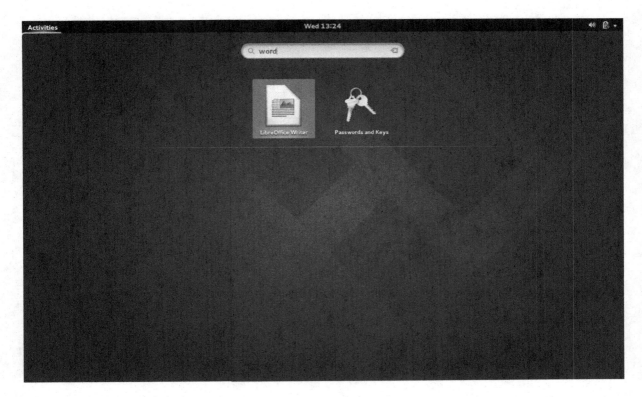

Figure 9-8. *Activities: search box*

The search box for the Activities overview can be configured from System Settings Search dialog (see Figure 9-9). Here, you can turn search on or off and specify which applications are to support searches. By default, these include Contacts, Documents, the Files file manager, Passwords and Keys, and the Web (Epiphany) web browser. To specify the folders to be searched, click the gear button on the lower left to open the Search Locations Dialog with switches for currently supported folders (see Figure 9-10). Click the plus button to add a folder of your choosing.

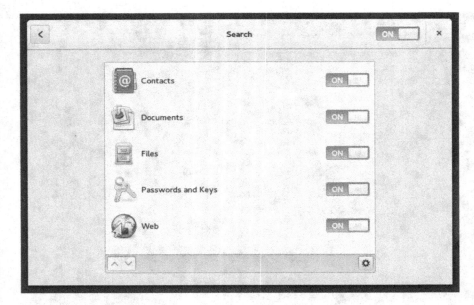

Figure 9-9. *Activities: Search configuration*

Figure 9-10. *Activities: Search Locations*

Managing Windows

The title bar and the toolbar for GNOME windows has been combined into a single header bar, as shown in the following for the file manager.

The minimize and maximize buttons have been dropped, and a single close button is always present. You can use Tweak tools to add the minimize and maximize buttons, if you wish. Some applications change the header bar if the function changes, presenting a different set of tools, as shown here for the GNOME Photos application.

Windows no longer have maximize and minimize buttons. These tasks can be carried out by a dragging operation or by double-clicking the header bar. To maximize a window, double-click its header bar or drag the header bar to the top edge of the screen. To minimize, drag the title away from the top edge of the screen. You can also use a window's menu entries to maximize or minimize it. Right-click the header bar or press Alt+spacebar to display the window menu.

Open application windows also have an Applications menu on the left side of the top bar. For many applications, this menu holds only a Quit entry (see Figure 9-11). Others, such as the file manager, list key tasks, such as Bookmarks, Preferences, and Help. The Firefox web browser only lists a Quit button, whereas the Epiphany web browser lists items for Bookmarks, History, and Preferences.

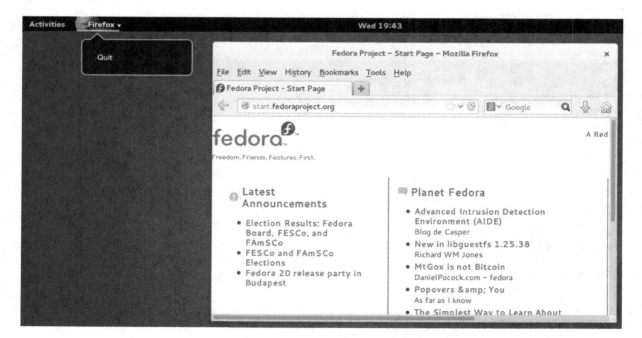

Figure 9-11. *Window with Applications menu*

To minimize an open window so that it no longer displays on the desktop, right-click the header bar and choose minimize. This will hide the window. You can then maximize the window later, using the window's thumbnails on the activities overview (Activities button).

To close a window, click its close box or press Alt+F4 (or choose Close from the Window menu). Many currently selected windows have an Applications menu in the top bar to the left. You can close an application by clicking the Applications menu button and choosing the Quit entry (see Figure 9-11).

To tile a window, click-and-drag its header bar to the left or right edge of the screen. When your mouse reaches the edge of the screen, the window is tiled to take up that half of the screen. You can do the same with another window for the other edge, showing two windows side by side.

To resize a window, move the mouse to the edge or corner until it changes to an edge or corner mouse, then click-and-drag.

The scrollbar to the right also features fine scrolling. When scrolling through a large number of items, you can fine scroll to slow the scrolling when you reach a point to search. To activate fine scrolling, click and hold the scrollbar handle, or press the Shift key while scrolling.

On the GNOME Tweak Tool's Windows tab, you can configure certain windows' actions and components. Attached Modal Dialogs will attach a dialog that an application opens to the application's window (see Figure 9-12). You can use the switch to turn this feature off, allowing you to move a modal dialog away from the application window. Actions on the title bar (Titlebar Actions) are also defined, such as double-click to maximize and secondary-click to display the menu. There are also switches to display the Maximize and Minimize buttons on the title bar. GNOME TweakTool is not installed by default. Use PackageKit or GNOME Software to install it.

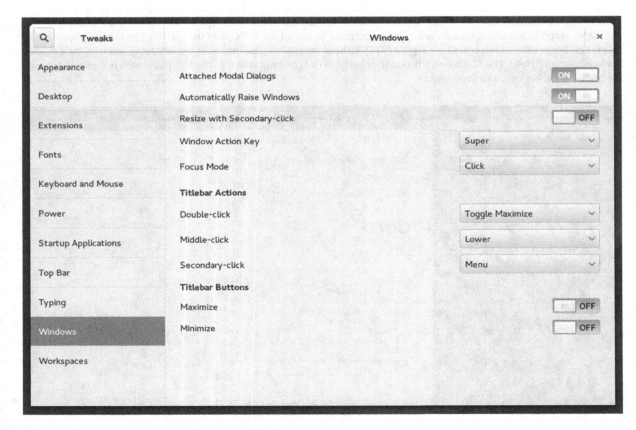

Figure 9-12. *GNOME Tweak Tool: Windows (dialogs and title bar)*

Workspaces

You can organize your windows into different workspaces. Workspaces are managed using the Workspace selector. In the overview, move your mouse to the right edge of the screen to display the workspace selector, a vertical panel showing thumbnails of your workspaces (see Figure 9-13). Workspaces are generated dynamically. The workspace selector will always show an empty workspace as the last workspace (see Figure 9-14). To add a workspace, click-and-drag a window in the overview to the empty workspace on the workspace selector. A new empty workspace appears automatically below the current workspaces.

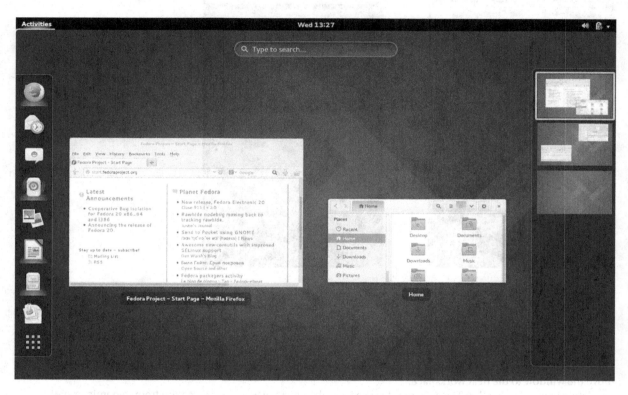

Figure 9-13. *Workspace selector*

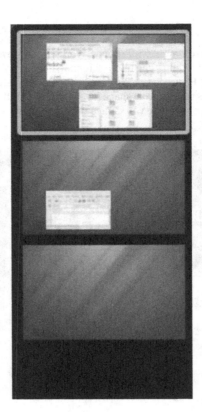
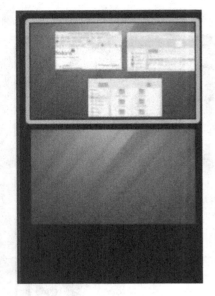

Figure 9-14. Adding workspaces

To remove a workspace, close all its open windows, or move the windows to other workspaces.

To move a window to a workspace, on the Windows overview, click-and-drag the window to the workspace selector (right edge) and then to the workspace you want. You can also use the Window menu and choose Move to Workspace Down or Move to Another Workspace. You can also use Ctrl+Alt+Shift and the up or down arrow keys to move the window to the next workspace.

You can use the GNOME Tweak Tool's Workspaces tab to change workspace creation from dynamic to static, letting you specify a fixed number of workspaces (see Figure 9-15).

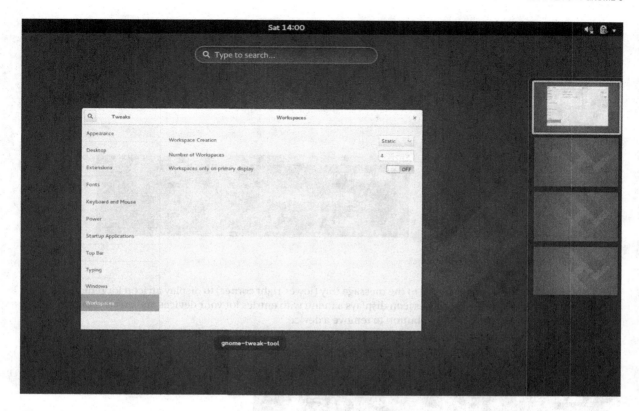

Figure 9-15. *GNOME Tweak Tool: Workspaces tab*

To move to another workspace, in the overview mode, move to the right edge to display the workspace selector, then click on the workspace you want. You can also use Ctrl+Alt with the up and down arrow keys to move to the next or previous workspaces.

Notifications and Message Tray

Notifications, such as software updates and removable device activation, are displayed in the message area at the bottom of the screen (automatically hidden). The notification will initially use a single line. Move your mouse on it to see the whole message. Notifications can be retrieved from the message tray, displayed by moving your mouse to the lower-right corner. Notifications also hold chat messages, organized by the user who sent them.

When you attach a removable device such as a USB drive or CD, a notification is displayed asking you what you want to do, such as open it with the file manager (see Figure 9-16).

Figure 9-16. *Notification for USB drive*

To remove the drive, you can move to the message tray (lower-right corner) to display an icon for removable devices. Clicking the Removable Devices icon displays a menu with entries for your devices and an eject button next to each (see Figure 9-17). Click an eject button to remove a device.

Figure 9-17. *Message tray with removable devices*

■ **Note** The gnome-shell manages system modal dialogs such as logout and policykit authentication.

GNOME Desktop Help

The GNOME Help browser (Yelp) provides a browser-like interface for displaying the GNOME Desktop Help and various GNOME applications, such as Brasero, Evince, and gedit (Utilities ➤ Help;. see Figure 9-18). It features a toolbar that enables you to move through the list of previously viewed documents. You can even bookmark specific items. You can search for topics using the search box, with results displayed in the drop-down menu. Initially, the Desktop Help manual is displayed. To see other help pages and manuals, choose All Documents from the Go menu (see Figure 9-19).

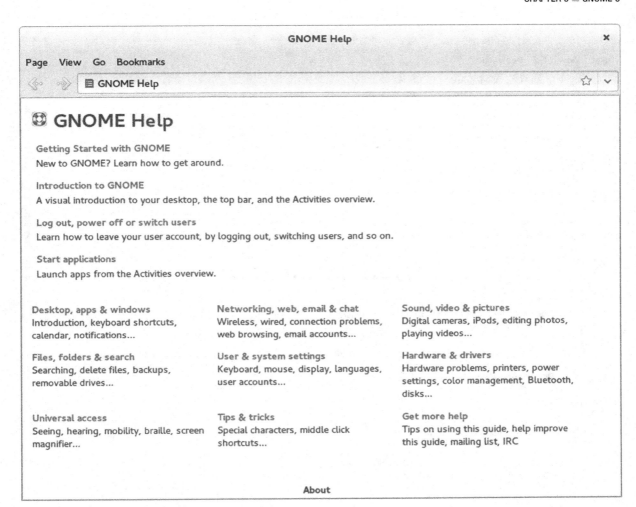

Figure 9-18. *GNOME Help browser*

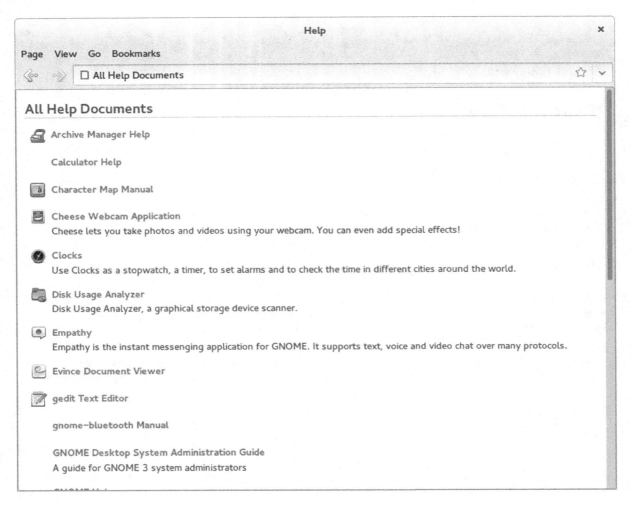

Figure 9-19. *GNOME Help: All Documents*

The GNOME Files File Manager

The GNOME file manager supports the standard features for copying, removing, and deleting items as well as setting permissions and displaying items. The name used for the file manager is *Files*, but the actual program name is still nautilus. When you select a file manager window, a Files menu appears as the Applications menu on the top bar to the left (see Figure 9-20). The Files menu has entries for opening a new file manager window, connecting to a remote FTP server, the file manager preferences, the default bookmarks management dialog, and help. The Enter Location entry changes the navigation bar to a text box where you can enter a directory pathname.

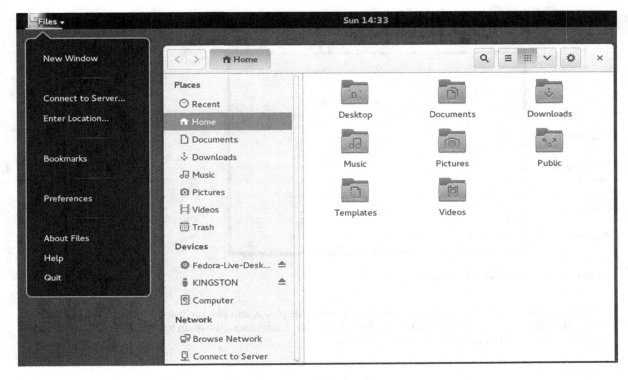

Figure 9-20. *File manager with Files applications menu*

Home Folder Subfolders

Fedora uses the Common User Directory Structure (`xdg-user-dirs` at `http://freedesktop.org`) to set up subfolders in the user home directory. Folders include Documents, Music, Pictures, Downloads, and Videos. These localized user folders are used as defaults by many desktop applications. Users can change their folder names or place them within each other using the GNOME file browser. For example, Music can be moved into Documents, Documents into Music. Local configuration is held in the `.config/user-dirs.dirs` file. System-wide defaults are set up in the `/etc/xdg/user-dirs.defaults` file.

You can manage these bookmarks using the file manager Bookmarks dialog, accessible from the Files menu as Bookmarks. From there, you can remove a bookmark or change its name and location.

File Manager Windows

When you click the Files icon on the dash, a file manager window opens showing your home folder. The file manager window displays several components, including a toolbar, a location bar, and a sidebar (see Figure 9-21). The sidebar displays sections for Places, Devices, Bookmarks, and Network items showing your file systems and default home folder subfolders. You can choose to display or hide the sidebar toolbar by selecting its entry in the View menu. The main pane (to the right) displays the icons or lists files and subfolders in the current working folder. When you select a file and folder, a status section at the bottom right of the window displays the number or name of the file or folder selected and the total size.

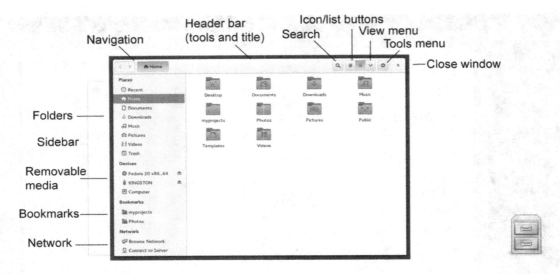

Figure 9-21. *File manager with sidebar*

When you open a new folder, the same window is used to display it, and you can use the forward and back arrows to move through previously opened folders (top left). As you open subfolders, the main toolbar displays buttons for your current folder and its parent folders, as shown here:

You can click a folder button to move to it directly. It also can display a location URL text box instead of buttons, from which you can enter the location of a folder, either on your system or on a remote one. Press Ctrl+l or, from the Files menu (Applications menu, top bar), select Enter Location. When you access another folder, you revert back to the folder button location bar.

File Manager Sidebar

The file manager sidebar shows file system locations that you would normally access: Places (computer folders), Devices (various devices), Bookmarks (bookmarks), and Network (network folders). (See Figure 9-22.) Selecting the Computer entry places you at the top of the file system, letting you move to any accessible part of it. In the Places section, you can search your default folders, such as Documents and Pictures. The Recent folder holds links to your recently used files. Should you bookmark a folder (Tools ➤ Bookmark This Location), the bookmarks will appear on the sidebar in a Bookmarks section. To remove or rename a bookmark, right-click its entry on the sidebar and choose Remove or Rename from the pop-up menu. The bookmark's name changes, but not the original folder name.

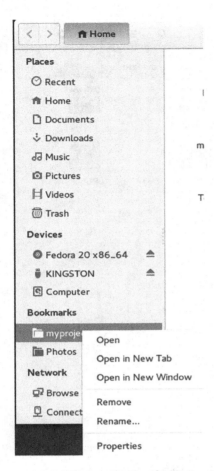

Figure 9-22. *File manager sidebar with menu*

Tabs

The GNOME file manager supports tabs with which you can open several folders in the same file manager window. To open a tab, select New Tab from the Tools menu (see Figure 9-23) or press Ctrl+t. You can use the entries in the Tabs menu to move from one tab to another, or to rearrange tabs. You can also use the Ctrl+PageUp and Ctrl+PageDown keys to move from one tab to another. Use the Shift+Ctrl+PageUp and Shift+Ctrl+PageDown keys to rearrange the tabs. To close a tab, click its close (x) button on the right side of the tab (see Figure 9-23), or press Ctrl+w. Tabs are detachable. You can drag a tab out to its own window.

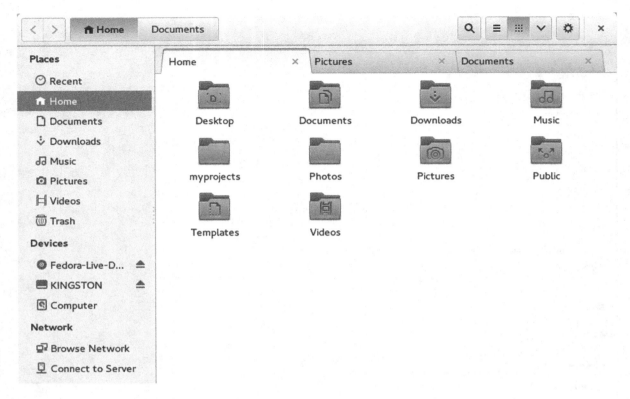

Figure 9-23. *File manager window with tabs*

Displaying Files and Folders

You can view a directory's contents as icons, as a compact list, or as a detailed list, which you can choose from the View icons at the right side. These icons are called Icons and List, as shown here:

Use the Ctrl key to change views quickly: Ctrl+1 for Icons and Ctrl+2 for list (there is no longer a Compact view). The List view provides the name, permissions, size, date, owner, and group. Buttons are displayed for each field across the top of the main pane. You can use these buttons to sort the list according to that field. For example, to sort the files by date, click the Date button; to sort by size, click Size. Click again to alternate between ascending and descending order.

Certain types of file icons display previews of their contents. For example, the icons for image files display a thumbnail of the image. A text file displays in its icon the first few words of its text.

You can click the down arrow button at the top right of a file manager window to display the View menu with entries for managing and arranging your file manager icons (see Table 9-2). The Arrange Items entries, such as By Name and By Type, allow you to sort your icons by name, size, type, and modification date. You can also simply reverse the order (see Figure 9-24).

Table 9-2. *File Manager View Menu*

Menu Item	Description
By Name, Size, Type, and Modification Date	Arranges files and directory by specified criteria
Reload	Refreshes file and directory list
Normal Size	Restores view of icons to standard size
Reset View to Defaults	Sets to default view and sorting
Reversed Order	Reverses the order of file list
Show Hidden Files	Shows administrative dot files
Show Sidebar	Displays sidebar with Places, Devices, Bookmarks, and Network items.
Zoom In	Provides a close-up view of icons, making them appear larger
Zoom Out	Provides a distant view of icons, making them appear smaller

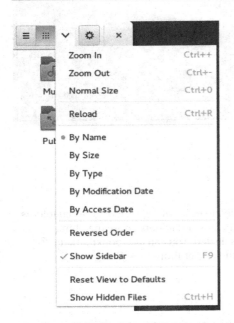
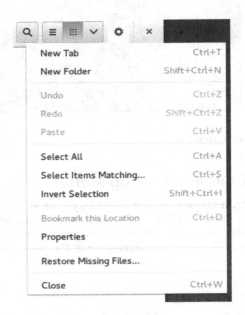

Figure 9-24. *File manager view and tools menus*

The View ➤ Zoom In entry enlarges your view of the window, making icons bigger. Zoom Out reduces your view, making them smaller. Normal Size restores them to the standard size. You can also use the Ctrl++ and Ctrl+- keys to zoom in and out.

Previews

The file manager supports previews for many different types of files. Select a file you want to preview, then press the spacebar. A dialog window opens, displaying the contents. Picture files show the image (see Figure 9-25). You can scroll through text and PDF files. Applications files such as LibreOffice files show information about the file. Video files are played, with controls to pause and to expand to full screen.

Figure 9-25. *File previews (spacebar)*

File Manager Tools and Pop-up Menus

From the Tools menu (gear button), you can paste files you have cut or copied to move or copy them between folders or make duplicates (see Table 9-3. The selection menu items let you select all files and folders, those matching a simple regular expression, and to invert a selection, choosing all those not selected. You can also bookmark the folder, restore missing files, and close the file manager window. Properties opens the Folder Properties dialog with Basic and Permissions tabs.

Table 9-3. *File Manager Tools Menu*

Menu Item	Description
New Folder	Creates a new subdirectory in the directory
New Tab	Creates a new tab
Paste	Pastes files that you have copied or cut, letting you move or copy files between folders, or make duplicates
Undo, Redo	Undoes or redoes a paste operation
Select All	Selects all files and folders in this folder

(continued)

Table 9-3. *(continued)*

Menu Item	Description
Select Items Matching	Quickly searches for files using basic pattern matching
Invert Selection	Selects all other files and folders not selected, deselecting the current selection
Bookmark this location	Bookmarks the folder by the file manager
Properties	Opens the Properties dialog for the directory.
Restore Missing Files	Restores deleted files from a Deja-Dup backup on a remote system or a local folder
Close	Closes the file manage window

You can click anywhere on the empty space on the main pane of a file manager window to display a pop-up menu with entries to create a new folder, restore missing files, and open the file manager properties dialog (see Table 9-4).

Table 9-4. *File Manager Pop-up Menu*

Menu Item	Description
New Folder	Creates a new subdirectory in the directory
Restore Missing Files	Restores deleted files from a Deja-Dup backup on a remote system or a local folder
Paste	Pastes files that you have copied or cut, letting you move or copy files between folders, or make duplicates
Properties	Opens the Properties dialog for the directory

■ **Note** If you move a file to a directory on another partition, it will be copied instead of moved.

Navigating in the File Manager

The file manager operates similarly to a web browser, using the same window to display opened directories. It maintains a list of previously viewed directories, and you can move back and forth through that list using the toolbar buttons. The left arrow button moves you to the previously displayed directory, and the right arrow button moves you to the next displayed directory. Use the sidebar to access your storage devices (USB, DVD/CD, and attached hard drives). From the sidebar, you can also access mounted network folders. From the Places section of the sidebar, you can access your home folders, trash, and recent files. The Computer entry on the Devices section opens your root (top) system directory.

To open a subdirectory, you can double-click its icon or right-click the icon and select Open from the File menu (File ➤ Open). To open the folder in a new tab, select Open in New Tab.

You can open any folder or file system listed in the sidebar by clicking it. You can also right-click an entry to display a menu with entries to Open in a New Tab and Open in a New Window (see Table 9-6). The Open in a New Window item is an easy way to access folders and devices from the file manager. The menu for the Trash entry lets you empty the trash. You can also remove and rename the bookmarks.

Entries for removable devices in the sidebar, such as USB drives, also have menu items for Eject and Safely Remove Drive. Internal hard drives have an Unmount option instead.

Managing Files and Folders

As a GNOME-compliant file manager, Files supports desktop drag-and-drop operations for copying and moving files. To move a file or directory, drag-and-drop from one directory to another, as you would on Windows or Mac interfaces. The move operation is the default drag-and-drop operation in GNOME. To copy a file to a new location, press the Ctrl key as you drag-and-drop.

Using a File's Pop-up Menu

You can also perform remove, rename, and link-creation operations on a file by right-clicking its icon and selecting the action you want from the pop-up menu that appears (see Table 9-5). For example, to remove an item, right-click it and select the Move To Trash entry from the pop-up menu. This places it in the Trash directory, where you can later delete it. To create a link, right-click the file and select Make Link from the pop-up menu. This creates a new link file that begins with the term "Link."

Table 9-5. *The File and Directory Pop-up Menu*

Menu Item	Description
Open	Opens the file with its associated application. Directories are opened in the file manager. Associated applications are listed.
Open in a New Tab	Opens a directory in a new tab in the same window
Open With	Selects an application with which to open this file. An Open With dialog lists the possible applications
Cut Copy	Cuts or copies the selected file
Make Link	Creates a link to that file in the same directory
Rename (F2)	Renames the file
Copy To	Copies a file to the Home folder, desktop, or to a folder displayed in another pane in the file manager window
Move To	Moves a file to the Home folder, desktop, or to a folder displayed in another pane in the file manager window
Move To Trash	Moves a file to the Trash directory, where you can later delete it
Revert to Previous Version	Restores from a previous Deja-Dup backup
Send To	E-mails the file
Compress	Archives the file using File Roller
Sharing Options	Displays the Folder Sharing dialog (Samba and NFS)
Properties	Displays the Properties dialog

Table 9-6. *The File Manager Sidebar Pop-up Menu*

Menu Item	Description
Open	Opens the file with its associated application. Directories are opened in the file manager. Associated applications are listed.
Open in a New Tab	Opens a directory in a new tab in the same window
Open in a New Window	Opens a directory in a separate window, accessible from the toolbar with a right-click
Remove	Removes the bookmark from the sidebar
Rename	Renames the bookmark

Renaming Files

To rename a file, you can either right-click the file's icon and select the Rename entry from the pop-up menu or click its icon and press the F2 function key. The name of the icon will be bordered, encased in a small text box. You can overwrite the old one or edit the current name by clicking a position in the name to insert text, as well as by using the Backspace key to delete characters. You can also rename a file by entering a new name in its Properties dialog box (Basic tab).

Grouping Files

You can select a group of files and folders by clicking the first item and then holding down the Shift key while clicking the last item, or by clicking and dragging the mouse across items you want to select. To select separated items, hold the Ctrl key down as you click the individual icons. If you want to select all the items in the directory, choose the Select All entry from the Edit menu (Edit ➤ Select All), or choose Ctrl+a. You can then copy, move, or delete several files at once. To select items that have a certain pattern in their name, choose Select Items Matching from the Tools menu to open a search box from which you can enter the pattern (Ctrl+s). Use the asterisk (*) character to match partial patterns, as in *let* to match on all file names with the pattern let in them. The pattern my* would match file names beginning with the my pattern, and *.png would match on all PNG image files (the period indicates a file name extension).

Opening Applications and Files MIME Types

You can start any application in the file manager by double-clicking either the application or a data file used for that application. If you want to open the file with a specific application, you can right-click the file and select one of the Open With entries. One or more Open With entries will be displayed for default and possible application, such as Open With gedit for a text file. If the application you want is not listed, you can select Open With ➤ Other Application to access a list of available applications. Drag-and-drop operations are also supported for applications. You can drag a data file to its associated application icon (say, on the desktop); the application then starts up using that data file.

To change or set the default application to use for a certain type of file, you open a file's Properties dialog and select the Open With tab. Here, you can choose the default application to use for that kind of file. Possible applications will be listed, organized as the default, recommended, related, and other categories. Click the one you want, and click the Set As Default button. Once you choose the default, it will appear in the Open With list for this file.

If you want to add an application to the Open With menu, click the Show Other Applications button to list possible applications. Select the one you want, and click the Add button. If there is an application on the Open With tab that you do not want listed in the Open With menu items, right-click it and choose Forget Association.

File and Directory Properties

In a file's Properties dialog, you can view detailed information on a file and set options and permissions (see Figure 9-26). A file's Properties dialog has three tabs: Basic, Permissions, and Open With. Folders will have an additional Share tab. The Basic tab shows detailed information, such as type, size, location, accessed, and date modified. The type is a MIME type, indicating the type of application associated with it. The file's icon is displayed at the top, with a text box showing the file's name. You can edit the file name in the Name text box. If you want to change the icon image used for the file or folder, click the icon image (next to the name) to open a Select Custom Icon dialog and browse for the one you want. The /usr/share/pixmaps directory holds the set of current default images, although you can select your own images (click pixmaps from the Places sidebar). Click an image file to see its icon displayed in the right pane. Double-click to change the icon image.

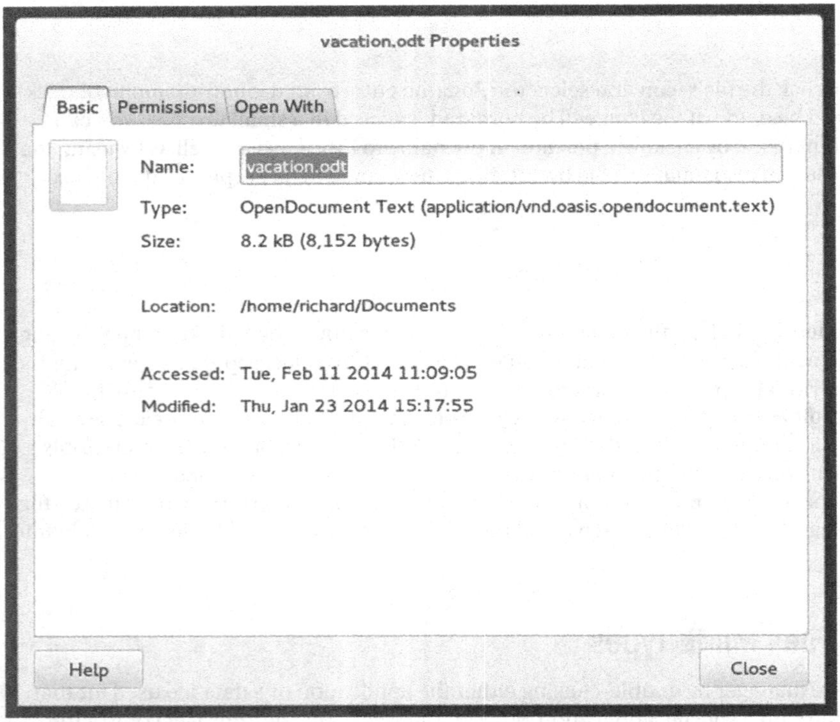

Figure 9-26. *File properties*

The Permissions tab for files shows the read, write, and execute permissions for owner, group, and others, as set for this file. You can change any of the permissions here, provided the file belongs to you. You configure access for the owner, the group, and others, using drop-down menus. You can set owner permissions as Read Only or Read and Write. For group and others, you can also set the None option, denying access. Clicking the group name displays a menu listing different groups, allowing you to select one to change the file's group. If you want to execute this as an application, you check the Allow Executing File As Program entry. This has the effect of setting the execute permission.

The Open With tab for files lists all the applications associated with this kind of file. You can select the one you want to use as the default. This can be particularly useful for media files, for which you may prefer a specific player for a certain file or a particular image viewer for pictures.

Certain kind of files will have additional tabs, providing information about the file. For example, an audio file will have an Audio tab listing the type of audio file and any other information, such as a song title or the compression method used. An image file will have an Image tab listing the resolution and type of image. A video file will contain an Audio/Video tab showing the type of video file, along with compression and resolution information.

The Permissions tab for folders operates much the same way, ith Access menus for Owner, Group, and Others. The Access menu controls access to the folder with options for None, List Files Only, Access Files, and Create and Delete Files. These correspond to the read and execute permissions given to directories. To set the permissions for all the files in the directory accordingly (not just the folder), click the "Change Permissions for Enclosed Files" button to open a dialog where you can specify the owner, group, and others permissions for files and folders in the directory.

File Manager Preferences

You can set preferences for your file manager in the Preferences dialog, accessible by selecting the Preferences item in any file manager window's Edit menu (Edit ➤ Preferences).

The Views tab allows you to select how files are displayed by default, such as a list, icon, or compact view. You also can set default zoom levels for icon, compact, and list views.

Behavior lets you choose how to select files, manage the trash, and handle scripts.

Display lets you choose what information you want displayed in an icon caption, such as the size or date.

The List Columns tab lets you choose both the features to display in the detailed list and the order in which to display them. In addition to the already-selected name, size, date, and type, you can add permissions, group, MIME type, and owner.

The Preview tab lets you choose whether you want small preview content displayed in the icons, such as the beginning text for text files.

■ **Tip** To display a Delete option on the file menus, from the Behavior tab of the File Management Preferences, click the Include a Delete Command that Bypasses Trash entry in the Trash section.

File Manager As an FTP Browser

The file manager works as an operational FTP browser. You can use the Connect to Server entry on the File menu to open a Connect to Server dialog, where you can enter the URL for the FTP site (you do not have to specify ftp://). The Service Type drop-down menu lists different kinds of FTP access. The default (Public FTP) is used for anonymous logins for most public FTP sites. In the Folder entry, you can specify a directory on the site, if you want. For a private FTP site, you can use FTP (With Login), which will display a User Name entry. For a shared windows folder, choose Windows Share, which displays entries for the share, folder, username, and domain. For sites requiring SSH encryption, use SSH.

Folders on the FTP site will be displayed, and you can drag files to a local directory to download them. You can navigate through the folders as you would with any file manager folder, opening directories or returning to parent directories. To download a file, just drag it from the FTP window to a local directory window. A small dialog will appear, showing download progress. To upload a file, drag it from your local folder to the window for the open FTP directory. Your file will be uploaded to that FTP site (if you have permission to do so). You can also delete files on the site's directories.

File Manager Search

Two primary search tools are available for your Fedora desktop—the GNOME dash search and the GNOME file manager search. With GNOME file manager, you enter a pattern to search. You can further refine your search by specifying locations and file types. Click the Search button (looking glass icon) on the toolbar to open a Search box. Enter the pattern to search, then press Enter. The results are displayed (see Figure 9-27). Drop-down menus for location and file type appear in the folder window, with + and - buttons for adding or removing location and file type search parameters. Click the plus (+) button to add more location and file-type search parameters. The search begins from the folder opened, but you can click the All Files button to search all files.

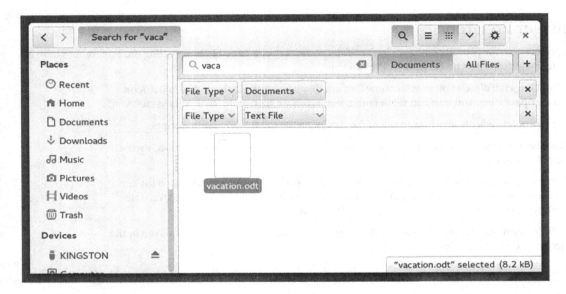

Figure 9-27. *GNOME file manager search*

GNOME Classic

As an alternative to the GNOME desktop, you can use the GNOME Classic desktop, which uses an interface similar to GNOME2 (see Figure 9-28). Install the `gnome-classic-session` package. When you log in again, you can choose GNOME Classic from the session menu. GNOME Classic displays a top panel with Applications and Places menus. The System Status Area menu is the same. Also, application menus continue to be displayed on the top panel, after the Places menu. The bottom panel has a task bar and a workspace switcher menu. Icons for applications can be displayed on the desktop. The Applications menu is organized into submenus by category, such as Graphics, Office, and Sound & Video. The Activities overview entry at the end of the Applications menu starts up the GNOME 3 overview interface.

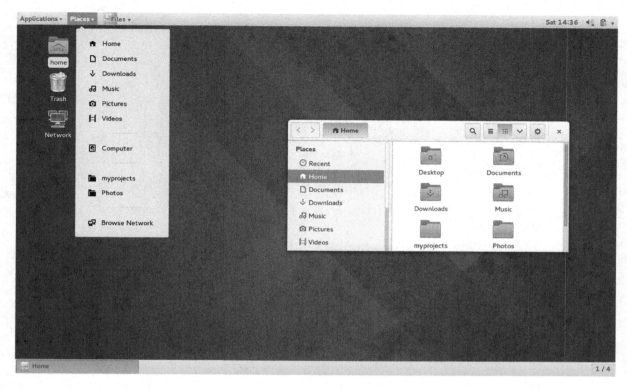

Figure 9-28. *GNOME Classic*

CHAPTER 10

■ ■ ■

The K Desktop Environment: KDE

The K Desktop Environment (KDE) includes the standard desktop features, such as a window manager and a file manager, as well as an extensive set of applications that cover most Linux tasks. The KDE desktop is developed and distributed by the KDE Project. KDE is open source software provided under a GNU Public License and, with its source code, is available free of charge.

Numerous applications written specifically for KDE are easily accessible from the desktop. These include editors, photo, and paint image applications, sound and video players, and office applications. Such applications usually have the letter *K* as part of their name, such as KWord or KMail. A variety of tools are provided with the KDE desktop. These include calculators, console windows, notepads, and even software package managers. On a system administration level, KDE provides several tools for configuring your system. Practically all your Linux tasks can be performed from the KDE desktop. KDE applications also feature a built-in help application. KDE includes support for the office application suite Calligra, which includes a presentation application, a spreadsheet application, an illustrator, and a word processor, among other components.

KDE, initiated by Matthias Ettrich in October 1996, is designed to run on any UNIX implementation, including Linux, Solaris, HP-UX, and FreeBSD. The official KDE web site is www.kde.org, which provides news updates and documentation. Several KDE mailing lists are available for users and developers, including announcements, administration, and other topics. A great many software applications are currently available for KDE at www.kde-apps.org. Development support and documentation can be obtained at http://developer.kde.org. Most applications are available on the Fedora repositories and can be installed directly from PackageKit. Various KDE web sites are listed in Table 10-1.

Table 10-1. *KDE Web Sites*

Web Site	Description
www.kde.org	KDE web site
http://spins.fedoraproject.org/kde	Fedora KDE spin
www.kde-apps.org	KDE software repository
http://developer.kde.org	KDE developer site
www.trolltech.com	Trolltech site for Qt libraries
www.calligra.org	Calligra KDE office project
www.kde-look.org	KDE desktop themes, select KDE entry
http://lists.kde.org	KDE mailing lists

You can install KDE on a Fedora desktop and use it as an alternative to the Fedora GNOME desktop, or you can install KDE directly, using the Fedora KDE spin. For the Fedora KDE spin, you can download the KDE ISO image file from the Fedora project download page for Desktops at http://fedoraproject.org/en/get-fedora-options#desktops.

To install KDE as an alternative desktop on a Fedora desktop (GNOME), you use the yum command with the groupinstall option in a terminal window, as the administrator. Other group packages that you may also want to install are kde-media, kde-apps, and kde-office. You can find the KDE groups listed in Packages (PackageKit) under "Package collections."

```
Su
yum groupinstall kde-desktop
yum groupinstall kde-media
yum groupinstall kde-apps
yum groupisntall kde-office
```

The K Desktop Environment (KDE)

New versions of KDE are released frequently. KDE releases are designed to enable users to upgrade their older versions easily. Your Fedora software updater will automatically update KDE from Fedora repositories, as updates become available. KDE uses as its library of desktop tools the Qt library, developed and supported by Trolltech (www.trolltech.com). Qt is considered one of the best desktop libraries available for UNIX/Linux systems. Using Qt has the advantage of relying on a commercially developed and supported desktop library. Trolltech provides the Qt libraries as open source software that is freely distributable.

The KDE 4 release is a major rework of the KDE desktop. KDE 4.11 is included with the Fedora 20 distribution. Check the KDE site for detailed information on KDE 4, including the visual guide.

```
http://kde.org/announcements/4.11/
```

Every aspect of KDE has been reworked with KDE 4. There is a new files manager, desktop, theme, panel, and configuration interface. The KDE window manager supports advanced compositing effects and the Oxygen artwork for user interface themes, icons, and windows.

The primary component of the KDE 4 desktop is the Plasma desktop shell. Plasma has containments and applets. Applets are also referred to as plasmoids. These plasmoids are applets that operate within containments. On KDE, there are two Plasma containments: the panel and the desktop. In this sense, the desktop and the panel are features of an underlying Plasma operation. They are not separate programs. Each has its own set of plasmoids (applets).

KDE Display Manager (KDM)

If you are using the KDMto log in, a box in which you can enter your username and password (see Figure 10-1) will be displayed at the center of the screen. Shutdown and Session menus are displayedbelow the login box The Session menu lets you change the desktop interface, such as GNOME, should it be installed. The Shutdown has entries for Switch User, Remote Login, and Shutdown. The Shutdown entry opens a dialog with selections to Restart or Turn Off the computer.

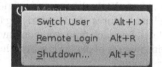

Figure 10-1. *KDE Display Manager (KDM), login screen with menus*

■ **Note:**   KDE can be started by other display managers such as the GNOME Display Manager (GDM) and LightDM.

Upon entering your username and password and pressing Enter or clicking the Play icon, your KDE session starts up. The login box displays the login splash screen showing the login progress.

You can change the theme of the login greeter using the Login Manager (System Settings ➤ System Administration ➤ Login screen). On the Theme tab, you can download and install new login themes (Get New Themes button) and then select the one you want to use. Click Apply to use the new theme. If you want to customize your login background, you can turn off the themed greeter on the General tab and then use the Background tab to use your own background image.

Configuration and Administration Access with KDE

KDE uses a different set of menus and access points than GNOME for accessing system administration tools. There are also different ways to access KDE configuration tasks, as well as KDE system administration tools not available through GNOME.

You access Fedora system administration tools from the Applications ➤ Administration entry. Here you will find Fedora administration tools such as Users and Groups, Printing, Display, and Network.

> **System Settings**—Accessible from the Kickoff menu with three entries: Favorites ➤ System Settings, Applications ➤ System ➤ System Settings, and Computer ➤ System Settings. This is the comprehensive KDE configuration tool, which lists all the KDE configuration tools for managing your desktop, file manager, and system, as well as KDE's own administration tools that can be used instead of the Fedora ones.

> **Administration**—Accessible from Applications ➤ Administration, this is a collection of Fedora administration tools. Here you will find tools like Firewall (firewall-config), Samba (system-config-samba), and Services (system-config-services). PackageKit (Software) is not listed. Instead, you use the KDE package manager, Apper, listed as Applications ➤ System ➤ Software Management.

Settings—Accessible from Applications ➤ Settings, this is a smaller collection of desktop configuration features for tasks such as setting the default printer, preferred applications, or PDA device setup. Also in this menu is the menu-updating tool, which lets you add non-KDE applications to the KDE menu.

System—Accessible from Applications ➤ System, this is where you find the KDE administration tools.

Plasma: Desktop, Panel, and Plasmoids (Applets)

Plasma has containments and applets. Applets are referred to as plasmoids. These plasmoids are applets that operate within containments. On KDE, there are two types of Plasma containments, the panel and the desktop. The desktop and the panel are features of an underlying Plasma operation. They are not separate programs; both can have plasmoids (applets). For each type, you can have several instances. You can have many different desktop containments, each with its own set of plasmoids installed. You can also have several panels on your desktop, using different collections of plasmoids.

Each containment has its own toolbox for configuration. The desktop has a toolbox at the top-right corner, and panels have a toolbox on the right side. The panel toolbox features configuration tools for sizing and positioning the panel. See Table 10-2 for keyboard shortcuts.

Table 10-2. *Desktop, Plasma, and KWin Keyboard Shortcuts*

Keys	Description
Alt+F2	Krunner, command execution. Entry can be any search string for a relevant operation, including bookmarks and contacts, not just applications.
Up/down arrows	Move among entries in menus, including the Kickoff and other menus
Left/right arrows	Move to submenus menus, including the Kickoff and QuickAccess submenus
Enter	Select a menu entry, including the Kickoff and QuickAccess menus
PageUp, PageDown	Scroll up quickly
Alt+F4	Close the current window
Alt+F3	Window menu for current window
Ctrl+r	Remove a selected plasmoid
Ctrl+s	Open a selected plasmoid's configuration settings
Ctrl+a	Open the Add Widgets window to add a plasmoid to the desktop
Ctrl+l	Lock your widgets so they can't be changed or removed and new ones can't be added
Alt+Tab	Cover Switch or Box Switch for open windows
Ctrl+F8	Desktop grid
Ctrl+F9	Present window's current desktop
Ctrl+F10	Present window's all desktops
Ctrl+F11	Desktop cube for switching desktops

Fedora KDE 4 also supports the activities interface, with its support for multiple plasma desktop containments (Activities). The Toolbox icon shows Add Widgets, Activities, and Lock Widgets entries. Use the Activities entry to add, remove, and select desktop containments.

The KDE Help Center

The KDE Help Center provides a browser-like interface for accessing and displaying both KDE Help files and Linux man and info files (see Figure 10-2). You can start the Help Center by selecting its entry at the bottom of the Kickoff Applications menu. The Help window displays a sidebar that holds two tabs: one listing contents and one providing a glossary The main pane displays currently selected documents. A help tree on the contents tab in the sidebar lets you choose the kind of help documents you want to access. Here, you can choose KDE manuals, man pages, info documents, and even application manuals. The Help Center includes a detailed user manual, an FAQ, and KDE web site access.

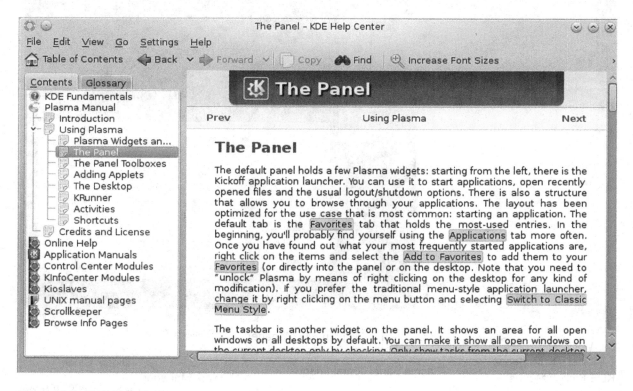

Figure 10-2. *KDE Help Center*

A navigation toolbar enables you to move through previously viewed documents. KDE Help documents contain links you can click to access other documents. The Back and Forward commands move you through the list of previously viewed documents. The KDE Help system provides an effective search tool for searching for patterns in Help documents, including man and info pages. Click the Find button to display a search toolbar where you can enter a query.

The KDE 4 Desktop

One of KDE's aims is to provide users with a consistent integrated desktop (see Figure 10-3). KDE provides its own window manager (KWM), file manager (Dolphin), program manager, and desktop and panel (Plasma). You can run any desktop application, such as Firefox, in KDE, as well as any GNOME application. In turn, you can run any KDE application, including the Dolphin file manager, in GNOME. The KDE 4 desktop features the Plasma desktop shell with a new panel, menus, and widgets and includes a dashboard function. Keyboard shortcuts are provided for many desktop operations, as well as for the plasmoid tasks (see Table 10-2).

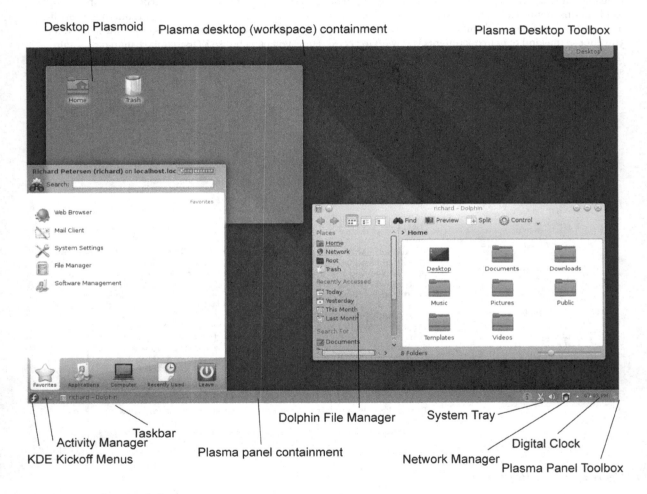

Figure 10-3. *The KDE desktop*

The desktop supports drag-and-drop and copy-and-paste operations. With the copy-and-paste operation, you can copy text from one application to another. You can place access to any directories on the desktop by simply dragging their icons from a file manager window to the desktop. A small menu will appear with options for Folder View or Icon. To create just an icon on the desktop, select the Icon entry. The Folder View option sets up a Folder View plasmoid for the folder, similar to the Desktop Folder shown in Figure 10-3. Items in the folder are displayed within the folder plasmoid as a menu from which you can make a selection.

To configure your desktop, you use the Workspace Appearance and Behavior tools in the System Settings dialog (Favorites ➤ System Settings). These include Workspace Appearance, Desktop Effects, Desktop Search, Default Applications, Accessibility, and Window Behavior. Workspace Appearance lets you choose themes and window decorations. Desktop Effects is where you set window effects and animation. The windows Behavior tool controls window display features such as task bars, virtual desktops, title bar actions, and screen edge actions. Fonts and Icons are set in the Applications Appearance dialog located in the Common Appearance and Behavior section.

Desktop Backgrounds (Wallpaper)

The background (wallpaper) is set from the desktop menu directly, not from the System Settings window. Right-click the desktop background to display the desktop menu and then select Desktop Activity Settings to open the Desktop Settings dialog (see Figure 10-4). The background is called wallpaper in KDE and can be changed from the View tab. You can select other wallpaper from the wallpaper listing or select your own image by clicking the Open button. Initially, you will have only the Ethais KDE default wallpaper. You can add more wallpaper by clicking the Get New Wallpapers button to open a Get Hot New Stuff dialog, which lists and downloads wallpaper posted on the www.kde-look.org site (see Figure 10-5). Each wallpaper entry shows an image, description, and rating. Buttons at the upper right of the dialog let you view the entries in details (list) mode or icon mode. Click the Install button to download the wallpaper and add it to your desktop setting's Wallpaper tab. The wallpaper is downloaded, and the Install button changes to Uninstall. You can refine your selection by size (category), newest, rating, and popularity (most downloads). To remove wallpaper, you can select installed wallpapers to find the entry quickly. You can also search by pattern for a wallpaper, such as baseball or sky.

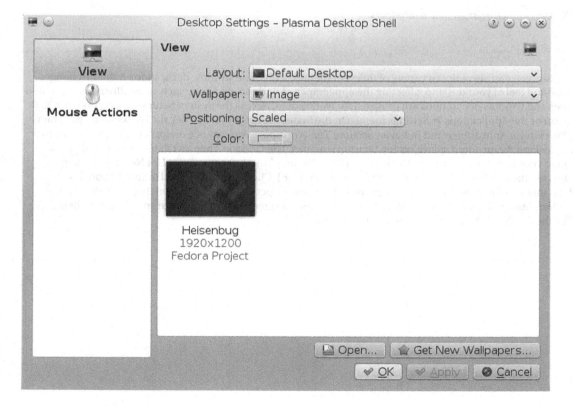

Figure 10-4. Desktop settings: Wallpaper

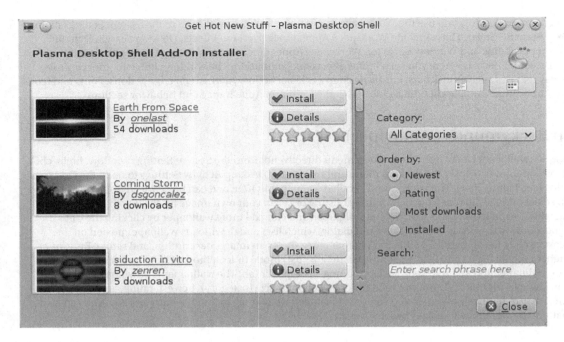

Figure 10-5. *Desktop settings: get new wallpapers*

Themes

For your desktop, you can also select a variety of different themes, icons, and window decorations A theme changes the entire look and feel of your desktop, affecting the appearance of desktop elements, such as scrollbars, buttons, and icons. Themes and window decorations are provided for workspaces. Access the System Settings dialog from the KDE Favorites menu or the Applications ➤ Settings menu. On the System Settings dialog, click the Workspace Appearance icon in the Workspace Appearance and Behavior section. The Workspace Appearance dialog lets you choose window decorations, desktop themes, and splash screen (startup) themes. The Desktop Themes tab lists installed themes, allowing you to choose the one you want. Click the Get New Themes button to open a Get Hot New Stuff dialog. It lists the desktop themes from www.kde-look.org (see Figure 10-6). Click a theme's Install button to download and install the theme. From the Window Decorations tab, you can select window decoration themes. Click the Get New Decorations button to download new decorations. The Splash Screen tab lists installed splash screen themes to choose. Click the Get New Themes button to install new ones.

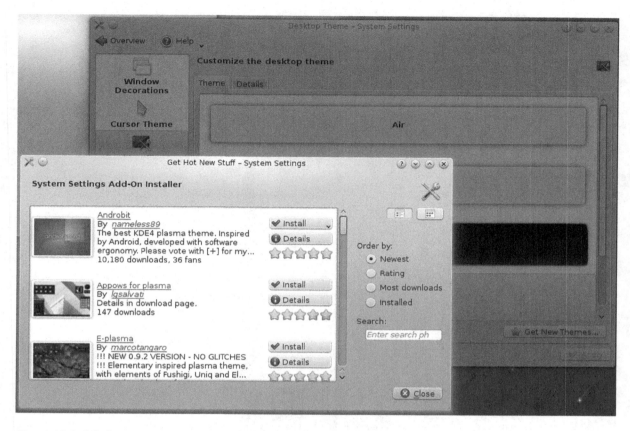

Figure 10-6. *Workspace Appearance ➤ Desktop Themes tab*

You can choose icon styles using Applications Appearance in the System Settings dialog's Common Appearance and Behavior section. Choose System Settings ➤ Applications Appearance. From the Icons tab, you can select an icon set or click the Get New Themes button to download new sets.

Leaving KDE

To leave KDE, you first click the Leave tab on the KDE Kickoff menu (see Figure 10-7). Here you will find options such as log out, lock, switch user, sleep, hibernate, restart, and shut down. There are Session and System sections. The Session section has entries for log out, lock, and switch user. The System section features system-wide operations, including shut down, restart, sleep, and hibernate. When you select a Leave entry, a dialog for that action appears on the desktop, which you then click. The Shutdown entry displays a Shutdown dialog.

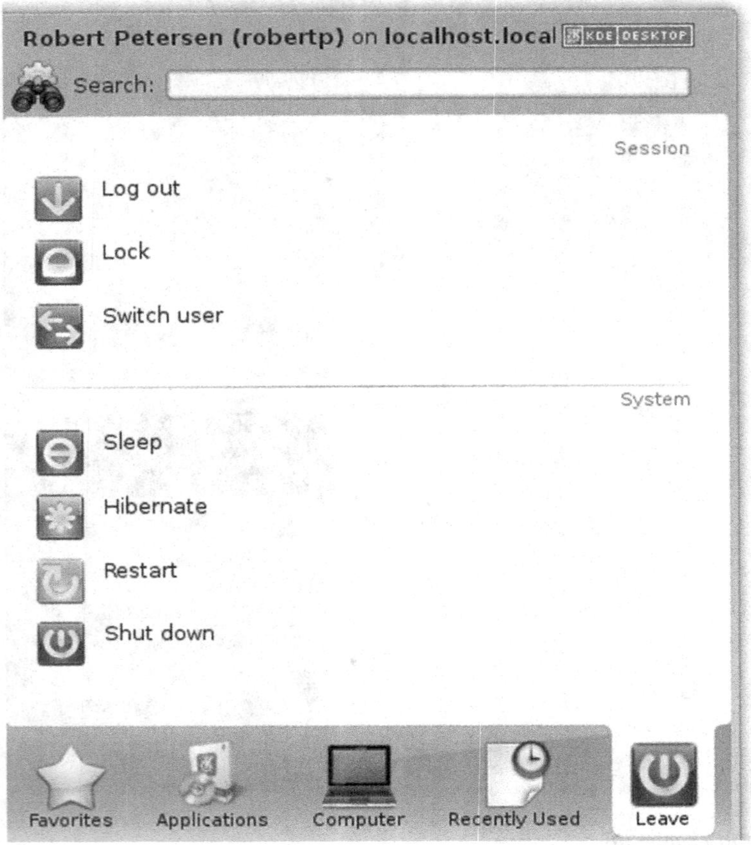

Robert Petersen (robertp) on localhost.local
KDE DESKTOP
Search:
Session
Log out
Lock
Switch user
System
Sleep
Hibernate
Restart
Shut down
Favorites
Applications
Computer
Recently Used
Leave

Figure 10-7. *The Kickoff menu: Leave option*

You can also right-click anywhere on the desktop and select the Leave entry from the pop-up menu (see Figure 10-8). If you leave any KDE applications or windows open when you quit, they are automatically restored when you start up again. If you just want to lock your desktop, you can select the Lock entry on the Kickoff Leave menu, and your screen saver will appear. To access a locked desktop, click on the screen, and a box appears that prompts you for your login password. When you enter the password, your desktop reappears.

Logging out in 28 seconds.
Logout
Turn Off Computer
Restart Computer
Cancel

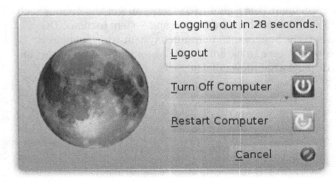

Figure 10-8. *The desktop menu: Leave option*

KDE Kickoff and QuickAccess Menus

The Kickoff application launcher (see Figure 10-9) organizes menu entries into tabs that are accessed by icons at the bottom of the Kickoff menu. There are tabs for Favorites, Applications, Computer, Recently Used, and Leave. You can add an application to the Favorites tab by right-clicking the application's Kickoff entry and selecting Add to Favorites. To remove an application from the Favorites menu, right-click it and select Remove from Favorites. The Applications tab shows application categories. Click the Computer tab to open a window with all your fixed and removable storage. The Recently Used tab shows recently accessed documents and applications. Kickoff also provides a Search box in which you can search for a particular application, instead of paging through menus. As you enter a submenu, a link for it is displayed below the search box, to the right. As you progress through submenus, they are listed here as links. You can move back to a previous menu directly by clicking on its link.

Figure 10-9. *The Kickoff menu: Favorites option*

To configure KDE, you use the KDE System Settings referenced by the System Settings item in the Favorites, Computer, or Applications ➤ Settings tabs.

The Computer menu has Applications and Places sections. The Applications section has an entry for System Settings. The Places section is similar to the Places menu in GNOME, with entries for your home folder, root folder, and the trash, as well as entries for removable devices such as USB drives and DVD/CDs.

The Applications menu has most of the same entries as those found on GNOME. The entries have been standardized for both interfaces (see Figure 10-10). You can find entries for categories such as Internet, Graphics, and Office. These menus list both GNOME and KDE applications you can use. However, some of the KDE menus contain entries for alternate KDE applications, such as KMail on the Internet menu. Other entries invoke the KDE version of a tool, such as the Terminal entry in the System menu, which invokes the KDE terminal window, KConsole.

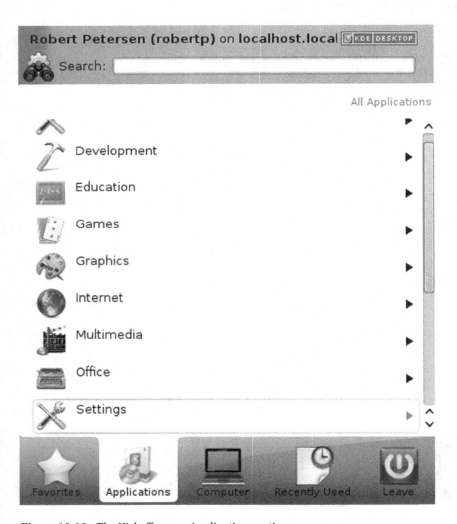

Figure 10-10. *The Kickoff menu: Applications option*

Krunner

For fast access to applications, bookmarks, contacts, and other desktop items, you can use Krunner. Krunner can even search bookmarks on the Marble atlas application. The Krunner plasmoid operates as a search tool for applications and other items. To find an application, enter a search pattern. A listing of matching applications is displayed.

Click an application entry to start the application. When you know the name of the application, part of the name, or just its basic topic, Krunner is a very fast way to access the application. To start Krunner, press Alt+F2, or right-click the desktop to display the desktop menu and select Run Command. Enter the pattern for the application you want to search for and press Enter. The patterns software and package would both display an entry for the Apper software manager. Entering the pattern office displays entries for all the LibreOffice.org applications (see Figure 10-11).

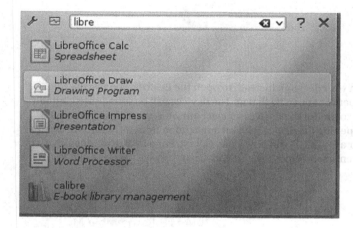

Figure 10-11. *Krunner application search*

Removable Devices: Device Notifier

Installed on the system tray to the right is the Device Notifier. When you insert a removable device such as a DVD/CD or a USB drive, the New Device Notifier briefly displays a dialog showing all your removable devices, including the new one. The Device Notifier icon is displayed on the system tray. You can click the New Device Notifier any time to display this dialog. Figure 10-12 shows the New Device Notifier displayed on the panel and its applet icon. The New Device Notifier is displayed only when at least one removable device is attached.

Figure 10-12. *Device Notifier and its panel plasmoid icon*

Removable devices are not displayed as icons on your desktop. Instead, to open the devices, you use the New Device Notifier. Click the Device Notifier icon in the panel to open its dialog. The devices will be unmounted initially with an unmount button displayed. Click this button to mount the device. An eject button is then displayed, which you can later use to unmount and eject the device. Opening the device with an application from its menu will mount the device automatically. Clicking the eject button for a DVD/CD will physically eject it. For a USB drive, the drive will be unmounted and prepared for removal. You can then safely remove the USB drive.

Click the device you want to open, such as your DVD/CD or your USB drive. If there is more than one application that can use this device, then a menu is displayed showing the options. For a DVD/CD, you have the options to open the disk with the file manager, copy it with the K3b application, or download photos from it with Gwenview (see Figure 10-12).

You can open a USB drive with the file manager, showing its contents. As you install more applications that can use a device, the applications will be added to the menu. Removable media will also be displayed on the file manager window's side pane. You can choose to eject removable media from the file manager instead of from the Device Notifier by right-clicking the removable media entry and selecting Safely Remove from the pop-up menu.

Network Manager

On KDE, the Network Manager plasma widget provides panel access for Network Manager. This is the same Network Manager application, but it has been adapted to the KDE 4 interface. Clicking the plasmoid icon in the panel opens a widget listing your current available connections (see Figure 10-13).

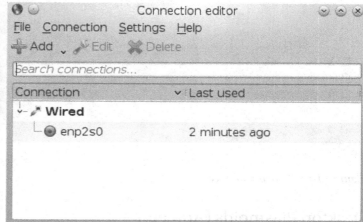

Figure 10-13. *Network connections*

To configure your connections manually, click the wrench button in the lower right to open the Connection editor, which lists your connections. To open the Network Manger editor for KDE, with the same General, Wired, Security, and IPv tabs for a wired or wireless connection, click the connection and then click the Edit button on the toolbar (see Figure 10-14). To add a new connection manually, click the Add button on the Connection editor to display a menu for different connection types.

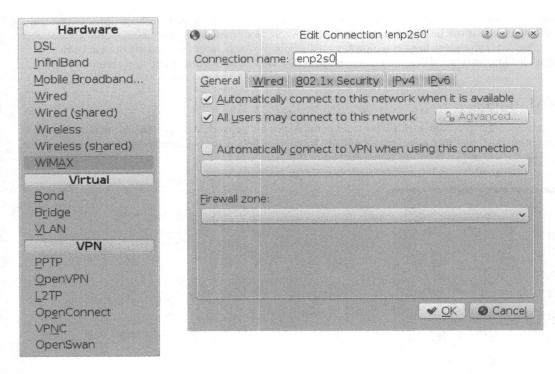

Figure 10-14. *Network Connections dialog*

Desktop Plasmoids (Applets)

The KDE 4 desktop features the Plasma desktop, which treats appletsdifferently. Plasma designates its applets as plasmoids. It is designed to deal with plasmoids on the same level as windows and icons. Just as a desktop can display windows, it can also display plasmoids. Plasmoids, or applets, are taking on more responsibility in desktop operations, running essential operations, even replacing, to a limited extent, the need for file manager windows. To this end, the dashboard tool can hide all other desktop items, showing just the plasmoids. When you first log in, your desktop will show one plasmoid, the Desktop folder view plasmoid (see Figure 10-15).

Figure 10-15. *Initial Fedora KDE screen, with Desktop folder, desktop menu, and desktop toolbox menu*

Managing Desktop Plasmoids

When you pass your mouse over a plasmoid, its sidebar is displayed with buttons for resizing, refreshing, settings, and closing the plasmoid. (See Figure 10-16 for the Clock plasmoid.) Click and drag the resize button to change the plasmoid size. Clicking the settings button (wrench icon) opens that plasmoid's settings dialog (see Figure 10-17).

Figure 10-16. *Clock plasmoid with task sidebar*

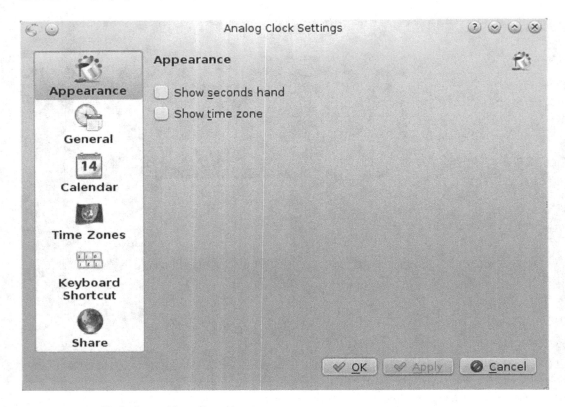

Figure 10-17. *Clock plasmoid configuration*

To add a widget (plasmoid) to the desktop, right-click anywhere on the desktop and select Add Widgets from the pop-up menu or choose Add Widgets from the desktop plasma toolbox menu in the upper-right corner (see Figure 10-15). This opens the Add Widgets dialog across the bottom of the desktop. It lists widgets you can add (see Figure 10-18). The Categories menu lets you see different widget categories such as Date and Time, Online Services, and Graphics. To move through them, use the bottom scrollbar, or the arrow buttons at the edges. Double-click a widget to add it to the desktop. As you pass over a widget, a dialog appears showing information about it.

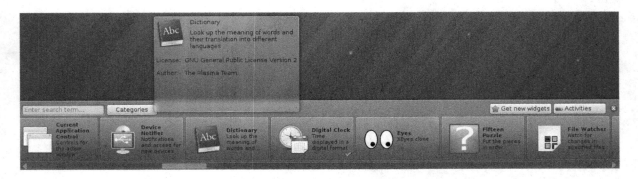

Figure 10-18. *Adding a plasmoid: Add Widgets*

The Desktop Folder, Digital Clock, Leave a Note, Calculator, and Folder View plasmoids are shown in Figure 10-19. The Desktop Folder plasmoid is just a folder view plasmoid set to the desktop folder. When you add a Folder View plasmoid, it will default to your home folder.

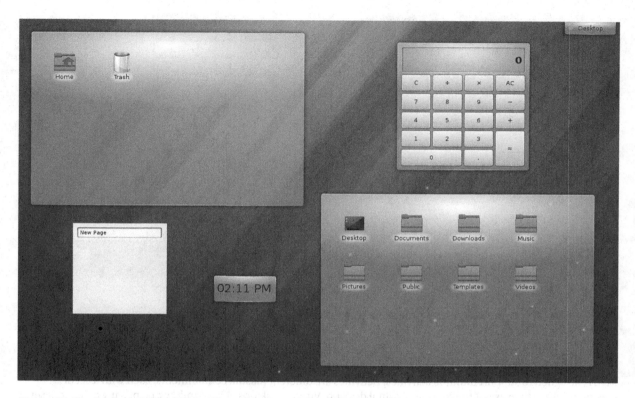

Figure 10-19. *Desktop Folder, Folder View, Calculator, Digital Clock, and Leave a Note plasmoids*

Dashboard

The dashboard is designed to display plasmoids (applets) only. It hides all windows and icons, showing all your desktop plasmoids. To start the dashboard, press Ctrl+F12. You can also add a Show Widget Dashboard widget to your panel or desktop. When in use, the screen will display the Widget Dashboard label at the top (see Figure 10-20). To return to the desktop, press Ctrl+F12 again or click the close button on the Widget Dashboard label at the top of the screen. Also, any plasmoid that interacts directly with the desktop, such as opening a folder in the folder plasmoid or clicking a desktop icon, will return you to the desktop automatically.

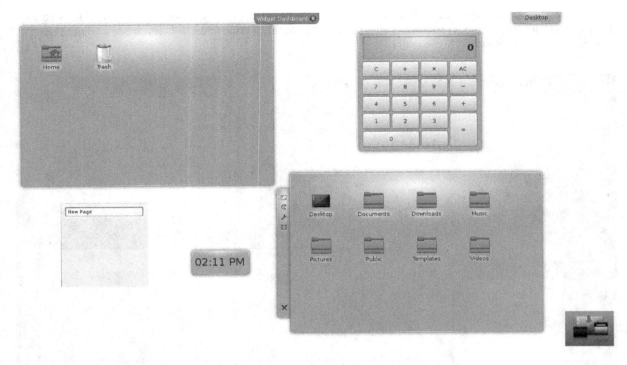

Figure 10-20. *The Dashboard (Ctrl+F12 or Show Widget Dashboard)*

Activities

KDE is designed to support multiple activities. Activities are different plasma containments, each with a set of plasmoids. An activity is not the same as a virtual desktop. Virtual desktops affect windows, displaying a different set of windows on each desktop. An activity has its own set of plasmoids (widgets). Technically, each activity is a Plasma containment that has its own collection of plasmoids. You can switch to a different activity (containment) and display a different collection of plasmoids on your desktop.

An activity is a way to set up a set of widgets (plasmoids) for a certain task. You could have one activity for office work, another for news, and yet another for media. Each activity can have its own set of appropriate widgets, like clock, calculator, dictionary, and document folder for an office activity. A media activity might have a Now Playing plasmoid for audio, Picture Frame for photos, and News for latest news. You can also choose a certain type of activity based on activity templates. KDE provides the desktop, folder view, search and launch, photo layout, and newspaper templates, although you can download more. The desktop template provides a desktop interface; the folder view is a full-screen view of one folder, search and launch displays application and task icons; and the newspaper layout template displays widgets in columns. Your original desktop is already configured as a desktop activity based on the desktop template.

Multiple activities are managed using the Activities toolbar, which is accessed through the Activities entry on the desktop toolbox menu or the Show Activities Manager button on the lower-left side of the panel. Both are shown here:

To add an activity, click the Activities entry in the toolbox or desktop menus, or click the Activities button on the lower-left side of the panel. An activities toolbar is displayed, listing your activities (see Figure 10-21). An activity icon for your desktop will already be displayed. Click the Create Activity button to add a new activity. From the pop-up menu, you can choose an empty desktop, a clone of the current activity, or from templates of different kinds of activities: Newspaper Layout, Folder View, Photos Activity, and Search and Launch. The Get New Templates entry lets you download additional templates. A New Activity icon then appears on the activity toolbar (see Figure 10-21). To switch to another activity, click its icon.

Figure 10-21. *Activity toolbar and icons*

Initially, an activity's name is New Activity. To change the name, click the configuration button (wrench icon) to the right of the icon, as shown here:

The activity editing mode displays the icon and the name and lets you edit the activity name, with Apply and Cancel buttons to the right (see Figure 10-22). To change the icon image, click the icon to open a Select Icon dialog from which you can choose an image. Once you have made your changes, click the Apply button.

Figure 10-22. *Changing an activity*

To add widgets to an activity, first click the activity to make it the current one, then click the Add Widgets button to display the Widgets toolbar. Widgets you add are placed in the current activity.

To disable (stop) an activity, click its Stop button to the right of its activity icon (a small white square next to the wrench icon). A Delete button with a red x is displayed to the right, and a Play button appears in the center of the icon, as shown in the following illustration. To reactivate the activity, click the Play button.

When you stop an activity, a Play button appears on the activity icon, and a Delete button appears to the right, with a red x. To remove an activity, first make sure it is stopped, then click the Delete button to the right. A Remove dialog appears with a Remove button, which you can click to remove the activity.

To switch from one activity to another, first display the Activities toolbar by choosing Activities from the desktop toolbox menu (right-click the desktop) or the Activities button on the panel. Then click the activity icon you want (see Figure 10-23). The new activity becomes your screen (see Figure 10-24). To change to another activity, open the Activities toolbar again and click the activity icon you want. Your original desktop is the first icon.

Figure 10-23. *Activity icons*

Figure 10-24. *Activity toolbar and screen of selected activity*

A Folder View activity functions like a file manager window, displaying a particular folder on the desktop. To configure a Folder View activity, right-click to display the desktop menu and choose Folder View Settings to display the Desktop Settings dialog. Icons are added for Location, Display, and Filter. On the Location tab, you can display the desktop folder, a place like the Home folder, or a folder of your choosing. On the Display tab, you set display features such as arrangement, sorting, and size. The Filter tab lets you display files of certain types or name patterns.

A Search and Launch activity sets up an interface containing icons for tasks and application groups such as Bookmarks, Contacts, Multimedia, Internet, Graphics, Games, and Office, (see Figure 10-25). To configure a Search and Launch activity, right-click to display the desktop menu and choose Configure Search and Launch to display the Desktop Settings dialog. The Desktop Settings dialog has additional Search plug-ins and Main Menu tabs. On the Main menu, you can add or remove application group and task icons.

Figure 10-25. Activity search and launch

The Newspaper Layout activity simply displays widgets in two columns. To configure a newspaper activity, right-click to display the desktop menu and choose Configure Page. This will display the Desktop Settings dialog.

To move easily between activities, you can add the Activity bar widget, either to the panel or to the desktop. On the panel, the Activity bar displays buttons for each activity. Click to move to a different activity. On the desktop, the Activity bar displays a dialog with an arrow button for moving from one activity to another.

KDE Windows

A KDE window has the same functionality you find in other window managers and desktops. You can resize the window by clicking and dragging any of its corners or sides. A click-and-drag operation on a side extends the window in that dimension, whereas a corner extends height and width at the same time. The top of the window has a title bar showing the name of the window, the program name in the case of applications, and the current directory name for the file manager windows. The active window has the title bar highlighted. To move the window, click the title bar and drag it where you want. Right-clicking the window title bar displays a pop-up menu with entries for window operations, such as closing or resizing the window. The Shade option will roll up the window to the title bar. Within the window, menus, icons, and toolbars for the particular application are displayed.

You can configure the appearance and operation of a window by selecting the Configure Window Behavior entry from the Window menu (right-click the title bar). Here, you can set appearance (Windows); button and key operations (Actions); the focus policy, such as a mouse click on the window or just passing the mouse over it (Focus); and how the window is displayed when moving it (Moving). All these features can also be configured using the System Settings Look & Feel Window Behavior dialog.

Opened windows are shown as buttons on the KDE task bar located on the panel. The task bar shows buttons for the different programs you are running or windows you have open. This is essentially a docking mechanism that lets you change to a window or application by clicking its button. When you minimize a window, it is reduced to its task bar button. You can then restore the window by clicking its task bar button.

To the right of the title bar are three small buttons for minimizing, maximizing, or closing the window (down, up, and x symbols). You can switch to a window at any time by clicking its task bar button. You can also maximize a window by dragging it to the top edge of the screen.

From the keyboard, you can use the Alt+Tab key combination to display a list of current open windows. Holding down the Alt key and sequentially pressing Tab moves you through the list.

A window can be displayed as a tile on one-half of the screen (see Figure 10-26). Another tile can be set up for a different window on the other side of the screen, allowing you to display two windows side by side on the full screen. You can tile a window by dragging it to the side of the screen (over the side edge to the middle of the window). A tile outline will appear. Add a second tile by moving a window to the other side edge, as shown in Figure 10-26. You can add more windows to a tile by moving them to that edge. Clicking on a window's task bar button will display it on its tile.

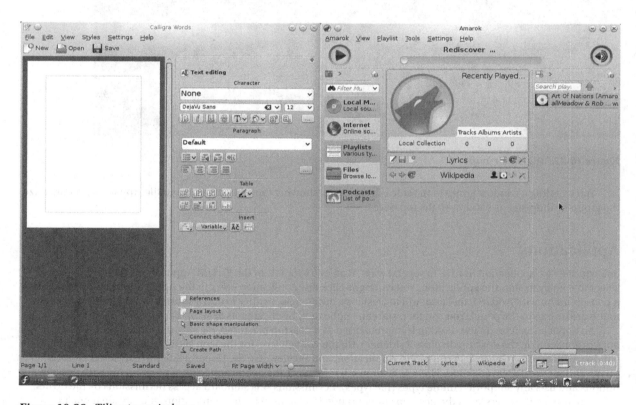

Figure 10-26. *Tiling two windows*

You can also group windows, displaying them as tabs within a single window. To add a window to a group, right-click its title bar and choose the Attach As Tab To option to display a submenu of open windows. Select the one you want to group the window with. The grouped windows are displayed as tabs within a single window. To remove a window from a group, right-click the title bar and select the Untab entry.

You can also add a widow to a group by moving its title bar with the middle mouse button (hold the right and left mouse buttons at once) to the title bar of another window. The title bar will become detached as you move it. Figure 10-27 shows the Amarok, Gwenview, and Calligra Words application windows grouped as tabs into a single window.

Figure 10-27. Window groups

You can drag a window group to the side edge to tile it, showing the tabbed group as a tile. You can also maximize the group by dragging its window to the top edge.

Applications

You can start an application in KDE in several ways. If an entry for it is in the Kickoff Applications menu, you can select that entry to start the application. You can right-click any application entry in the Applications menu to display a pop-up menu with Add to Panel and Add to Desktop entries. Select either to add a shortcut icon for the application to the desktop or to the panel. You can then start an application by clicking its desktop or panel icon.

An application icon on the desktop is implemented as a desktop plasmoid. Passing the mouse over the application icon on the desktop displays a sidebar with the wrench icon for the icon settings. This opens a Setting window with tabs for General, Permissions, Application, and Preview. On the General tab, you can select an icon image and set the displayed name. The Application tab references the actual application program file with possible options and lists any supported mime types (file types). Permissions sets standard access permissions by the owner, group, or others. Preview shows the desktop configuration information for the application, such as the name in various languages, the program name and location, the file name of the icon used for the application, the application's software category, and any comments.

You can also run an application by right-clicking the desktop and selecting Run Command (or pressing Alt+F2), which will display the Krunner tool consisting of a box in which to enter a single command. Previous commands can be accessed from a pop-up menu. You need only enter a pattern to search for the application. Results are displayed in the Krunner window. Choose the one you want.

Virtual Desktops: Desktop Pager

KDE supports virtual desktops, extending the desktop area on which you can work. You can have a web browser running on one desktop and be using a text editor in another. KDE can support up to 16 virtual desktops, although the default is 4. Your virtual desktops can be displayed and accessed using the KDE Desktop Pager. It is not installed by default. Use Add Widgets for the Panel (Panel options menu) to install it. In these examples it is located on the left side of the panel. The KDE Desktop Pager represents your virtual desktops as miniature screens showing small squares for each desktop. It works much like the GNOME Workspace Switcher. On Fedora, by default, there are two squares, one on top of the other. To move from one desktop to another, click the square for the destination desktop. The selected desktop will be highlighted. Just passing your mouse over a desktop image on the panel will open a message displaying the desktop number, along with the windows open on that desktop.

If you want to move a window to a different desktop, first open the window's menu by right-clicking the window's title bar. Then select the To Desktop entry, which lists the available desktops. Choose the one you want.

You can also configure KDE so that if you move the mouse over the edge of a desktop screen, it automatically moves to the adjoining desktop, as if the desktop were arranged next to each. You enable this feature by enabling the Switch Desktop on Edge feature in the System Settings ➤ Window Behavior ➤ Screen Edges tab. This feature also allows you to move windows over the edge to an adjoining desktop.

To change the number of virtual desktops, you right-click the Desktop Pager on the panel and select the Pager Settings entry in the pop-up menu. This opens the Desktop Settings dialog, which displays tabs for General and Virtual Desktops (see Figure 10-28). You can also access the Desktop Settings Virtual Desktop tab from System Settings ➤ Workspace Behavior ➤ Virtual Desktops. By default, the Fedora KDE desktop will set up two virtual desktops for you. On the Desktop Settings dialog's Virtual Desktops ➤ Desktops tab, the text box labeled Number of Desktops controls the number of active desktops. Use the arrows or enter a number to change the number of active desktops. You can change any of the desktop names by clicking an active name and entering a new one. The Switching tab lets you configure animations and shortcuts. Four desktops are shown here:

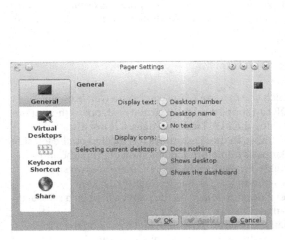
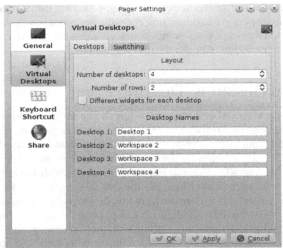

Figure 10-28. Virtual desktop configuration and Pager plasmoid icon

To change how the Pager displays desktops on the panel, use the Pager Settings dialog, General tab. From there, you can configure the Pager to display numbers or names for desktops. You can also decide on the number of rows to use. Choosing just one row will display the desktops side by side, as shown here:

■ **Tip** Use the Ctrl key in combination with a function key to switch to a specific desktop. For example, Ctrl+F1 switches to the first desktop, and Ctrl+F3 switches to the third desktop.

KDE Panel

The KDE panel, located at the bottom of the screen, provides access to most KDE functions (see Figure 10-29). The panel is a specially configured Plasma containment, just as the desktop is a Plasma containment. The panel includes icons for menus, directory windows, specific programs, and virtual desktops. These are plasmoids that are configured for use on the panel. At the left end of the panel is a button for the Kickoff menu, a Fedora *F* icon.

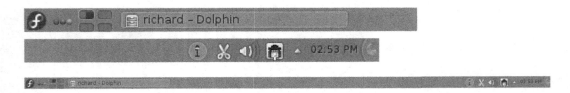

Figure 10-29. KDE panel

To add an application to the panel, right-click its entry in the Kickoff menu, to open a pop-up menu, and select Add to Panel.

To add a widget to the panel, right-click any panel widget on the panel, to open a pop-up menu, and select the Panel Options submenu, from which you can select the Add Widgets entry. This opens the Add Widgets window, which lists the widgets you can add to the panel (see Figure 10-30). A drop-down menu at the top of the window lets you see different widget categories, such as Date and Time, Online Services, and Graphics. You can also see recently used widgets and set up favorite widgets.

Figure 10-30. *KDE Add Widgets for panel*

■ **Note**   To open the Add Widgets dialog, you can click the panel toolbox at the right side of the panel and click the Add Widgets button.

The Plasma panel supports several kinds of windows and tasks widgets, including the task bar, system tray, and pager. The system tray holds widgets for desktop operations such as sound settings (KMix), update notifier, the network manager, the clipboard (Klipper), power (battery) detection, and device notifier (see Figure 10-31). A pop-up menu (arrow icon) on the right side of the system tray displays widgets that do not fit, such as printers and search service. To configure the system tray, right-click the system tray border on the left and choose System Tray Settings. This opens the System Tray Configuration dialog, from which you can decide the items to display or the entries to make visible or remove.

Figure 10-31. *KDE panel plasmoids, including system tray and device notifier*

To the right of the system tray is the digital clock. To the left are widgets such as the notifications and jobs widget (i icon) and any other widgets you may have added. Figure 10-31 shows, from left to right, the show plasma dashboard, notifications and jobs, the system tray (update notifier, clipboard, sound volume, device notifier, Bluetooth, network manager, and pop-up menu for printer and search), and the digital clock.

KDE Panel Configuration

To configure a panel, changing its position, size, and display features, you use the panel's toolbox. The panel toolbox is located at the right side of the panel. Click it to open an additional configuration panel with buttons for adding widgets, moving the panel, and changing its size and position. There is also a More Settings menu for setting visibility and alignment features. Figure 10-32 shows the configuration panel as it will appear on your desktop. Figure 10-33 provides a more detailed description, including the More Settings menu entries.

Figure 10-32. *KDE panel configuration*

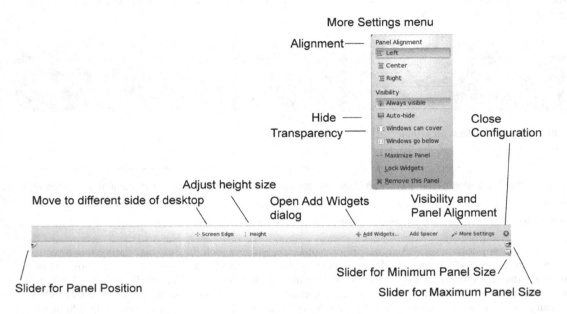

Figure 10-33. *KDE panel configuration details and display features*

With the configuration panel activated, you can move plasmoids around the panel. Clicking a plasmoid will overlay a movement icon, letting you move the plasmoid icon to a different location on the panel.

The lower part of the configuration panel is used for panel position settings. On the left side is a slider for positioning the panel on the edge of the screen. On the right side are two sliders for the minimum (bottom) and maximum (top) size of the panel.

The top part of the panel has a button for changing the location and the size of the panel. The Screen Edge button lets you move the panel to another side of the screen (left, right, top, bottom). Just click and drag. The Height button lets you change the panel size.

The Add Widgets button will open the Add Widgets dialog, which enables you to add new plasmoids to the panel.

The More Settings menu lets you set visibility and alignment features. You can choose an Auto-Hide setting, which will hide the panel until you move the mouse to its location. The Windows Can Cover option lets a window overlap the panel. For smaller panels, you can align to the right, left, or center of the screen edge.

The More Settings menu also has an entry to Remove This Panel. Use this entry to delete a panel you no longer want. When you are finished with the configuration, click the red x icon on the upper-right side.

KWin: Desktop Effects

KWin desktop effects can be enabled on the System Settings Desktop Effects dialog (System Settings ➤ Desktop Effects). The switching effects for windows and desktops can be selected on the Desktop Effects tab. For desktop switching, you can choose Slide, Fade Desktop, and Desktop Cube Animation. The All Effects tab lists all available effects (see Figure 10-34). The more dramatic effects are found in the Windows Management section. Desktop Effects requires the support of a capable graphics chip (GPU).

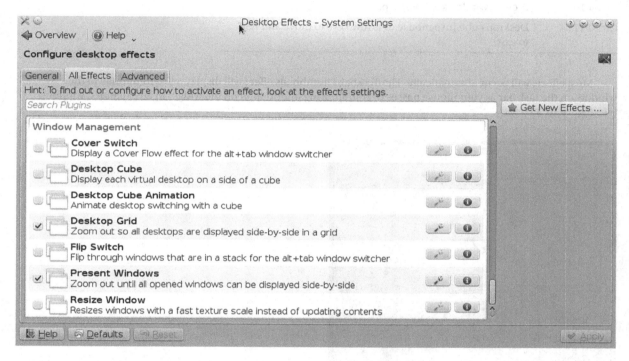

Figure 10-34. *Desktop All Effects selection and configuration*

Window switching using Alt+Tab is controlled on the Windows Behavior dialog's Task Switcher tab, not from Desktop Effects. From the Visualization menu, you can choose effects such as Cover Switch, Flip Switch, Grid, and Thumbnails.

Several windows effects are selected by default, depending on whether your graphics card can support them. A check mark is placed next to active effects. If there is wrench icon in the Effects entry, it means the effect can be configured. Click the icon to open its configuration dialog. For several effects, certain keys must be used to start them. The more commonly used effects are Taskbar Thumbnail, Cover Switch, Desktop Grid, Present Windows, and Desktop Cube. The keys for these effects are listed in Table 10-3.

Table 10-3. *KWin Desktop Effects Keyboard Shortcuts (KWin must be enabled)*

Key	Operation
Alt+Tab	Cover Switch or Box Switch for open windows
Ctrl+F8	Desktop grid (use mouse to select a desktop)
Ctrl+F9	Present windows, current desktop
Ctrl+F10	Present windows, all desktops
Ctrl+F11	Desktop cube (use mouse or arrow keys to move and ESC to exit)

Most effects will occur automatically. The Taskbar Thumbnails effect will display a live thumbnail of the window on the task bar as your mouse passes over it, showing information on the widget in an expanded window (see Figure 10-35).

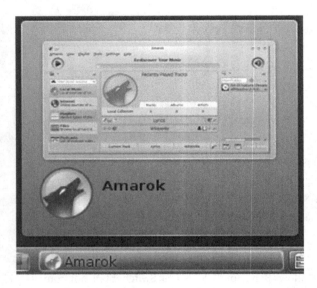

Figure 10-35. *The Taskbar Thumbnails effect, showing thumbnails of minimized applications*

On the Windows Behavior dialog's Task Switcher tab, from the Visualization menu, you can choose from the drop-down menu the window switching effect you want to use. Choices include Thumbnails, Grid, Small Icons, Cover Switch, and Flip Switch, as well as smaller listings, such as informative, compact, text icons, and small icons. The Alt+Tab keys implement the effect you have chosen. Continually pressing the Tab key while holding down the Alt key moves you through the windows. Box Switch displays windows in a boxed dialog; Cover Switch arranges unselected windows stacked to the sides; and Flip Switch arranges the windows to one side (see Figure 10-36).

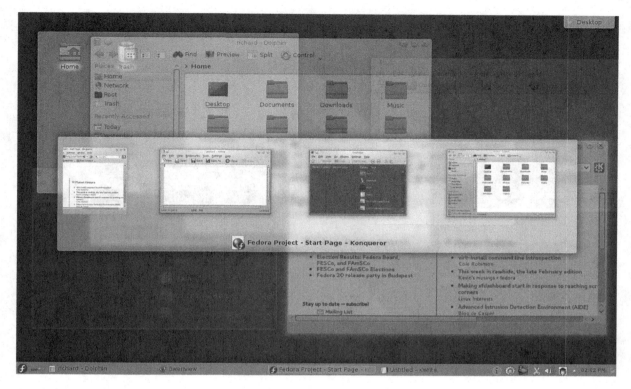

Figure 10-36. *Box Switch using Alt+Tab*

The Present Windows effect displays images of your open windows on your screen, with the selected one highlighted (see Figure 10-37). You can use your mouse to select another. This provides an easy way to browse your open windows. You can also use Ctrl+F9 to display windows on your current virtual desktop statically and use the arrow key to move between them. Use Ctrl+F10 to display all your open windows across all your desktops. Press the ESC key to return to the desktop.

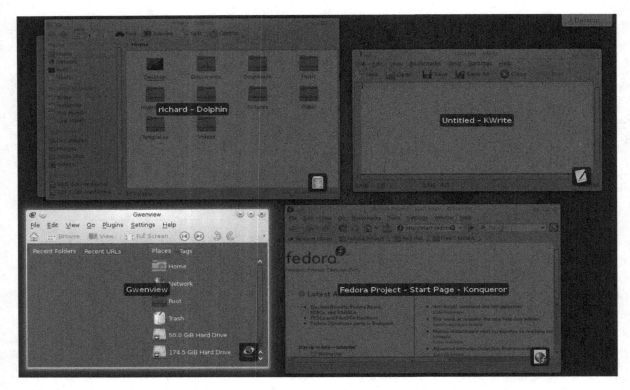

Figure 10-37. *Present Windows (Windows effects) Ctrl+F9 for current desktop and Ctrl+F10 for all desktops*

On the Desktop Effects dialog's All Effects tab, you can enable additional windows management features. Desktop Grid will show a grid of all your virtual desktops (Ctrl+F8), letting you see all your virtual desktops on the screen at once (see Figure 10-38). You can then move windows and open applications between desktops. Clicking a desktop makes it the current one. The plus and minus keys allow you to add or remove virtual desktops.

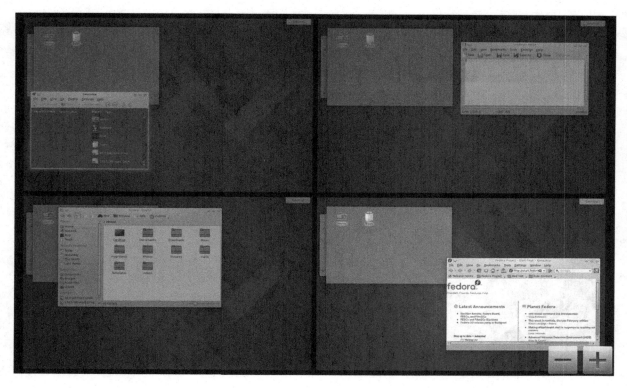

Figure 10-38. *Desktop Grid using Ctrl+F8*

Desktop Cube will show a cube of all your virtual desktops, letting you move to different desktops around a cube (see Figure 10-39). Stop at the side you want to select. Press Ctrl+11 to start the Desktop Cube. You can then move around the cube with the arrow keys or by clicking and dragging your mouse. When you are finished, press the ESC key to return to the desktop.

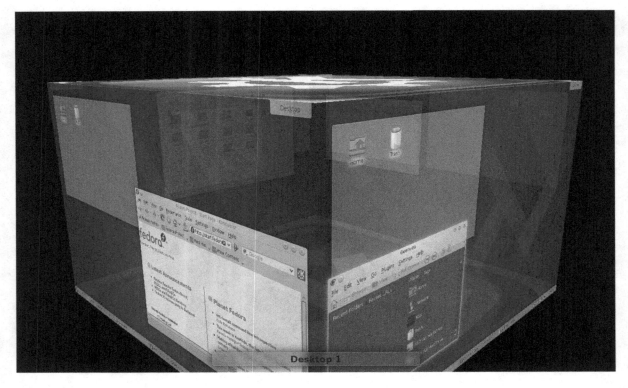

Figure 10-39. *Desktop Cube using Ctrl+F11, drag-mouse, or right/left arrow keys*

Desktop Cube Animation will use cube animation whenever you switch to a different desktop using the Desktop Pager.

KDE File Manager: Dolphin

Dolphinis KDE's dedicated file manager (see Figure 10-40). A navigation bar shows the current directory either in a browser or edit mode. In browser mode, it shows icons for the path of your current directory, and in the edit mode it shows the pathname in a text-editable box. You can use either to move to different folders and their subfolders. Use the Ctrl+l key or click to the right of the folder buttons to use the edit mode. You can also choose Location Bar ➤ Editable Location from the configuration menu (the Ctrl+l key will toggle between the edit and browser modes). Clicking the check mark at the end of the editable text box returns you to the browser mode.

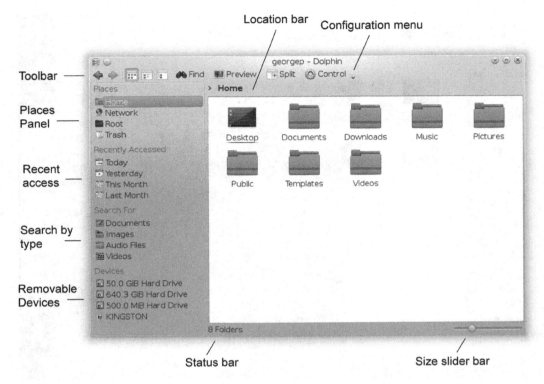

Figure 10-40. *The KDE file manager (Dolphin)*

The Dolphin menu bar is hidden by default and, instead, the menus are displayed when you click the configuration button on the right side of the toolbar (see Figure 10-41). Should you want to use the menu bar instead, from the configuration menu, choose Show Menubar. The Configuration menu button disappears and the menu bar appears with the File, Edit, View, Go, Tools, Settings, and Help menus. To hide the menu bar again, choose Settings ➤ Show Menubar.

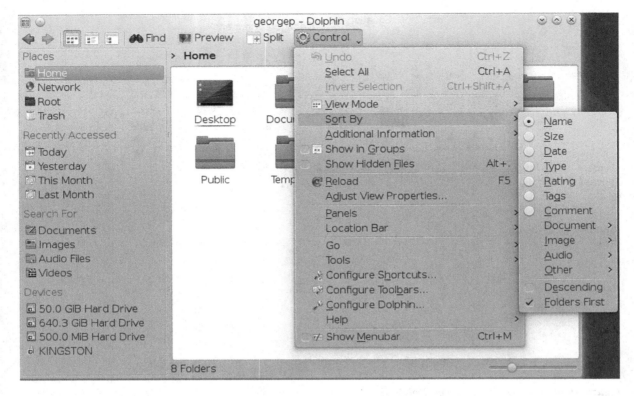

Figure 10-41. *The KDE file manager menus*

You can also sort by metadata such as documents, audio, video, image, time and date, file ratings, and tags. The Custom link in the Time and Date entries opens a calendar, which you can use to select a specific date. The Search Panel works with both the search and filter bars. Before you can use the Search Panel, you must enable Nepomuk file indexing (Nepomuk Indexing Controller on the system tray). Indexing is resource intensive, and can degrade performance on smaller systems and laptops.

You can open a file either by clicking it or by right-clicking it and choosing the Open With submenu to list applications to open it with. If you want to select the file or folder, you have to hold down the Ctrl key while you click it. A single click will open the file. If the file is a program, that program starts up. If it is a data file, such as a text file, the associated application is run using that data file. Clicking a text file displays it with the Kate editor, while clicking an image file displays it with the Gwenview image viewer. Selecting a DEB package opens it with the Muon Software Center, which you can then use to install the package. If you want to use a double-click instead, to open a file or folder, you can set the double-click option on the Dolphin Preferences dialog, Navigation tab (Configure Dolphin in the configuration menu).

If Dolphin cannot determine the application to use, it opens a dialog box prompting you to enter the application name. You can click the Browse button to use a directory tree to locate the application program you want.

Dolphin can display panels to either side (Dolphin refers to these as *panels*, although they operate more like standalone tabs). The Places panel will show icons for often-used folders such as Home, Network, and Trash, as well as removable devices. To add a folder to the Places panel, just drag it there. The files listed in a folder can be viewed in several ways, such as icons, detailed listing (Details), and columns (View Mode menu). See Table 10-4 for the keyboard shortcuts.

Table 10-4. *KDE File Manager Keyboard Shortcuts*

Keys	Description
Alt+left arrow, Alt+right arrow	Go backward and forward in history
Alt+up arrow	One directory up
Enter	Open a file/directory
Left/right/up/down arrows	Move among the icons
PageUp, PageDown	Scroll quickly
Ctrl+c	Copy selected file to clipboard
Ctrl+v	Paste files from clipboard to current directory
Ctrl+s	Select files by pattern
Ctrl+l	Text box location bar
Ctrl+f	Find files
Ctrl+q	Close window

The Additional information submenu in the Control menu (or View menu) lets you display additional information about files, such as the size, date, type, and comments. Type-specific information can also be displayed, such as album, track, and duration for audio files, and word and line counts for documents. You can also display the full path, permissions, and group information (Other submenu).

You can display additional panels by selecting them from the configuration menu's Panels submenu (see Figure 10-42). The Information panel displays detailed information about a selected file or folder, and the Folders panel displays a directory tree for the file system. The panels are detachable from the file manager window. Be sure to choose Unlock Panels to make the panels in the Panels menu detachable.

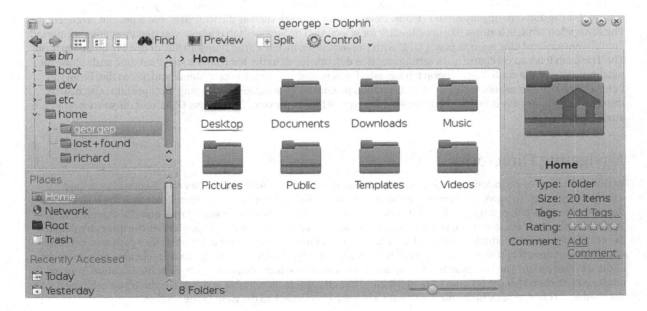

Figure 10-42. *The KDE file manager, with sidebars attached and detached*

Dolphin supports split views, where you can open two different folders in the same window. Click the Split button in the toolbar. You can then drag folders and files from one folder to the other (see Figure 10-43).

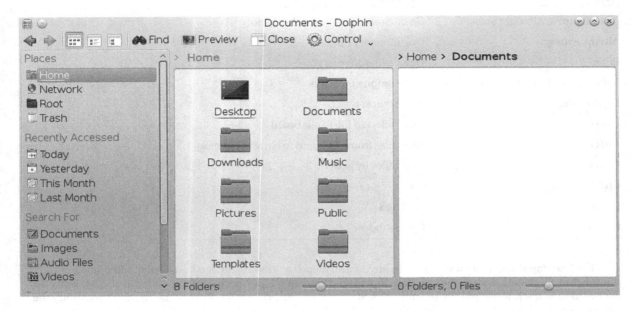

Figure 10-43. *The KDE file manager with split views*

To configure Dolphin, click Configure Dolphin from the configuration menu. This opens the Dolphin Preferences dialog with tabs for Startup, View Modes, Navigation, Services, Trash, and General. On the Startup tab, you can specify features such as the split view and the default folder to start up with. On the View Modes tab, you can set display features for the different display modes (Icons, Details, and Column), such as the icon size, font type, and arrangement. The Navigation tab sets features like double-click for selection. The Services tab is where you specify actions supported for different kinds of files, such as play a DVD with DragonPlayer, install a TrueType font file, or display tiff image files. The Trash tab lets you configure trash settings such as deleting items in the trash after a specified time and setting the maximum size of the trash. The General tab has tabs for Behavior, Preview, Context Menu, and Status Bar. From the Behavior tab you can enable tooltips, set confirmation prompts for file deletion or closing multiple tabs, and display the selection marker. Preview lets you choose which type of files to preview. The image, JPEG, and directories types are already selected.

Navigating Directories

Within a file manager window, a single click on a directory icon moves to that directory and displays its file and subdirectory icons. To move back up to the parent directory, click the back arrow button located on the left end of the navigation toolbar. A single click on a directory icon moves you down the directory tree, one directory at a time. By clicking the back arrow button, you move up the tree. The Navigation bar can display either the directory path for the current folder or an editable location box where you can enter a pathname. For the directory path, you can click any displayed directory name to move you quickly to an upper level folder. To use the location box, click to the right of the directory path. The Location box is displayed. You can also select Location Bar ➤ Editable Location from the configuration menu (or press Ctrl+l). The navigation bar changes to an editable text box, in which you can type a pathname. To change back to the directory path, click the check mark to the right of the text box.

As with a web browser, the file manager remembers the previous directories it has displayed. You can use the back and forward arrow buttons to move through this list of prior directories. You can also use several keyboard shortcuts to perform operations, such as pressing Alt+back arrow to move up a directory and the arrow keys to move to different icons.

Copy, Move, Delete, Rename, and Link Operations

To perform an operation on a file or directory, you first have to select it by clicking the file's icon or listing. To select more than one file, hold down the Ctrl key while you click the files you want. You can also use the keyboard arrow keys to move from one file icon to another.

To copy and move files, you can use the standard drag-and-drop method with your mouse. To copy a file, you locate it by using the file manager. Open another file manager window to the directory to which you want the file copied. Then drag and drop the File icon to that window. A pop-up menu appears with selections for Move Here, Copy Here, or Link Here. Choose Copy Here. To move a file to another directory, follow the same procedure, but select Move Here from the pop-up menu. To copy or move a directory, use the same procedure as for files. All the directory's files and subdirectories are also copied or moved. Instead of having to select from a pop-up menu, you can use the corresponding keys: Ctrl for copy, Shift for move, and Ctrl+Shift for link—same as for GNOME.

To rename a file, Ctrl-click its icon and press F2, or right-click the icon and select Rename from the pop-up menu. A dialog opens in which you can enter the new name for the file or folder.

You delete a file either by selecting it and deleting it or placing it in the Trash folder to delete later. To place a file in the Trash folder, drag and drop it to the Trash icon on your desktop, or right-click the file and choose Move To Trash from the pop-up menu. You can later open the Trash folder and delete the files. To delete all the files in the Trash folder, right-click the Trash icon in Dolphin file manager sidebar and select Remove Trash from the pop-up menu. To restore files in the Trash bin, open the Trash window and right-click the file to restore and select Restore.

Each file or directory has properties associated with it that include permissions, the filename, and its directory. To display the Properties dialog for a given file, right-click the file's icon and select the Properties entry. On the General tab, you can see the name of the file. To change the file name, replace the name with a new one. Permissions are set on the Permissions tab. Here, you can set read, write, and execute permissions for user, group, or other. The Group entry enables you to change the group for a file.

Search Bar and Filter Bar

KDE has combined the former KFind and Dolphin search tools into one simplified search bar. KDE also supports a filter bar to search files and folders in the current folder. You can also use the Filter Panel to refine searches by metadata, such as type, date, ratings, and tags.

Search Bar

To search for files, click the Find button on the icon bar to open the search bar, which displays a search text box. You can also choose Find from the Edit menu, or press Ctrl+f. The search bar displays a search text box, in which you enter the pattern of the file or folder you are searching for. Click the red x button to the left to close the find bar, and use the black x button in the text box to clear the search pattern.

Buttons below the search box provide options to qualify the search. The Filename button (the default) searches on the file name. The Content button searches the contents of text files for the pattern. The From Here button searches the user's home folders, and the Everywhere button (the default) searches the entire file system (see Figure 10-44).

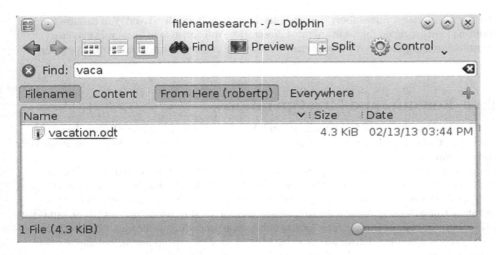

Figure 10-44. *The KDE search bar*

The search results are displayed in the main pane. You can click a file to have it open with its appropriate application. Text files are displayed by the Kate text editor; images are viewed by Gwenview; and applications are run. The search program also enables you to save your search results for later reference (click the Save button to the right). When you are finished searching, click the Close button.

When you pass your mouse over an icon listed in the Query Results dialog, information about it is displayed on the information panel to the right. Links are shown for adding tags and comments. Right-clicking this panel lets you open a Configure dialog, where you can specify what information to display.

The search operation makes use of the KDE implementation of Nepomuk Semantic Desktop's metadata indexing, a powerful desktop indexer that makes use of file information, user tags and comments on the file, and file usage associations like the e-mail used to send a file as an e-mail attachment. The Nepomuk project aims to implement a semantic desktop, organizing desktop information so it can be accessed easily and shared collaboratively.

To manage the Nepomuk file indexing, open the Nepomuk Indexing Controller from the system tray. You can choose to resume or suspend indexing. To configure Nepomuk, choose System Settings ➤ Workspace Appearance and Behavior ➤ Desktop Search (you can also choose Configure File Indexing from the Nepomuk system tray entry). This opens the Desktop Search control module, with tabs for Basic Settings, Desktop Query, Backup, and Advanced Settings. On the Basic Settings tab, you can enable the Strigi desktop search, which can search files by content.

Filter Bar

For a quick search of the current folder, you can activate the Filter bar (choose Tools ➤ Show Filter Bar or Ctrl+i), which opens a Filter search box at the bottom of the window (be sure to show the menubar). Enter a pattern, and only those file and directory names containing that pattern are displayed. Click the x button at the right of the Filter box to clear it (see Figure 10-45).

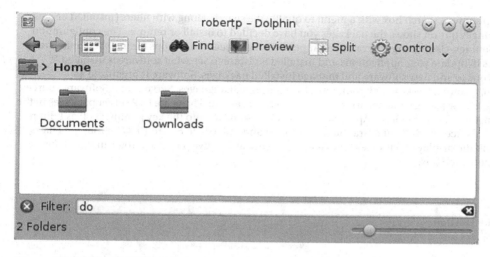

Figure 10-45. *The KDE filter bar*

KDE Software Management: Apper

For software management, you can use *Apper*, the new KDE software management application. This replaces the older KPackageKit software manager. You can access Apper from Applications ➤ Administration ➤ Software Management. The Apper dialog shows a toolbar and two sections of icons—Lists and Categories (see Figure 10-46).

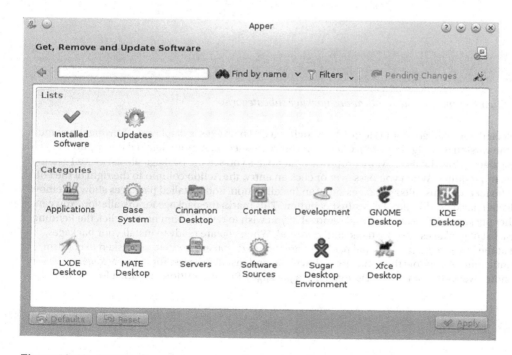

Figure 10-46. *Apper software manager: package categories*

The toolbar at the top shows a search box with a menu to qualify the search, along with filters (installed or new packages). A Pending Changes button shows the packages you have decided to install or remove. The configuration button lists History and Settings. Use Settings to configure Apper. The Lists section has icons for Installed Software and Updates. Use Updates to update your applications and Installed Software to see what software is installed.

Use the Categories icons to add new software and manage installed packages. Software is organized as Applications, Base System, Content, Desktop Environments, Development, Languages, Servers, and Software Sources. Clicking an icon opens a window listing subcategories for that topic. You can quickly locate FTP server packages in the Servers window by clicking the FTP Server icon. Applications organizes software into the key groups, such as Editors, Games and Entertainment, Office/Productivity, Graphics, and Sound and Video (see Figure 10-47). From the Filters menu, you can further limit the display of packages for installed, newest, and native packages. You can search for packages directly using the search box.

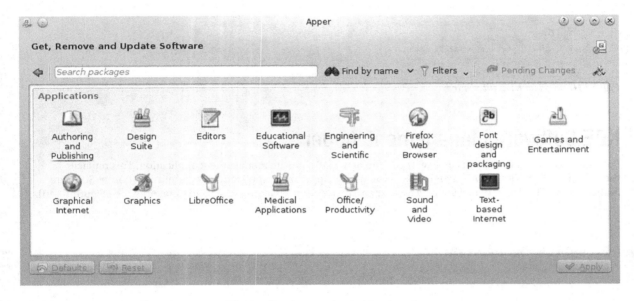

Figure 10-47. Apper software manager: The Applications package subcategories

Once you have selected a subcategory or performed a search, a list of packages is displayed, showing the name, brief description, and the version (see Figure 10-48). Click on an entry to select it. A more detailed description of the selected package appears below the list. A More drop-down menu lets you see the package file list as well as the packages it depends on and requires. When you pass over or click an entry, the Action column to the right of the entry shows what action can be taken. Uninstalled packages show an Install button, and installed packages show a Remove button. To install a selected package, double-click its Install button. This marks the package for installation. You can continue to choose other packages for installation and removal. If you wish to review your choices, click the Pending Changes button to see a list of packages to be installed and removed. When you are ready to install your packages, click the Apply button at the lower right. If additional packages are required, you are notified and asked to confirm, then queried for authentication. A window then shows the download and install progress for your packages (see Figure 10-49). Removal works the same way. Double-click a package's Remove button to mark it for removal. Then click Apply.

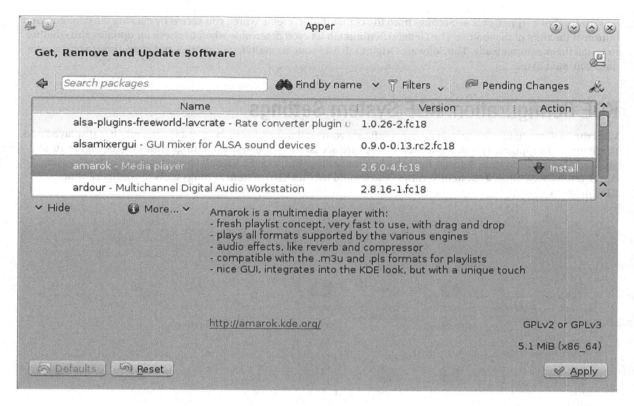

Figure 10-48. *Apper software manager: selected package*

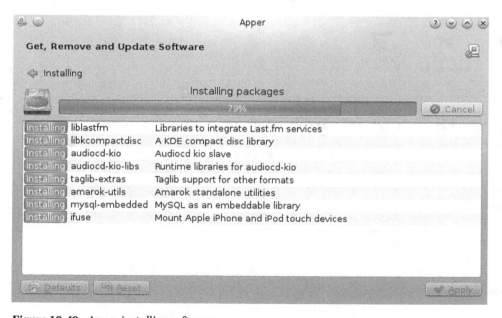

Figure 10-49. *Apper installing software*

To configure Apper, choose Settings from the configuration menu, which you access by clicking the configuration button at the right of the toolbar. The General Settings tab lets you determine when to check for updates and whether to install them automatically. The Software Origins tab lists your accessible repositories and allows you to choose the ones you want to use.

KDE Configuration: KDE System Settings

With the KDE configuration tools, you can configure your desktop and system, changing the way it is displayed and the features it supports. The configuration dialogs are accessed on the System Settings window (see Figure 10-50). You can access this System Settings from the System Settings entry in the Kickoff Favorites menu or by choosing Applications ➤ Settings ➤ System Settings. You should use the KDE System Settings tools to configure your KDE desktop.

Figure 10-50. KDE System Settings

The System Settingswindow shows system dialog icons arranged in several sections: Common Appearance and Behavior, Workspace Appearance and Behavior, Network and Connectivity, Hardware, and System Administration. Click an icon to display a dialog with a sidebar icon list for configuration tabs, with the tabs selected shown on the right. The selected tab may also have tabs (see Figure 10-51).

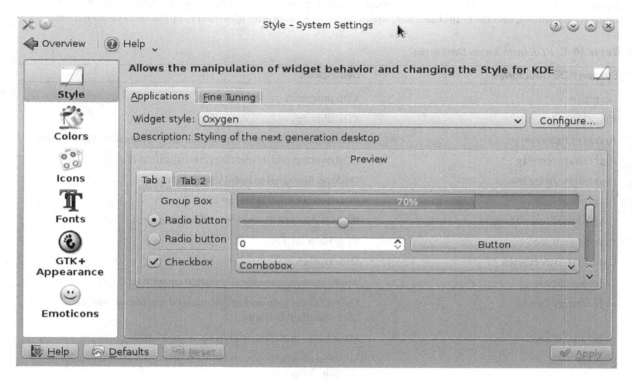

Figure 10-51. *KDE System Settings: Applications Appearance: Style*

The Network and Connectivity section holds icons for configuring the networking, Bluetooth connections, and sharing. The Common Appearance and Behavior section has icons for personal information (About Me), account details, shortcuts, file associations, and your location. Workspace Appearance and Behavior lets you set desktop effects, themes, accessibility, default applications, desktop search, and windows features. System Administration lets you change the settings for user management, the date and time, font management, software management, startup and shutdown (sessions), and login screen (KDM, not GDM). Hardware lets you set the printer configuration, power management, multimedia devices (sound), your display resolution, and information sources.

If you installed KDE as an added desktop, and did not peform a full install of KDE, be sure to install the kdeadmin package to install the KDE task manager (KCron), KUser, and KSystemLog.

Alternatively, you can display the System Settings window using the classic tree format. Click the System Settings Configure button to open the configuration dialog and select Classic Tree from the General tab. Setting sections are displayed as expandable trees on the left pane, with packages for a selected section displayed on the right.

KDE Directories and Files

When KDE is installed on your system, its system-wide application, configuration, and support files may be installed in the same system directories as other desktop and user applications (see Table 10-5). On Fedora, KDE is installed in the standard system directories, with some variations, such as /usr/bin for KDE program files; /usr/lib/kde4, which holds KDE libraries; and /usr/include/kde, which contains KDE header files used in application development.

Table 10-5. *KDE Installation Directories*

System KDE Directories	Description
/usr/bin	KDE programs
/usr/lib/kde4	KDE libraries
/usr/include/kde	Header files for use in compiling and developing KDE applications
/usr/share/config	KDE desktop and application configuration files
/usr/share/mimelnk	Desktop files used to build the main menu
/usr/share/apps	Files used by KDE applications
/usr/share/icons/oxygen	Icons used in KDE desktop and applications
/usr/share/doc	KDE Help system
User KDE Directories	**Description**
.kde/AutoStart	Applications automatically started up with KDE
.kde/share/config	User KDE desktop and application configuration files for user-specified features
.kde/share/apps	Directories and files used by KDE applications
Desktop	Desktop files for icons and folders displayed on the user's KDE desktop
.kde/share/config/plasma--desktop-appletsrc	Plasma applet configuration

The .kde directory holds files and directories used to maintain your KDE desktop. As with GNOME, the Desktop directory holds KDE desktop files whose icons are displayed on the desktop. Configuration files are located in the .kde/share/config directory. Here, you can find the general configuration files for different KDE components—kwinrc holds configuration commands for the window manager, kmailrc for mail, and kdeglobals for keyboard shortcuts and other global definitions. You can place configuration directives directly in any of these files; .kde/share/mimelnk holds the desktop files for the menu entries added by the user. The .kde/share/apps directory contains files and directories for configuring KDE applications, including KMail and Rekonq.

Each user has a Desktop directory that holds KDE link files for all icons and folders on the user's desktop (see Table 10-5). These include the Trash folders and the CD-ROM and home directory links.

The directories located in the share directory contain files used to configure system defaults for your KDE environment (the system share directory is located at /usr/share). The share/apps directory contains files and directories set up by KDE applications; share/config contains the configuration files for particular KDE applications. These are the system-wide defaults that can be overridden by users' own configurations in their own .kde/share/config directories. The share/icons directory holds the default icons used on your KDE desktop and by KDE applications. The user's home directory, the .kde directory, holds a user's own KDE configuration for the desktop and its applications.

CHAPTER 11

■ ■ ■

Shells

The **shell** is a command interpreter that provides a line-oriented interactive and noninteractive interface between the user and the operating system. You enter commands on a command line. They are interpreted by the shell and then sent as instructions to the operating system (interactive). The command-line interface is accessible from GNOME and KDE through a terminal window. You can also place commands in a script file, to be consecutively executed much like a program (non-interactive). This interpretive capability of the shell provides for many sophisticated features. For example, the shell has a set of file-expansion characters that can generate file names. The shell can redirect input and output, as well as run operations in the background, freeing you to perform other tasks.

Several different types of shells have been developed for Linux: the Bourne-Again shell (BASH), the Korn shellthe TCSH shelland the Z shell. All shells are available for your use, although the BASH shell is the default. You need only one type of shell to do your work. Fedora Linux includes all the major shells, although it installs and uses the BASH shell as the default. If you use the command-line shell, you will be using the BASH shell, unless you specify another. This chapter discusses the BASH shell, which shares many of the same features as other shells.

You can find out more about shells at their respective web sites, as listed in Table 11-1. In addition, a detailed online manual is available for each installed shell. Use the man command and the shell's keyword to access them— bash for the BASH shell, ksh for the Korn shell, tsch for the TSCH shell, and zsh for the Z shell. For example, the command man bash will access the BASH shell online manual.

Table 11-1. *Linux Shells*

Shell	Web Site
www.gnu.org/software/bash	BASH web site, with online manual, FAQ, and current releases
www.gnu.org/software/bash/manual/bash.html	BASH online manual
www.zsh.org	Z shell web site, with referrals to FAQ and current downloads
www.tcsh.org	TCSH web site, with detailed support, including manual, tips, FAQ, and recent releases
www.kornshell.com	Korn shell site with manual, FAQ, and references

---

▪ **Note**   You can find out more about the BASH shell at www.gnu.org/software/bash. A detailed online manual is available on your Linux system, using the man command with the bash keyword.

The Command Line

The Linux command-line interface consists of a single line into which you enter commands with any of their options and arguments. From GNOME or KDE, you can access the command-line interface by opening a terminal window (Applications ➤ Accessories ➤ Terminal). Should you start Linux with the command-line interface, you will be presented with a BASH shell command line when you log in.

By default, the BASH shell has a dollar sign ($) prompt, but Linux has several other types of shells, each with its own prompt (such as % for the C shell). The root user will have a different prompt, the #. A shell *prompt,* such as the one shown following, marks the beginning of the command line:

```
$
```

At the prompt, you can enter a command, along with options and arguments. For example, with an -l option, the ls command will display a line of information about each file, listing such data as its size and the date and time it was last modified. In the following example, the user enters the ls command, followed by a -l option. The dash before the -l option is required. Linux uses it to distinguish an option from an argument.

```
$ ls -l
```

If you wanted only the information displayed for a particular file, you could add that file's name as the argument, following the -l option.

```
$ ls -l mydata
-rw-r--r-- 1 chris weather 207 Feb 20 11:55 mydata
```

▪ **Tip**   Some commands can be complex and take some time to execute. If you mistakenly execute the wrong command, you can interrupt and stop it with the interrupt key (press Ctrl+c).

You can enter a command on several lines by typing a backslash (\) just before you press Enter. The backslash "escapes" the Enter key, effectively continuing the same command line to the next line. In the next example, the cp command is entered on three lines. The first two lines end in a backslash, effectively making all three lines one command line.

```
$ cp -i \
mydata \
/home/george/myproject/newdata
```

You can also enter several commands on the same line, by separating them with a semicolon (;). In effect, the semicolon operates as an execute operation. Commands will be executed in the sequence in which they are entered. The following command executes an ls command followed by a date command:

$ **ls ; date**

You can also conditionally run several commands on the same line with the && operator. A command is executed only if the previous command is true. This feature is useful for running several dependent scripts on the same line. In the next example, the ls command runs only if the date command is successfully executed.

$ **date && ls**

■ **Tip** Commands can also be run as arguments on a command line, using their results for other commands. To run a command within a command line, you encase the command in back quotes.

Command-Line Editing

The BASH shell which is your default shell, has special command-line editing capabilities that you may find helpful as you learn Linux (see Table 11-2). You can easily modify commands you have entered before executing them, moving anywhere on the command line and inserting or deleting characters. This is particularly helpful for complex commands.

Table 11-2. *BASH Command-Line Editing Operations*

Movement Command	Operation
Ctrl+f, right-arrow	Moves forward a character
Ctrl+b, left arrow	Moves backward a character
Ctrl+a or Home	Moves to beginning of line
Ctrl+e or End	Moves to end of line
Alt+f	Moves forward a word (not on terminal window)
Alt+b	Moves backward a word
Ctrl+l	Clears screen and places line at top
Editing Command	**Operation**
Ctrl+d or Del	Deletes character cursor is on
Ctrl+h or Backspace	Deletes character before the cursor
Ctrl+k	Cuts remainder of line from cursor position
Ctrl+u	Cuts from cursor position to beginning of line
Ctrl+w	Cuts previous word

(continued)

Table 11-2. (*continued*)

Movement Command	Operation
Ctrl+c	Cuts entire line and starts a new one
Alt+d	Cuts the remainder of a word
Alt+Del	Cuts from the cursor to the beginning of a word
Ctrl+y	Pastes previous cut text
Alt+y	Pastes from set of previously cut text
Ctrl+y	Pastes previous cut text
Ctrl+v	Inserts quoted text; used for inserting control or meta (Alt) keys as text, such as Ctrl-b for backspace or Ctrl-t for tabs
Alt+t	Transposes current and previous word
Alt+l	Lowercases current word
Alt+u	Uppercases current word
Al+-c	Capitalizes current word
Ctrl+Shift+_	Undoes previous change

You can press Ctrl+f or use the right arrow key to move forward a character, or the Ctrl+b or left arrow key to move back a character. Ctrl+d or Del deletes the character the cursor is on, and Ctrl+h or Backspace deletes the character preceding the cursor. To add text, you use the arrow keys to move the cursor to where you want to insert text and type the new characters.

You can even cut words with the Ctrl+w or Alt+d keys and then press the Ctrl+y keys to paste them back in at a different position, effectively moving the words. As a rule, the Ctrl version of the command operates on characters, and the Alt version works on words, such as Ctrl+t to transpose characters, and Alt+t to transpose words. At any time, you can press Enter to execute the command. For example, if you make a spelling mistake when entering a command, rather than reentering the entire command, you can use the editing operations to correct the mistake. The actual associations of keys and their tasks, along with global settings, are specified in the /etc/inputrc file.

The editing capabilities of the BASH shell command line are provided by Readline. Readline supports numerous editing operations. You can even bind a key to a selected editing operation. Readline uses the /etc/inputrc file to configure key bindings. This file is read automatically by your /etc/profile shell configuration file when you log in. Users can customize their editing commands by creating an .inputrc file in their home directory (this is a dot file). It may be best to first copy the /etc/inputrc file as your .inputrc file and then edit it. The /etc/profile will first check for a local .inputrc file before accessing the /etc/inputrc file. You can find out more about Readline in the BASH shell reference manual at www.gnu.org/manual/bash.

Command and Filename Completion

The BASH command line has a built-in feature that performs command and filename completion. Automatic completions can be affected by pressing the Tab key. If you enter an incomplete pattern as a command or file name argument, you can press the Tab key to activate the command and filename completion feature, which completes the pattern. A directory will have a forward slash (/) attached to its name. If more than one command or file has the same prefix, the shell simply beeps and waits for you to press the Tab key again. It then displays a list of possible command completions and waits for you to add enough characters to select a unique command or file name. For situations in which you know multiple possibilities are likely, you can just press the ESC key instead of two Tabs. In the next example, the user issues a cat command with an incomplete file name. When the user presses the Tab key, the system searches for a match and, when it finds one, fills in the file name. The user can then press Enter to execute the command.

```
$ cat pre <tab>
$ cat preface
```

The automatic completions also work with the names of variables, users, and hosts. In this case, the partial text has to be preceded by a special character, indicating the type of name. A listing of possible automatic completions follows:

> File names begin with any text or /.
>
> Shell variable text begins with a $ sign.
>
> Username text begins with a ~ sign.
>
> Hostname text begins with a @.
>
> Commands, aliases, and text in files begin with normal text.

Variables begin with a $ sign, so any text beginning with a dollar sign is treated as a variable to be completed. Variables are selected from previously defined variables, such as system shell variables. Usernames begin with a tilde (~). Hostnames begin with a @ sign, with possible names taken from the /etc/hosts file. For example, to complete the variable HOME given just $HOM, simply press a Tab key.

```
$ echo $HOM <tab>
$ echo $HOME
```

If you entered just an H, then you could press the Tab key twice to see all possible variables beginning with H. The command line is redisplayed, letting you complete the name.

```
$ echo $H <tab> <tab>
$HISTCMD $HISTFILE $HOME $HOSTTYPE HISTFILE $HISTSIZE $HISTNAME
$ echo $H
```

You can also specifically select the kind of text to complete, using corresponding command keys. In this case, it does not matter what kind of sign a name begins with.

For example, the pressing Alts+~ will treat the current text as a username. Pressing Alt+@ will treat it as a hostname, and Alt+$, as a variable. Pressing Alt+! will treat it as a command. To display a list of possible completions, press the Ctrl+x key with the appropriate completion key, as in Ctrl+x+$ to list possible variable completions. See Table 11-3 for a complete listing.

Table 11-3. *Command-Line Text Completion Commands*

Command (Ctrl+r for Listing Possible Completions)	Description
Tab	Automatic completion
Tab Tab or ESC	Lists possible completions
Alt+/, Ctrl+r+/	Filename completion, normal text for automatic
Alt+$, Ctrl+r+$	Shell variable completion, $ for automatic
Alt+~, Ctrl+-r+~	Username completion, ~ for automatic
Alt+@, Ctrl+r+@	Hostname completion, @ for automatic
Alt+!, Ctrl+r+!	Command-name completion, normal text for automatic

History

The BASH shell keeps a history list of your previously entered commands. You can display each command, in turn, on your command line by pressing the up arrow key. Press the down arrow key to move down the list. You can modify and execute any of these previous commands when you display them on the command line. The list of history command is kept in your **.bash_history** file.

■ **Tip** The ability to redisplay a command is helpful when you have already executed a command you had entered incorrectly. In this case, you would be presented with an error message and a new, empty command line. By pressing the up arrow key, you can redisplay the previous command, make corrections to it, and then execute it again. This way, you don't have to enter the whole command again.

History Events

In the BASH shell, the *history* utility keeps a record of the most recent commands you have executed. The commands are numbered, starting at 1, and a limit exists to the number of commands remembered. The default is 500. The history utility is a kind of short-term memory, keeping track of the most recent commands you have executed. To see the set of your most recent commands, type history on the command line and press Enter. A list of your most recent commands is then displayed, preceded by a number. Table 11-4 lists the different commands for referencing the history list.

```
$ history
1 cp mydata today
2 vi mydata
3 mv mydata reports
4 cd reports
5 ls
```

Table 11-4. *History Commands and History Event References*

History Command	Description
Ctrl+n or down arrow	Moves down to the next event in the history list
Ctrl+p or up arrow	Moves up to the previous event in the history list
Alt+<	Moves to the beginning of the history event list
Alt+>	Moves to the end of the history event list
Alt+n	Forward search, next matching item
Alt+p	Backward search, previous matching item
Ctrl+s	Forward search history, forward incremental search
Ctrl+r	Reverse search history, reverse incremental search
fc *event-reference*	Edits an event with the standard editor and then executes it Options: -l lists recent history events; same as history command -e editor event-reference invokes a specified editor to edit a specific event
History Event Reference	
!*event num*	References an event with an event number
!!	References the previous command
!*characters*	References an event with beginning characters
!?*pattern*?	References an event with a pattern in the event
!-*event num*	References an event with an offset from the first event
!*num-num*	References a range of events

Each of these commands is technically referred to as an event. An *event* describes an action that has been taken—a command that has been executed. The events are numbered according to their sequence of execution. The most recent event has the highest number. Each of these events can be identified by its number or beginning characters in the command.

The history utility lets you reference a former event, placing it on your command line so that you can execute it. The easiest way to do this is to use the up arrow and down arrow keys to place history events on the command line, one at a time. You need not display the list first with history. Pressing the up arrow key once places the last history event on the command line. Pressing it again places the next history event on the command line. Pressing the down arrow key places the previous event on the command line.

You can use certain control and meta keys to perform other history operations, such as searching the history list. A meta key is the Alt key, and the ESC key on keyboards that have no Alt key. The Alt key is used here. Pressing Alt+< will move you to the beginning of the history list; Alt+n will search it. Ctrl+s and Ctrl+r will perform incremental searches, displaying matching commands as you type in a search string.

▪ **Tip** If more than one history event matches what you have entered, you will hear a beep, and you can then enter more characters to help uniquely identify the event.

You can also reference and execute history events using the ! history command. The ! is followed by a reference that identifies the command. The reference can be either the number of the event or a beginning set of characters in the event. In the next example, the third command in the history list is referenced first by number and then by the beginning characters:

```
$ !3
mv mydata reports
$ !mv my
mv mydata reports
```

You can also reference an event using an offset from the end of the list. A negative number will offset from the end of the list to that event, thereby referencing it. In the next example, the fourth command, vi mydata, is referenced using a negative offset, and then executed. Remember that you are offsetting from the end of the list—in this case, event five—up toward the beginning of the list, event one. An offset of 4 beginning from event five places you at event two.

```
$ !-4
vi mydata
```

To reference the last event, you follow it with an !, as in !!. In the following example, the command !! executes the last command the user executed—in this case, ls:

```
$ !!
ls
mydata today reports
```

You can also perform a search of the listing of previous commands by entering Ctrl-r on the command line. You are prompted to enter a pattern for a search.

```
$ (revrse-isarch) 'vi' : vi mydata
```

Filename Expansion *, ?, [ ]

File names are the most common arguments used in a command. Often, you will know only part of the file name, or you will want to reference several file names that have the same extension or begin with the same characters. The shell provides a set of special characters that search out, match, and generate a list of file names. These are the asterisk, the question mark, and brackets (*, ?, [ ]). Given a partial file name, the shell uses these matching operators to search for files and expand to a list of file names found. The shell replaces the partial file name argument with the expanded list of matched file names. This list of file names can then become the arguments for commands such as ls, which can operate on many files. Table 11-5 lists the shell's file-expansion characters.

Table 11-5. Shell Symbols

Common Shell Symbol	Execution
Enter	Executes a command line
;	Separates commands on the same command line
`command`	Executes a command
$(command)	Executes a command
[ ]	Matches on a class of possible characters in file names

(continued)

Table 11-5. (*continued*)

Common Shell Symbol	Execution
\	Quotes the following character; used to quote special characters
|	Pipes the standard output of one command as input for another command
&	Executes a command in the background
!	References a history command
File-Expansion Symbol	**Execution**
*	Matches on any set of characters in file names
?	Matches on any single character in file names
[ ]	Matches on a class of characters in file names
Redirection Symbol	**Execution**
>	Redirects the standard output to a file or device, creating the file if it does not exist and overwriting the file if it does exist
>!	The exclamation point forces the overwriting of a file if it already exists
<	Redirects the standard input from a file or device to a program
>>	Redirects the standard output to a file or device, appending the output to the end of the file
Standard Error-Redirection Symbol	**Execution**
2>	Redirects the standard error to a file or device
2>>	Redirects and appends the standard error to a file or device
2>&1	Redirects the standard error to the standard output

Matching Multiple Characters

The asterisk (*) references files beginning or ending with a specific set of characters. You place the asterisk before or after a set of characters that form a pattern to be searched for in file names.

If the asterisk is placed before the pattern, file names that end in that pattern are searched for. If the asterisk is placed after the pattern, filenames that begin with that pattern are searched for. Any matching file name is copied into a list of file names generated by this operation.

In the next example, all file names beginning with the pattern "doc" are searched for, and a list is generated. Then all file names ending with the pattern "day" are searched for, and a list is generated. The last example shows how the * can be used in any combination of characters.

```
$ ls
doc1 doc2 document docs mydoc monday Tuesday
$ ls doc*
doc1 doc2 document docs
$ ls *day
monday Tuesday
$ ls m*d*
Monday
$
```

File names often include an extension specified with a period and followed by a string denoting the file type, such as .c for C files, .cpp for C++ files, or even .jpg for JPEG image files. The extension has no special status and is only part of the characters making up the file name. Using the asterisk makes it easy to select files with a given extension. In the next example, the asterisk is used to list only those files with a .c extension. The asterisk placed before the .c constitutes the argument for ls.

```
$ ls *.c
calc.c main.c
```

You can use * with the rm command to erase several files at once. The asterisk first selects a list of files with a given extension, or beginning or ending with a given set of characters, and then it presents this list of files to the rm command to be erased. In the following example, the rm command erases all files beginning with the pattern "doc":

```
$ rm doc*
```

■ **Caution**   Use the * file-expansion character carefully and sparingly with the rm command. The combination can be dangerous. A misplaced * in an rm command without the -i option could easily erase all the files in your current directory. The -i option will first prompt you to confirm whether the file should be deleted.

Matching Single Characters

The question mark (?) matches only a single incomplete character in file names. Suppose you want to match the files doc1 and docA, but not the file called document. Whereas the asterisk will match file names of any length, the question mark limits the match to one extra character. The following example matches files that begin with the word "doc," followed by a single differing letter:

```
$ ls
doc1 docA document
$ ls doc?
doc1 docA
```

Matching a Range of Characters

Whereas the * and ? file-expansion characters specify incomplete portions of a file name, the brackets ([ ]) enable you to specify a set of valid characters to search for. Any character placed within the brackets will be matched in the filename. Suppose you want to list files beginning with "doc" but ending only in *1* or *A*. You are not interested in filenames ending in *2* or *B*, or any other character. Here is how it is done:

```
$ ls
doc1 doc2 doc3 docA docB docD document
$ ls doc[1A]
doc1 docA
```

You can also specify a set of characters as a range, rather than listing them one by one. A dash placed between the upper and lower bounds of a range of characters selects all characters within that range. The range is usually determined by the character set in use. In an ASCII character set, the range "a-g" will select all lowercase alphabetic characters from *a* through *g,* inclusive. In the next example, files beginning with the pattern "doc" and ending in characters *1* through *3* are selected. Then, those ending in characters *B* through *E* are matched.

```
$ ls doc[1-3]
doc1 doc2 doc3
$ ls doc[B-E]
docB docD
```

You can combine the brackets with other file-expansion characters to form flexible matching operators. Suppose you want to list only file names ending in either a .c or .o extension but no other extension. You can use a combination of the asterisk and brackets: * [co]. The asterisk matches all file names, and the brackets match only file names with extension .c or .o.

```
$ ls *.[co]
main.c  main.o  calc.c
```

Matching Shell Symbols

At times, a file-expansion character is actually part of a file name. In these cases, you have to quote the character by preceding it with a backslash (\) to reference the file. In the next example, the user must reference a file that ends with the ? character, called answers?. The ? is, however, a file-expansion character and would match any file name beginning with "answers" that has one or more characters. In this case, the user quotes the ? with a preceding backslash to reference the file name.

```
$ ls answers\?
answers?
```

Placing the file name in double quotes will also quote the character.

```
$ ls "answers?"
answers?
```

This is also true for filenames or directories that have whitespace characters such as the space character. In this case, you can either use the backslash to quote the space character in the file or directory name or place the entire name within double quotes.

```
$ ls My\ Documents
My Documents
$ ls "My Documents"
My Documents
```

Generating Patterns

Although not a file-expansion operation, {} is often useful for generating names that you can use to create or modify files and directories. The braces operation only generates a list of names. It does not match on existing file names. Patterns are placed within the braces and separated with commas. Any pattern placed within the braces will be used to generate a version of the pattern, using either the preceding or following pattern, or both. Suppose you want to generate a list of names beginning with "doc," but ending only in the patterns "ument," "final," and "draft." Here is how it is done:

```
$ echo doc{ument,final,draft}
document docfinal docdraft
```

Because the names generated do not have to exist, you could use the { } operation in a command to create directories, as follows:

```
$ mkdir {fall,winter,spring}report
$ ls
fallreport springreport winterreport
```

Standard Input/Outputand Redirection

The data in input and output operations is organized like a file. Data input at the keyboard is placed in a data stream arranged as a continuous set of bytes. Data output from a command or program is also placed in a data stream and arranged as a continuous set of bytes. This input data stream is referred to in Linux as the standard input, while the output data stream is called the standard output. A separate output data stream is reserved solely for error messages; it is called the standard error.

Because the standard input and standard output have the same organization as that of a file, they can easily interact with files. Linux has a redirection capability that lets you easily move data in and out of files. You can redirect the standard output so that instead of displaying the output on a screen, you can save it in a file. You can also redirect the standard input away from the keyboard to a file, so that input is read from a file instead of from your keyboard.

When a Linux command is executed that produces output, this output is placed in the standard output data stream. The default destination for the standard output data stream is a device—in this case, the screen. Device, such as the keyboard and screen are treated as files. They receive and send out streams of bytes with the same organization as that of a byte-stream file. The screen is a device that displays a continuous stream of bytes. By default, the standard output will send its data to the screen device, which will then display the data.

For example, the ls command generates a list of all file names and outputs this list to the standard output. Next, this stream of bytes in the standard output is directed to the screen device. The list of file names is then printed on the screen. The cat command also sends output to the standard output. The contents of a file are copied to the standard output, whose default destination is the screen. The contents of the file are then displayed on the screen. Table 11-6 lists the different ways you can use the redirection operators.

Table 11-6. *The Shell Operations*

Command	Execution
Enter	Executes a command line
;	Separates commands on the same command line
command\ opts args	Enters a backslash before a carriage return, to continue entering a command on the next line
`command`	Executes a command
Special Characters for Filename Expansion	**Execution**
*	Matches on any set of characters
?	Matches on any single characters
[]	Matches on a class of possible characters
\	Quotes the following character; used to quote special characters

(continued)

Table 11-6. (*continued*)

Command	Execution
Redirection	**Execution**
command > *filename*	Redirects the standard output to a file or device, creating the file if it does not exist and overwriting the file if it does exist
command < *filename*	Redirects the standard input from a file or device to a program
command >>*filename*	Redirects the standard output to a file or device, appending the output to the end of the file
command 2> *filename*	Redirects the standard error to a file or device
command 2>>*filename*	Redirects and appends the standard error to a file or device
command 2>&1	Redirects the standard error to the standard output in the Bourne shell
command >& *filename*	Redirects the standard error to a file or device in the C shell
Pipe	**Execution**
command | *command*	Pipes the standard output of one command as input for another command

Redirecting the Standard Output: > and >>

Suppose that instead of displaying a list of files on the screen, you would like to save this list in a file. In other words, you would like to direct the standard output to a file rather than the screen. To do this, you place the output redirection operator, the greater-than sign (>), followed by the name of a file on the command line, after the Linux command. In the following example, the output of the ls command is redirected from the screen device to a file:

```
$ ls -l *.c > programlist
```

The redirection operation creates the new destination file. If the file already exists, it will be overwritten with the data in the standard output. You can set the noclobber feature to prevent overwriting an existing file with the redirection operation. In this case, the redirection operation on an existing file will fail. You can overcome the noclobber feature by placing an exclamation point after the redirection operator. You can place the noclobber command in a shell configuration file to make it an automatic default operation. The following example sets the noclobber feature for the BASH shell and then forces the overwriting of the oldarticle file if it already exists:

```
$ set -o noclobber
$ cat myarticle >! oldarticle
```

Although the redirection operator and the file name are placed after the command, the redirection operation is not executed after the command. In fact, it is executed before the command. The redirection operation creates the file and sets up the redirection before it receives any data from the standard output. If the file already exists, it will be destroyed and replaced by a file of the same name. In effect, the command generating the output is executed only after the redirected file has been created.

In the next example, the output of the ls command is redirected from the screen device to a file. First the ls command lists files, and in the next command, ls redirects its file list to the listf file. Then the cat command displays the list of files saved in listf. Notice that the list of files in listf includes the listf file name. The list of file names generated by the ls command includes the name of the file created by the redirection operation—in this case, listf. The listf file is first created by the redirection operation, then the ls command lists it along with other files. This file list output by ls is then redirected to the listf file, instead of being printed on the screen.

```
$ ls
mydata intro preface
$ ls > listf
$ cat listf
mydata intro listf preface
```

■ **Tip**   Errors occur when you try to use the same file name for an input file for the command and for the redirected destination file. In this case, because the redirection operation is executed first, the input file, because it exists, is destroyed and replaced by a file of the same name. When the command is executed, it finds an input file that is empty.

You can also append the standard output to an existing file using the >> redirection operator. Instead of overwriting the file, the data in the standard output is added at the end of the file. In the next example, the myarticle and oldarticle files are appended to the allarticles file. The allarticles file will then contain the contents of both myarticle and oldarticle.

```
$ cat myarticle >> allarticles
$ cat oldarticle >> allarticles
```

The Standard Input

Many Linux commands can receive data from the standard input. The standard input itself receives data from a device or a file. The default device for the standard input is the keyboard. Characters typed on the keyboard are placed in the standard input, which is then directed to the Linux command. Just as with the standard output, you can also redirect the standard input, receiving input from a file rather than the keyboard. The operator for redirecting the standard input is the less-than sign (<). In the next example, the standard input is redirected to receive input from the myarticle file, rather than the keyboard device (use Ctrl+d to end the typed input). The contents of myarticle are read into the standard input by the redirection operation. Then the cat command reads the standard input and displays the contents of myarticle.

```
$ cat < myarticle
hello Christopher
How are you today
$
```

You can combine the redirection operations for both standard input and standard output. In the next example, the cat command has no file name arguments. Without file name arguments, the cat command receives input from the standard input and sends output to the standard output. However, the standard input has been redirected to receive its data from a file, while the standard output has been redirected to place its data in a file.

```
$ cat < myarticle > newarticle
```

Pipes: |

You may encounter situations in which you have to send data from one command to another. In other words, you may want to send the standard output of a command to another command, rather than to a destination file. Suppose you want to send a list of your file names to the printer to be printed. You need two commands to do this: the ls command to generate a list of file names and the lpr command to send the list to the printer. In effect, you have to take the output of the ls command and use it as input for the lpr command. You can think of the data as flowing from one command to another. To form such a connection in Linux, you use what is called a *pipe*. The *pipe operator* (|, the vertical bar character) placed between two commands forms a connection between them. The standard output of one command becomes the standard input for the other. The pipe operation receives output from the command placed before the pipe and sends this data as input to the command placed after the pipe. As shown in the next example, you can connect the ls command and the lpr command with a pipe. The list of file names output by the ls command is piped into the lpr command.

```
$ ls | lpr
```

You can combine the pipe operation with other shell features, such as file-expansion characters, to perform specialized operations. The next example prints only files with a .c extension. The ls command is used with the asterisk and .c to generate a list of file names with the .c extension. Then this list is piped to the lpr command.

```
$ ls *.c | lpr
```

In the preceding example, a list of file names was used as input. What is important to note is that pipes operate on the standard output of a command, whatever that might be. The contents of whole files or even several files can be piped from one command to another. In the following example, the cat command reads and outputs the contents of the mydata file, which are then piped to the lpr command:

```
$ cat mydata | lpr
```

Linux has many commands that generate modified output. For example, the sort command takes the contents of a file and generates a version with each line sorted in alphabetic order. The sort command works best with files that are lists of items. Commands such as sort that output a modified version of its input are referred to as *filters*. Filters are often used with pipes. In the next example, a sorted version of mylist is generated and piped into the more command for display on the screen. The original file, mylist, has not been changed and is not sorted. Only the output of sort in the standard output is sorted.

```
$ sort mylist | more
```

The standard input piped into a command can be more carefully controlled with the standard input argument (-). When you use the dash as an argument for a command, it represents the standard input.

■ **Tip** The **xargs** command lets you easily run complex commands with multiple options using data from the standard output generated from pipes or redirection operators.

Linux Files

You can name a file using any letters, underscores, and numbers. You can also include periods and commas. Except in certain special cases, you should never begin a file name with a period. Other characters, such as slashes, question marks, or asterisks, are reserved for use as special characters by the system and should not be part of a file name. File names can be as long as 256 characters. File names can also include spaces, although to reference such file names from the command line, be sure to encase them in quotes. On a desktop such as GNOME or KDE, you do not have to use quotes. A file name cannot have the same name as a subdirectory within the same directory. Directories are treated as type of file.

You can include an extension as part of a file name. A period is used to distinguish the file name proper from the extension. Extensions can be useful for categorizing your files. You are probably familiar with certain standard extensions that have been adopted by convention. For example, C source code files always have a .c extension. Files that contain compiled object code have an .o extension. You can make up your own file extensions. The following examples are all valid Linux file names. Keep in mind that to reference the name with spaces on the command line, you have to encase it in quotes, for example, "New book review."

```
preface
chapter2
9700info
New_Revisions
calc.c
intro.bk1
New book review
```

Special initialization files are also used to hold shell configuration commands. These are the hidden, or dot, files, which begin with a period. Dot files used by commands and applications have predetermined names, such as the .mozilla directory used to hold your Mozilla data and configuration files. Recall that when you use ls to display your file names, the dot files will not be displayed. To include the dot files, you must use ls with the -a option.

The ls -l command displays detailed information about a file. First, the permissions are displayed, followed by the number of links, the owner of the file, the name of the group to which the user belongs to, the file size in bytes, the date and time the file was last modified, and the name of the file. Permissions indicate who can access the file: the user, members of a group, or all other users. The group name indicates the group permitted to access the file object. The file type for mydata is that of an ordinary file. Only one link exists, indicating the file has no other names and no other links. The owner's name is chris, the same as the login name, and the group name is weather. Other users probably also belong to the weather group. The size of the file is 207 bytes, and it was last modified on February 20 at 11:55 a.m. The name of the file is mydata.

If you want to display this detailed information for all the files in a directory, simply use the ls-l command without an argument.

```
$ ls -l
-rw-r--r-- 1 chris weather 207 Feb 20 11:55 mydata
-rw-rw-r-- 1 chris weather 568 Feb 14 10:30 today
-rw-rw-r-- 1 chris weather 308 Feb 17 12:40 monday
```

All files in Linux have one physical format, a byte stream, which is simply a sequence of bytes. This allows Linux to apply the file concept to every data component in the system. Directories are classified as files, as are devices. Treating everything as a file allows Linux to organize and exchange data more easily. The data in a file can be sent directly to a device, such as a screen, because a device interfaces with the system using the same byte-stream file format used by regular files.

This same file format is used to implement other operating system components. The interface to a device, such as the screen or keyboard, is designated as a file. Other components, such as directories, are themselves byte-stream files, but they have a special internal organization. A directory file contains information about a directory, organized in a special directory format. Because these different components are treated as files, they can be said to constitute different *file types*. A character device is one file type. A directory is another file type. The number of these file types may vary according to your specific implementation of Linux. Five common types of files exist, however: ordinary files, directory files, first-in first-out (FIFO) pipes, character device files, and block device files. Although you may rarely reference a file's type, it can be useful to know when searching for directories or devices.

Although all ordinary files have a byte-stream format, they may be used in different ways. The most significant difference is between binary and text files. Compiled programs are examples of binary files. However, even text files can be classified according to their different uses. You can have files that contain C programming source code or shell commands, or even a file that is empty. The file could be an executable program or a directory file. The Linux file command helps you determine what a file is used for. It examines the first few lines of a file and tries to determine a classification for it. The file command looks for special keywords or special numbers in those first few lines, but it is not always accurate. In the following example, the file command examines the contents of two files and determines a classification for them:

```
$ file monday reports
monday: text
reports: directory
```

If you have to examine the entire file byte by byte, you can do so with the od (octal dump) command, which performs a dump of a file. By default, it prints every byte in its octal representation. However, you can also specify a character, decimal, or hexadecimal representation. The od command is helpful when you have to detect any special character in your file or if you want to display a binary file.

The File Structure

Linux organizes files into a hierarchically connected set of directories. Each directory may contain either files or other directories. In this respect, directories perform two important functions. A directory holds files, much like files held in a file drawer, and a directory connects to other directories, much as a branch in a tree is connected to other branches. Because of the similarities to a tree, such a structure is often referred to as a *tree structure*.

The Linux file structure branches into several directories, beginning with a root directory, /. Within the root directory, several system directories contain files and programs that are features of the Linux system. The root directory also contains a directory called home that contains the home directories of all the users in the system. Each user's home directory, in turn, contains the directories the users have made for their own use. Each of these can also contain directories. Such nested directories branch out from the user's home directory. Table 11-7 lists the basic system directories.

Table 11-7. *Standard System Directories in Linux*

Directory	Function
/	Begins the file system structure, called the root
/home	Contains users' home directories
/bin	Holds all the standard commands and utility programs
/usr	Holds those files and commands used by the system; this directory breaks down into several subdirectories
/usr/bin	Holds user-oriented commands and utility programs
/usr/sbin	Holds system administration commands
/usr/lib	Holds libraries for programming languages
/usr/share/doc	Holds Linux documentation
/usr/share/man	Holds the online man files
/var/spool	Holds spooled files, such as those generated for printing jobs and network transfers
/sbin	Holds system administration commands the system
/var	Holds files that vary, such as mailbox files
/dev	Holds file interfaces for devices such as the terminals and printers (dynamically generated by udev; do not edit)
/etc	Holds system configuration files and any other system files

---

▪ **Note** The user's home directory can be any directory, though it is usually the directory that bears the user's login name. This directory is located in the directory named /home on your Linux system. For example, a user named dylan will have a home directory called dylan located in the system's /home directory. The user's home directory is a subdirectory of the directory called /home on your system.

Home Directories

When you log in to the system, you are placed within your home directory. The name given to this directory by the system is the same as your login name. Any files you create when you first log in are organized within your home directory. Within your home directory, you can create more directories. You can then change to these directories and store files in them. The same is true for other users on the system. Each user has a home directory, identified by the appropriate login name. Users, in turn, can create their own directories.

You can access a directory either through its name or by making it your working directory. Each directory is given a name when it is created. You can use this name in file operations to access files in that directory. You can also make the directory your working directory. If you do not use any directory names in a file operation, the working directory will be accessed. The working directory is the one from which you are currently working. When you log in, the working directory is your home directory, which usually has the same name as your login name. You can change the working directory by using the cd command to move to another directory.

Pathnames

The name you give to a directory or file when you create it is not its full name. The full name of a directory is its *pathname*. The hierarchically nested relationship among directories forms paths, and these paths can be used to identify and reference any directory or file uniquely or absolutely. Each directory in the file structure can be said to have its own unique path. The actual name by which the system identifies a directory always begins with the root directory and consists of all directories nested below that directory.

In Linux, you write a pathname by listing each directory in the path, separated from the last by a forward slash. A slash preceding the first directory in the path represents the root. The pathname for the chris directory is /home/chris. If the chris directory has a subdirectory called reports, then the entire pathname for the reports directory would be /home/chris/reports. Pathnames also apply to files. When you create a file within a directory, you give the file a name. The actual name by which the system identifies the file, however, is the file name combined with the path of directories from the root to the file's directory. As an example, the pathname for monday is /home/chris/reports/monday (the root directory is represented by the first slash). The path for the monday file consists of the root, home, chris, and reports directories and the file name monday.

Pathnames may be absolute or relative. An *absolute pathname* is the complete pathname of a file or directory beginning with the root directory. A *relative pathname* begins from your working directory; it is the path of a file relative to your working directory. The working directory is the one you are currently operating in. Using the previous example, if chris is your working directory, the relative pathname for the file monday is reports/monday. The absolute pathname for monday is /home/chris/reports/monday.

The absolute pathname from the root to your home directory can be especially complex and, at times, even subject to change by the system administrator. To make it easier to reference, you can use the tilde (~) character, which represents the absolute pathname of your home directory. You must specify the rest of the path from your home directory. In the next example, the user references the monday file in the reports directory. The tilde represents the path to the user's home directory, /home/chris, then the rest of the path to the monday file is specified, as follows:

```
$ cat ~/reports/monday
```

System Directories

The root directory that begins the Linux file structure contains several system directories that contain files and programs used to run and maintain the system. Many also contain other subdirectories with programs for executing specific features of Linux. For example, the directory /usr/bin contains the various Linux commands that users execute, such as lpr. The directory /bin holds system level commands.

Listing, Displaying, and Printing Files: ls, cat, more, less, and lpr

One of the primary functions of an operating system is the management of files. You may be required to perform certain basic output operations on your files, such as displaying them on your screen or printing them. The Linux system provides a set of commands that perform basic file-management operations, such as listing, displaying, and printing files, as well as copying, renaming, and erasing files. These commands are usually made up of abbreviated versions of words. For example, the ls command is a shortened form of "list" and lists the files : in your directory. The lpr command is an abbreviated form of "line print" and will print a file. The cat, less, and more commands display the contents of a file on the screen. Table 11-8 lists these commands with their different options. When you log in to your Linux system, you may want a list of the files in your home directory. The ls command, which outputs a list of your file and directory names, is useful for this. The ls command has many possible options for displaying file names according to specific features.

Table 11-8. *Listing, Displaying, and Printing Files*

Command or Option	Execution
Ls	Lists file and directory names
cat *filenames*	Used to display a file. It can take file names for its arguments. It outputs the contents of those files directly to the standard output, which, by default, is directed to the screen
more *filenames*	Displays a file screen by screen. Press the spacebar to continue to the next screen and the q key to quit
less *filenames*	Also displays a file screen by screen. Press the spacebar to continue to the next screen and the q key to quit
lpr *filenames*	Sends a file to the line printer to be printed; a list of files may be used as arguments. Use the -P option to specify a printer
lpq	Lists the print queue for printing jobs
lprm	Removes a printing job from the print queue

Displaying Files: cat, less, and more

You may also have to look at the contents of a file. The cat and more commands display the contents of a file on the screen. The name *cat* stands for "concatenate."

```
$ cat mydata
computers
```

The cat command outputs the entire text of a file to the screen at once. This presents a problem when the file is large, because its text quickly speeds past on the screen. The more and less commands are designed to overcome this limitation, by displaying one screen of text at a time. You can then move forward or backward in the text at your leisure. You invoke the more or less command by entering the command name, followed by the name of the file you want to view (less is a more powerful and configurable display utility).

$ **less mydata**

: When more or less invoke a file, the first screen of text is displayed. To continue to the next screen, you press the f key, the spacebar, or PageUP keys. To move back in the text, you press the b or PageDown keys. You can quit at any time by pressing the q key.

Printing Files: lpr, lpq, and lprm

With the printer commands, such as lpr and lprm, you can perform printing operations such as printing files or canceling print jobs (see Table 11-8). When you have to print files, use the lpr command to send files to the printer connected to your system. In the following example, the user prints the mydata file:

$ **lpr mydata**

If you want to print several files at once, you can specify more than one file on the command line after the lpr command. In the following example, the user prints the mydata and preface files:

$ **lpr mydata preface**

Printing jobs are placed in a queue and printed one at a time in the background. You can continue with other work as your files print. You can see the position of a particular printing job at any given time with the lpq command, which gives the owner of the printing job (the login name of the user who sent the job), the print job ID, the size in bytes, and the temporary file in which it is currently held.

If you have to cancel an unwanted printing job, you can do so with the lprm command, which takes as its argument either the ID number of the printing job or the owner's name. It then removes the print job from the print queue. For this task, lpq is helpful, as it provides you with the ID number and owner of the printing job you must use with lprm.

Managing Directories: mkdir, rmdir, ls, cd, pwd

You can create and remove your own directories, as well as change your working directory, with the mkdir, rmdir, and cd commands. Each of these commands can take as its argument the pathname for a directory. The pwd command displays the absolute pathname of your working directory. In addition to these commands, the special characters represented by a single dot, a double dot, and a tilde can be used to reference the working directory, the parent of the working directory, and the home directory, respectively. Taken together, these commands enable you to manage your directories. You can create nested directories, move from one directory to another, and use pathnames to reference any of your directories. Those commands commonly used to manage directories are listed in Table 11-9.

Table 11-9. *Directory Commands*

Command	Execution
mkdir *directory*	Creates a directory
rmdir *directory*	Erases a directory
ls -F	Lists the directory name with a preceding slash
ls -R	Lists the working directory as well as all subdirectories
cd *directory*	Changes to the specified directory, making it the working directory. cd without a directory name changes back to the home directory: $ cd reports
pwd	Displays the pathname of the working directory
directory */filename*	A slash is used in pathnames to separate each directory name. In the case of pathnames for files, a slash separates the preceding directory names from the file name.

..	References the parent directory. You can use it as an argument or as part of a pathname:
	$ cd ..
	$ mv ../larisa oldarticles

.	References the working directory. You can use it as an argument or as part of a pathname: $ ls
~/*pathname*	The tilde is a special character that represents the pathname for the home directory. It is useful when you have to use an absolute pathname for a file or directory: $ cp monday ~/today
j *pattern*	Use the autojump command to quickly jump to a frequently used directory using a matching pattern
jumpstat	Statistics showing frequently used directories accessible with autojump

Creating and Deleting Directories

You create and remove directories with the mkdir and rmdir commands. In either case, you can also use pathnames for the directories. In the next example, the user creates the directory reports. Then the user creates the directory articles, using a pathname.

```
$ mkdir reports
$ mkdir /home/chris/articles
```

If there the interveing parent directories in a pathname do not yet exist, you can have them created automatically with the **-p** option. In the following example, the intevening parent subdirectories **project/newproject**, inidicated by the pathname, do not yet exist. Using the **-p** option creates them automatically, creating the **project**, **newproject**, and **proposals** subdirectories. Without the **-p** option you would recieve an error stating the directories do not exist.

```
$ mkdir -p  /home/chris/project/newproject/proposal
```

You can remove a directory with the rmdir command followed by the directory name. In the following example, the user removes the directory reports with the rmdir command:

```
$ rmdir reports
```

To remove a directory and all its subdirectories, you use the rm command with the -r option. This is a very powerful command and could be used to erase all your files. You will be prompted for each file. To remove all files and subdirectories without prompts, add the -f option. The following example deletes the reports directory and all its subdirectories:

```
rm -rf reports
```

Displaying Directory Contents

You have seen how to use the ls command to list the files and directories within your working directory. To distinguish between file and directory names, however, you must use the ls command with the -F option. A slash is then placed after each directory name in the list.

```
$ ls
weather reports articles
$ ls -F
weather reports/ articles/
```

The ls command also takes as an argument any directory name or directory pathname. This enables you to list the files in any directory without first having to change to that directory. In the next example, the ls command takes as its argument the name of a directory, reports. Then the ls command is executed again, only this time, the absolute pathname of reports is used.

```
$ ls reports
monday Tuesday
$ ls /home/chris/reports
monday Tuesday
$
```

Moving Through Directories

The cd command takes as its argument the name of the directory to which you want to move. The name of the directory can be the name of a subdirectory in your working directory or the full pathname of any directory on the system. If you want to change back to your home directory, you need to enter only the cd command by itself, without a file name argument.

```
$ cd reports
$ pwd
/home/chris/reports
```

As a complement to the cd command, you can use the autojump command. Install the autojump package. autojump keeps a record of your frequently accessed directories. You can then use the j command with a partial-matching pattern to quickly jump (cd) to that directory.

```
$ j rep
$ pwd
/home/chris/reports
```

Jumpstart keeps a database of your cd operations and uses it to determine the directory you want. The jumpstat command displays the ranked directories.

Referencing the Parent Directory

A directory always has a parent (except, of course, for the root). For example, in the preceding listing, the parent for reports is the chris directory. When a directory is created, two entries are made: one represented with a dot (.), and the other with double dots (..). The dot represents the pathnames of the directory, and the double dots represent the pathname of its parent directory. Double dots, used as an argument in a command, reference a parent directory. The single dot references the directory itself.

You can use the single dot to reference your working directory, instead of using its pathname. For example, to copy a file to the working directory retaining the same name, the dot can be used in place of the working directory's pathname. In this sense, the dot is another name for the working directory. In the next example, the user copies the weather file from the chris directory to the reports directory. The reports directory is the working directory and can be represented with a single dot.

```
$ cd reports
$ cp /home/chris/weather .
```

The .. symbol is often used to reference files in the parent directory. In the next example, the cat command displays the weather file in the parent directory. The pathname for the file is the .. symbol (for the parent directory), followed by a slash and the file name.

```
$ cat ../weather
raining and warm
```

■ **Tip**   You can use the cd command with the .. symbol to step back through successive parent directories of the directory tree from a lower directory.

File and Directory Operations: find, cp, mv, rm, ln

As you create more and more files, you may want to back them up, change their names, erase some of them, or even give them added names. Linux provides several file commands that you can use to search for, copy, rename, or remove files (see Table 11-11. If you have a large number of files, you can also search them to locate a specific one. The commands are shortened forms of full words, consisting of only two characters. The cp command stands for "copy" and copies a file; mv stands for "move" and renames or moves a file; rm stands for "remove" and erases a file; and ln stands for "link" and adds another name for a file, often used as a shortcut to the original. One exception to the two-character rule is the find command, which performs searches of your file names to find a file. All these operations can be handled by the GUI desktops, such as GNOME and KDE.

■ **Note**   To quickly searching for a file, you can use the **locate** command. The locate command reads from a database of file locations compiled daily by **updatedb**.

Searching Directories: find

Once a large number of files has been stored in many different directories, you may have to search them to locate a specific file, or files, of a certain type. The find command enables you to perform such a search from the command line. The find command takes as its arguments directory names, followed by several possible options that specify the type of search and the criteria for the search. It then searches within the directories listed and their subdirectories for files that meet these criteria. The find command can search for a file by name, type, owner, and even the time of the last update (see Table 11-10).

```
$ find directory-list -option criteria
```

Table 11-10. *The find Command*

Command or Option	Execution
Find	Searches directories for files according to search criteria. This command has several options that specify the type of criteria and actions to be taken
-name *pattern*	Searches for files with the *pattern* in the name
-lname *pattern*	Searches for symbolic link files
-group *name*	Searches for files belonging to the group *name*
-gid *name*	Searches for files belonging to a group according to group ID
-user *name*	Searches for files belonging to a user
-uid *name*	Searches for files belonging to a user according to user ID
-mtime *num*	Searches for files last modified *num* days ago
-context *scontext*	Searches for files according to security context (SELinux)
-print	Outputs the result of the search to the standard output. The result is usually a list of file names, including their full pathnames
-type *filetype*	Searches for files with the specified file type. File type can be b for block device, c for character device, d for directory, f for file, or l for symbolic link
-perm *permission*	Searches for files with certain permissions set. Use octal or symbolic format for permissions
-ls	Provides a detailed listing of each file, with owner, permission, size, and date information
-exec *command*	Executes *command* when files are found

▪ **Tip** From the GNOME desktop, you can use the Search tool in the Places menu to search for files. From the KDE desktop, you can use the Find tool in the file manager.

The -name option has as its criteria a pattern and instructs find to search for the file name that matches that pattern. To search for a file by name, you use the find command with the directory name, followed by the -name option and the name of the file.

```
$ find directory-list -name filename
```

The find command also has options that merely perform actions, such as outputting the results of a search. If you want find to display the file names it has located, you simply include the -print option on the command line, along with any other options. The -print option instructs find to write to the standard output the names of all the files it locates. (You can also use the -ls option instead to list files in the long format.) In the next example, the user searches for all the files in the reports directory with the name monday. Once located, the file, with its relative pathname, is printed.

```
$ find reports -name monday -print
reports/monday
```

The find command prints the file names using the directory name specified in the directory list. If you specify an absolute pathname, the absolute path of the found directories will be output. If you specify a relative pathname, only the relative pathname is output. In the preceding example, the user specified a relative pathname, reports, in the directory list. Located file names were output beginning with this relative pathname. In the next example, the user specifies an absolute pathname in the directory list. Located file names are then output using this absolute pathname.

```
$ find /home/chris -name monday -print
/home/chris/reports/monday
```

■ **Tip**　Should you need to find the location of a specific program or configuration file, you could use find to search for the file from the root directory. Log in as the root user and use / as the directory. This command searches for the location of the more command and files on the entire file system: find / -name more -print.

Searching the Working Directory

If you want to search your working directory, you can use the dot in the directory pathname to represent it. The double dots represent the parent directory. The next example searches all files and subdirectories in the working directory, using the dot to represent the working directory. If your working directory is your home directory, this is a convenient way to search through all your own directories. Notice that the located file names that are output begin with a dot.

```
$ find . -name weather -print
./weather
```

You can use shell wildcard characters as part of the pattern criteria for searching files. The special character must be quoted, however, to avoid evaluation by the shell. In the next example, all files (indicated by the asterisk, *) with the .c extension in the programs directory are searched for and then displayed in the long format, using the -ls action:

```
$ find programs -name '*.c' -ls
```

Locating Directories

You can also use the find command to locate other directories. In Linux, a directory is officially classified as a special type of file. Although all files have a byte-stream format, some files, such as directories, are used in special ways. In this sense, a file can be said to have a file type. The find command has an option called -type that searches for a file of a given type. The -type option takes a one-character modifier that represents the file type. The modifier that represents a directory is a d. In the following example, both the directory name and the directory file type are used to search for the directory called travel:

```
$ find /home/chris -name travel -type d -print
/home/chris/articles/travel
$
```

File types are not so much different types of files as they are the file format applied to other components of the operating system, such as devices. In this sense, a device is treated as a type of file, and you can use find to search for devices and directories, as well as ordinary files. Table 11-10 lists the different types available for the find command's -type option.

You can also use the find operation to search for files by ownership or security criteria, like those belonging to a specific user or those with a certain security context. The -user option lets you locate all files belonging to a certain user. The following example lists all files that the user chris has created or owns on the entire system. To list those only in users' home directories, you use /home for the starting search directory. This would find all those in a user's home directory, as well as any owned by that user in other user directories.

```
$ find / -user chris -print
```

Copying Files

To make a copy of a file, you simply give cp two file names as its arguments (see Table 11-11). The first file name is the name of the file to be copied—the one that already exists. This is often referred to as the source file. The second file name is the name you want for the copy. This will be a new file containing a copy of all the data in the source file. This second argument is often referred to as the destination file. The syntax for the cp command follows:

```
$ cp source-file destination-file
```

Table 11-11. *File Operations*

Command	Execution
cp *filename filename*	Copies a file. cp takes two arguments: the original file and the name of the new copy. You can use pathnames for the files to copy across directories.
cp -r *directory directory*	Copies a subdirectory from one directory to another. The copied directory includes all its own subdirectories.
mv *filename filename*	Moves (renames) a file. The mv command takes two arguments: the first is the file to be moved. The second argument can be the new file name or the pathname of a directory. If it is the name of a directory, then the file is moved to that directory, changing the file's pathname.
mv *directory directory*	Moves directories. In this case, the first and last arguments are directories.
ln *filename filename*	Creates added names for files referred to as links. A link can be created in one directory that references a file in another directory.
rm *filenames*	Removes (erases) a file. Can take any number of file names as its arguments. Literally removes links to a file. If a file has more than one link, you must remove all of them to erase a file.

In the following example, the user copies a file called proposal to a new file called oldprop:

```
$ cp proposal oldprop
```

You could unintentionally destroy another file with the cp command. The cp command generates a copy by first creating a file and then copying data into it. If another file has the same name as the destination file, that file is destroyed, and a new file with that name is created. By default, Fedora configures your system to check for an existing copy by the same name (cp is aliased with the -i option). To copy a file from your working directory to another directory, you have to use that directory name as the second argument in the cp command. In the next example, the proposal file is overwritten by the newprop file. The proposal file already exists.

```
$ cp newprop proposal
```

You can use any of the wildcard characters to generate a list of file names to use with cp or mv. For example, suppose you need to copy all your C source code files to a given directory. Instead of listing each one individually on the command line, you could use an * character with the .c extension to match on and generate a list of C source code files (all files with a .c extension). In the following example, the user copies all source code files in the current directory to the sourcebks directory:

```
$ cp *.c sourcebks
```

If you want to copy all the files in a given directory to another directory, you could use * to match on and generate a list of all those files in a cp command. In the next example, the user copies all the files in the props directory to the oldprop directory. Notice the use of a props pathname preceding the * special characters. In this context, props is a pathname that will be appended before each file in the list that * generates.

```
$ cp props/* oldprop
```

You can, of course, use any of the other special characters, such as ., ?, or [ ]. In the following example, the user copies both source code and object code files (.c and .o) to the projbk directory:

```
$ cp *.[oc] projbk
```

When you copy a file, you can give the copy a name that is different from the original. To do so, place the new file name after the directory name, separated by a slash.

```
$ cp filename directory-name/new-filename
```

Moving Files

You can use the mv command either to rename a file or move a file from one directory to another. When using mv to rename a file, you simply use the new file name as the second argument. The first argument is the current name of the file you are renaming. If you want to rename a file when you move it, you can specify the new name of the file after the directory name. In the following example, the proposal file is renamed with the name version1:

```
$ mv proposal version1
```

As with cp, it is easy for mv to erase a file accidentally. When renaming a file, you might accidentally choose a file name already used by another file. In this case, that other file will be erased. The mv command also has an -i option that checks first to see if a file with that name already exists.

You can also use any of the special characters to generate a list of file names to use with mv. In the following example, the user moves all source code files in the current directory to the newproj directory:

```
$ mv *.c newproj
```

If you want to move all the files in a given directory to another directory, you can use * to match on and generate a list of all those files. In the following example, the user moves all the files in the reports directory to the repbks directory:

```
$ mv reports/* repbks
```

■ **Note**   The easiest way to copy files to a CD-R/RW or DVD-R/RW disk is to use the built-in file manager burning capability. Simply insert a blank disk, open it as a folder, and drag and drop files onto it. You will be prompted automatically to burn the files.

Copying and Moving Directories

You can also copy or move whole directories at once. Both cp and mv can take as their first argument a directory name, enabling you to copy or move subdirectories from one directory into another (see Table 11-11). The first argument is the name of the directory to be moved or copied, and the second argument is the name of the directory within which it is to be placed. The same pathname structure used for files applies to moving or copying directories.

You can just as easily copy subdirectories from one directory to another. To copy a directory, the cp command requires you to use the -r option, which stands for "recursive." It directs the cp command to copy a directory, as well as any subdirectories it may contain. In other words, the entire directory subtree, from that directory on, will be copied. In the next example, the travel directory is copied to the oldarticles directory. Now two travel subdirectories exist, one in articles and one in oldarticles.

```
$ cp -r articles/travel oldarticles
$ ls -F articles
/travel
$ ls -F oldarticles
/travel
```

Erasing Files and Directories the rm Command

As you use Linux, you will find the number of files you use increases rapidly. Generating files in Linux is easy. Applications such as editors, and commands such as cp, can easily be used to create files. Eventually, many of these files may become outdated and useless. You can then remove them with the rm command. The rm command can take any number of arguments, enabling you to list several file names and erase them all at the same time. In the next example, the file oldprop is erased:

```
$ rm oldprop
```

Be careful when using the rm command, because it is irrevocable. Once a file is removed, it cannot be restored (there is no undo). With the -i option, you are prompted separately for each file and asked whether you really want to remove it. If you enter y, the file will be removed. If you enter anything else, the file is not removed. In the next example, the rm command is instructed to erase the files proposal and oldprop. The rm command then asks for confirmation for each file. The user decides to remove oldprop but not proposal.

```
$ rm -i proposal oldprop
Remove proposal? n
Remove oldprop? y
$
```

Links: The ln Command

You can give a file more than one name using the ln command. You might do this because you want to reference a file using different file names to access it from different directories. The added names are often referred to as *links*. Linux supports two different types of links, hard and symbolic. Hard links are literally another name for the same file, whereas symbolic links function like shortcuts referencing another file. Symbolic links are much more flexible and can work over many different file systems, while hard links are limited to your local file system. Furthermore, hard links introduce security concerns, as they allow direct access from a link that may have public access to an original file that you may want protected. Links are usually implemented as symbolic links.

Symbolic Links

To set up a symbolic link, use the ln command with the -s option and two arguments: the name of the original file and the new, added file name. The ls operation lists both file names, but only one physical file will exist.

```
$ ln -s original-filename added-filename
```

In the next example, the today file is given the additional name weather. It is just another name for the today file.

```
$ ls
Today
$ ln -s today weather
$ ls
today weather
```

You can give the same file several names by using the ln command on the same file many times. In the next example, the file today is assigned the names weather and weekend:

```
$ ln -s today weather
$ ln -s today weekend
$ ls
today weather weekend
```

If you list the full information about a symbolic link and its file, you will find that the information displayed is different. In the next example, the user lists the full information for both lunch and /home/george/veglist, using the ls command with the -l option. The first character in the line specifies the file type. Symbolic links have their own file type, represented by an l. The file type for lunch is l, indicating it is a symbolic link, not an ordinary file. The number after the term "group" is the size of the file. Notice that the sizes differ. The size of the lunch file is only 4 bytes. This is because lunch is only a symbolic link—a file that holds the pathname of another file—and a pathname takes up only a few bytes. It is not a direct hard link to the veglist file.

```
$ ls -l lunch /home/george/veglist
lrw-rw-r-- 1 chris group 4 Feb 14 10:30 lunch
-rw-rw-r-- 1 george group 793 Feb 14 10:30 veglist
```

To erase a file, you have to remove only its original name (and any hard links to it). If any symbolic links are left over, they will be unable to access the file. In this case, a symbolic link would hold the pathname of a file that no longer exists.

Hard Links

You can give the same file several names by using the `ln` command on the same file many times. To set up a hard link, you use the `ln` command with no `-s` option and two arguments: the name of the original file and the new, added file name. The `ls` operation lists both file names, but only one physical file will exist.

```
$ ln original-filename added-filename
```

In the next example, the `monday` file is given the additional name `storm`. It is just another name for the `monday` file.

```
$ ls
today
$ ln monday storm
$ ls
monday storm
```

To erase a file that has hard links, you must remove all its hard links. The name of a file is actually considered a link to that file; hence, the command `rm` removes the link to the file. If you have several links to the file and remove only one of them, the others stay in place, and you can reference the file through them. The same is true even if you remove the original link—the original name of the file.

CHAPTER 12

■ ■ ■

Additional Desktops

Several alternative desktops are available for use on Fedora. Table 12-1 lists several popular alternative desktops that you can use for Fedora. You can use these desktops as additional ones that you can install on your Fedora system. At the login screen, the Sessions menu lets you choose which desktop you want to use, just as with KDE. You can download them from PackageKit (System Tools ➤ Software). Look for the meta package with the extension -desktop, such as xfce-desktop and cinnamon-desktop. This meta package will download the entire collection of packages for that desktop interface. Many of the desktops have their own desktop spin ISO images, which you can download and burn onto a DVD/CD. They also operate as Live CDs. The Xfce and LXDE spins can be downloaded from the Fedora Project download page. SoaS can be downloaded from its web site at http://spins.fedoraproject.org/soas. You can also install a desktop directly using the **yum install** command and the dektop name.

Table 12-1. *Additional Desktops*

Web Site	Description
www.xfce.org/	Xfce desktop. Simple lightweight desktop
http://lxde.org/	LXDE desktop. Small desktop for low-power systems
http://spins.fedoraproject.org/soas/	Sugar on a Stick (SoaS) desktop. Education desktop for children
http://mate-desktop.org/	Mate desktop. Enhanced GNOME 2 desktop interface.
http://cinnamon.linuxmint.com/	Cinnamon desktop. Mint desktop base on GNOME 3 with both GNOME 2 and GNOME 2 features

The Xfce Desktop

Xfce is a lightweight desktop designed to run fast without the kind of overhead required for full-featured desktops such as KDE and GNOME. You can think of it as a window manager with desktop functionality. It includes its own file manager and panel, but the emphasis is on modularity and simplicity. Like GNOME, Xfce is based on GTK+ GUI tools. The desktop consists of a collection of modules, such as the tuner file manager, xfce4-panel panel, and the xfwm4 window manager. Keeping with its focus on simplicity, Xfce features only a few common applets on its panel. Its small scale makes it appropriate for laptops or dedicated systems that have no need for complex overhead found in other desktops. Xfce is useful for desktops, such as multimedia desktops, designed for just a few tasks.

To install Xfce as an alternative desktop on a system, select the Xfce package in the Package Collection category on PackageKit (Software).

You can also use Xfce as a Live CD, which you can download from http://fedoraproject.org/en/get-fedora-options#desktops.

The Xfce Live CD is available in 32-bit and 64-bit versions, such as `Fedora-20x86_64-Live-XFCE.iso`. You can then burn the CD and run it as a Live CD. Click the Install icon to install an Xfce-based Fedora system on your computer. Double-click the Install icon to install an LXDE-based Fedora system on your computer. Follow the same basic steps for installing Fedora as for the Fedora Live DVD. The Installation Summary screen shows items for Installation Destination, Date & Time, and Keyboard. Be sure to choose the disks to install on and to check the time zone. Once installed, you use the GDM login screen to log in.

The desktop displays icons for your home directory, file system, and trash (see Figure 12-1). Xfce displays a top and bottom panel. The top panel will have buttons for an applications menu at the letf., From this menu, you can access any Fedora software applications, along with Fedora administration tools. To the right of the menu is the taskbar, showing buttons for open windows. The left side of the panel shows workspace switcher, time and date, network connections (Network Manager), and the session menus displaying the user name. The session menu has entries for shut down, log out, lock screen, suspend, and switch user. The bottom panel has icons for hide/show desktop, terminal, file manager, web browser, applications finder, and a directory menu for your home folder.

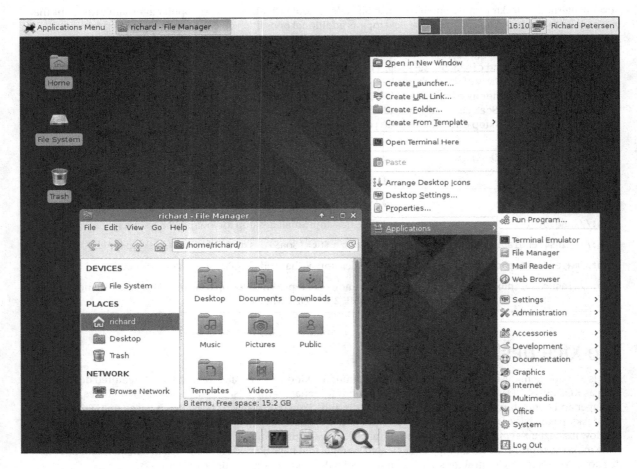

Figure 12-1. *Xfce desktop*

ou can add more items by clicking the panel and selecting Add New Items. This opens a window with several applets, such as the clock,workspace switcher, applications menu, and launcher. The launcher applet lets you specify an application to start and choose an icon image for it. To move an applet, right-click it and choose Move from the pop-up menu. Then move the mouse to the new insertion location and click.

Xfce file manager is called *Thunar* The file manager will open a side pane in the shortcuts view that lists entries not only for the home directory but also for your file system, desktop, and trash contents. The File menu lets you perform folder operations, such as creating new directories. From the Edit menu, you can perform tasks on a selected file, such as renaming the file or creating a link for it. You can change the side pane view to a tree view of your file system by selecting from the menu bar View ➤ Side Pane ➤ Tree (Ctrl+t). The Shortcuts entry changes the view back (Ctrl+b).

To configure the Xfce interface, you use the Xfce Settings Manager, accessible from the Applications menu at Settings ➤ Settings Manager. It will be the first entry. This opens the Settings window, which shows icons for your desktop, display, panel, andappearance, among others (see Figure 12-2). Use the Appearance tool to select themes, icons, and toolbar styles (Settings). The Panel tool lets you add new panels and control features, such as fixed for freely movable and horizontally or vertically positioned.

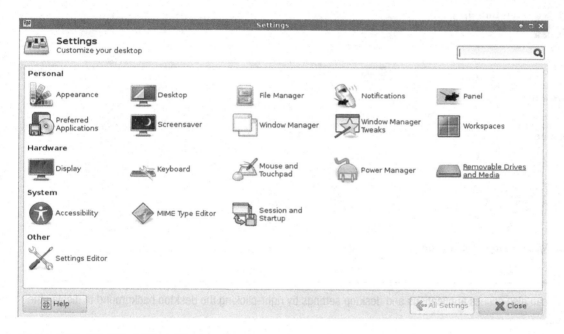

Figure 12-2. *The Xfce Settings Manager*

To configure the desktop, select the Desktop icon in the Settings window or right-click the desktop and select Desktop Settings from the pop-up menu (you can also select Settings ➤ Desktop). This opens the Desktop window, from which you can select the background image (Background tab), control menu behavior (Menus tab), and set icon sizes (Icons tab) (see Figure 12-3).

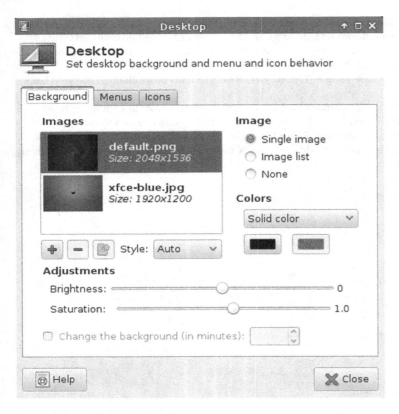

Figure 12-3. Xfce Desktop configuration

■ **Note** You can also access applications and desktop settings by right-clicking the desktop background to display the desktop menu.

The LXDE Desktop

LXDE is another small desktop designed for use on minimal or low-power systems such as laptops, netbooks, or older computers. To install LXDE as an alternative desktop on a system, select the LXDE desktop package on PackageKit (Software).

You can also use LXDE as a Live CD, which you can download from http://fedoraproject.org/en/get-fedora-options#desktops.

The LXDE Live CD is available in 32-bit and 64-bit versions, such as Fedora-20x86_64-Live-LXDE.iso. You can then burn the CD and run it as a Live CD. Double-click the Install icon to install an LXDE-based Fedora system on your computer. Follow the same basic steps for installing Fedora as for the Fedora Live DVD. The Installation Summary screen shows items for Installation Destination, Date & Time, and Keyboard. Be sure to choose the disks to install on and to check the time zone.

The desktop displays a single panel at the bottom with application applets to the right, followed by the windows task bar and system applets (see Figure 12-4). The desktop shows only the Documents folder for the user, not the home directory. From the Fedora Applications menu, you can access any applications.

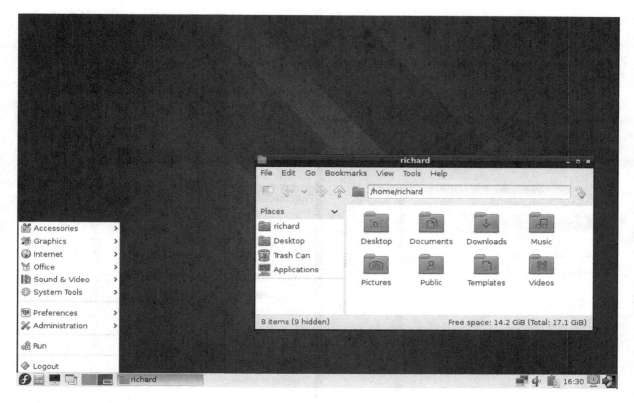

Figure 12-4. *LXDE desktop*

The panel shows applets for the Fedora applications menu, the PC-Man file manager, the terminal window, minimize windows, desktop pager, and window list. On the right side of the panel are the network connection monitor, and the system tray with Network Manager, volume control, clipboard, clock, lock desktop, and the logout button (see Figure 12-5).

Figure 12-5. *LXDE bottom panel*

The logout entry on the Fedora applications menu, and the logout button on the right side of the panel, open a dialog with buttons for logout, shutdown, suspend, hibernate, and reboot.

LXDE uses the PC-Manfile manager, as shown in Figure 12-4. The button bar performs browser tasks such as moving backward and forward to previously viewed folders. The Home button moves you to your home folder. The folder button with the yellow star will open tabs, allowing you to open several folders in the same window. The side pane has a location (Places) and directory tree view. You can switch between the two using the button at the top of the pane. You can also choose from the View ➤ Side Pane menu.

To configure your panelright-click the panel and select Panel Settings. This opens the Panel Preferences window with tabs for Geometry, Appearance, Panel Applets, and Advanced (see Figure 12-6). The Geometry tab lets you set the position and size of the panel. The Appearance tab lets you set the background, theme, and font for the panel. The

Panel Applets tab is where you can add applets to the panel. The applets are referred to as plug-ins. Currently loaded applets are listed, along with format features such as spaces. You have the option to stretch a particular applet to take up any available space on the panel. By default, only the task bar (Window List) is configured to do this. To remove an applet or feature, select it and click the Remove button. If an applet or feature can be configured, the Edit button will become active when you select the applet. You can then click the Edit button to open the applet's configuration dialog. This will vary among applets. To set the time display format, select the clock and click Edit to open the Digital Clock settings dialog. Applets settings can also be edited directly from the panel. Right-click the applet and choose the Settings entry, such as Digital Clock Settings for the digital clock applet.

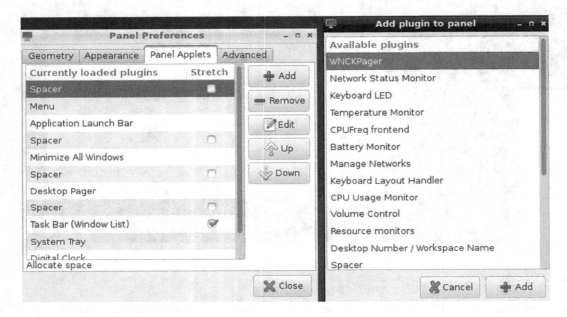

Figure 12-6. *LXDE's Panel Preferences and plug-ins*

To add a new applet to the panel, click the Add button to open the Add Plugin to Panel window, which will list all available applets and panel features like spaces and separators. Select the one you want and click the Add button (see Figure 12-6, right).

To configure the desktop, right-click anywhere on the desktop and choose Desktop Settings from the pop-up menu. This opens the Preferences window with tabs for Appearance and Advanced (see Figure 12-7). The Appearance tab lets you set the background and font. The Advanced tab lets you display window manager menus.

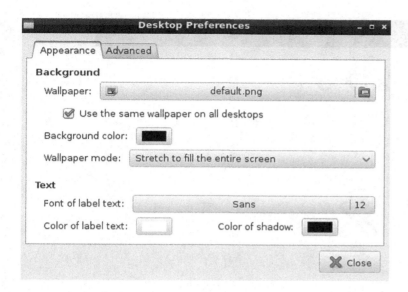

Figure 12-7. *LXDE's Desktop Preferences*

The Sugar on a Stick (SoaS) Desktop

The Sugar on a Stick (SoaS) learning platform is designed for OLPC(One Laptop per Child) computers.

To install Sugar on an installed Fedora system, select the Sugar Desktop Environment package in the Package Collection category on PackageKit (Software).

As a separate Live USB spin, the Fedora 20 OLPC desktop has been integrated into the Sugar on a Stick (SoaS) project at http://wiki.sugarlabs.org/go/Sugar_on_a_Stick.

You can find out more about the Fedora spin of Sugar on a Stick at http://spins.fedoraproject.org/soas/#home.

To create a Live USB, first download the ISO image from http://spins.fedoraproject.org/soas/#downloads.

The Sugar on a Stick live ISO image is available in 32-bit and 64-bit versions, such as Fedora-20x86_64-Live-SoaS.iso. You can then burn the image to a USB drive as a Live USB using Live USB Creator (see Chapter 1).

The Sugar on a Stick project also provides a creation kit (http://download.sugarlabs.org/soas/docs/creation-kit), which you can use to create your own customized Sugar on a Stick system.

The Sugar desktop initially displays a panel with a circular favorites menu (see Figure 12-8). Each icon will start a simple application, beginning at the top with the calculator, text editor, chat, a moon description, terminal window, web browser, and log. The top panel has buttons on the right for the circular favorites menu, or the list version.

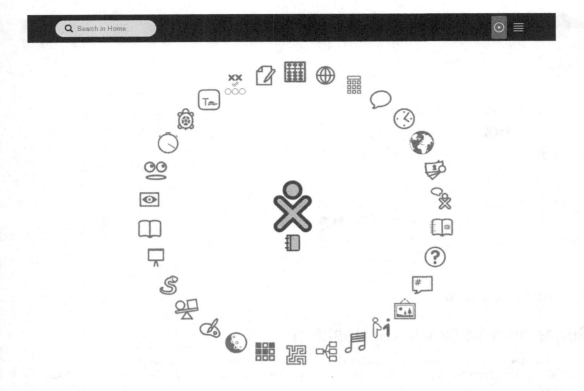

Figure 12-8. Sugar desktop: Favorites

See the following links for Sugar instructions and information: `http://laptop.org/8.2.0/manual/`, `http://laptop.org/8.2.0/manual/Sugar_Interface.html` and `http://laptop.org/8.2.0/manual/Sugar_LaunchingActivities.html`.

To quit Sugar, pass your mouse over your person image at the center of the main screen and leave it there, or right-click the person image. A pop-up menu will appear with the Logout, Shutdown, Restart, and Control Panel entries.

You use the Frame to move around Sugar. The Frame works much like the Panel. It remains hidden until you choose to use it. Move the mouse to a corner, and the Frame will appear. (You can configure it to display if you move the mouse to any side.) You can display the Frame from any activity. The top side of the Frame displays icons for accessing modes. The Home mode is your home screen and uses the "circle around the dot" button. To the left are group and neighborhood view buttons for displaying persons who are accessible on your network. To the right are the Activities button, which displays all your current activities, and the Journal button. The top frame will also display buttons for all your currently running activities. You can use these buttons to quickly move between activities (see Figure 12-9).

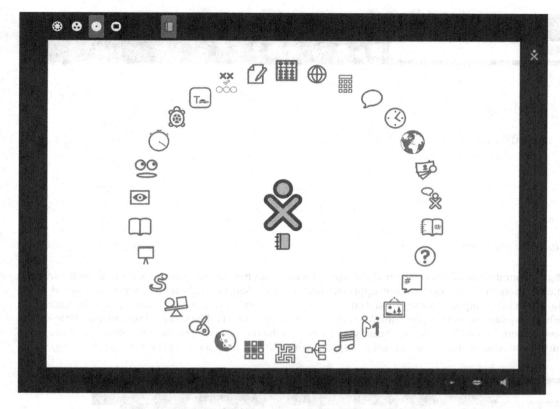

Figure 12-9. *Sugar desktop showing the Frame*

The bottom side of the Frame shows the device status, such as network connection, speech (microphone) and sound (speakers), The left side is used as a clipboard. The right side shows any other accessible users in the neighborhood or group view.

Below the person image is the Journal icon. Use this as your file manager; it also has bookmark and history capabilities. The *journal* is a history of all activities performed on the laptop. All your previous activities are listed. You can change their names and select them for saving. Right-click an activity to Resume, Copy, or Erase. Also, at the right side of an Activity entry is an arrow key that opens the activity's properties. Here, a panel at the top has buttons to Resume, Copy, or Erase. The screen has an image of the activity. There are also boxes labeled Description (for activity description), Tags (search terms), and Participants (shared projects).

To copy an activity, such as a text file or image, to a USB drive, first insert the USB drive. A USB icon will appear on the lower left. Then just click and drag the activity to the USB icon. Before removing the USB drive, place your mouse over it until a pop-up menu appears and select the Unmount entry. Select it, and the USB icon will disappear.

To return to the home screen, move your mouse to a corner to display the Frame and then click the home screen button (the circle around the dot).

When you run an activity, a button bar lets you choose different sets of actions, and those actions are displayed as buttons, menus, or applets in a top panel. Activities are the equivalent of applications. The text editor will have buttons for the Write Activity and several editing operations, such as Cut/Paste, Fonts, Paragraph Format, Lists, and Tables (see Figure 12-10). The panel on top will display different applets, according to the button selected. The Cut/Paste panel supports Undo and Redo, Cut and Paste, and Search operations; while the Fonts panel lets you set the font and size. The Write Activity button displays options to save or quit. Click the Journal icon to save your activity, or press Ctrl+s. To quit, click the octagonal shape on the right side of the top panel, or press Ctrl+q.

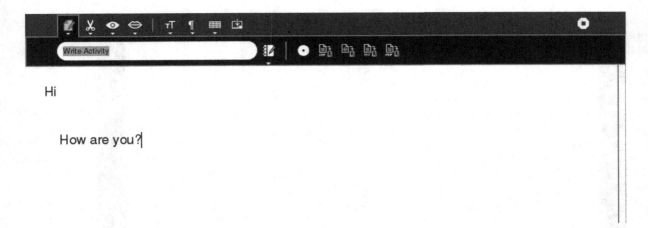

Hi

How are you?|

Figure 12-10. *Sugar text editor*

To configure your desktop, first access the control panel. Place your mouse over your person image on the main screen and hold it there until the pop-up menu appears. Then select My Settings. This opens a screen with icons for About Me, About My Computer, Background, Date & Time, Frame, Keyboard, Language, Modem Configuration, Network, Software Update, and Configure Your Web Services (see Figure 12-11). The tasks are very simple. Date & Time sets the time zone. About Me lets you change your name and the color of your person icon. Network allows you to disable the network connection to save power and specify your collaboration server (jabber.sugarlabs.org).

Figure 12-11. *Sugar: My Settings*

The Mate Desktop

The Mate desktop continuse the development of the older GNOME 2 interface (see Figure 12-12), providing an enhanced version of GNOME 2. Most operations can be performed using the Applications, Places, and System menus. There is both a top and a bottom panel. The top-right panel holds applets for sound, Network Manager, and the date. The bottom panel holds the windows task bar and the pager for workspaces. Mate uses a different file manager from GNOME, called Caja, but it operates much like a GNOME 2 file manager. The file manager window has sidebars with places and tree views. You can use the File, Edit, View, and Go menus to perform most operations. There is a home button and computer button for the home folder and for a computer window, respectively. The desktop also displays icons for both the computer window and the home folder. The computer window shows all your devices.

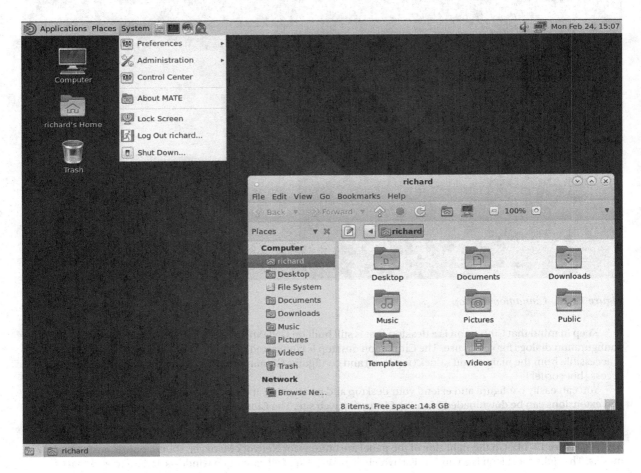

Figure 12-12. *Mate desktop (GNOME 2)*

The Cinnamon Desktop

The Cinnamon desktop is based on GNOME and was developed for the Linux Mint distribution (see Figure 12-13). It uses a variation of the GNOME 3 window manager (Mutter) called Muffin and a variation of the GNOME 3 nautilus file manager called Nemo. Cinnamon, although based on GNOME 3, is designed to work much like a traditional desktop, using a panel, menu, and applets. To install Cinnamon as an alternative desktop on a system, select the

`Cinnamon Desktop` package on PackageKit (Software). Although the panel operates much like the older GNOME 2 panel, Cinnamon also includes overview modes (a GNOME 3 feature) for workspace (expo) and window selection (scale). You can find out more about Cinnamon at :`http://cinnamon.linuxmint.com`.

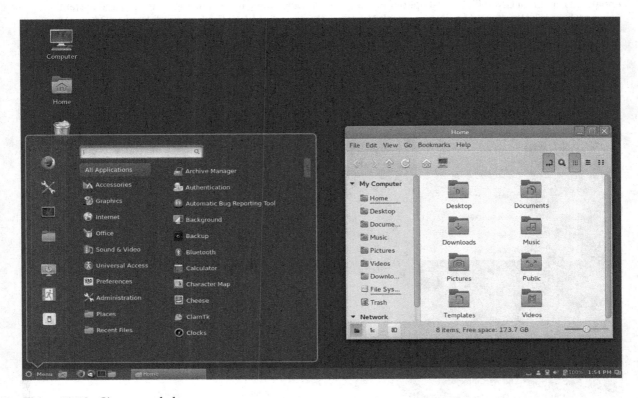

Figure 12-13. *Cinnamon desktop*

Keep in mind that Cinnamon is a desktop that is still built on GNOME 3. As such, there are two setting configuration dialogs for you to use. The Cinnamon desktop is configured using the Cinnamon Settings dialog, which is accessible from the main menu's dock (top icon) and configures Cinnamon features such as applets and overview access (hot corner).

You can easily configure and extend your desktop and panel using applets and extensions. Additional applets and extensions can be downloaded from the Cinnamon web site. The Cinnamon Settings dialogs for applets and extensions have links to those pages.

The Cinnamon desktop features a bottom panel with buttons for menus, applications, and the windows task bar (see Figure 12-14). On the right side of the panel are buttons for Network Manager, sound, power, and calendar menus. The right-most icon is a window list, which displays a list of all your open windows and their workspaces.

Figure 12-14. *Cinnamon's bottom panel*

Panel configuration tasks such as adding applications, selecting applets, setting up menus, and creating new panels are handled from the Panel pop-up menu. Just right-click on the empty space on your panel (the middle) to display a menu with entries for Settings, Troubleshoot, Panel Edit mode, and Panel settings. The pop-up menu lists an addtional entry for "Add applets to the panel." From Settings, you can access commonly used Cinnamon settings such as Applets, Themes, and Menu. From Troubleshoot, you can restart Cinnamon or restore its defaults. You can also turn on the Panel Edit mode, which allows you to change the position of any button on the panel. Using the Cinnamon Settings panel dialog, you can change the position of the panel to the top of the screen or have two panels as GNOME 2 did. You can also change the panel size.

Right-clicking the empty space of the panel displays the same menu with Settings, Troubleshoot, and Panel Edit Mode entries, but with added entries for Panel settings and adding applets to the panel. Clicking the Applets entry opens the Cinnamon Settings ➤ Applets dialog (see Figure 12-15). Using the check boxes, you can add or remove applets. A large number of additional applets can be added that are supported by third-party developers. These are listed on the "Get More Online" tab. The Sort by menu lets you sort the listing by name, score (most popular), and date (latest). An applet entry has a "more info" link, which opens your Web browser to the Mint page describing the applets and comments by users about it. Click on the install button to perform the download and install of all selected applets.

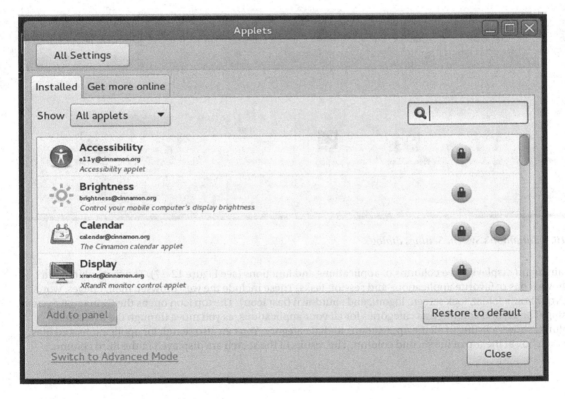

Figure 12-15. *Cinnamon's applets settings*

Clicking the Setting button on the main menu's favorites (first icon) opens the System Settings dialog showing all your Cinnamon desktop configuration tools (see Figure 12-16).

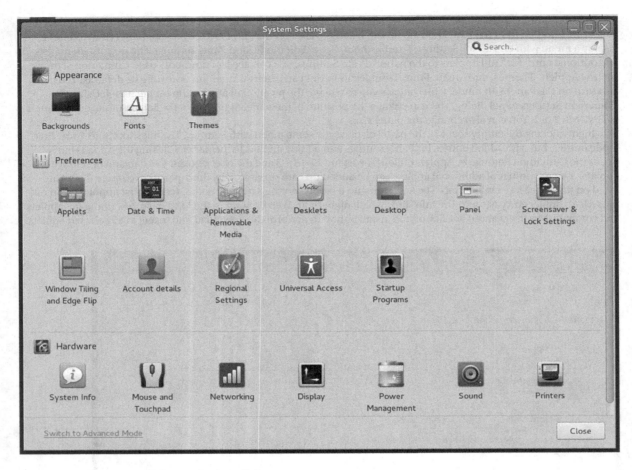

Figure 12-16. *Cinnamon's System Settings dialog*

The main menu displays three columns of applications and functions (see Figure 12-17). The first column is a dock that shows icons of favorite applications and session tasks. These include the web browser, mail, images, word processing, your home folder, lock screen, logout, and shutdown (last icon). The top icon opens the Cinnamon System Settings dialog. The second column lists categories for all your applications, as you move through the categories; the third column shows a listing of all the applications in that category. You can also search for applications and files using the search box at the top of the second column. The results of the search are displayed in the third column.

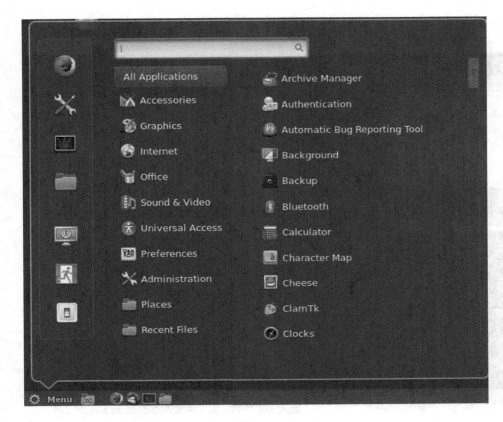

Figure 12-17. *Cinnamon's main menu and favorites*

Workspaces are accessed on Cinnamon from the Expo overview, which you activate by moving your mouse to the top-left corner of the desktop. This opens a workspace switcher displaying your workspaces (see Figure 12-18). Click on a workspace to change to it. A plus button to the right adds new workspaces. When you pass your mouse over a workspace, a close button appears in the upper-right corner, which you can use to remove the workspace. You can move windows from one workspace to another by clicking and dragging them. You can also rename a workspace, by clicking on the text box for its name and entering a new one. To leave the workspace switcher, click a workspace you want to move to, or move the mouse to the hot corner, to return to your current workspace.

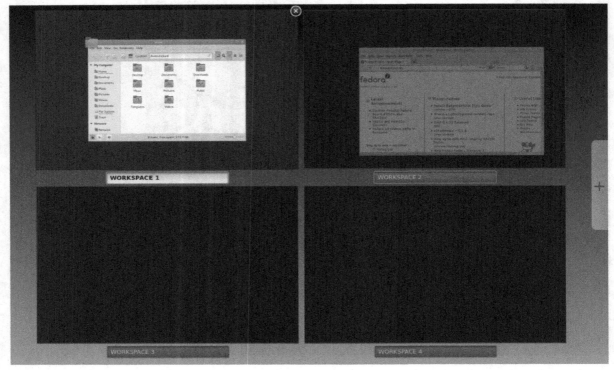

Figure 12-18. Cinnamon workspace switcher overview

You configure access to the workspace switcher (Expo overview) using the Cinnamon Settings Hot Corner dialog. Hot Corner is set to workspace selection by default. However, you can change it to window selection (Scale overview). In this case, thumbnails of your open windows are displayed, and you choose the one you want. Clicking the corner will still open the workspace switcher. The Hot Corner Settings dialog also lets you change the corner to use and enables you to display a hot corner icon.

You can also enable the Scale and Expo applets, which display buttons for the scale and expo overviews. These buttons let you switch to the window selection overview or the window switcher overview from the panel, as shown here:

The Cinnamon file manager, Nemo, works much like previous GNOME file managers, with home and computer buttons and buttons for the icon, list, and compact views (see Figure 12-19). It is based on the GNOME 3 file manager but restores much of the functionality found in the older file manager releases. File, Edit, View, and Go menus let you perform most functions, much like earlier versions of GNOME. The sidebar works much like the current GNOME file manager, with Bookmarks, My Computer, Devices, and Network sections. Right-clicking an entry in the sidebar lets you open it in a new window or tab.

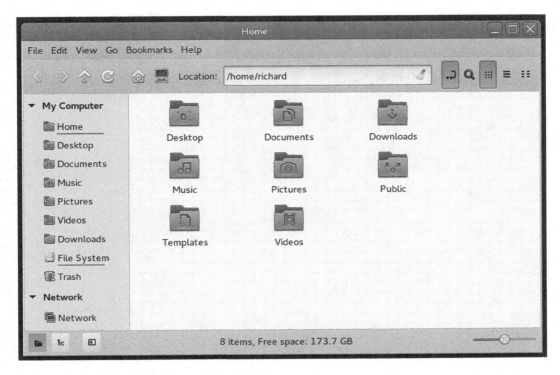

Figure 12-19. *Cinnamon file manager (Nemo)*

The button before the find button lets you toggle to a location text box view, where you can enter a folder path name. The Computer window (computer icon or Computer entry in the Go menu) displays your devices.

Window Managers

In addtion to desktops, there are also several popular window managers available for Fedora, including openbox and fluxbox. The Openbox window manager provides a very minimal interface (http://openbox.org). Openbox initially just displays the desktop background image. Access to all applications and system tools is obtained through the desktop menu. Right-click anywhere on the desktop to display the Openbox menu with entries for Applications, Preferences, Administration, Terminal, exit and logout.

Fluxbox, baseed on the blackbox window manager, provide features such as window tabing, grouping, and editable windows (http://fluxbox.org).

CHAPTER 13

■ ■ ■

Fedora System Tools

Fedora provides several helpful system tools for monitoring—disk management, logs, scheduling, and security (see Table 13-1).

Table 13-1. *Fedora System Tools*

Package Name	Application	Description
system-config-selinux	SELinux Management	Manages and configures SELinux policy
gpk-update	Software update	Package updater (see Chapter 4)
gnome-system-monitor	System Monitor	GNOME System Monitor
gnome-system-log	System Log	GNOME system log viewer
gnome-terminal	Terminal	GNOME terminal window
baobab	Disk Usage Analyzer	Baobab Disk Usage Analyzer
gnome-disk-utility	Palimpsest Disk Utility	Palimpsest DeviceKit disk manager
sealert	SELinux Troubleshooter	setroubleshoot, SELinux alert browser
gnome-power-statistics	Power Statistics	Power usage
Schedule	Scheduled Tasks	GNOME Cron schedule manager

System Monitoring

You can use several tools to monitor your system. On the desktop you can use the GNOME System Monitor, and, from a terminal window, several command line tools are available. The GNOME System Monitor displays system information and monitors system processes (Utilities ➤ System Monitor). It has three tabs: Processes, Resources, and File Systems (see Figure 13-1).

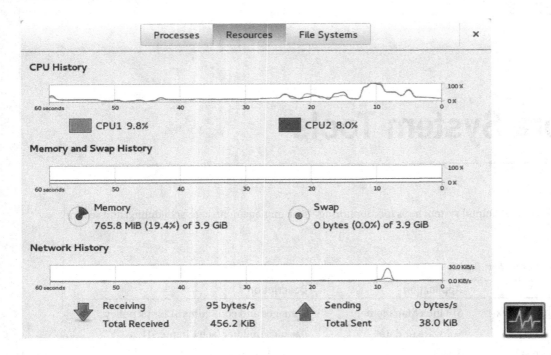

Figure 13-1. *GNOME System Monitor*

■ **Note**   System information, such as the Fedora release, hardware information, and system status, held on the System tab in previous GNOME System Monitor versions, is now available on the System Settings Details dialog's Overview tab.

The Resources tab displays graphs for CPU History, Memory and Swap History, and Network History. If your system has a multi-core CPU, the CPU History graph shows the usage for each CPU. The Memory and Swap Memory graph shows the amount of memory in use. The Network History graph displays both the amount of sent and received data, along with totals for the current session.

The File Systems tab lists your file systems, including where they are mounted, their type, and the amount of disk space used and how much is free. You can sort the list by any category. Device, directory, and type names are listed alphabetically. Total, free, available, and used space can be sorted numerically in ascending or descending order. Double clicking on a file system entry will open that file system in a file manager window.

The Processes tab lists your processes, letting you sort or search for processes. You can use field buttons to sort by name, process ID, user, and memory. The View pop-up menu lets you select all processes, just your own or active processes. You can easily stop any process by selecting it and then clicking the End Process button. Right-clicking an item displays actions you can take on the process, such as stopping it, killing it, or changing its priority. The Open Files option opens a window listing all the files that the process is using. The Memory Maps display, selected from the View menu, shows information on virtual memory, inodes, and flags.

From a terminal window, you can use tools such as **vmstat**, **free**, **top**, and **iostat** to monitor your system. The **vmstat** command outputs a detailed listing indicating the performance of different system components, including CPU, memory, I/O, and swap operations. A report is issued as a line with fields for the different components. If you provide a time period as an argument, it repeats at the specified interval—usually a few seconds. The **top** command provides a listing of the processes on your system that are the most CPU intensive, showing what processes are using most of your resources. The listing is in real time and updated every few seconds. Commands are provided for changing a process's status, such as its priority. The **free** command lists the amount of free RAM memory on your system, showing how much is used and how much is free, as well as what is used for buffers and swap memory. The **iostat** command displays your disk usage, and **sar** shows system activity information.

Managing Processes

Should you have to force a process or application to quit, you can use the GNOME System Monitor Processes tab to find, select, and stop it. You should be sure of the process you want to stop. Ending a critical process could cripple your system.

Application processes will bear the name of the application, and you can use those to force an application to quit. Ending processes manually is usually preformed for open-ended operations that you are unable to stop normally. In Figure 13-2, the Firefox application has been selected. Clicking the End Process button on the lower left will force the Firefox web browser to end (you can also right-click the entry and select End from the menu).

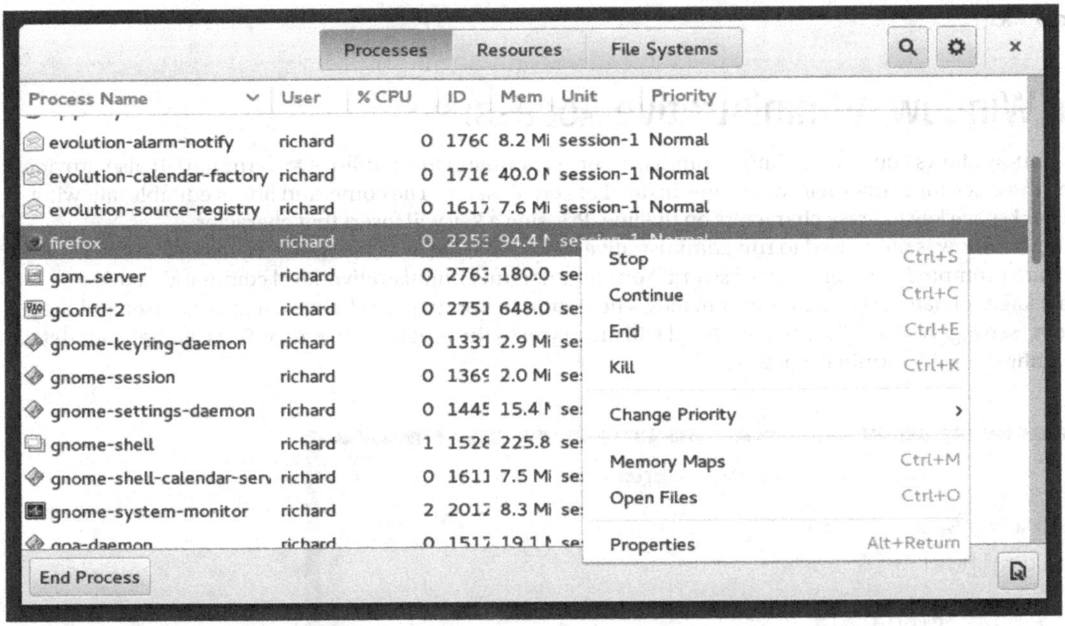

Figure 13-2. *GNOME System Monitor, Processes tab*

You can also use the kill command in a terminal window to end a process. The kill command takes as its argument a process ID. Be sure you obtain the correct one. Entering the incorrect process ID could also cripple your system. Use the ps command to display a process ID. You cna search for a process using the -C option or the -aux options. The ps command with the -C option searches for a particular application name. The -o pid= option displays only the process ID, instead of the process ID, time, application name, and tty. Once you have the process ID, you can use the kill command, with the process ID as its argument, to end the process.

```
$ ps -C firefox -o pid=
5555
$ kill 5555
```

One way to ensure the correct number is to use the ps command to return the process number directly as an argument to a kill command. The process is then stopped by first executing the ps command to obtain the process ID for the firefox process (back quotes), and then using that process ID in the kill command to end the process. The -o pid= option displays only the process ID.

```
kill `ps -C firefox -o pid=`
```

To search for a process using a pattern, you can use a ps command with the -aux option to list all processes and pipe the output to a grep command with a specified pattern. The following command lists all X Window System processes:

```
ps -aux | grep 'X'
```

Terminal Window Administrative Access: su

The terminal window allows you to enter Linux commands on a command line (Utilities ➤ Terminal). It also provides you with a shell interface for using shell commands instead of your desktop. The command line is editable, allowing you to use the Backspace key to erase characters on the line. Pressing a key will insert that character.

The terminal window is often used to run administrative tasks. First, log in as the root user, using the su command. You are prompted to enter your password. You can then run administrative-level commands, such as yum to install packages or nano to configure system files. The terminal prompt then changes to the root user and the current directory (see Figure 13-3). The cd command will move you to the root user directory. See Chapter 3 for details on using and configuring the terminal window.

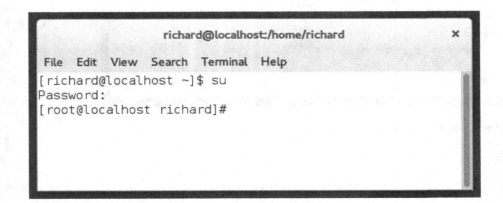

Figure 13-3. Terminal window

If the root password is not known, and the **sudo** command is enabled (see Chapter 14), you can use the **sudo** command in combination with the **su** command for the same effect.

```
sudo su.
```

Schedule Tasks

Scheduling regular maintenance tasks, such as backups, is managed by the cron service on Linux and implemented by a cron daemon. A daemon is a continually running server that constantly checks for certain actions to take. These tasks are listed in the crontab file. The cron daemon constantly checks the user's crontab file to see if it is time to take these actions. Any user can set up a crontab file. The root user can set up a crontab file to take system administrative actions, such as backing up files at a certain time each week or month.

Creating cron entries can be a complicated task, using the crontab command to make changes to crontab files in the /etc/crontab directory. Instead, you can use several desktop cron-scheduler tools to easily set up cron actions. Two of the more useful tools are KCron and GNOME Schedule, which creates an easy-to-use interface for creating scheduled commands.

GNOME Schedule

GNOME Schedule provides an easy-to-use interface for managing scheduled tasks (see Figure 13-4; install Scheduled Tasks on GNOME Software or the gnome-schedule package on PackageKit). Once installed you can access it as Scheduled Tasks.

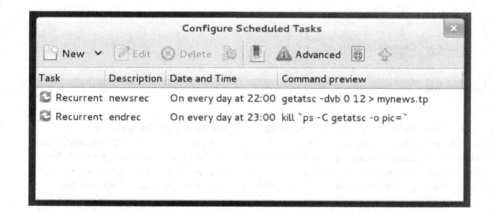

Figure 13-4. *GNOME Schedule*

Use the New button to schedule a task. You are first asked if you want to create the task as a recurrent item, a one-time task, or a task from a template. The Create a New Scheduled Task window then opens, from which you can specify the time and date and whether to repeat the task weekly or monthly (see Figure 13-5). You can use the Basic radio button to set defaults for Hourly, Daily, Weekly, or Monthly entries. Then click Advanced to specify a time.

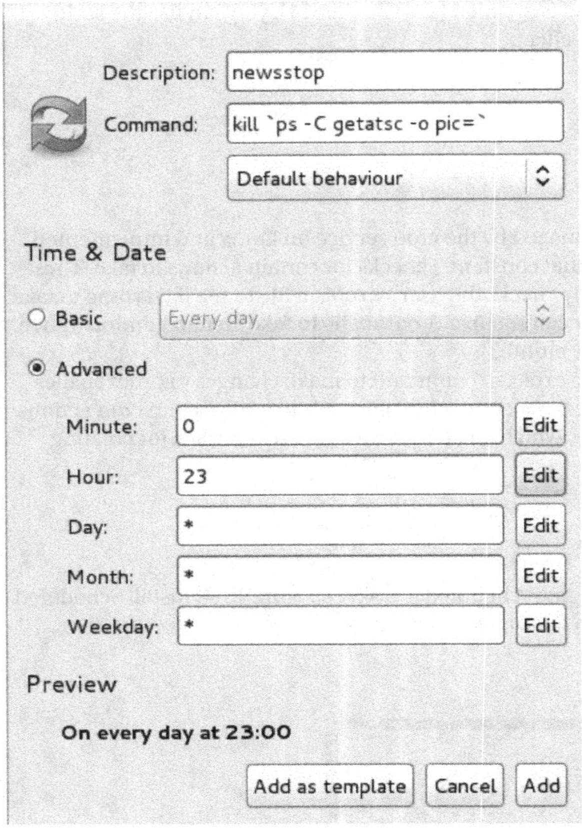

Figure 13-5. *GNOME Schedule new task*

The template feature lets you set up a new schedule with information for a previous one, using the same or similar commands but a different time. Click the Template button to add a new template. This opens a window similar to the Create Task window in Figure 13-5. Once you have created the template, you can use it to generate scheduled tasks. When creating a task, from the initial menu, choose A Task from a Predefined Template. This option opens the Choose Template window. Clicking the Use Template button opens the Create Task window, from which you can modify your task.

To delete a task, simply select the entry in the Scheduled Tasks window and click the Delete button. To run a task immediately, select and click the Run Task button.

On the Scheduled Tasks window, you can click the Advanced button to see the actual cron entries created by GNOME Schedule.

KDE Task Scheduler (KCron)

On KDE you can use the KDE Task Scheduler (KCron) to set up user- and system-level scheduled tasks (install the kdeadmin package). You access the Task Scheduler on the System Settings window, System Settings ➤ Task Scheduler (System Administration section). The Task Scheduler window will list your scheduled tasks. Click the New Task button to open a New Task window in which you can enter the command to run, add comments, and then specify the time in months, days, hours, and minutes from simple arranged buttons. On the Task Scheduler window, you can select a task and use the side buttons to modify it, delete the task, run it now, or print a copy of it. For tasks using the same complex commands or arguments, you can create a variable and then use that variable in a command. Variables are listed in the Environment Variables section. To use a variable in a scheduled task, precede its name with the $ character when you enter the command. Entering just the $ symbol in the Command text box will display a drop-down list of predefined system variables you can use, such as $PATH and $USER.

System Logs, journals, and journald

Various system logs for tasks performed on your system are stored and managed by the journald logging daemon. In effect, logs are now considered to be journals accessible by a systemd daemon, journald. From the command line (terminal window), you can use the journalctl command to access messages. The -f option displays the last few messages and is equivalent to displaying the last few messages in the old /var/log/messages file. The following command lists the last few messages:

journalctl -f

To see logs from the last system startup (boot), you use the -b option.

journalctl -b

To see messages for a particular service, you use the -u option and the name of the unit's service file, such as samba.service. The following lists the messages for the samba server.

journalctl -u samba.service

With the --since and --until options, you can further specify a time.

journalctl -u samba.service --since=12:00

If you want, you can still install and run the older rsyslogd, which stores message in the /var/log/messages file.

GNOME Log File Viewer

To view these logs you can use the GNOME Log File Viewer, Utilities ➤ Log File Viewer (System Log on GNOME Software and the gnome-system-log package on PackageKit). A sidebar lists the different logs. Selecting one displays the log in the right pane (see Figure 13-6). A search button on the top right opens a search box, in which you can search for messages in the selected log. A menu button on the top right lets you perform tasks such as zooming, copying, selecting, and filtering. The Log File Viewer queries the journald daemon for log reports using journalctl.

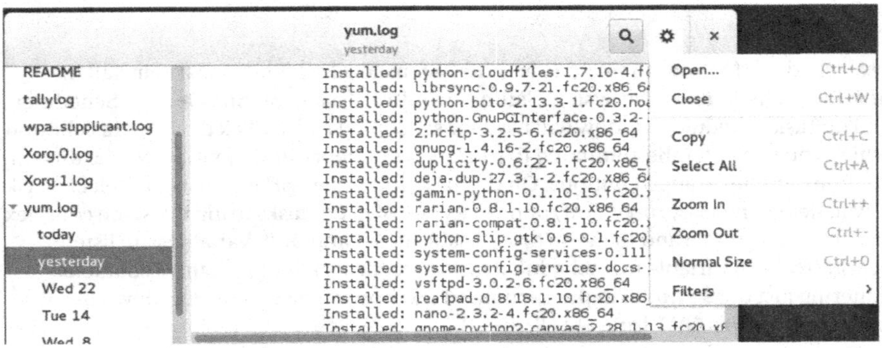

Figure 13-6. *GNOME Log File Viewer*

Disk Usage Analyzer

The Disk Usage Analyzer lets you see how much disk space is used and available on all of your mounted hard disk partitions (see Figure 13-7), Utilities ➤ Disk Usage Analyzer. It also checks all LVM and RAID arrays. Usage is shown in a simple graph, letting you see how much overall space is available. On the scan dialog, you can choose to scan your home directory. You can choose your home folder, your entire file system (disk drive icon), an attached device such as a USB drive, or a remote folder (Scan Remote Folder button). When you scan a directory or the file system, disk usage for your directory is analyzed and displayed. Each file system is shown with a graph for its usage, as well as its size and the number of top-level directories and files. Then the directories are shown, along with their size and contents (files and directories).

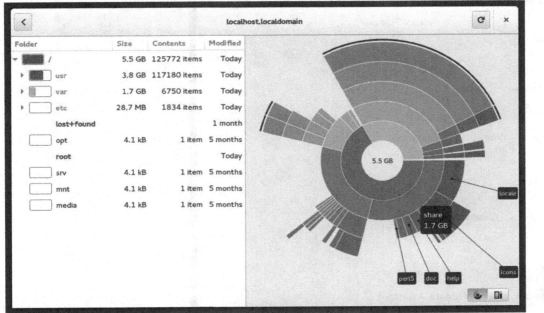

Figure 13-7. *Disk Usage Analyzer*

A representational graph for disk usage is displayed on the right pane. The graph can be a Ring Chart or a Treemap. The Ring Chart is the default. Choose the one you want from the button on the lower right. For the Ring Chart, directories are shown, starting with the top-level directories at the center and moving out to the subdirectories. Passing your mouse over a section in the graph displays its directory name and disk usage, as well as all its subdirectories. The Treemap chart shows a box representation, with greater disk usage in larger boxes, and subdirectories encased within directory boxes.

Virus Protection

Though viruses are rare on Linux, especially on Fedora, which has advanced security features such as SELinux, they can still occur. As a precaution you can install the free and open source Clam Anti-Virus virus protection software (www.clamav.net). On Gnome Software choose ClamTK or, for KDE, KlamAV. On PackageKit choose the clamav, clamav-filesystem, clamav-lib, clamav-update, clamav-data, on either ClamTK (clamtk package, GNOME) or KlamAV (KDE) front ends. Once installed, you can access it as ClamTK. With ClamTK, you can scan specific files and directories, as well as your home directory (see Figure 13-8). Searches can be recursive, including subdirectories. You have the option to also check dot configuration files. Infected files are quarantined. The ClamTK dialog has four sections: Configuration, History, Updates, and Analysis. Updates can be automatic or manual. Click the Help button on the upper right to open the ClamTK Virus Scanner documentation with details on scanning updates, and settings.

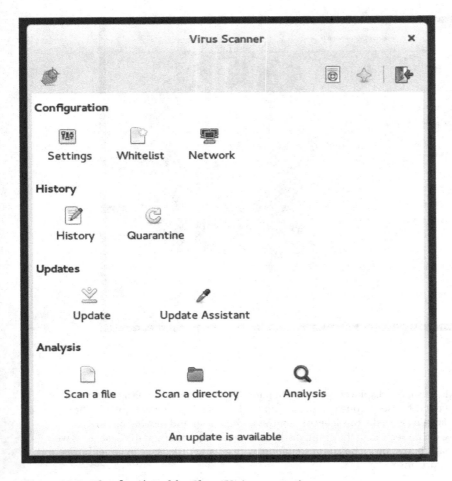

Figure 13-8. The `clamtk` *tool for ClamAV virus protection*

To permit updates, you first have to edit the `/etc/freshclam.conf` file to remove the example entry. Open a terminal window and log in as the root user, then enter the `nano` or `vi` command to edit the file.

```
su
nano /etc/freshclam.conf
```

Find the example entry at the top and comment it out or remove it. Insert a space between the `#` and `Example` text to comment it, as shown following:

```
# Comment or remove the line below
# Example
```

You can also install the `clamav-milter` and `clamav-scanner` packages, which work with your e-mail application, to detect viruses.

Disk Utility and Udisks

Disk Utility (Palimpsest) is a Udisks-supported user configuration interface for your storage media, such as hard disks, USB drives, and DVD/CDs, (gnome-disk-utility package). Supported tasks include disk labeling, mounting, disk checks, and encryption. You can also perform more advanced tasks, such as managing partitions. Disk Utility is accessible from Utilities ➤ Disks. Users can use Disk Utility to format removable media such as USB drives. Disk Utility is also integrated into the file manager, letting you format removable media directly.

The Disk Utility window shows a sidebar (Devices) with entries for your storage media (see Figure 13-9). Clicking an entry displays information for the media on the right pane. Removable devices, such as USB drives, display an eject button and a task menu with an entry to format the disk. If you are formatting a partition, such as that on removable media, you can specify the file system type to use.

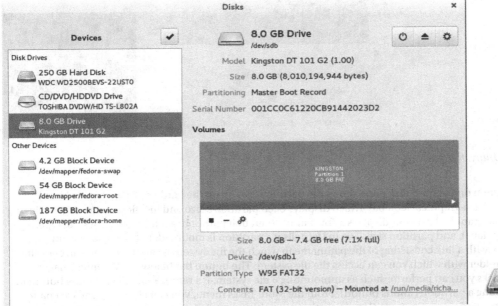

Figure 13-9. *Disk Utility (Palimpsest)*

■ **Warning**   Disk Utility (Palimpsest) will list your fixed hard drives and their partitions, including the partitions on which your Fedora Linux system is installed. Be careful not to delete or erase these partitions.

If you select a hard disk device, information about the hard disk is displayed on the right pane, such as the model name, size, partitioning, serial number, and, for hard disks, a status assessmentsee Figure 13-10). Click the task button to display the task menu on the upper right with tasks you can perform on the hard drive: Format, Benchmark, and SMART (Self-Monitoring, Analysis, and Reporting Technology) Data & Self-Tests.

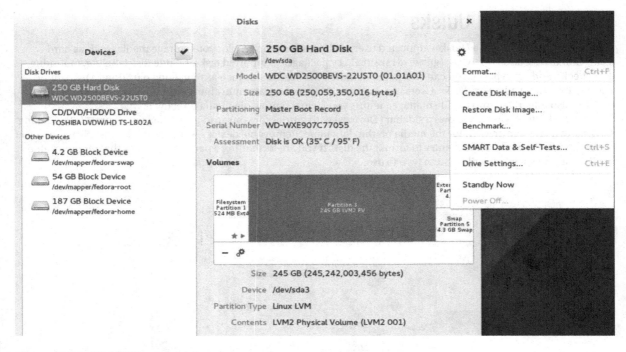

Figure 13-10. *Disk Utility, hard drive*

The Volumes section on the hard disk pane shows the partitions set up on the hard drive (see Figure 13-11). Partitions are displayed in a graphical icon bar, which displays each partition's size and location on the drive. Clicking a partition entry on the graphical icon bar displays information about that partition, such as the file system type, device name, partition label, and partition size. The In Use tells if a partition is mounted. If it is in use, it shows a Yes: Mounted At entry with a link consisting of the pathname in which the file system is mounted. You can click this pathname to open a folder with which you can access the file system. The button bar below the Volumes images provides additional tasks you can perform, such as unmounting a file system, if a removable drive, (square button in Figure 13-9) and deleting a partition (minus button). From the More Tasks menu, you can choose entries to change the partition label, type, and mount options. Certain partitions, such as extended and swap partitions, display limited information and have few allowable tasks.

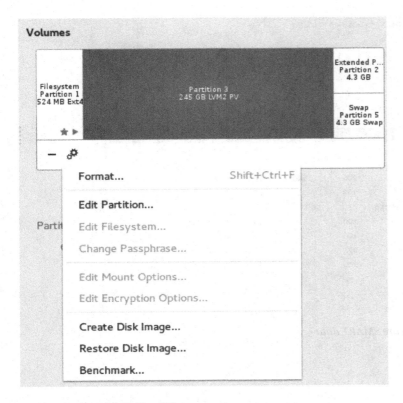

Figure 13-11. *Disk Utility, Volumes section*

For more detailed hardware information about a hard drive, you can choose the "SMART Data & Self-Tests" entry from the task menu (gear button) in the hard drive's Drives section. This opens a SMART data dialog with hardware information about the hard disk (see Figure 13-12), including temperature, power cycles, selft-test status, the self-test assessment, and the overall health of the disk. The Attributes section lists SMART details, such as the read error rate, spinup time, and write error rate. Click the switch to on to enable the tests, and off to disable testing. Click the "Refresh" button to manually run the tests. Click the "Start Self-test" button to open a menu with options for short, extended, and conveyance tests.

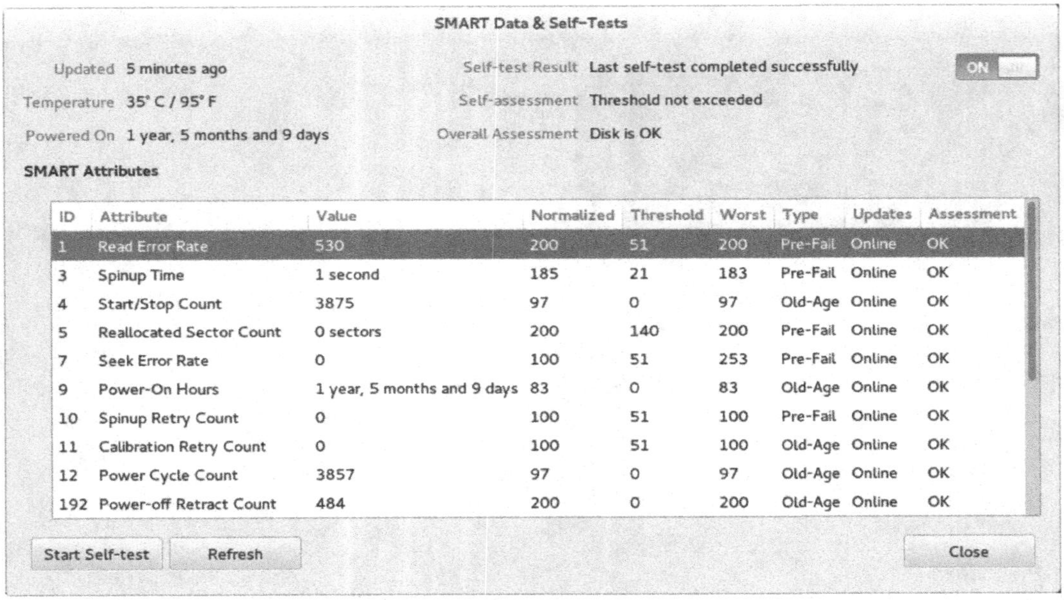

SMART Data & Self-Tests

Updated	5 minutes ago
Temperature	35° C / 95° F
Powered On	1 year, 5 months and 9 days

Self-test Result	Last self-test completed successfully
Self-assessment	Threshold not exceeded
Overall Assessment	Disk is OK

ON

SMART Attributes

ID	Attribute	Value	Normalized	Threshold	Worst	Type	Updates	Assessment
1	Read Error Rate	530	200	51	200	Pre-Fail	Online	OK
3	Spinup Time	1 second	185	21	183	Pre-Fail	Online	OK
4	Start/Stop Count	3875	97	0	97	Old-Age	Online	OK
5	Reallocated Sector Count	0 sectors	200	140	200	Pre-Fail	Online	OK
7	Seek Error Rate	0	100	51	253	Pre-Fail	Online	OK
9	Power-On Hours	1 year, 5 months and 9 days	83	0	83	Old-Age	Online	OK
10	Spinup Retry Count	0	100	51	100	Pre-Fail	Online	OK
11	Calibration Retry Count	0	100	51	100	Old-Age	Online	OK
12	Power Cycle Count	3857	97	0	97	Old-Age	Online	OK
192	Power-off Retract Count	484	200	0	200	Old-Age	Online	OK

Start Self-test   Refresh   Close

Figure 13-12. *Disk Utility, hard disk hardware SMART data*

Hardware Sensors

A concern for many users is the temperature and usage of computer components. You install different software packages to enable certain sensors (see Table 13-2). For the CPU, system, fan speeds, and any other motherboard supported sensors, you use the lm_sensors service. Download and install the lm_sensors package. First, you must configure your sensor detection. In a terminal window, log in as the root user (su) and enter the following (answer yes to the prompts):

su
sensors-detect

Table 13-2. *Sensor Packages and Applications*

Sensor Application	Description
lm_sensors	Detects and accesses computer (motherboard) sensors, such as CPU and fan speed. Runs sensors-detect once to configure
hddtemp	Detects hard drive temperatures
ksenors	KDE sensor applet

This service will detect hardware sensors on your computer. It will run as the lm_sensors service.

For hard drive temperature detection, you install hddtemp. You will have to enable the hddtemp daemon, using the service command as the root user, and then you can start the server.

```
su
service hddtemp enable
service hddtemp start
```

If your hard disks are not detected, you can to configure the /etc/sysconfig/hddtemp file to detect specific hard drives. Add the device name of the drives, using [abcd] to match the last letter, as in /dev/sd[abcd] for the sda, sdb, sdc, and sdd hard drives. In the following example, the device name /dev/sd[adcd] was inserted into the HDDTEMP_OPTIONS entry after 127.0.0.1, the localhost IP address used to reference your system.

```
HDDTEMP_OPTIONS="-l 127.0.0.1 /dev/sd[abcd]"
```

To edit the hddtemp file, you must open a terminal window and log in as the root user. Then use an editor such as nano or vi. The nano editor is easier to use. (Press Ctrl+o to save and Ctrl+x to exit; use arrow keys to navigate.)

```
su root
nano /etc/sysconfig/hddtemp
```

You can then download and install the ksensors package, the KDE applet for displaying sensor information. On GNOME, you can access it as KSensors. KSensors will reside in the message tray (lower-right corner), showing the temperature of the first item in its panel. Click the eicon to open the KSensors panel. On KDE, access Ksensors from Applications ➤ System ➤ Hardware Monitor, where it will appear as an icon on the system tray. Once opened, right-click the KSensors dialog and choose Configure from the pop-up menu to open the KSensors configuration dialog (see Figure 13-13). On the sidebar, choose a sensor category such as Hard Disks, radeon (AMD video card), or nouveau (Nvidia video card) sensors. On the right pane, you can choose from a Sensors, and Preferences tab. The Preferences tab sets the update frequency and temperature scale. The Sensors tab has subtabs that let you change the name (General), make something visible on the panel (Panel) or dock (Dock), or set an alarm(Alarm). For the System Inforamtion tab, a System Panels tab replaces the Sensors tab with there are subtabs for system information such as CPU Speed and RAM used, which you can make visible and set the tile and colors. To have a temperature displayed on the KSensors panel, but sure to click its visible checkbox on its Panel tab,a nd then click on the Apply button. Once configured, click the KSensors icon in the message tray to open the KSensors panel (see Figure 13-14).

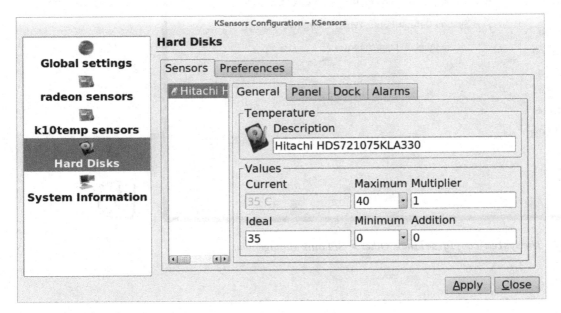

Figure 13-13. KSensors Configuration

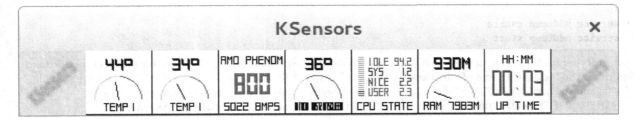

Figure 13-14. KSensors

SELinux: Configuration with system-config-selinux

With system-config-selinux, you can manage and configure your SELinux policies, although you cannot create new policies. You can install system-config-linux using the Packages package manager. Its package name is policycoreutils-gui. You can access system-config-selinux as SELinux Management. The SELinux Administration window lists several panes with a sidebar menu for Status, Boolean, File Labeling, User Mapping, SELinux User, Network Port, Policy Module, and Process Domain (see Figure 13-15). system-config-selinux will invoke the SELinux-management tools, such as sestatus and semanage, with appropriate options to make configuration changes.

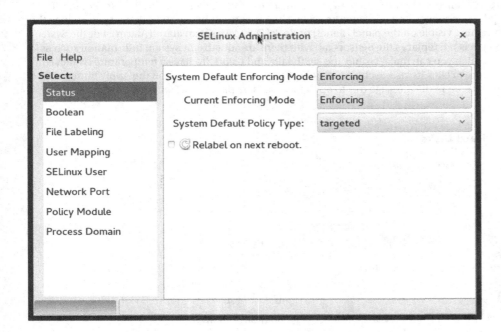

Figure 13-15. The system-config-selinux, Other ➤ SELinux Management

The Status pane sets the default and current enforcing modes. Here you can enable or disable SELinux, as well as specify the policy type. By default, the enforcing modes are set to Enforcing. You have the choice of Disable, Permissive, and Enforcing. If you are experiencing difficulties accessing your system, you can set the enforcing modes to Permissive or Disabled. Permissive will allow access, but issue warning messages. Disabled will completely shut down SELinux. The policy is normally targeted, focusing on network services like Samba and Apache. You can download and install more restrictive policies, but you may need a detailed understanding of SELinux to manage them.

This pane also features the relabeling option. Sometimes when you install new server software or update your system, you may need to relabel some of your files and directories. Relabeling will mark the files and directories to correct security access. Check Relabel on Next Reboot to perform the relabeling. It may take some time.

You can also quickly turn the enforcing mode on an off from a terminal window with the **setenforce** command. The 0 argument turns it off, and the 1 argument turns it on.

Use the **getenforce** command to see what your current enforcement mode is.

```
getenforce
```

■ **Note** Configuration for general SELinux server settings is carried out in the **/etc/selinux/config** directory. Currently there are only two settings available: the state and the policy. You set the SELINUX variable to the enforcement mode, such as enforcing or permissive, and the SELINUXTYPE variable to the kind of policy you want.

User Mapping shows the mapping of user login names to SELinux users. Initially, there will be two mappings: the root user and the default user.

The Boolean pane lists various options for targeted services, such as web and FTP servers, NFS, and Samba (see Figure 13-16). With these, you can further modify how each service is controlled. There are expandable menus for different services, such as FTP, Apache web server, and Samba. For example, the FTP entry lets you choose whether to allow access to home directories or to NFS transfers.

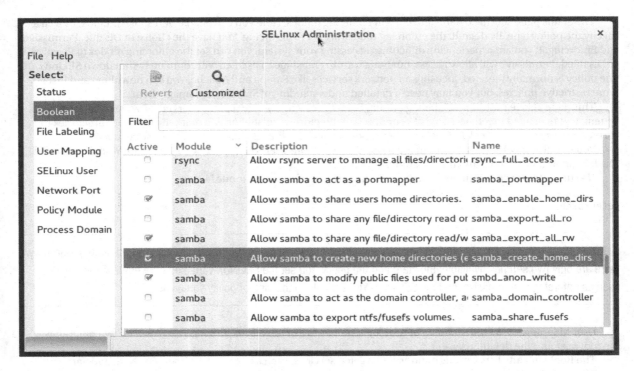

Figure 13-16. *system-config-selinux SELinux Boolean pane*

To allow access to many network services, you must not only allow access through your firewall but also through SELinux. The Boolean pane has entries for the different network services. Samba, in particular, has to have its Boolean entries set before you can access Samba shares.

The File Labeling pane will list your system directories and files, showing their security contexts and types. You can edit a file's properties by selecting the entry and then clicking Properties. This displays a dialog with File Name, Type, SELinux Type, and Multi-Level Security (MLS) levels. MLS gives a security level value to resources. Only users with access to certain levels can access the corresponding files and applications. You can change the SELinux type or the MLS level. For a permissive policy, the MLS level will be s0, allowing access to anyone. You can also add or delete entries.

The SELinux Users pane shows the different kinds of SELinux users. Initially, there will be several user types, including root, system_u, and user_u. The root user has full and total administrative access to the entire system. The system_u user allows users to take on administrative access where needed. The user_u user is for normal users. Each entry lists its SELinux user, SELinux prefix, MLS level, MLS range, and SELinux roles. MLS level is the access level (s0 on a permissive policy), and MLS range is the range of access from SystemLow to SystemHigh. A given user has certain roles available. The root user has the system_r, sysadm_r, and staff_r roles, allowing that person system access, administration capability, and staff user access. The user_u users also have a system_r role, allowing those users to perform system administration, if they have the root user password.

The Network Port pane lists the network protocol, the SELinux type, and the MLS security level for ports on your system. Select an entry and click Properties to change the SELinux type or the MLS level for the port. The Group View button will display the SELinux type, along with a list of the ports they apply to. This view does not display the MLS level, as these apply to ports individually.

The Policy Module pane lists the different SELinux policy modules. Here, you will see modules for different applications, such as Thunderbird and Evolution, as well as device service such as USB. Listed also are desktops such as GNOME. The pane allows you to add or remove modules. You can also enable or additional audit rules for a module for logging.

SELinux Troubleshooting and audit2allow

Fedora includes the SELinux troubleshooter, which notifies users of problems that SELinux detects. Whenever SELinux denies access to a file or application, the kernel issues an AVC (Access Vector Cache) notice. These are analyzed by the SELinux troubleshooter to detect problems that users may have to deal with. When a problem is detected, a SELinux troubleshooter notification is displayed in the desktop message tray, along with the troubleshooter icon, as shown here:

Clicking the icon or notice will open the SELinux troubleshooter window. You can also access it at any time as SELinux Troubleshooter. You can find out more information about SELinux troubleshooter at `https://fedorahosted.org/setroubleshoot/`.

The SELinux troubleshooter window displays the current notice (see Figure 13-17). Use the Next and Previous buttons to page through notices. The number of the displayed notice is shownbetween the Previous and Next buttons.

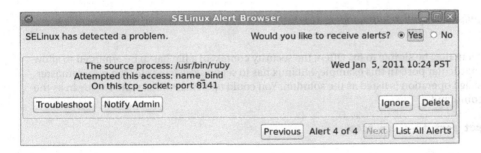

Figure 13-17. SELinux troubleshooter

Clicking the Troubleshoot button displays detailed information about the notice, listing what you may be trying to do and possible solutions (see Figure 13-18). To see a full description of the problem and solution in a separate window, click the Details button to the right of the solution description (see Figure 13-19).

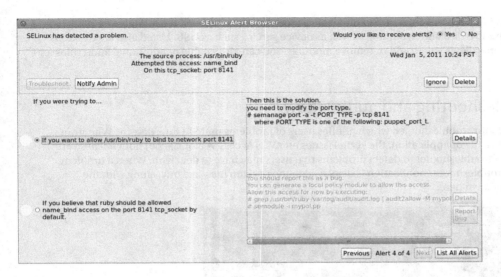

Figure 13-18. *SELinux troubleshooter, troubleshoot listing*

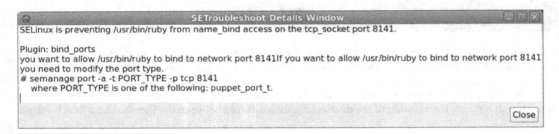

Figure 13-19. *SELinux troubleshooter, full details window*

In many cases, the problem may be simple to fix. Often, the security context of a file has to be renamed to allow access, or access set up to a particular port. In this example, SELinux has to set up port access for the puppetmaster service on port 8141. A semanage operation is listed as the solution. You could open a terminal window, log in as the root user (su), and run the command.

```
semanage port -a -t puppet_port_t -p tcp 8141
```

You could also use the SELinux Management tool to make the changes. In this case, you'd choose the Network Port tab and click the Add button to open the Add Network Port dialog.

For a security context change, you use the chcon command. In the following example, access is granted by Samba to the /mymedia directory.

```
chcon -R -t samba_share_t '/mymedia'
```

To see a full listing of error messages at once, click the List All Alerts button to display a list of alert notices, along with their date, the number of times the error has occurred, its category, and a brief explanation (see Figure 13-20). The Delete button lets you delete alerts.

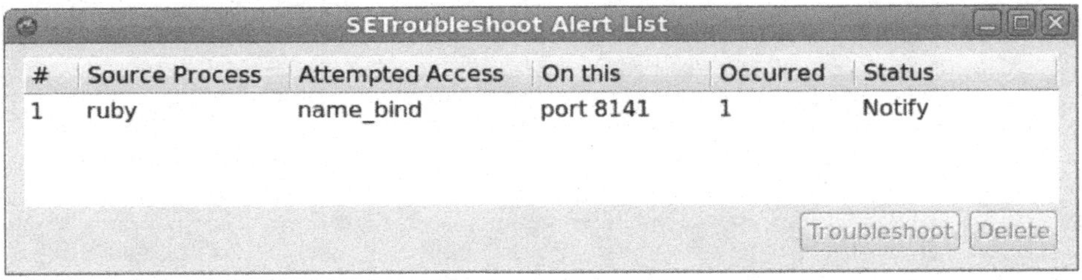

SETroubleshoot Alert List
Source Process Attempted Access On this Occurred Status
1 ruby name_bind port 8141 1 Notify
Troubleshoot
Delete

Figure 13-20. SELinux troubleshooter alert list

More complicated problems, especially ones that are unknown, may require you to create a new policy module, using the AVC messages in the audit log. To do this, you can use the `audit2allow` command. The command will take an audit AVC message and generate commands to allow SELinux access. The audit log used on Fedora is `/var/log/audit/audit.log`. This log is output to `audit2allow`—you then can use its `-M` option to create a policy module.

```
cat /var/log/audit/audit.log | audit2allow -M local
```

You then use the `semodule` command to load the module.

```
semodule -i local.pp
```

If you want to first edit the allowable entries, you can use the following code to create a `.te` file of the local module, `local.te`, which you can then edit.

```
audit2allow -m local -i  /var/log/audit/audit.log   >  local.te
```

Once you have edited the `.te` file, you can then use `checkmodule` to compile the module, then `semodule_package` to create the policy module, `local.pp`. Then you can install it with `semodule`. You first create a `.mod` file with `checkmodule` and then a `.pp` file with `semodule_package`.

```
checkmodule -M -m -o local.mod local.te
semodule_package -o local.pp  -m local.mod
semodule -i local.pp
```

In the preceding example, the policy module is called `local`. If you later want to create a new module with `audit2allow`, you should either use a different name or append the output to the `.te` file, using the `-o` option.

CHAPTER 14

■ ■ ■

System Administration

To make effective use of your Fedora Linux system, you must know how to configure certain features and services. Administrative operations, such as adding users and installing software, can be performed with user-friendly system tools. This chapter discusses basic system administration operations that you need to get your system up and running, as well as to perform basic maintenance, such as adding new users. You can make changes or additions easily, using the administrative tools described in this chapter.

Configuration operations can be performed from a desktop interface, such as GNOME or KDE, or they can be performed using a simple shell command line, on which you type configuration commands. You can also manually access system configuration files, editing them and making entries yourself. For example, some file system-mounted configuration entries are kept in the /etc/fstab.conf file. You can edit this file and type the mount operations for file systems. Configuration tools are accessible only to the root user. Although these tools are accessible from any user account, you will first be prompted for the root user password before you can use them.

■ **Tip**   If you have difficulties with your system configuration, check the www.fedorasolved.org site for possible solutions. The site offers help ranging from solutions to video and network problems to solutions for games, browsers, and multimedia.

Fedora Administrative Tools

On Fedora, administration is handled by a set of separate, specialized administrative tools developed and supported by Fedora, such as those for user management and printer configuration (see Table 14-1). Users & Groups lets you create and modify users and groups. Printing lets you install and reconfigure printers. All tools provide intuitive graphical user interfaces that are easy to use. The actual names normally begin with the term system-config. For example, the printer configuration tool is listed as Printing, but its actual name is system-config-printer. You can separately invoke any tool by entering its name in a terminal window.

Table 14-1. *Administrative Tools*

/Command	Application	Description
authconfig-gtk	Authentication	Sets authentication settings
system-config-date	sytem-config-date	Changes system date/time
gnome-control-center datetime	Date & Time	System Settings date and time configuration tool
firewall-config	Firewall	Configures your network firewall
system-config-lvm	Logical Volume Management	Configures LVM file system volumes
system-config-printer	Printing	Printer configuration tool
gnome-control-center printers	Printers	System Settings printer configuration tool
system-config-rootpassword	Root Password	Changes the root user password
system-config-samba	Samba	Configures Samba
system-config-services	Services	Manages such services as starting and stopping servers
system-config-users	Users & Groups	User and Group configuration tool.
gnome-control-center user-accounts	User Accounts	System Settings user configuration tool
policycoreutils-gui	SELinux Management	SELinux configuration
gnome-control-center network	Network	System Settings network configuration tool
nm-connections-editor	Network Connections	Network Manager configuration tool

With GNOME 3, several administrotion tools have been developed that will be supersceding corresponding older system-config tools. For example, the GNOME Control Center user accounts is the defalt user management tool, insted of the older system-config-users. For printing you can use the GNOME Control Center printing tool, instead of system-config-printer. The GNOME Control Center was covered in chapter 3, as most of its tools are used for desktop configuration, instead of administration purposes. Tools that have administrative functions, such as the user accounts tool, are described in the administrative chapters(14,15, and 16). You can access any of the GNOME Control Center tools from the System Settings dialog as described in Chapter3.

Some tools overlap with the new GNOME 3 System Settings tools, such as Users for user accounts and Printers for printing. To set the date, you can use either the System Settings Date & Time or system-config-date (Sundry ➤ Date & Time).

Superuser Control: The Root User

To perform system administration operations, you must supply the root user password, making you the superuser. Because a superuser has the power to change almost anything on the system, such a password is usually given only to those whose job is to manage the system. With the superuser password, you can log in to the system as a system administrator and configure the system in different ways. You can also access administrative tools for specific tasks from any account, temporarily giving you superuser access for just that administrative operation. As a superuser, you can perform tasks such as starting up and shutting down the system, adding or removing users, formatting file systems, backing up and restoring files, and you may also specify the system's hostname.

Administrative Access from Normal User Accounts

To access an administrative tool, you simply log in to a normal account and choose the tool you want. A dialog is then displayed that will prompt you to enter the root user password. Once you do so, the administrative tool you chose starts up, allowing its functions to have full root user access (see Figure 14-1). The same kind of permission is required for updates. When you're logged in to any normal account, you will be notified of any new updates. When you open the Software Update tool, you will first be prompted by the same dialog for a root user password. For each different administrative tool you start, you must separately enter the root user password.

Figure 14-1. *Administrative access authentication dialog*

Logging In to the Root User Account Directly: su

There are situations in which you might want to log in directly to the root user account. If you are performing several administrative tasks at once, or if you have to modify configuration files directly, root user account access may work best. The root user is a special account reserved for system management operations with unrestricted access to all components of your Linux operating system. You can log in as the root user from a terminal window or from the command-line login prompt.

If you log in from the command-line interface, you can run corresponding administrative commands, such as rpm to install packages or useradd to add a new user. From your desktop, you can also run command-line administrative tools, using a terminal window. The command-line interface for the root user employs a special prompt, the sharp sign, #. In the following example, the user logs in to the system as the root user and receives the # prompt.

```
login: root
password:
#
```

su

When logged in as a normal user on the desktop, you can then log in as a root user, using a terminal window and the su command (**su** stands for switch user). This is helpful if you just need to quickly run a command as a root user. You can use the su command with the root username, or the su command alone (the root username will be assumed). You will be prompted to enter the root user password.

su root
password:

In the following example, the user logs in as the root user and then runs the nmb script using the service command, which requires root user access.

su
password:
service nmb start

To exit from a su login operation, when you are finished with that account, simply enter exit.

exit

If you log in as the root user with the su command in a terminal window, you cannot run desktop applications from that terminal window as the root user. You can, however, run the leafpad editor from a root user terminal window, allowing you to use leafpad to edit configuration files. leafpad is a simple desktop editor.

su
leafpad /etc/default/grub

■ **Note**   The su command can actually be used to log in to any user, provided you have that user's password.

Root Password

Because a superuser has the power to change almost anything on the system, the root user password is usually a carefully guarded secret, changed very frequently and given only to those whose job it is to manage the system. With the correct password, you can log in to the system as a system administrator and configure the system in different ways. You can also add or remove users, add or remove whole file systems, back up and restore files, and even designate the system's name and address.

To change the root user password, you can use the Root Password dialog (system-config-rootpassword package). You can also use the passwd command in a terminal window, once you have logged in as the root user. Both will check your password to see if you have selected one that can be easily cracked.

Controlled Administrative Access: sudo

The sudo command allows ordinary users to have limited root user administrative access for a specific task. Users can perform a superuser operation without having full root-level control. You can find out more about sudo at www.sudo.ws. Normal users are not configured for sudo access by default, though the root user, if specified, is. For normal user access, you must first configure that user to have sudo access. This requires editing the /etc/sudoers file. Once you have sudo access, you can use administrative tools as the root user, giving you direct root user access with desktop capabilities.

sudo Configuration

Access with the sudo command is controlled by the /etc/sudoers file. This file lists users and the commands they can run, along with the password for access. If the NOPASSWD option is set, then users will not require a password. ALL, depending on the context, can refer to all hosts on your network, all root-level commands, or all users. To make changes or add entries, you have to edit the file with the special sudo editing command, visudo. This invokes the vi editor to edit the /etc/sudoers file. Unlike a standard editor, visudo will lock the /etc/sudoers file and check the syntax of your entries. You are not allowed to save changes, unless the syntax is correct. Use the vi editing commands to make changes (see Chapter 5). If you want to use a different editor, you can assign it to the EDITOR shell variable. Log in first as the root user, using the su command, then enter visudo.

```
su
visudo
```

A sudoers entry has the following syntax. The host is a host on your network. You can specify all hosts with the ALL term. The command can be a list of commands, some or all qualified by options such as whether a password is required. To specify all commands, you can also use the ALL term.

```
user    host=command
```

The following gives the user robert full root-level access to all commands on all hosts:

```
robert  ALL = ALL
```

Use vi commands to edit the file. You can move to the root user entry and then press the o command to open a new line. Type the new user entry and then press the ESC key. Press Shift+zz when you've finished editing.

In addition, you can let a user run as another user on a given host. Such alternate users are placed within parentheses before the commands. For example, if you want to give robert access to the mypic host as the user fineart, you use the following:

```
robert mypic = (fineart) ALL
```

By default, sudo will deny access to all users, including the root. For this reason, the default /etc/sudoers file sets full access for the root user to all commands. The ALL=(ALL) ALL entry allows access by the root to all hosts as all users to all commands.

```
root    ALL=(ALL)    ALL
```

To specify a group name, you prefix the group with a % sign, as in %mygroup. This way, you can give the same access to a group of users. The /etc/sudoers file contains samples for a %wheel group.

To give robert access on all hosts to the system-config-users tool, you would use the following:

```
robert ALL=/usr/bin/system-config-users
```

If a user wanted to see which commands he or she can run, that user would use the sudo command with the -l option.

```
sudo -l
```

Using sudo

Once the user is configured, the user can use sudo to run an administrative command. The user precedes the command with the sudo command. The user is then issued a time-sensitive ticket to allow access.

```
sudo date
```

The sudo command becomes very useful when you have to perform an otherwise ordinary task with root user access. This allows you to avoid having to log in as the root user, yet still allows you to have extensive root user access over the system. One very common use is to employ the gedit graphical text editor to edit system configuration files. There is no specific administrative tool to do this, so ordinarily, you would have to log in as the root user to perform this task. With the sudo command, however, you can edit any system configuration file from a normal account. The following example would let you edit the /etc/fstab file, used for automatic file system mounting. Open a terminal window and enter the command. You will be prompted for the user password, then gedit will start as a functional desktop editor.

```
sudo gedit /etc/fstab
```

You could even run the file manager as a sudo operation, allowing the file manager full administrative access from any normal account. The file manager will open to the root user account.

```
sudo files
```

One advantage of using sudo over su is that sudo allows you to use certain desktop applications, such as gedit, as the root user, whereas su only allows command-line operation.

Controlled Access with PolicyKit: polkit-1

Designed by the Freedesktop.org project, PolicyKit allows ordinary users and applications access to administration-controlled applications and devices. Currently, it supports several key administrative operations, including Network Manager, Udisks, PackageKit, Firewall, Samba, and system monitor. Though this could be done with other operations, such as group permissions, PolicyKit aims to provide a simple and centralized interface for granting users access to administration-controlled devices and tools. PolicyKit is used to grant access to shared devices managed by Udisks. This includes most of the devices on your system, including removable ones.

PolicyKit can allow for more refined access. Instead of an all-or-nothing approach, whereby a user has to gain full root-level control over the entire system just to access a specific administration tool, PolicyKit can allow access to specific administrative applications. All other access can be denied. A similar kind of refined control is provided with PAM and sudo, allowing access to specific administrative applications, but administrative password access is still required, and root-level access, though limited to that application, is still granted. You can find out more about PolicyKit at http://hal.freedesktop.org/docs/polkit.

PolicyKit configuration and support is already set up for you. A new version of PolicyKit, polkit-1, is now used for PolicyKit operations. Configuration files for these operations are held in /usr/share/polkit-1. There is, as of yet, no desktop tool available for configuring these settings. The desktop tool polkit-gnome only provides GNOME dialogs for providing authentication, when required by an application or device.

Changing PolicyKit Options

With PolicyKit, administration-controlled devices and applications are set up to communicate with ordinary users, allowing them to request certain actions. If the user is allowed to perform the action, the request is then authorized, and the action is performed.

Difficulties occur if you want to change the authorization setting for certain actions, such as mounting internal hard drives. Currently, you can change the settings by manually editing the configuration files in the /usr/share/polkit-1/actions directory, but this is risky. To make changes, you first must know the action to change and the permission to set. The man page for polkit will list possible authorizations. The default authorizations are allow_any for anyone, allow_inactive for a console, and allow_active for an active console only (user logged in). These authorizations can be set to the following specific values:

auth_admin	Administrative user only, authorization always required
auth_admin_keep	Administrative user only, authorization kept for a brief period
auth_self	User authorization required
auth_self_keep	User authorization required, authorization kept for a brief period
yes	Always allow access
no	Never allow access

You will have to know which PolicyKit action to modify and which file to edit. The action is listed in the PolicyKit dialog, which prompts you to enter the password (expand the Details arrow) when you try to use an application. The File will be the first segments of the action, with the suffix policy attached. For example, the action for mounting internal drives is

```
org.freedesktop.udisks2.filesystem-mount-system-internal
```

Its file is

```
org.freedesktop.udisks2.policy
```

The file is located in the /usr/share/polkit-1/actions directory. Its full pathname is:

```
/usr/share/polkit-1/actions/org.freedesktop.udisks2.policy
```

By default, PolicyKit is configured to require authorization, using the root password before a user can mount an internal hard drive partition. Should you want to allow users to mount partitions without an authorization request, the org.freedesktop.udisks2.policy file in the /usr/share/polkit-1 directory has to be modified to change the allow_active default for the filesystem-mount-system action from auth_admin_keep to yes. The auth_admin_keep option requires administrative authorization.

Enter the following to edit the org.freedesktop.udisks.policy file in the /usr/share/polkit-1/actions directory with the nano text editor. First log in as the root user, su.

```
su
nano /usr/share/polkit-1/actions/org.freedesktop.udisks2.policy
```

If you are configured as a valid `sudo` user in the `/etc/sudoers` file, you can use the `sudo` command instead, which allows you to use desktop editors such as `gedit`.

```
sudo gedit /usr/share/polkit-1/actions/org.freedesktop.udisks2.policy
```

Locate the `action id` labeled as

```
<action id ="rg.feedesktop.udisks2.filesystem-mount-system">
  <description>Mount a filesystem on a system device</description>
```

This is usually the second action ID. At the end of that action section, you will find the following entry. It will be located within a defaults subsection, `<defaults>`.

```
<allow_active>auth_admin</allow_active>
```

Replace `auth_admin_keep` with yes.

```
<allow_active>yes</allow_active>
```

Save the file. Users will no longer have to enter a password to mount internal partitions.

Authentication: authconfig-gtk

To confirm that user identities are valid, your network may provide several authentication services. These can be enabled on your system using `authconfig-gtk` (Sundry ➤ Authentication). The `authconfig-gtk` tool is not installed by default with the desktop install. The `authconfig-gtk` tool has three tabs: Identity & Authentication, Advanced Options, and Password Options (see Figure 14-2). On the Identity & Authentication tab, the User Account Database drop-down menu is used to specify a service such as NIS and LDAP, which maintains configuration information about systems and users on your network. If your network maintains LDAP, NIS, and Winbind authentication servers, you can enable support for them here, specifying their servers and domains. Entries available on the Identity & Authentication dialog will change according to the database you choose (see Figure 14-3). The LDAP and FreeIPA databases display a text box in which you can enter the address for your LDAP server. When you select a service from the User Account Database menu, the Identity & Authentication tab expands to list Authentication Configuration options. From the Authentication Method drop-down menu, you can select a Kerberos or password method. Kerberos is the default and will display entries for specifying the Kerberos KDC and administration server addresses.

Figure 14-2. `authconfig-gtk`

The Advanced Options tab allows you to configure settings such as the user account database to use and the authentication method (SHA512, SHA256, and so on) used for the system. Smart Card support is also available in the configuration tool. Using the Advanced Options tab, you can also enable support for fingerprint readers and local access control files (/etc/security/access.conf). Additionally, you can configure password hashing used by the system. The Password Options tab allows you to configure the minimum password length.

Using this tool, you can configure the various options available for authenticating users on your system. By default, the settings are already configured with local authentication using shadow and MD5 passwords enabled, as shown in the figures. If you select a network authentication option, you will need to supply the servers and other information needed to connect to and use the selected service. After making your modifications, click the Apply button to save your changes and apply the new authentication configuration.

Default Permissions and umask

By default, whenever you create a directory or file, it is given predetermined permissions. A directory is given the permission 755, which allows all users read and execute access, but only the owner read, write, and execute access. A file is given the more restrictive permission 644, which allows read and write for the owner, but only read access for the group and others.

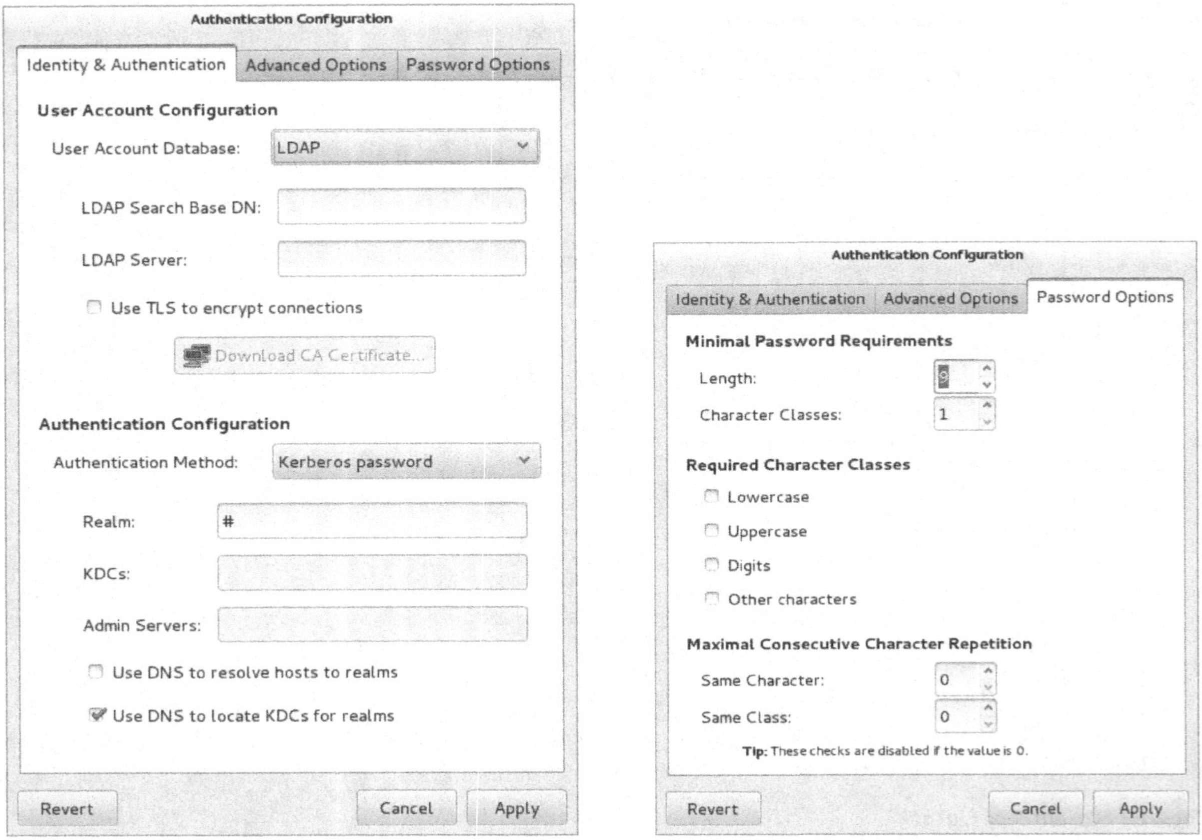

Figure 14-3. *authconfig-gtk: LDAP and password options*

The Advanced Options tab lets you set authentication options, such as a password-hashing algorithm. From a pop-up menu, you can select the password encryption codec. SHA512 is the default. Other options provide for more controlled access, such as not creating user home directories until the user first logs in, or checking /etc/security/access.conf for users to deny or allow access. You can also enable fingerprint reader support. The Password Options tab lets you set required password features, such as length, digits, uppercase, same characters, and character classes (see Figure 14-3, right).

The System Security Services daemon (SSSD) provides offline access for users relying on remote authentication, such as an LDAP server. The SSSD will cache the authentication method, allowing you to log in offline. Before SSSD, users had to maintain a corresponding local account from which to gain access when offline. SSSD is installed by default. You start it using the sssd daemon. Configuration is integrated into authconfig-gtk. Configuration files are located at /etc/sssd. See https://fedorahosted.org/sssd/ for more details.

Desktop Login to the Root User

Access to the root user is disallowed by default by the GNOME Display Manager (GDM), your login window. This feature is designed as a security precaution, and it is recommended that you leave it in place. Should you want to access the root user desktop, you can configure your system to restore root user access from the login window. See the following site for details: http://fedoraproject.org/wiki/Enabling_Root_User_For_GNOME_Display_Manager.

To enable access, you edit the /etc/pam.d/gdm file as the root user. This is the PAM configuration file for the GDM. Then comment out the following line by placing a # sign before it, as shown. It will be the second line. To later disable root user access, just remove the comment sign.

```
# auth required pam_succeed_if.so user != root quiet
```

Date and Time

You can set the system date and time using System Settings Date & Time (discussed in Chapter 3), the shell date command, or the older system-config-date tool. You probably set the date and time when you first installed your system. You should not have to do so again. However, if you entered the time incorrectly or moved to a different time zone, you could use this utility to change your time.

Using the system-config-date Utility

The system-config-date utility displays two tabs: one for the date and time and one for the time zone (see Figure 14-4). The Date and Time tab displays a calendar for manually setting the time or a list of network time servers for setting the time automatically over a network. The Time Zone tab displays a map with locations. Select the one nearest you to set your time zone. Install system-config-date using GNOME Software or PackageKit. system-config-date is accessible from the Sundry subview on Applications.

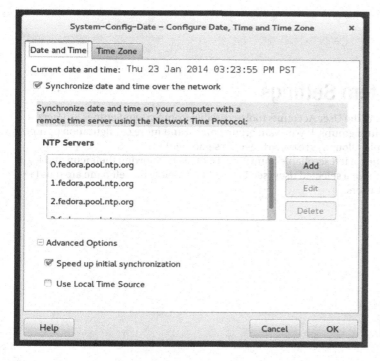

Figure 14-4. system-config-date

On the Date and Time tab, by default the "Synchronize date and time over the network" item is checked, enabling the Network Time Protocol (NTP) service. The Date and Time tab displays a list of NTP servers. Using NTP allows a remote server to set the date and time, instead of using local settings. NTP allows for the most accurate synchronization of your system's clock. It is also used to manage the time and date for networked systems, freeing the administrator from having to synchronize clocks manually. You can download current documentation and NTP software from the www.ntp.org site.

From the list of time servers, you can select the server to use. NTP servers operate through pools that will randomly select an available server to increase efficiency. A set of pools designated for use by Fedora is already installed for you, beginning with 0.fedora.pool.ntp.org. If access with one pool is slow, change to another. The pool servers support worldwide access. Pools for specific geographical locations can be found at the NTP Public Services Project site (Time Servers link), http://ntp.isc.org. A closer server could be faster. The Advanced Options allows you to speed up initial synchronization and lets you use a local time source if you have one, such as a radio-controlled time device for your computer.

If you uncheck the "Synchronize date and time over the network" check box, the tab displays a calendar and a time box. Use the calendar to select the year, month, and date. Then use the time box to set the hour, minute, and second.

Using the date Command

You can use the date command on your root user command line to set the date and time for the system. As an argument to date, you list (with no delimiters) the month, day, time, and year. In the next example, the date is set to 2:59 p.m., April 4, 2014. That's 04 for April, 04 for the day, 1459 for the time (2:59 p.m.), and 08 for the year 2014

```
date 0404145914
Fri Apr 4 02:59:22 PST 2014
```

User Accounts: Users, System Settings

You can configure and create user accounts using the User Accounts tool accessible from System Settings as Users. User Accounts does not provide any way to control groups. If you want group control and more configuration options, you can use the GNOME Users and Groups application (system-config-users package).

The User Accounts dialog displays two panes, a left scrollable pane for a list of users, showing their icon and login name, and a right pane, showing information about a selected user (see Figure 14-5). Below the left pane are plus (+) and minus (-) buttons, for adding and deleting users.

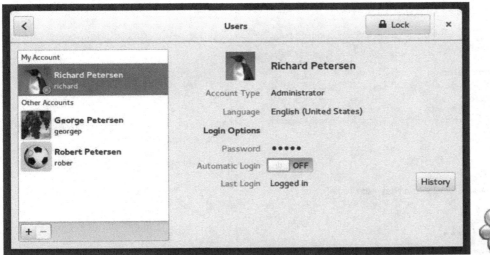

Figure 14-5. *User Accounts*

When User Accounts is active, the applications menu on the GNOME top bar displays a Settings menu with Help and Quit options. Choosing the Help entry opens the User Account help pages in GNOME desktop help, with detailed steps for most tasks and an explanation of administrative privileges.

PolicyKit controls administrative access for the Users tool. When you first click a task button such as the plus or minus, an Authenticate dialog will open and prompt you to enter your user password. You will also be prompted to authenticate if you try to change a user password, account type, icon, or name.

When you add a new account, a dialog opens, allowing you to set the account type (standard or administrator), the full name of the user, and the username (see Figure 14-6). For the username, you can enter a name or choose from a recommended list of options. You can also choose to set the password at this time. Click Add to create the user. The new account appears on the right pane, showing the name, icon, account type, language, password, and an automatic login option.

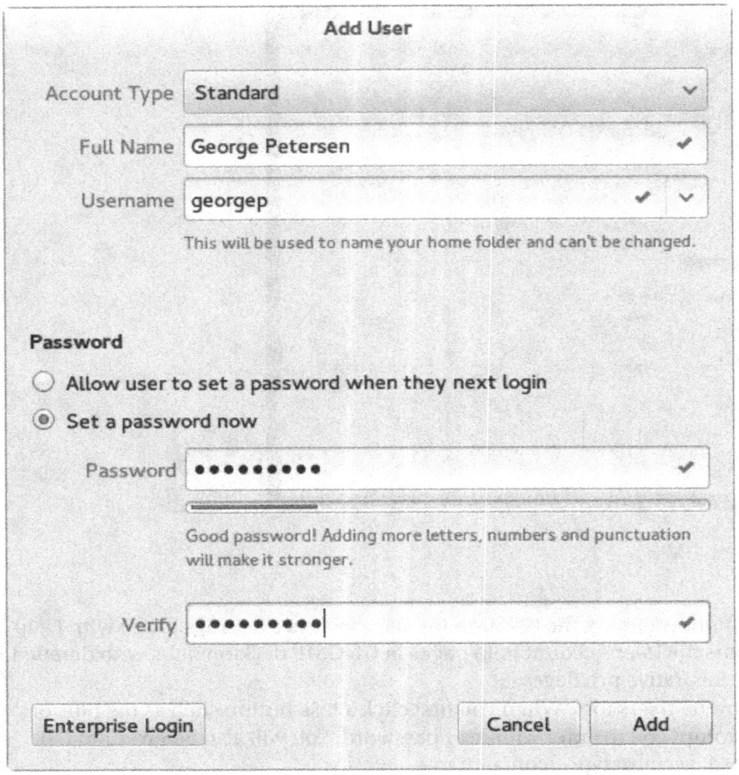

Figure 14-6. *Add a new user*

The account remains inactive until you specify a password (see Figure 14-7). You can do this when you add the account or later. You can also change the password for an account. Click the password entry to open a dialog in which you can enter the new password (see Figure 14-8). On the right side of an empty Password text box a password generator button is displayed that will generate a password for you when clicked. Once clicked, a generated password is entered into the text box and the button disappears, replaced by a checkmark. Deleteing the password to show an empty box, once again displayes the password generator button. Once the password is selected, the account becomes enabled.

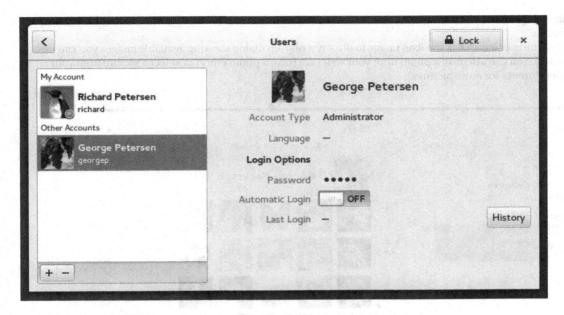

Figure 14-7. *Users, inactive user*

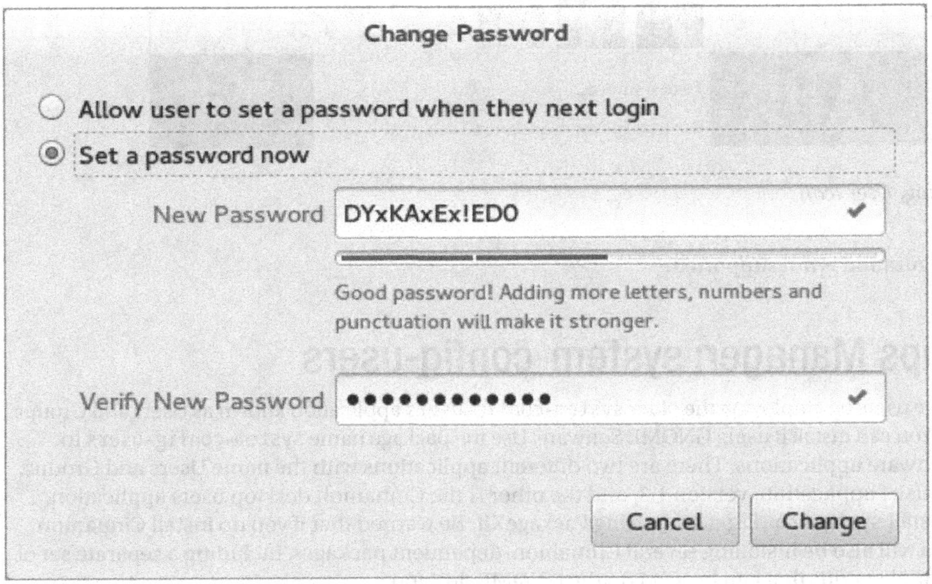

Figure 14-8. *Users, password dialog*

You can change the account type, language, password, and icon by clicking on their entries. You will be prompted for authorization.

To change the user icon, click the icon image to display a pop-up dialog showing available images you can use (see Figure 14-9). You can also take a photo from your web cam (take a photo entry) or select a picture from your Pictures folder (browse for more pictures).

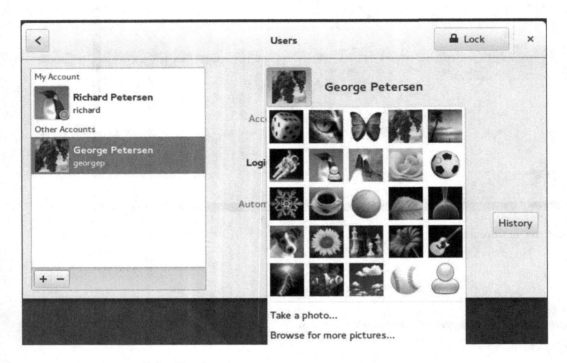

Figure 14-9. *Accounts dialog, User Icon*

Currently, group configuration is not supported.

Users and Groups Manager: system-config-users

You can also add and manage users by employing the older system-config-users application known as Users and Groups. It is not installed by default. You can install it using GNOME Software. Use the package name system-config-users to locate it on the GNOME Software applications. There are two different applications with the name Users and Groups. One is the system-config-user application, version 1.3, and the other is the Cinnamon desktop users application, version 2.0. You can also install system-config-users using PackageKit. Be warned that if you do install Cinnamon Users and Groups (2.0), you will also be installing several Cinnamon-dependent packages, including a separate set of Cinnamon system-setting applications that can be used on the GNOME desktop.

Once installed, you can access User and Groups as Users and Groups. The system-config-users window displays tabs for listing both users and groups (see Figure 14-10). A button bar lists various tasks you can perform, including adding new users or groups, editing current ones (Properties), or deleting a selected user or group. You are prompted for authentication once, when you first open Users and Groups. You can then make changes as you wish.

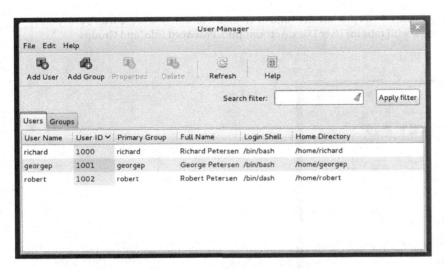

Figure 14-10. *Users and Groups:* `system-config-users`

Users and Groups: New Users

To create a new user, click Add User to open a window with entries for the username, password, and login shell, along with options for creating a home directory and a new group for that user (see Figure 14-11).

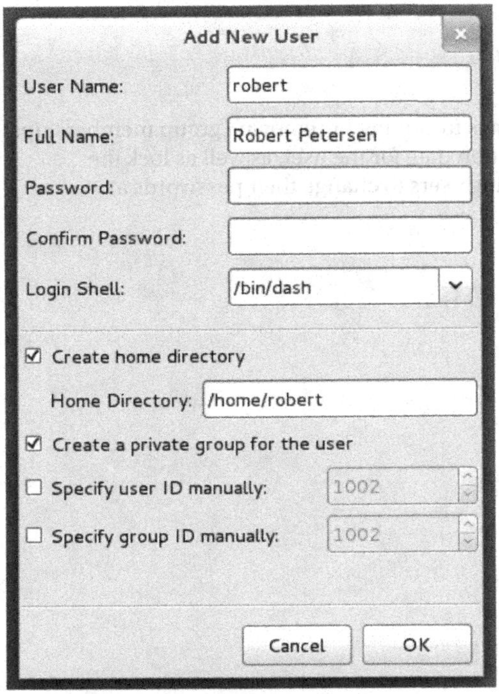

Figure 14-11. *Users and Groups: Add New User*

Once you have created a user, you can edit its properties to add or change features. Select the user's entry and click Properties. This displays a window with tabs for User Data, Account Info, Password Info, and Groups (see Figure 14-12).

Figure 14-12. *Users and Groups: User Properties window: User Data tab*

On the Groups tab, you can select the groups that the user belongs to, adding or removing group memberships (see Figure 14-13). The Accounts Info tab allows you to set an expiration date for the user, as well as lock the local password. Password Info can enable password expiration, forcing users to change their passwords at certain intervals.

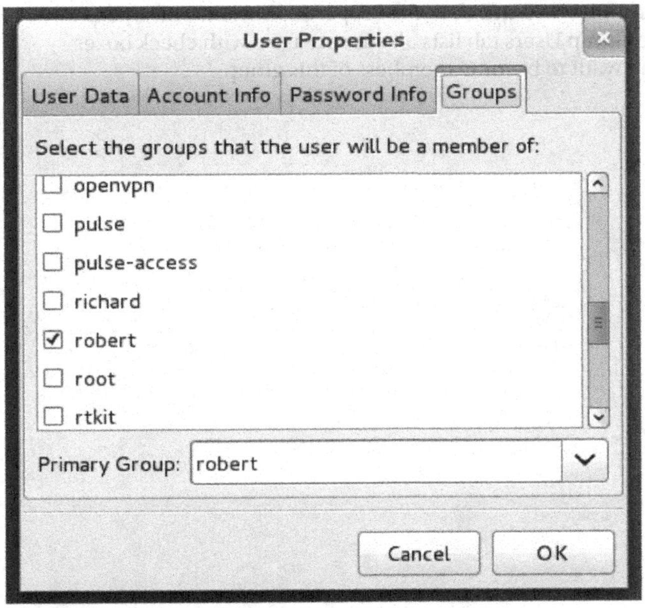

Figure 14-13. *Users and Groups: User Properties window: Add groups to a user*

Users and Groups: Groups

To add a group, click the Add Group button to open a small window in which you can enter the group name. The new group will be listed in the Groups listing (see Figure 14-14). Groups can be used in file and folder permissions to restrict access to a group of users.

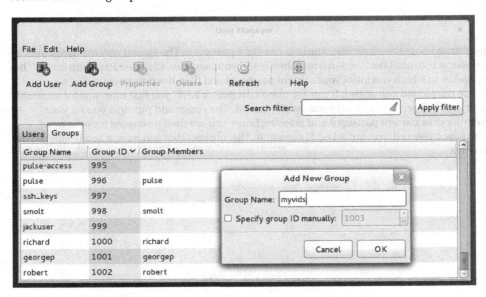

Figure 14-14. *Users and Groups: Groups panel*

To add users as members of the group, select the group's entry and click the Properties button. This opens a window with tabs for Group Data and Group Users. The Group Users tab lists all current users with check boxes (see Figure 14-15). Click the check boxes of the users you want to become members of this group.

Figure 14-15. *Users and Groups: Group Properties: Group Users panel*

If you want to remove a user as a member, click the check box to remove its check. Click OK to affect your changes. If you want to remove a group, select its entry in the Groups panel and then click the Delete button.

You can also add groups to a user by selecting a user in the Users tab and opening its Properties window. Then select the Groups tab and select the groups you want that user to belong to.

Passwords

One common operation performed from the command line is to change a password. The easiest way to change your password on the GNOME desktop is to use User Accounts and then select your account. Click the Password entry. The Changing Password dialog opens, in which you enter your current password and then the new password.

Alternatively, you can use the passwd command. If you are using GNOME or KDE, you first must open a terminal window (Terminal). Then, at the shell prompt, enter the passwd command. The command prompts you for your current password. After entering your current password and pressing Enter, you are then prompted for your new password. After entering the new password, you are asked to reenter it. This ensures that you have actually entered the password you intended to enter.

```
$ passwd
Old password:
New password:
Retype new password:
$
```

Display Configuration

Your desktop display is implemented by the X Window System. The version used on Fedora is X.org (x.org). X.org provides its own drivers for various graphics cards and monitors. You can find out more about X.org at www.x.org.

X.org will automatically detect most hardware. The /etc/X11/Xorg.conf file will usually hold only keyboard and graphics card information. All other information, such as monitors, will be automatically determined. Should you want to change the screen resolution, use the System Settings Displays tool.

Vendor Drivers

As an alternative, you could download and install the drivers and video configuration tools supplied by graphics card vendors such as ATI or Nvidia These are provided by RPM Fusion's nonfree repository (http://rpmfusion.org), when they become available. Due to licensing issues, they are not part of the Fedora repository. Once they are installed, you can use their configurations tools to configure your display. The vendor drivers often provide many more options—3D acceleration, for example—than the X.org drivers, although the X.org drivers tend to be more stable.

Because the vendor drivers are designed to work across all distributions, they may conflict with the Fedora X Window System configuration. It is recommended that you use the RPM Fusion packages for the ATI (AMD) or Nvidia drivers. These are the same vendor drivers, but with slight configuration modification to ensure Fedora compatibility.

RPM Fusion also provides the Livna Display Configuration tool for enabling AIGLX and XGL. AIGLX is accelerated indirect GLX, which is required for the compiz and beryl OpenGL window managers. Unlike XGL, AIGLX is fully open source and integrated into the X.org drivers.

If your X Window System fails to start, you can log in to the command-line interface version (runlevel) by editing your boot loader and placing a 3 at the end of the kernel line. Use the e key to edit a line, and b to boot when finished.

Bluetooth

Bluetooth is a wireless connection method for locally connected devices such as keyboards, mice, printers, and even PDAs and Bluetooth-capable cell phones. You can think of it as a small local network dedicated to your peripheral devices, eliminating the need for wires. BlueZ is the official Linux Bluetooth protocol and is integrated into the Linux kernel. The BlueZ protocol was developed originally by Qualcomm and is now an open source project, located at www.bluez.org. It is included with Fedora in the bluez and bluez-libs packages, among others. Check the BlueZ site for a complete list of supported hardware, including adapters, PCMCIA cards, and serial connectors. Configuration and management is handled by gnome-bluetooth and kdebluetooth. To connect mobile phones to a system using Bluetooth, you can use the GNOME Phone Manager (gnome-phone-manager).

Both GNOME and KDE provide Bluetooth configuration and management tools. GNOME provides the GNOME Bluetooth subsystem, which features a device manager, a plug-in for the file manager to let the GNOME file browser access Bluetooth devices, and a file server. You can find out more about GNOME Bluetooth at http://live.gnome.org/GnomeBluetooth and https://fedoraproject.org/wiki/Documentation/Bluetooth.

The Bluetooth menu is displayed on your top panel. Click it to display a menu of options for your Bluetooth devices (see Figure 14-16). Currently configured Bluetooth devices are listed. The Bluetooth Settings option displays the Bluetooth dialog window. You can also access Bluetooth dialog from the System Settings dialog.

Figure 14-16. *GNOME Bluetooth menu*

When a Bluetooth device is first connected, a message is displayed, with a notice to enter your Bluetooth passkey (see Figure 14-17). Clicking it opens the Bluetooth passkey dialog. Once you enter the PIN number, you are asked to grant access.

Figure 14-17. *GNOME Bluetooth device passkey dialog*

The Bluetooth Settings dialog lists any connected Bluetooth devices (see Figure 14-18). A Bluetooth switch at the top right lets you turn Bluetooth on or off. Above the left frame, detected Bluetooth adaptors for which you can switch visibility on or off are listed. Detected devices are listed in the Devices frame below. Selecting a device displays its type and address (in the right frame), as well as a connection switch you can use to turn the device on or off.

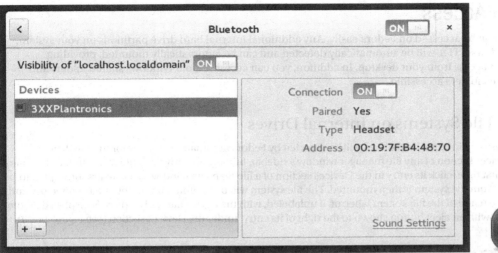

Figure 14-18. *GNOME Bluetooth preferences*

Many devices, such as headsets, will be detected automatically when you connect to your system, requesting a pin number. You can add a device manually by clicking the plus button below the Devices list on the Bluetooth dialog, to start up the Bluetooth New Device Wizard, detecting a new device (you choose "Set up New Device" from the Bluetooth menu). The wizard performs a search and setup of a device. The "Devices Search" dialog will search for connected devices (see Figure 14-19). From the "Device Type" drop-down menu, you can select a type of device. The PIN options button opens a dialog in which you can choose a pin number.

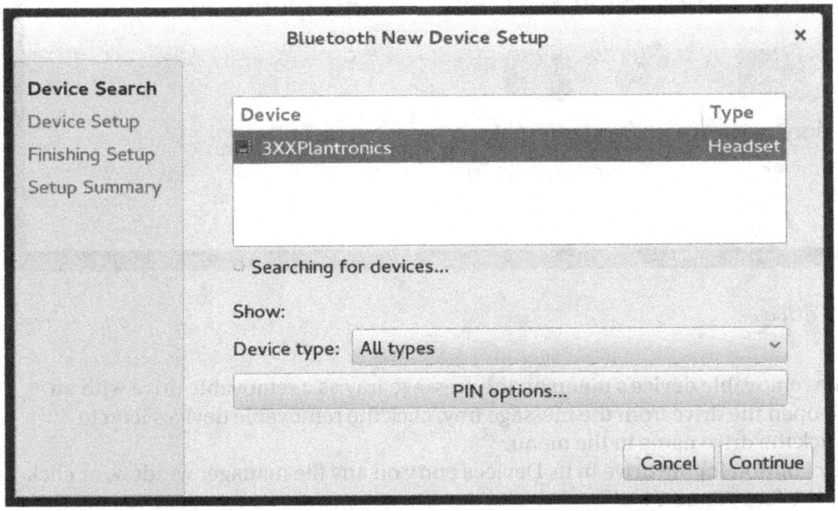

Figure 14-19. *GNOME Bluetooth Device Wizard*

Bluetooth audio devices can be managed by PulseAudio, just like any other audio device. They will be listed in the Sound dialog (Sound Settings on the Bluetooth menu, or System Settings) on the Input and Output tabs.

File System Access

Various file systems can be accessed on Fedora easily. Any additional internal hard drive partitions on your system, both Linux and Windows NTFS, will be automatically detected and can be automatically mounted, providing immediate and direct access from your desktop. In addition, you can access remote Windows shared folders and make your own shared folders accessible.

Access Linux File Systems on Internal Drives

Other Linux file systems on internal hard drives will be detected by Fedora automatically. Icons for them will be displayed on the Devices section of any file manager window's sidebar. Initially, the drive will not be mounted. To mount a file system for the first time, click its entry in the Devices section of a file manager window. You are first prompted to enter your password. Your file system is then mounted. The file system will be mounted under the /media directory and given a folder with the name of the file system label, or, if unlabeled, with the device name. The drive is displayed on the file manager window, with an eject button shown to the right of its entry, under the Devices section (see Figure 14-20).

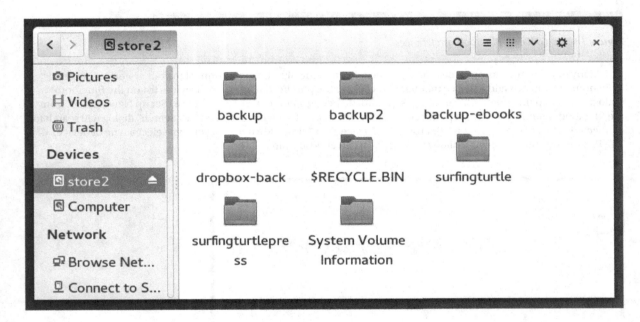

Figure 14-20. Mounted internal hard drive

The hard drive is also listed in the removable device's menu on the message tray as a removable drive with an eject button to unmount the drive. To open the drive from the message tray, click the removable devices icon to display the mounted devices. Then click the drive name in the menu.

To remove the drive, click the eject button for the drive in its Devices entry on any file manager window, or click the eject button on its message tray entry (see Figure 14-21).

Figure 14-21. *Internal hard drive message tray entry with eject button*

Any user with administrative access on the primary console is authorized to mount file systems. You can use the PolicyKit agent to expand or restrict this level of authorization, as well as enabling access for specific users. Users without administrative access are prompted for authentication. Once granted, authentication access will remain in place for a limited time, allowing you to mount other file systems without having to enter your password. These file systems will then be automatically mounted, provided you have left the Remember Authorization checked in the Authenticate window.

Access to Local Windows NTFS File Systems

Linux NTFS (Windows file system support is installed automatically. Your NTFS partitions are mounted using FUSE, Filesystem in Userspace. The same authentication control used for Linux file systems applies to NTFS file systems. Icons for the NTFS partitions will be displayed in the Devices section of a file manager window. Click an entry to mount it. Your NTFS file system is then mounted as a removable device with an eject button appearing in its file manager window (see Figure 14-20). Click the eject button to unmount the device.

The partitions will be mounted under the /media directory with their labels used as folder names. If they have no labels, they are given the UUID (Universally Unique Identifier) name as listed in the /dev/disks/by-uuid directory. The UUID is a complex number that uniquely identifies the hard disk device. The NTFS partitions are mounted using ntfs-3g drivers.

Access to Local Network Windows NTFS File Systems

Shared Windows folders and printers on any of the computers connected to your local network are automatically accessible from your Fedora desktop. The DNS discovery service (Avahi) automatically detects hosts on your home or local network and will let you access any of their shared folders directly.

To access the shared folders, click the Browse Network entry in the Network section of a file manager sidebar (see Figure 14-22). Click the Windows network icon to see just the Windows machines (see Figure 14-23).

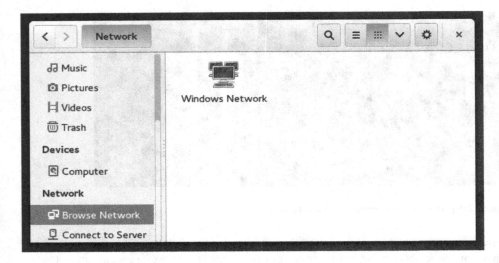

Figure 14-22. Network places

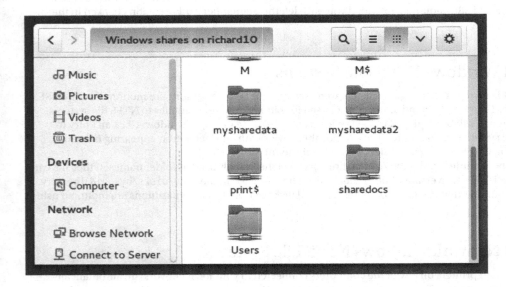

Figure 14-23. Remote shares

However, local systems cannot access your shared folders until you install a sharing server—Samba for Windows systems and NFS for Linux/UNIX systems. Should you attempt to share a directory, an error notice will be displayed, asking you to install Samba or NFS. Once selected, the shared folders will be shown.

Permissions on GNOME

On GNOME, you can set a directory or file permission using the Permissions panel in its Properties window (see Figure 14-24).

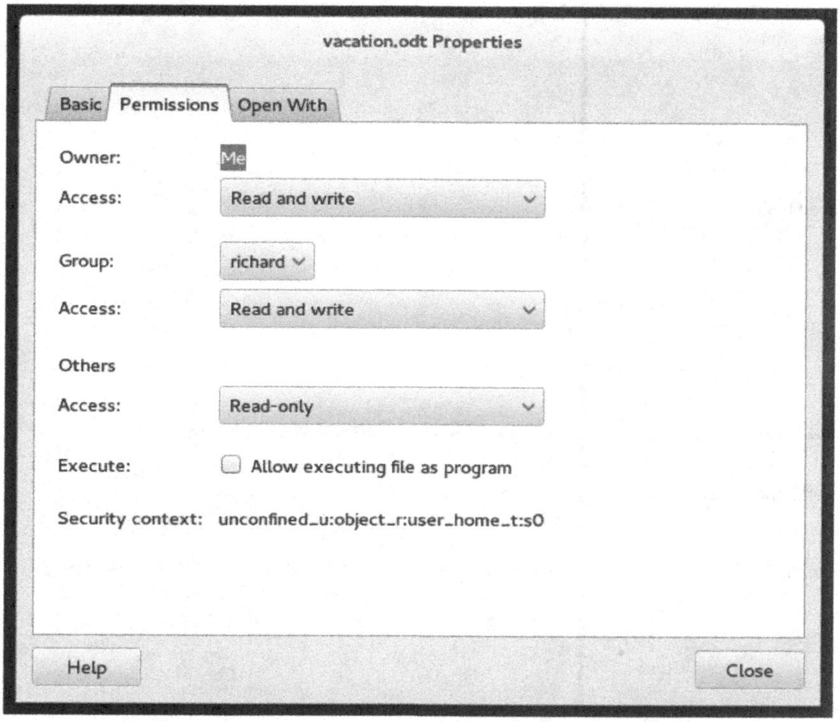

Figure 14-24. *File permissions*

For files, right-click the file icon or entry in the file manager window and select Properties. Then select the Permissions tab. Here you will find pop-up menus for read and write permissions, along with rows for Owner, Group, and Others. You can set owner permissions as Read-Only or Read and Write. For the Group and Others, you can also set the None option, denying access. The group name expands to a pop-up menu listing different groups; select one to change the file's group. If you want to execute this as an application (say, a shell script), check the Allow Executing File As Program entry. This has the effect of setting the execute permission.

The Permissions tab for folders (directories) Properties dialog operates much the same way, with Access menus for Owner, Group, and Others (see Figure 14-25, left). The Access menu controls access to the folder with options for "List files only", "Access files", and "Create and delete files." These correspond to the read, read and execute, and read/write/execute permissions given to directories. The File Access option lets you set permissions for all those files in the directory. They are the same as for files: for the owner, Read or Read and Write. The group and others access menus add a None option to deny access. To set the permissions for all the files in the directory accordingly (not just the folder), click the Change Permissions for Enclosed Files button to open a dialog in which you can specify the owner, group, and others permissions for files and folders in the directory (see Figure 14-25, right).

Figure 14-25. *Folder permissions*

Automatic File System Mounts with /etc/fstab

Although most file systems are automatically mounted for you, there may be instances where you require a file system to be mounted manually. Using the mount command
you can do this directly, or you can specify the mount operation in the /etc/fstab file to have it mounted automatically. Make sure your file system is labeled. Fedora now uses labels to identify file systems, not device names. If you have to find out the device name of an unlabeled disk, you can use the fdisk command, or the GParted or QTParted tools, to list all your hard disks, their partitions, and their current device names. You can then use the ext2label command to label a file system. GParted and QTParted are not installed by default, but they are available on the Fedora Software repository (use Software to install them).

All file systems are uniquely identified by their UUID. These are listed in the /dev/disk/by-id directory (or with the sudo blkid command). Fedora will use the UUID to identify any unlabeled file system. In the /etc/fstab file, the file system partition devices are listed as a comment and then followed by the actual file system mount operation, using the UUID. The following example mounts the boot file system on a partition identified as 81acc8a8-128a-4860-bae3-999bfee5e0f5 to the /boot directory as an ext4 file system with default options (defaults):

```
UUID=81acc8a8-128a-4860-bae3-999bfee5e0f5 /boot ext4 defaults 1
```

LVM file systems are already labeled. LVM file system device names are located in the /dev directory with a directory for the volume group and device names within that directory for each logical volume in that group. If you use the default LVM configuration for your root and swap partitions, there will be a fedora subdirectory in the /dev directory (fedora is the default name). As an example, the file system fedora would have an LVM directory /dev/

fedora/. This directory would hold links for the root and swap volumes, root and swap. These link to the actual device files in the /dev directory. The /dev/mapper directory also links the device files, such as /dev/mapper/fedora-root. This is the reference used in the /etc/fstab file to mount the LVM root partition.

```
/dev/mapper/fedora-root     /         ext4     defaults        1 1
```

If you installed Fedora 20 as fresh install (not an upgrade), you may have to use a mount operation to mount any LVM file systems you had previously. In this case, you would place an entry for the mount operation in the /etc/fstab file. The LVM device name is in the /etc/fstab file. In the following example, the Linux file system labeled mydata1 is mounted to the /mydata1 directory as an ext4 file system type. In addition, an LVM file system, mymedia, is mounted to the /mymedia directory. The logical volume mymedia is part of the logical group, mymedia, which is a directory in the /dev directory, /dev/mymedia/myvideo.

/etc/fstab
```
UUID=81acc8a8-128a-4860-bae3-999bfee5e0f5 /boot ext4    defaults        1 2
/dev/mapper/fedora-root                   /     ext4    defaults        1 1
/dev/mapper/fedora-swap                swap swap        defaults        0 0
/dev/mymedia/myvideo              /mymedia ext4         defaults        1 1
LABEL=mydata1                     /mydata1 ext4         defaults        1 1
```

To mount manually, use the mount command and specify the type with the -t ext4 option. Use the -L option to mount by label. List the file system first and then the directory name to which it will be mounted. For a NTFS partition, type ntfs. The mount option has the format:

```
mount -t type  filesystem  directory
```

The following example mounts the mydata1 file system to the /mydata1 directory:

```
mount -t ext4  -L mydata1  /mydata1
```

Editing Configuration Files Directly

Although the administrative tools will handle all configuration settings for you, there may be times when you need to make changes by directly editing the configuration files. These are usually text files in the /etc directory or dot files in a user home directory, such as .bash_profile. System configuration files are normally located in the /etc, /usr/share, and /etc/default directories. To change system configuration files, you will need administrative access, requiring you to first log in as the root user. User configuration files are located in dot files in the user's home directory and don't require any administrative access. They can be accessed directly by the user.

Because you can no longer log in to a desktop user interface as the root user, you must log in through the command-line interface. To edit any of the system-wide configuration files, such as those in the /etc directory, you must first have root user access. You can log in as the root user from a terminal window, using the su command. Alternatively, you can use the sudo command once sudo is configured.

As you can no longer log in to the desktop (unless manually configured) as root, you cannot edit system files with a desktop editor like gedit. Instead, you must use a command-line interface editor like vi, nano, Leafpad, or Emacs. Most command-line editors provide a screen-based interface that makes displaying and editing a file fairly simple. Two standard command-line editors are installed by default on your system, vi and nano. In addition, you can install Leafpad or Emacs. Leafpad is easier to use from a terminal window than nano. It will provide mouse support for menus and for editing. Emacs is much more powerful, but, like vi, is more complex.

The nano editor is a simple screen-based editor that lets you visually edit your file, using arrow and page keys to move around the file. You use control keys to perform actions. Pressing Ctrl+x will exit and prompt you to save the file; pressing Ctrl+o will save it. You start nano with the nano command. To edit a configuration file, you will require administrative access, so you first have to log in as the root user, su. Figure 14-26 shows the nano editor being used to edit the /etc/default/grub file.

```
su
nano /etc/default/grub
```

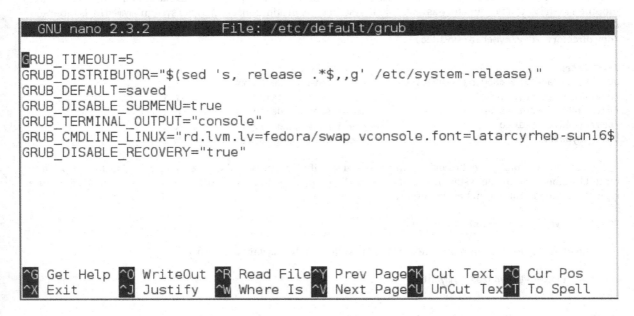

Figure 14-26. nano editor and system configuration files

Leafpad provides basic mouse support, letting you edit a file easily. Enter the command leafpad in a terminal window with the name of the file you want to edit. Be sure to log in as the root user first, using the su command. The following command would edit the grub file (see Figure 14-27). If you use the sudo command (with sudo configured), you can use gedit instead.

```
su
leafpad /etc/default/grub
```

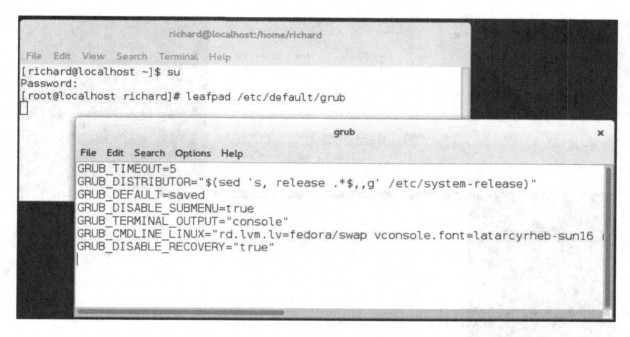

Figure 14-27. *Leafpad editor and system configuration files*

You cannot use the gedit text editor to edit system configuration files (unless you use the sudo command instead of su). Nor can you log in as the root user with the GNOME or KDE desktops.

User configuration files (dot files) can be changed by individual users directly. To edit user configuration files, you can use a standard editor, such as vi or Emacs, though one of the easiest ways to edit them is to use the gedit editor on the GNOME desktop.

For gedit, user configuration files do not show up automatically. Dot files like .bash_profile have to be chosen from the file manager window, not from the gedit open operation. First, configure the file manager to display dot files. Open any file manager window and, from the View menu, choose Show Hidden Files. All your user configuration files will be displayed. Usually you can then just double-click the file to open it in the gedit text editor. Alternatively, you can right-click the file and select Open with "Text Editor" from the pop-up menu (see Figure 14-28). Gedit will let you edit several files at once, opening a tabbed pane for each. You can use gedit to edit any text file, including ones you create yourself.

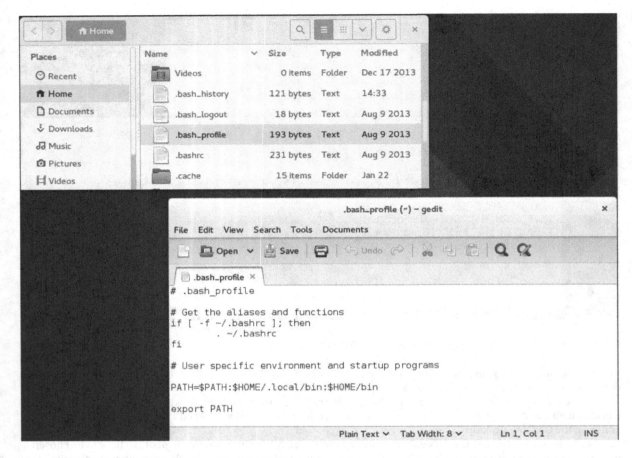

Figure 14-28. *Gedit text editor and configuration files*

■ **Caution**   Be careful when editing your configuration files. Editing mistakes can corrupt your configurations. It is advisable to make a backup of any configuration files you are working on first, before making major changes to the original.

Backup Management: rsync, Déjà Dup, and Amanda

Backup operations have become an important part of administrative duties. Several backup tools are provided on Linux systems, including Amanda and the traditional dump/restore tools, as well as the rsync command for making individual copies. Déjà Dup is a front end for the duplicity backup tool, which uses rsync to generate backup archives. Amanda provides server-based backups, letting different systems on a network back up to a central server. BackupPC provides network and local backup using configured rsync and tar tools. The dump tools let you refine your backup process, detecting data changed since the last backup. Table 14-2 lists web sites for Linux backup tools. Backintime is a simple backup tool that takes snapshots of directories. Bacula allows you to manage backups across a network.

Table 14-2. Backup Resources

Web Site(s)	Application
http://rsync.samba.org	rsync remote copy backup
http://amanda.org	Amanda network backup
http://dump.sourceforge.net	Dump and restore tools
http://backuppc.sourceforge.net	BackupPC network or local backup, using configured rsync and tar tools
https://launchpad.net/deja-dup www.nongnu.org/duplicity	Déjà Dup front end for duplicity, which uses rsync to perform basic backups

Individual Backups: archive and rsync

You can back up and restore particular files and directories with archive tools such as tar, restoring the archives later. For backups, tar is usually used with a tape device. To automatically schedule backups, you can schedule appropriate tar commands with the cron utility. The archives also can be compressed for storage savings. You can then copy the compressed archives to any medium, such as a DVD, USB drive, or tape. On GNOME, you can use File Roller to create archives easily (Archive Manager).

If you want to remote-copy a directory or files from one host to another, making a particular backup, you can use rsync, which is designed for network backups of particular directories or files, intelligently copying only those files that have been changed, rather than the contents of an entire directory. In archive mode, it can preserve the original ownership and permissions, provided corresponding users exist on the host system. The following example copies the /home/george/myproject directory to the /backup directory on the host rabbit, creating a corresponding myproject subdirectory. The -t specifies that this is a transfer. The remote host is referenced with an attached colon, rabbit:.

```
rsync -t /home/george/myproject    rabbit:/backup
```

As a precaution, you could first perform a dry run to see what actions your rsync operation will perform. Use the -n option to perform the dry run, and add the -v option for details (verbose).

```
rsync -nvt /home/george/myproject    rabbit:/backup
```

If, instead, you wanted to preserve the ownership and permissions of the files, you would use the -a (archive) option. Adding a -z option will compress the file. The -v option provides a verbose mode.

```
rsync -avz  /home/george/myproject    rabbit:/backup
```

A trailing slash on the source will copy the contents of the directory, rather than generating a subdirectory of that name. Here the contents of the myproject directory are copied to the george-project directory:

```
rsync -avz  /home/george/myproject/    rabbit:/backup/george-project
```

The rsync command is configured to use the SSH remote shell by default. You can specify it or an alternate remote shell to use with the -e option. For secure transmission, you can encrypt the copy operation with ssh. Either use the -e ssh option or set the RSYNC_RSH variable to ssh.

```
rsync -avz -e ssh  /home/george/myproject    rabbit:/backup/myproject
```

As when using `rcp`, you can copy from a remote host to the one you are on.

```
rsync -avz  lizard:/home/mark/mypics/  /pic-archice/markpics
```

You can also run rsync as a server daemon. This will allow remote users to sync copies of files on your system with versions on their own, transferring only changed files, rather than entire directories. Many mirror and software FTP sites operate as rsync servers, letting you update files without having to download the full versions again. Configuration information for rsync as a server is kept in the /etc/rsyncd.conf file. On Fedora, rsync as a server is managed through systemdi, using the /usr/lib/systemd/system/ v file, which starts rsync with the-daemon option. You can enable it with systemctl command.systemctl enable rsyncd.service

You can then start and stop it with the service command in a terminal window. Be sure to login as root with the su command.

```
service rsyncd start
```

■ **Tip** Although it is designed for copying between hosts, you can also use `rsync` to make copies within your own system, usually to a directory in another partition or hard drive. In fact, there are several different ways of using `rsync`, including adding on the fly compression for faster transfers. Check the `rsync` man page for detailed descriptions of each.

Déjà Dup

Déjà Dup is a front end for the duplicity backup tool, which uses `rsync` to generate backup archives (www.nongnu.org/duplicity/). It is not installed with the desktop. Install the software named Backup on GNOME Software. You can access Déjà Dup from the Applications overview (Utilities ➤ Backup). Initially, you are prompted either to restore your files or to show your backup settings (see Figure 14-29). Clicking Restore performs an immediate restore operation. If you encrypted your backups, you have to provide the encryption password.

Figure 14-29. *Déjà Dup initial backup dialog*

The Déjà Dup Settings dialog shows tabs for Overview, Storage, Folders, and Schedule (see Figure 14-30). The Overview tab provides information about your backup configuration, showing the folders to back up, those ignored, and the dates of the last and next backups. A switch allows you to turn automatic backups on and off. Click the Help button to display the Déjà Dup manual.

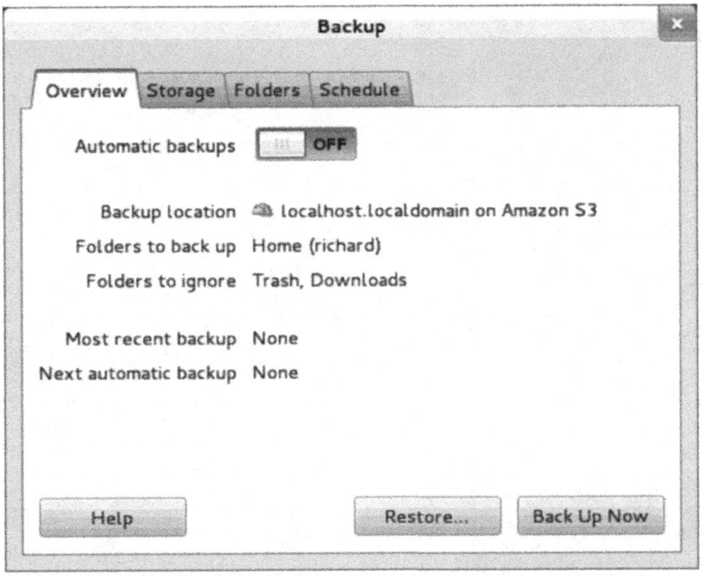

Figure 14-30. *Déjà Dup settings: overview*

The Storage tab lets you specify a location to store your backups (see Figure 14-31). By default, this is set to the local folder. You can choose different locations to use instead, such as an FTP account, Amazon S3 cloud account, SSH server, Samba (Windows) share, or a local folder. Choose the one you want from the "Backup location" menu. With each choice, you are prompted for the appropriate configuration information (see Figure 14-32).

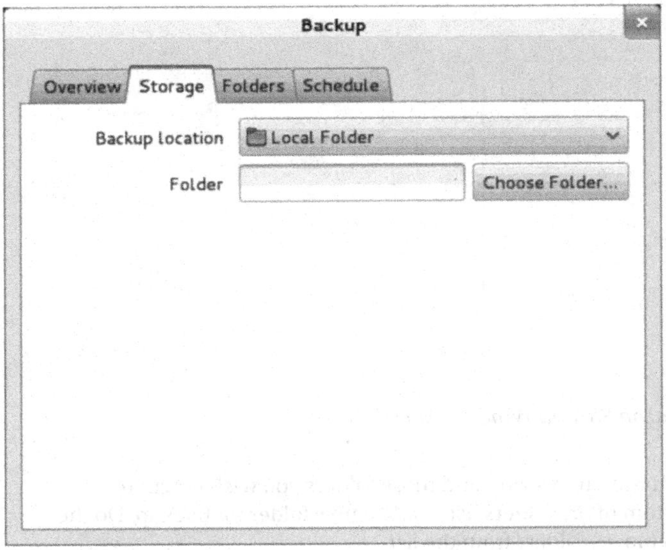

Figure 14-31. *Déjà Dup settings: storage*

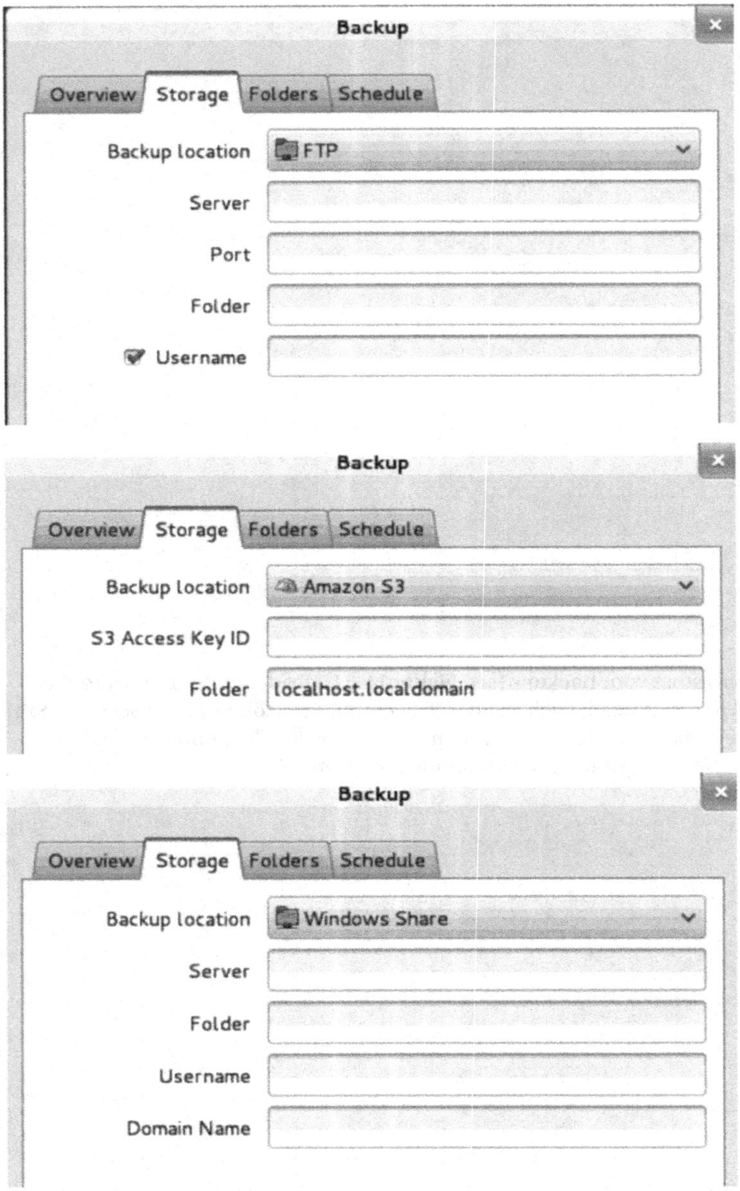

Figure 14-32. *Déjà Dup settings: storage for FTP, Amazon S3, and Windows share*

The Folders tab lets you specify which folders you want to back up and those folders you wish to ignore (see Figure 14-33). Click the plus button (+) at the bottom of the folders list to add a new folder for backup. Do the same to specify folders to ignore. The minus button removes folders from the list.

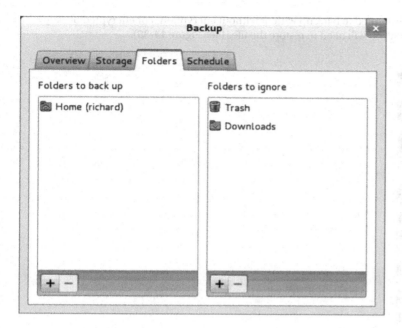

Figure 14-33. *Déjà Dup settings: backup folders*

On the Schedule tab, you specify the frequency of your backups and how long to keep them (see Figure 14-34). Backups can be performed daily, weekly, every two weeks, or monthly. They can be kept for a week, month, several months, a year, or forever.

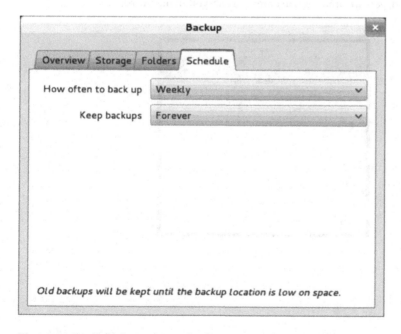

Figure 14-34. *Déjà Dup settings: backup schedule*

When you perform a backup, you are prompted to back up with or without encryption. For encrypted backups, you are prompted to enter a password, which you will need to restore the files (see Figure 14-35).

Figure 14-35. *Déjà Dup backup: encryption*

When restoring, you are prompted to specify the location you are backing up from, the backup date to restore from, and whether to restore to the original location or a specific folder. A summary shows the backup selections (see Figure 14-36). If the backup is encrypted, you are prompted to enter the encryption password.

Figure 14-36. *Déjà Dup restore*

BackupPC

BackupPC provides an easily managed local or network backup of your system or hosts on a system using configured rsync or tar tools. There is no client application to install, just configuration files. BackupPC can back up hosts on a network, including servers, or just a single system. Data can be backed up to local hard disks or to network storage, such as shared partitions or storage servers. You can configure BackupPC using your web page configuration interface. This is the hostname of your computer with the /backuppc name attached, such as http://rabbit.turtle.com/backuppc. Detailed documentation is installed at /usr/share/doc/BackupPC. You can find out more about BackupPC at http://backuppc.sourceforge.net.

BackupPC uses both compression and detection of identical files to significantly reduce the size of the backup, allowing several hosts to be backed up in limited space. Once an initial backup is performed, BackupPC will only back up changed files, reducing the time of the backup significantly.

BackupPC is managed by the systemd server. Use the service command as root to manage, enable, and start it. Configuration files are located at /etc/BackupPC. The config.pl file holds BackupPC configuration options, and the hosts file lists hosts to be backed up.

Amanda

To back up hosts connected to a network, you can use the Advanced Maryland Automatic Network Disk Archiver (Amanda) to archive hosts. Amanda uses tar tools to back up all hosts to a single host operating as a backup server. Backup data is sent by each host to the host operating as the Amanda server, where they are written out to a backup medium such as tape. With an Amanda server, the backup operations for all hosts become centralized in one server, instead of each host having to perform its backup. Any host that has to restore data simply requests it from the Amanda server, specifying the file system, date, and file names. Backup data is copied to the server's holding disk and from there to tapes. Detailed documentation and updates are provided at http://amanda.org. For the server, be sure to install the amanda-server package, and for clients, use the amanda-clients package.

Managing Services: systemd and service

Most services are servers, such as web or proxy servers. Other services provide security, such as SSH or Kerberos. Services such as the Apache web server, Samba server, and the FTP server are now handled by the systemd daemon. You can decide which services to use with the chkconfig and service commands and the system-config-services tool.

If a service, such as the VsFTP server or Samba, is not enabled at installation, it will not appear on the chkconfig or system-config-services tool. You must first enable it manually, using the service tool as the root user. Use the enable command to enable the service. The following command enables the vsftp server and the Samba server (smb):

```
su
service vsftpd enable
service smb enable
```

The service command is now simply a front end for the systemctl command, which performs the actual operation using systemd. The following commands are equivalent to the previous example. The systemctl command uses the service's systemd configuration file, located at the /lib/systemd/system directory.

```
systemctl enable vsftpd.service
systemctl enable smb
```

Once they're enabled, you can use service, chkconfig, and system-config-services to start and stop services.

For some services, such as the Apache web server (httpd), you may have to use systemctl instead of service to enable the server.

```
systemctl enable httpd.service
```

system-config-services

The system-config-services tool (Services) can be used to manage services, provided it has been enabled by systemctl. On GNOME Software, it is called Services, and on PackageKit, it goes by the package name, system-config-services. Once opened, the side pane displays a listing of installed daemons and servers (see Figure 14-37). A status icon indicates whether a service is enabled and if it is running. The right pane will display the current status of a selected service and its description.

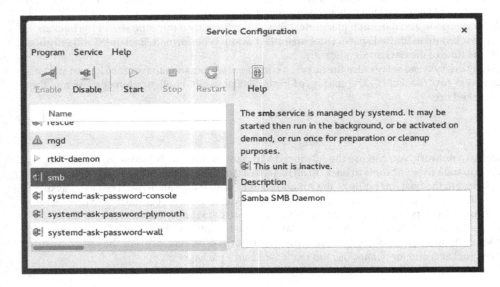

Figure 14-37. *Services:* system-config-services

Several services are already selected by default, such as network, which runs your network. To initially enable a service so that it appears on system-config-services, such as Samba, you have to first use the service or systemctl as the root user to enable the service.

chkconfig

To configure a service to start up automatically, you can also use the chkconfig tool, which is run on a command line. The chkconfig command uses the on and off options to select and deselect services for startup.

```
chkconfig httpd on
```

Manual Service Control

To start and stop services manually, you can use either system-config-services or the service command. Use the service's script with the stop argument to stop it, the start argument to start it, and the restart argument to restart it. The scripts are run from a terminal window. You must first log in as the root user, using the su command. You can use the service command with the service script name and option. The following will restart the nmb Samba service:

```
service nmb restart
```

CHAPTER 15

■ ■ ■

Network Configuration

Network configuration is managed by Network Manager. Network configuration differs, depending on the kind of connection you have, such as a wired connection (Ethernet), a DSL modem, or a wireless connection. GNOME System Settings Network is the primary network configuration tool for Fedora, which can be used to configure all your network connections manually. You can configure a variety of network connections, including wired settings, DSL, and wireless, for the IPv4 and IPv6 protocols. As an alternative, you can still use the older Network Manager's Network Connections application (Sundry ➤ Network Connections). Table 15-1 lists several different network configuration tools.

Table 15-1. *Fedora Network Configuration Tools*

Network Configuration App	Description
Network Manager	Automatically configures wireless and wired network connections. Can also manually edit them
System Settings Network	GNOME System Settings Network configuration utility (System Settings ➤ Network)
nm-connection-editor	Network Connections: the older Network Manager configuration utility (Sundry ➤ Network Connections)
kde-plasma-networkmanagement	KDE version of Network Manager
firewall-config	Sets up a network firewall
system-config-samba	Configures Samba shares
system-config-nfs	Configures NFS shares
wvdial	PPP modem connection, enter on a command line
wconfig	Wireless connection, enter on a command line

Network Information: Dynamic and Static

Most networks now support dynamic configuration using either the older Dynamic Host Configuration Protocol (DHCP) or the new IPv6 protocol and its automatic address configuration. In this case, you need only check the DHCP entry in most network configuration tools. For IPv6, you check the Enable IPv6 Configuration entry in the Network Connections device configuration window. For DHCP, a DHCP client on each host will obtain network connection information from a DHCP server serving that network. IPv6 generates its addresses directly from the device and router information, such as the device hardware MAC address.

If you have a static connection (no DHCP or IPv6 support), you have to provide connection information such as your IP address and DNS servers. If you are using a DSL dynamic, ISDN, or modem connection, you will also have to supply provider, login, and password information, whether your system is dynamic or static. You may also have to supply specialized information, such as DSL or modem compression methods or a dial-up number. You can obtain most of your static network information from your network administrator or ISP (Internet service provider). The connection information commonly needed follows:

- **The device name for your network interface:** For LAN and wireless connections, this is usually an Ethernet card with the name eth0 or eth1. For a modem, DSL, or ISDN connection, this is a PPP device named ppp0 (ippp0 for ISDN). Virtual private network (VPN) connections are also supported.

- **Hostname:** This is the name by which your computer is identified on the network.

- **Domain name:** This is the name of your network.

- **The Internet Protocol (IP) address assigned to your machine:** This is needed only for static Internet connections. Dynamic connections use the DHCP protocol to automatically assign an IP address for you. Every host (computer) on the Internet is assigned an IP address. Local networks often use the older IPv4 format, which has a set of four numbers, separated by periods. Most networks now use the new IP protocol version 6, IPv6, which uses a different and more complex numbering format.

- **Your network IP address:** Static connections only. This is the IP address of your network. In the IPv4 format, it is the same as the IP address, but with zeros for the last segment.

- **The netmask:** Static connections only. This is usually 255.255.255.0 for most IPv4 networks.

- **The broadcast address for your network, if available (optional):** Static connections only. In IPv4 networks, this is the same as your IP address with the number 255 for the last segment.

- **The IP address of your network's gateway computer:** Static connections only. This is the computer with a server that connects your local network to a larger one like the Internet.

- **Name servers:** Static connections only. The IP address of the name servers your network uses. These enable the use of URLs.

- **NIS domain and IP address for an NIS server:** Necessary if your network uses an NIS server (optional).

- **User login and password information:** Needed for dynamic DSL, ISDN, and modem connections.

User and System-Wide Network Configuration: Network Manager

Network Manager will automatically detect your network connections, both wired and wireless. It is the default method for managing your network connections. Network Manager makes use of the automatic device detection capabilities of udev to configure your connections. Should you instead have to configure your network connections manually, you would use Network Connections, the Network Manager connections editor (nm-connections-editor).

Network Manager is user specific. When a user logs in, it selects the network connection preferred by that user. For wireless connections, the user can choose from a list of current possible connections. For wired connections, a connection can be started automatically, when the system starts up. Initial settings will be supplied from the system-wide configuration.

Configurations can also be applied system-wide to all users. When editing or adding a network connection, the edit or add dialog displays an Available to All Users check box in the lower-left corner. Click this check box and then click the Apply button to make the connection configuration system-wide. A PolicyKit authentication dialog will first prompt you to enter your root password.

Network Manager can configure any network connection. This includes wired, wireless, and all manual connections. Network Interface Connection (NIC cards) hardware is detected using udev. Information provided by Network Manager is made available to other applications over D-Bus.

■ **Note**   The KDE version of Network Manager, KNetworkManager, also detects network connections. In addition, it allows you to configure PPP dial-up connections and manage wireless connections. To start KNetworkManager, select its entry in Applications ➤ Network Tools.

With multiple wireless access points for Internet connections, a system could have several different network connections to choose from, instead of a single-line connection such as DSL or cable. This is particularly true for notebook computers that access different wireless connections at different locations. Instead of manually configuring a new connection each time one is encountered, the Network Manager tool can automatically configure and select a connection to use.

By default, an Ethernet connection will be preferred, if available. For wireless connections, you will have to choose the one you want.

Network Manager is designed to work in the background, providing status information for your connection and switching from one configured connection to another, as needed. For initial configuration, it detects as much information as possible about the new connection.

Network Manager operates as a daemon with the name NetworkManager. If no Ethernet connection is available, Network Manager will scan for wireless connections, checking for Extended Service Set Identifiers (ESSIDs). If an ESSID identifies a previously used connection, then it is automatically selected. If several are found, then the most recently used one is chosen. If only a new connection is available, the Network Manager waits for the user to choose one. A connection is selected only if the user is logged in. If an Ethernet connection is later made, the Network Manager will switch to it from wireless.

The NetworkManager daemon can be turned on or off, using the service command as the root user.

```
su
service NetworkManager start
service NetworkManager stop
```

Network Manager Manual Configuration using GNOME Network

The GNOME Network utility, available from System Settings, can be used to configure all your network connections manually. Automatic wireless and wired connections were covered in Chapter 3. For detailed manual configuration, Network features the dialogs similar to those used in Network Connections. Network displays a dialog with tabs for Wi-Fi, Wired, and Network proxy (see Figure 15-1).

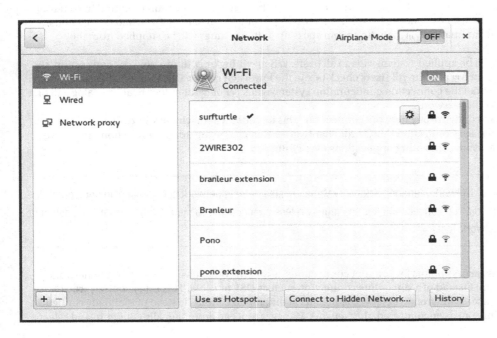

Figure 15-1. *Network (System Settings): Wi-Fi tab*

On the Wi-Fi tab, available wireless connections are listed to the right. Selecting an entry will create a gear button for it, which you can click to open the network configuration dialog with tabs for Details, Security, Identity, IPv4, IPv6, and Reset. The Details tab show strength, speed, security methods, IP and hardware addresses, routes, and the DNS server IP address. To edit the connection manually, you use the Security, Identity, and IP tabs. The Security tab displays a menu from which you can choose a security method and a password (see Figure 15-2).

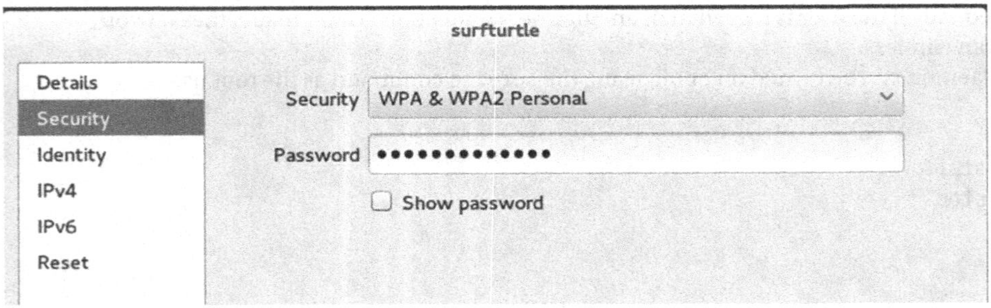

Figure 15-2. *Network wireless configuration: Security tab*

On the Identity tab, you can specify the SSID name, choose a firewall zone, and choose to connect automatically when you log in and whether to make the connection system-wide (available to other users; see Figure 15-3).

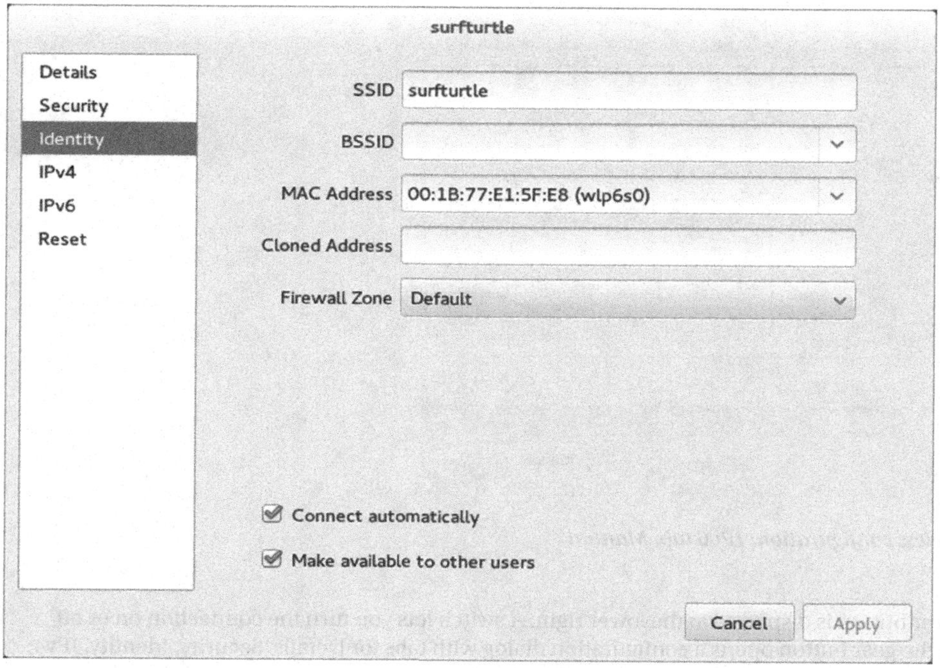

Figure 15-3. *Network wireless configuration: Identity tab*

On the IPv4 Settings tab, a switch allows you to turn the IP connection on or off. There are sections for Addresses, the DNS servers, and Routes. An Addresses menu lets you choose the type connection you want. By default, it is set to Automatic. If you change it to Manual, new entries appear for the address, netmask, and gateway. On the IPv6 tab, the netmask is replaced by prefix (see Figure 15-4). You can turn off Automatic switches for the DNS and Routes sections to make them manual. The DNS section has a plus button to let you add more DNS servers.

Wired

Details	IPv6	ON
Security	Addresses	Manual ∨
Identity		
IPv4		
IPv6	Address	
Reset	Prefix	🗑
	Gateway	
		+
	DNS	Automatic ON
	Server	🗑
		+

Cancel   Apply

Figure 15-4. *Network wireless configuration: IPv6 tab, Manual*

On the Wired tab, a gear button is displayed at the lower right. A switch lets you turn the connection on or off (see Figure 15-5). Clicking the gear button opens a configuration dialog with tabs for Details, Security, Identity, IPv4, IPv6, and Reset (see Figure 15-6).

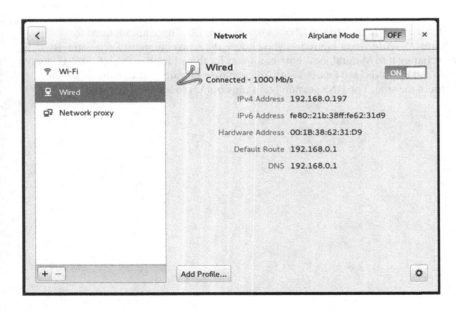

Figure 15-5. *Network (System Settings): Wired tab*

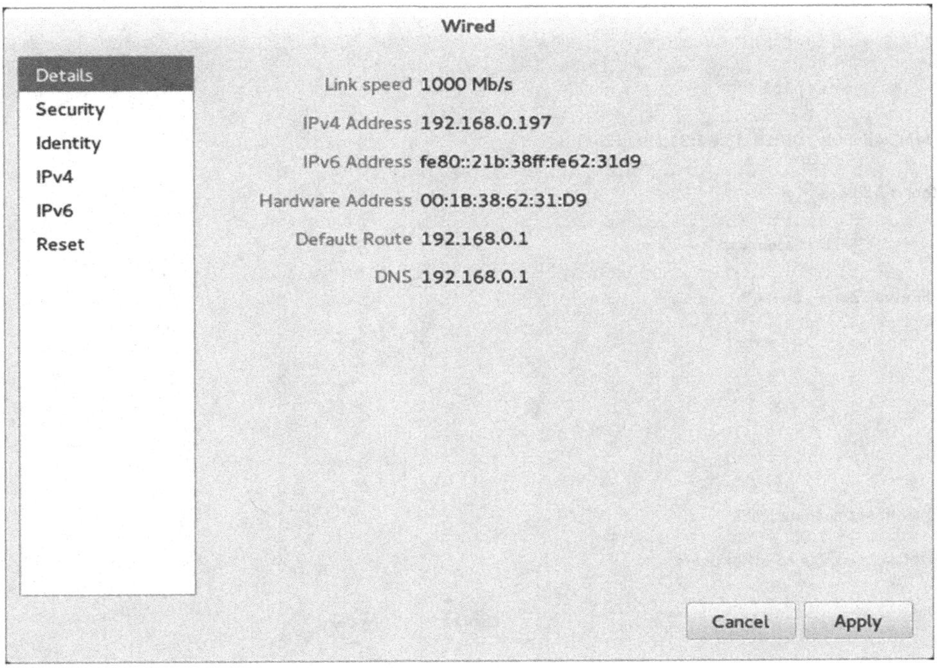

Figure 15-6. *Network wired configuration dialog*

You can use the Security, Identity, and IP tabs to manually configure the connection. The Security tab lets you turn on 802.1x security and choose an authentication method, as well as provide a username and password (see Figure 15-7).

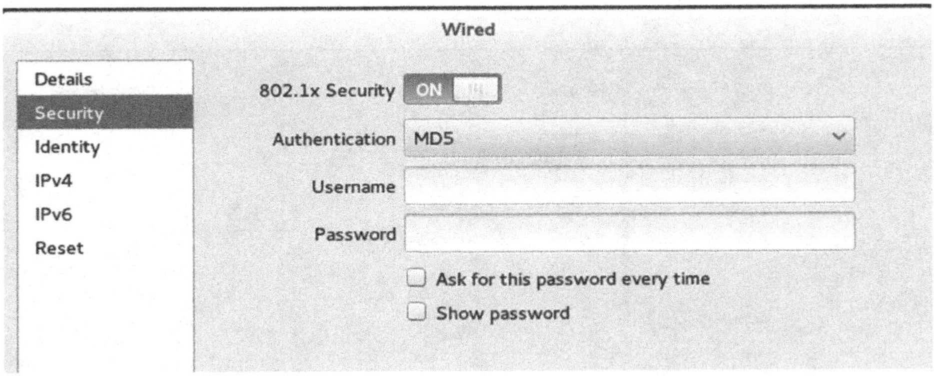

Figure 15-7. *Network wired configuration: Security tab*

On the Identity tab, you can choose the firewall zone, set the name, choose the hardware address, set the MTU blocks, and choose to connect automatically and whether to make the connection system-wide (see Figure 15-8).

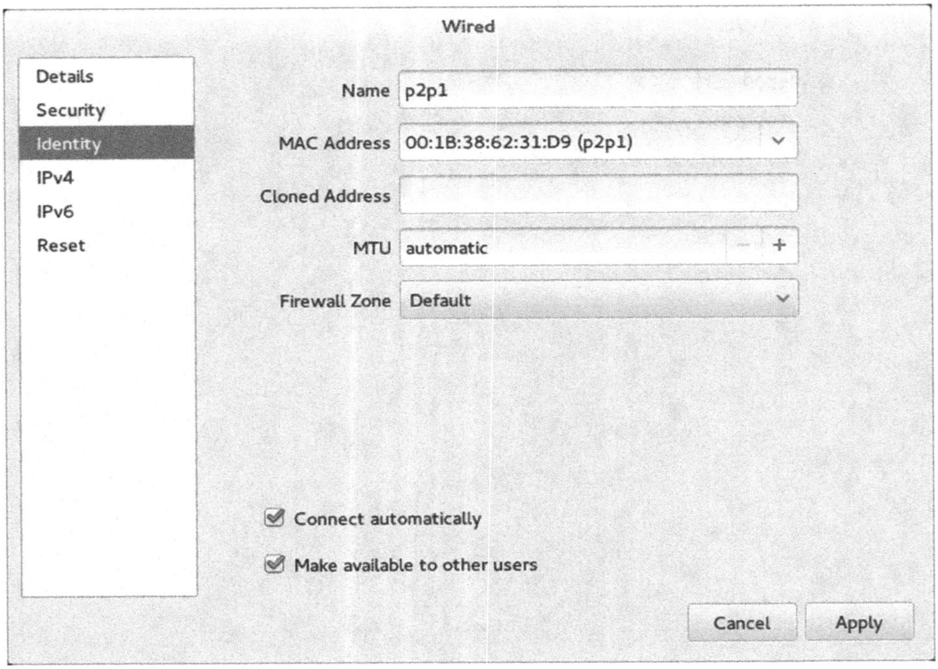

Figure 15-8. *Network wired configuration: Identity tab*

On the IP tabs, a switch allows you to turn the connection on or off. The tab has sections for Addresses, DNS servers, and Routes. DNS and Routes have a switch for automatic. Turning the switch off allows you to manually enter a DNS server address or routing information. From the Addresses menu, you can also choose to make the connection automatic or manual. When manual, new entries appear that let you enter the address, netmask, and gateway (see Figure 15-9). On the IPv6 tab, the netmask entry is replaced by a prefix entry.

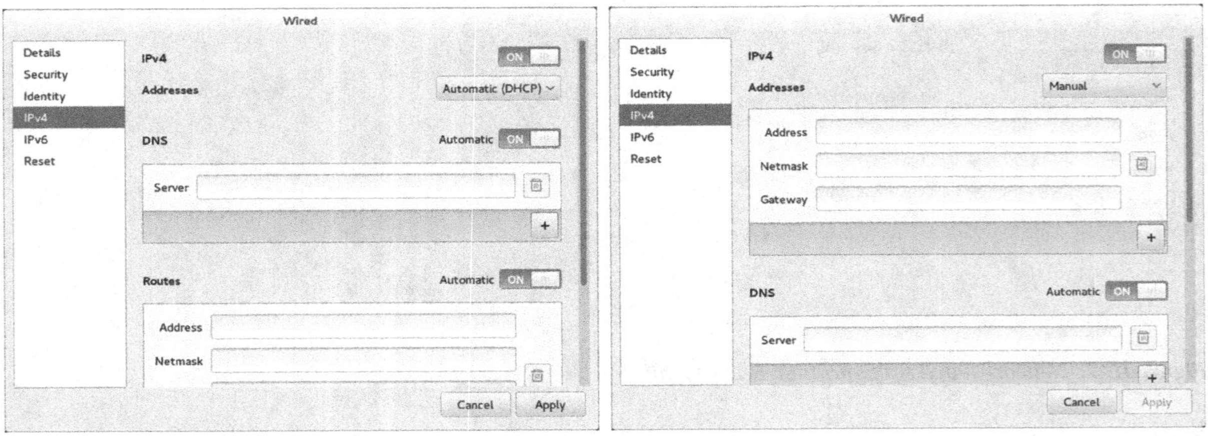

Figure 15-9. *Network wired configuration: IPv4 tab*

On the Network dialog, you can add a new connection by clicking the plus button on the lower-left corner. A dialog opens to let you enter as a VPN, Bond, Bridge, or VLAN connection. A VPN connection opens another dialog listing supported VPN connection types, such as Point-to-Point or OpenVPN (see Figure 15-10). The Bond, Bridge, and VLAN entries open the Network Connections dialogs for those connections.

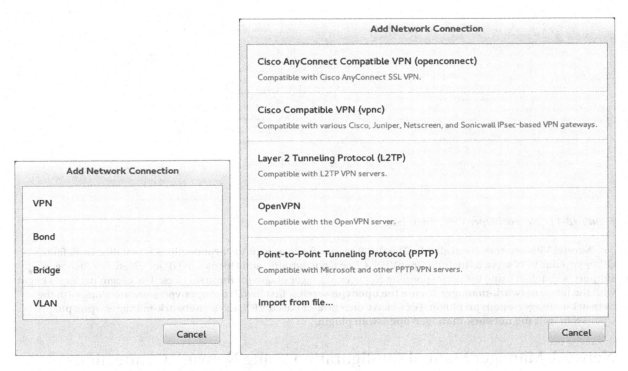

Figure 15-10. Network, new connections and VPN connections

You can then configure the VPN connections in the "Add Network Connection" dialog, which shows three tabs: Identity, IPv4, and IPv6 (see Figure 15-11). The IP tabs are the same as for wireless and wired configuration dialogs. On the Identity tab, you can enter the name, gateway, and authentication information. Click the Advanced button for detailed connection configuration.

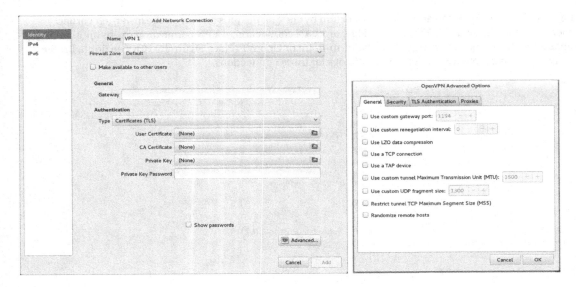

Figure 15-11. *Network OpenVPN connection*

Several VPN services are available. The PPTP service for Microsoft VPN connections is installed by default. Other popular VPN services include OpenVPN, Cisco Concentrator, and Openswan (IPSec). Network Manager support is installed using the corresponding Network Manager plugin for these services. The plugin packages begin with the name **network-manager**. To use the **openvpn** service, first install the **openvpn** software along with the **network-manager-openvpn** plugin. For Cisco Concentrator based VPN, us the **network-manager-vpnc** plugin. Openswan uses the **network-manager-openswan** plugin.

Network Manager Manual Configuration Using Network Connections

You can also use the older Network Connections utility (`nm-connection-editor`) to edit any network connection, accessible from the Sundry ➤ Network Connections on the Applications overview. It should already be installed. Established connections are listed, with Add, Edit, and Delete buttons for adding, editing, and removing network connections (see Figure 15-12). Your current network connections should already be listed.

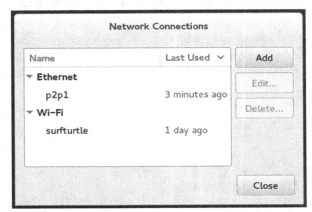

Figure 15-12. *Network configuration*

When you add a connection, you can choose its type from a drop-down menu (see Figure 15-13). The menu organizes connection types into three categories: Hardware, Virtual, and VPN (Virtual Private Network; see Figure 15-14). Hardware connections cover both wired (Ethernet, DSL, and InfiniBand) and wireless (Wi-Fi, WiMAX, and Mobile Broadband) connections. VPN lists the supported VPN types, such as OpenVPN, PPTP, and Cisco. You can also import a previously configured connection. Virtual supports VLAN and Bond virtual connections.

Figure 15-13. *Choosing a connection type for a new network connection*

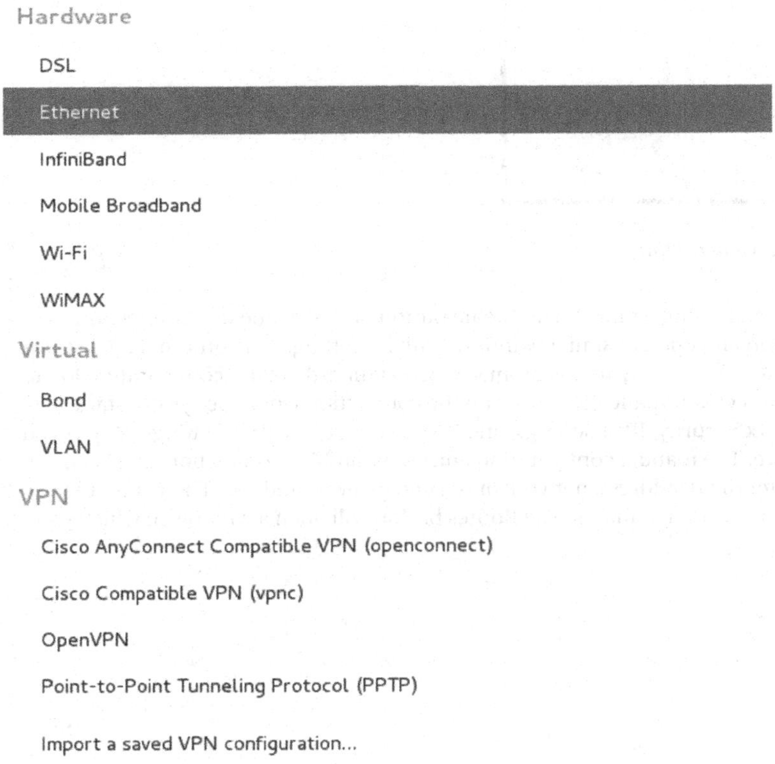

Hardware

   DSL

   Ethernet

   InfiniBand

   Mobile Broadband

   Wi-Fi

   WiMAX

Virtual

   Bond

   VLAN

VPN

   Cisco AnyConnect Compatible VPN (openconnect)

   Cisco Compatible VPN (vpnc)

   OpenVPN

   Point-to-Point Tunneling Protocol (PPTP)

   Import a saved VPN configuration...

Figure 15-14. *New connection types*

Configuration editing dialogs display a General tab from which you can make your configuration available to all users and automatically connect when the network connection is available. You can also choose to use a VPN connection and specify a firewall zone. Figure 15-15 shows the General tab on a wired connection.

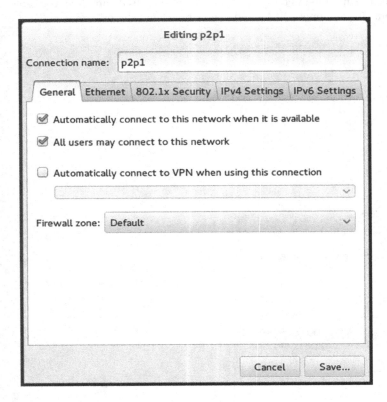

Figure 15-15. *Configuration editing dialog: General tab*

Editing an Ethernet connection opens an Editing window. The Create button on the "Choose a Connection Type" dialog is used to add a new connection and opens a similar window, with no settings. The Ethernet tab lists the MAC hardware address and the MTU. The MTU is usually set to automatic. The standard default configuration for a wired Ethernet connection uses DHCP. Connect automatically will set up the connection when the system starts up. There are five tabs, General, Ethernet, 8.02.1x Security, IPv4 Settings, and IPv6 Settings. The IPv4 Settings tab lets you select the kind of wired connection you have. The manual configuration entries for an IPv4 connection are shown in Figure 15-16. Click the Add button to enter the IP address, network mask, and gateway address. Then enter the address for the DNS servers and your network search domains. The Routes button will open a window in which you can manually enter any network routes.

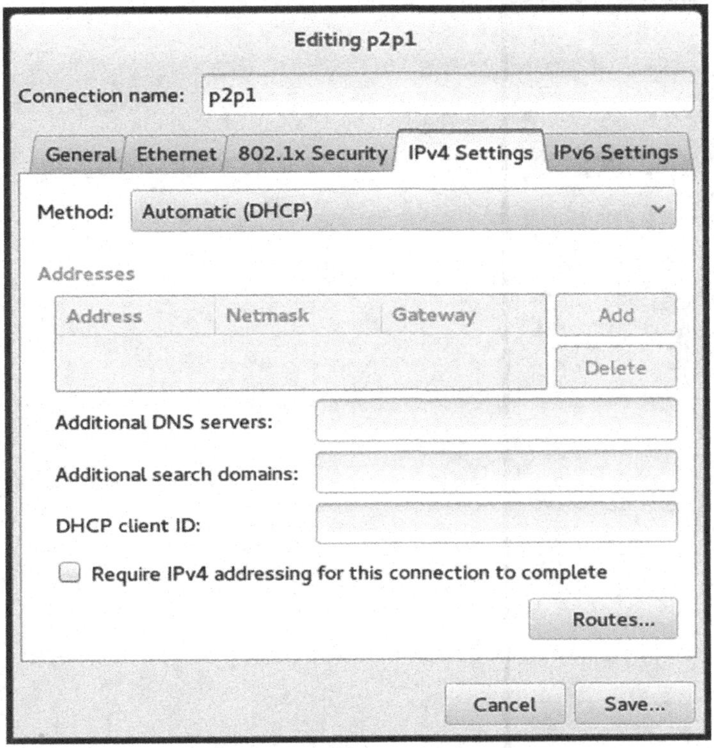

Figure 15-16. *IPv4 wired configuration*

For a wireless connection, you enter wireless configuration data, such as your ESSID, password, and encryption method. For wireless connections, you choose Wi-Fi or WiMAX as the connection type. The Editing Wi-Fi connection window opens with tabs for your wireless information, security, and IP settings (see Figure 15-17). On the Wi-Fi tab, you specify your SSID, along with your mode and MAC address.

Editing Wi-Fi connection 1

Connection name: [Wi-Fi connection 1]

| General | Wi-Fi | Wi-Fi Security | IPv4 Settings | IPv6 Settings |

SSID: [   ]

Mode: [Infrastructure   ▾]

BSSID: [▾]

Device MAC address: [▾]

Cloned MAC address: [   ]

MTU: [automatic   − +] bytes

[Cancel] [Save...]

Figure 15-17. Wireless configuration

On the Wi-Fi Security tab, you enter your wireless connection security method. The commonly used method, WEP, is supported, along with WPA personal. The WPA personal method only requires a password. More secure connections, such as Dynamic WEP and Enterprise WPA, are also supported. These will require much more configuration information, such as authentication methods, certificates, and keys.

For a new broadband connection, choose the Mobile Broadband entry in the connection type menu. A 3G wizard starts up to help you set up the appropriate configuration for your particular 3G service. Configuration steps are listed on the left pane. If your device is connected, you can select it from the drop-down menu on the right pane.

Once a service is selected, you can further edit the configuration by clicking its entry in the Mobile Broadband tab and clicking the Edit button. The Editing window opens with tabs for Mobile Broadband, PPP, IPv4, and IPv6 settings. On the Mobile Broadband tab, you can enter your number, username, and password. Advanced options include the APN, Network, and PIN. The APN should already be entered.

On the Network Manager panel applet menu, the VPN Connection entry submenu will list configured VPN connections for easy access. The Configure VPN entry will open the Network Connections window to the VPN section, from which you can then add, edit, or delete VPN connections. The Disconnect VPN entry will end the current active VPN connection. To add a VPN connection, choose a VPN connection type from the connection type menu.

The Editing VPN Connection dialog opens with two tabs: VPN and IPv4 Settings. On the VPN tab, you enter VPN connection information, such as the gateway address and any additional VPN information that may be required. For an OpenVPN connection, you will have to provide the authentication type, certificates, and keys. Clicking the Advanced button opens the Advanced Options dialog. An OpenVPN connection will have tabs for General, Security, and TLS Authentication. On the Security tab, you can specify the cipher to use.

Networks are configured and managed with the lower level tools: **ifconfig**, route, and netstat. The **ifconfig** tool operates from your root user desktop and enables you to configure your network interfaces fully, adding new ones and modifying others. The ifconfig and route utilities are lower-level programs that require more specific knowledge of your network to use effectively. The netstat tool provides you with information about the status of your network connections.

Command-Line PPP Access: wvdial

From the command-line interface, you can use the wvdial dialer to set up PPP connections for dial-up modems. The wvdial program loads its configuration from the /etc/wvdial.conf file. You can edit this file and enter modem and account information, including modem speed and serial device, as well as ISP phone number, username, and password. The wvdial.conf file is organized into sections, beginning with a section label enclosed in brackets. A section holds variables for different parameters that are assigned values, such as username = chris. The default section holds default values inherited by other sections, so you needn't repeat them.

With the wvdialconf utility, you can create a default wvdial.conf file automatically; wvdialconf detects your modem and sets the default values for basic features. You can then edit the wvdial.conf file and modify the phone, username, and password entries with your ISP dial-up information. Remove the preceding semicolon (;) to unquote the entry. Any line beginning with a semicolon is ignored as a comment.

```
$ wvdialconf
```

The following example shows the /etc/wvdial.conf file:

/etc/wvdial.conf
```
[Modem0]
Modem = /dev/ttyS0
Baud = 57600
Init1 = ATZ
SetVolume = 0
Dial Command = ATDT

[Dialer Defaults]
Modem = /dev/ttyS0
Baud = 57600
Init1 = ATZ
SetVolume = 0
Dial Command = ATDT
```

To start wvdial, enter the command wvdial, which then reads the connection configuration information from the /etc/wvdial.conf file; wvdial dials the ISP and initiates the PPP connection, providing your username and password, when requested.

```
$ wvdial
```

You can set up connection configurations for any number of connections in the /etc/wvdial.conf file. To select one, enter its label as an argument to the wvdial command, as shown here:

```
$ wvdial myisp
```

Setting Up Your Firewall: firewall-config

You can run your firewall on a standalone system directly connected to the Internet or on a gateway system that connects a local network to the Internet. Most networks now use dedicated routers for Internet access, which have their own firewalls. If, instead, you decide to use a Linux system as a gateway, it will have at least two network connections, one for the local network and an Internet connection device for the Internet.

Fedora 20 uses the Firewalld firewall daemon, instead of the older static system-config-firewall. To configure Firewalld, you can use the firewalld-config graphical interface. You can also use firewalld-cmd command from the command line. To set up your firewall, run firewall-config (Sundry ➤ Firewall; see Figure 15-18). The firewall is configured using zones displayed on the Zones tab. To configure a particular service, use the Services tab.

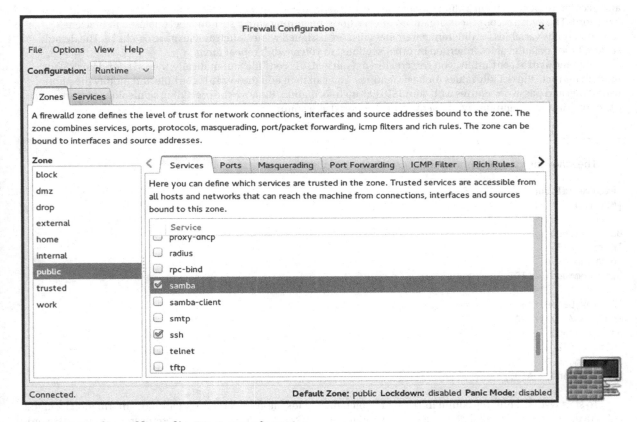

Figure 15-18. firewall-config: *Runtime configuration*

With firewall-config you can configure either a Runtime configuration or Permanent configuration. Select one from the Current View drop-down. The Runtime configuration shows your current runtime setup, whereas a Permanent configuration does not take effect until you reload or restart. If you wish to edit your zones and services, you need to choose the Permanent configuration. This view displays a zone toolbar for editing the zone, at the bottom of the zone scroll box, and an Edit Services button on the Services tab for editing service protocols, ports, and destination addresses.

Additional tabs can be displayed from the View menu for configuring ICMP types, whitelists, and for adding firewall rules directly (Direct configuration).

A firewall configuration is set up for a given zone, such as a home, work, internal, external, or public zone. Each zone can have its own configuration. Zones are listed in the Zone scrollbox on the left side of the `firewall-config` window (see Figure 15-19). Select the one you want to configure. The `firewall-config` window opens to the default, Public. You can choose the default zone from the System Default Zone dialog, which you open from the Options menu as Change Default Zone.

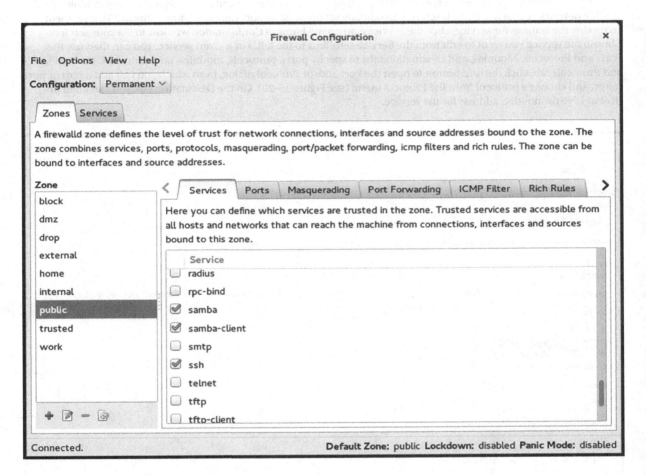

Figure 15-19. `firewall-config`: *Permanent configuration*

If you choose Permanent configuration from the Current View Menu, a toolbar for zones is displayed below the Zone scrollbox, as shown in the preceding figure. The plus button lets you add a zone; minus removes a zone. The pencil/page button lets you edit a zone. The add and edit buttons open the Base Zone Settings dialog, in which you enter or edit the zone name, version, description, and the target. The default target is ACCEPT. Other options are REJECT and DROP. The Load Zone Defaults button (yellow arrow) loads default settings, removing any you have made.

Each zone, in turn, can have one or more network connections. From the Options menu, choose Change Zones of Connections to open the Network Connections dialog, from which you can add a network connection.

For a given zone, you can configure services, ports, masquerading, port forwarding, and ICMP filter. The features many users want to change are the services. A Linux system is often used to run servers for a network. If you are creating a strong firewall but still want to run a service such as a web server, an FTP server, Samba desktop browsing, or SSH encrypted connections, you must specify it in the Services tab. Samba desktop browsing lets you access your Samba shares, such as remote Windows file systems, from your GNOME or KDE desktops.

For a selected service, you can specify service settings such as the ports and protocols it uses, any modules, and specific network addresses. Default settings are already set up, such as port 139 for Samba, using the TCP protocol. To modify the settings for service, click the Services tab on the Firewall Configuration window to list your services. Choose the service you want to edit from the Service scrollbox to the left. For a given service, you can then use the Ports and Protocols, Modules, and Destination tabs to specify ports, protocols, modules, and addresses. On the Ports and Protocols tab, click the Add button to open the Port and/or Protocol dialog, from which you can add a port or port range, and choose a protocol from the Protocol menu (see Figure 15-20). On the Destination tab, you can enter an IPv4 or IPv6 destination address for the service.

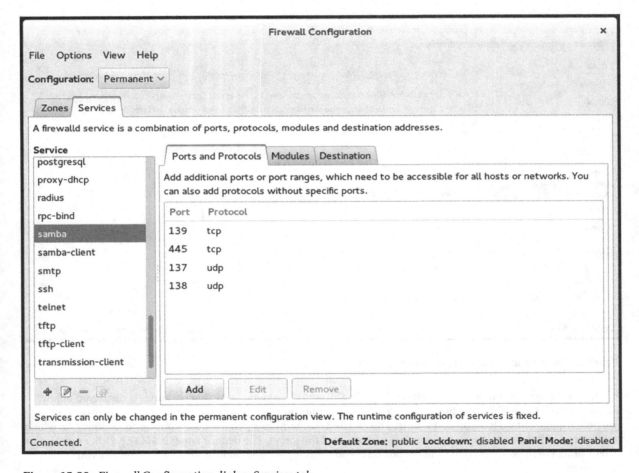

Figure 15-20. *Firewall Configuration dialog: Services tab*

The Ports tab lets you specify ports that you may want opened for certain services, such as BitTorrent. Click the Add button to open a dialog in which you can select the port number, along with the protocol to control (TCP or UDP), or enter a specific port number or range.

If your system is being used as gateway to the Internet for your local network, you can implement masquerading to hide your local hosts from outside access from the Internet. This also requires IP forwarding, which is automatically enabled when you choose masquerading. Local hosts will still be able to access the Internet, but they will masquerade as your gateway system. You would select for masquerading the interface that is connected to the Internet. Masquerading is available only for IPv4 networks, not IPv6 networks.

The Port Forwarding tab lets you set up port forwarding, channeling transmissions from one port to another, or to a different port on another system. Click the Add button to add a port, specifying its protocol and destination.

The ICMP Filters tab allows you to block ICMP messages. By default, all ICMP messages are allowed. Blocking ICMP messages makes for a more secure system. Certain types of ICMP messages are often blocked, as they can be used to infiltrate or overload a system, such as the ping and pong ICMP messages.

If you have specific firewall rules to add, use the Direct Configuration tab (displayed from the View ➤ Direct Configuration menu).

IPtables firewallIf you wish, you can still use iptables instead of FirewallD to manage firewalls. Older customized firewall configurations may still want to use the older iptables static firewall. IPtables systemd unit files manage static IPtables rules, much like System V scripts did in previous releases. The iptables command keeps firewall rules in **/etc/sysconfig/iptables**, which is checked for (ConditionPathExists). The iptables operation runs an iptables.init script to start and stop the firewall. The script reads runtime configuration from **/etc/sysconfig/iptables-config**.

You can still use the older **system-config-firewall** desktop tool to configure iptables static firewalls. Download and install the system-config-firewall packages. You can start it from the Sundry | Firewall. Keep in mind that it conflicts with FirewallD. You will have to first stop firewalld before you can use system-config-firewall.

service firewalld stop

To set up your firewall, run system-config-firewall (Sundry | Firewall). It should be the second firewall icon. The top button bar has buttons for a Firewall wizard, Apply button to effect any changes, Reload to restore your saved firewall, and Disable and Enable buttons. You can enable or disable your firewall with the Enable and Disable buttons. If the Firewall is active, only the Disable button can be used, and vice versa.

Setting Up Windows Network Access: Samba

Most local and home networks include some systems working on Microsoft Windows and others on Linux. You may be required to let a Windows computer access a Linux system or vice versa. If you want to allow other Windows users to access folders on your Fedora desktop, you will have to install and configure the Samba server.

Be sure that Samba is installed and enabled. Open Packages (PackageKit) and click the Server entry or search for samba. Install the samba, samba-client, and system-config-samba packages. Selecting samba for installation will automatically select any needed dependent packages.

Be sure that the firewall on your Windows system is not blocking Samba. Run firewall-config (Sundry ➤ Firewall). Make sure that the Samba service and Samba client entries are checked, allowing Samba to operate on your system (see preceding Figure 15-19). Click Apply to make the changes. To enable access immediately, restart your firewall.

The Samba server consists of two daemons: smb and nmb. You may first have to enable and then start these daemons, using the systemctl and service commands as the root user. Open a terminal window (Terminal), access the root user with the su command, and then enter a systemctl command for the smb and nmb servers with the enable command to enable the server. Finally, use the service command with the start option to start it. Once enabled, the server should start automatically whenever your system starts up. Samba is managed by systemd.

```
su
systemctl enable nmb
systemctl enable smb
service nmb start
service smb start
```

Also, make sure that Samba access is permitted by SELinux (system-config-selinux). Use the SELinux Management tool and on the Boolean tab and enable Samba access (see Figure 14-16). There are several Samba entries. To share folders, Windows folders, and NFS folders you would check the following:

```
Allow samba to share any file/directory read/write
Allow samba to export ntfs/fusefs volumes
Allow samba to export NFS volumes
```

Should you receive a security alert, you can change the Samba SELinux file context manually, using the chcon and semanage commands. The commands to enter will be listed in the Fix Command section of the security alert's Show Full Error Output scroll window. The Samba share directory's SELinux file context is set to samba_share_t. The semanage command preserves the change through relabeling. In the following example, the SELinux file context for the /mymedia share is set:

```
chcon -R -t samba_share_t '/mymedia'
semanage fcontext -a  -t samba_share_t '/mymedia'
```

■ **Note**   If SELinux continues to block your connections, you could disable SELinux by placing it in the Permissive mode, system-config-selinux (Status tab).

Samba has two methods of authentication, shares and users. User authentication requires that there be corresponding accounts in the Windows and Linux systems. They can have the same name, although a Windows user can be mapped to a Linux account. A share can be made, open to any user and function, as an extension of the user's storage space. The user method is recommended.

The system-config-samba tool provides an easy way to configure your Samba server from your desktop (Samba). With a few clicks, you can add Samba users and set up Samba shares. The system-config-samba tool lists all the shares for your server (see Figure 15-21). Use buttons at the top to manage your shares, adding new ones or deleting current ones. If you delete a share, the actual directories are not removed; they just lose their status as shared directories.

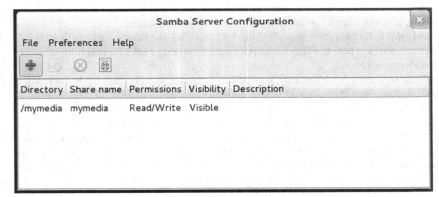

Figure 15-21. system-config-samba

To configure your Samba server, select Server Settings from the Preferences menu to open the Server Settings window. This window has two panels: Basic and Security. On the Basic panel, you enter the Samba server workgroup name. This will be the same name used as the workgroup by all your Windows systems. The default names given by Windows are MSHOME or WORKGROUP. Use the name already given to your Windows network. For home networks, you can decide on your own. Make sure all your computers use the same network name.

On the Security tab, specify the authentication mode, the password encryption option, and the name of the guest account, along with the authentication server. By default, user security is used. You could also use share or server security. These are more open, but both have been deprecated and may be dropped in later versions. The authentication mode specifies the access level, which can be user, share, server, ADS, or domain. User-level access restricts access by user password, whereas share access opens access to any guest. Normally, you would elect to encrypt passwords, rather than have them passed over your network in plain text.

For user authentication, you must associate a Windows user with a particular Samba user. Samba maintains its own password listing for users. To provide Samba access to a user, you must register the user as a Samba user. Select Samba Users from the Preferences menu to open the Samba Users window, clicking the Add User button. Here, you enter the UNIX username, the Windows username, and the Samba password. There is an additional box for confirming the Samba password. The UNIX Username is a pop-up window listing all the users on your Samba server.

Select Samba Users in the system-config-samba Preferences menu. This opens the Samba Users window listing all current Samba users. These correspond to user accounts already set up on your system. To add a Samba user, click the Add User button on the right. This opens a Create New Samba User window with four entries. Here you enter the UNIX username, the Windows username, and the Samba password. There is an additional box for confirming the Samba password. The UNIX Username is a pop-up window listing all the users on the Linux system hosting your Samba server.

First, select a Linux user to use from the UNIX Username pop-up menu, then enter the corresponding Windows user. The Windows username can be different from the Linux account (Linux username). You then enter a password that the Windows user can employ to access Linux. This is the Samba password for that user. Samba maintains its own set of passwords that users will require in order to access a Samba share. When Windows users want to access a Samba share, they will need their Samba passwords.

Once you create a Samba user, its name will appear in the list of Samba users on the Samba Users window. To later modify or delete a Samba user, use the same Samba Users window. You select the user from the list and click the Edit User button to change entries such as the password, or click the Delete User button to remove the Samba user.

To set up a simple share, click Add Share, which opens a Create a Share window. On the Basic tab, you select the Linux directory to share (click Browse to find it) and then specify whether it will be writable and visible. You also provide a name for the share, as well as any description you want. On the Access tab, you can restrict access to certain users or allow access to all users. All Samba users on your system will be listed with check boxes in which you can select those to whom you want to give access. Once created, the share will appear in the main system-config-samba window. The share's directory, share name, its visibility, read/write permissions, and description will be shown. To later modify a share, click its entry and then click the Properties menu to open an Edit Samba Share window with the same Basic and Access tabs you used to create the share.

## CHAPTER 16

Printing

This chapter covers the printing-configuration tools: the GNOME 3 Printers tool (System Settings ➤ Printers) and the older `system-config-printer` tool (Sundry ➤ Print Settings). Most printers are detected for you automatically. You can use the System Settings Printers tool to turn them on or off and access their print queues. As an alternative, you can still use the older `system-config-printer`. Both are front ends for the Common UNIX Printing System (CUPS), which provides printing services (`www.cups.org`).

When you attach a local printer to your system for the first time, the GNOME 3 Printers tool automatically detects the printer and installs the appropriate driver, r. A message appears briefly in the message tray, indicating that a new printer has been detected. The printer is then listed in both the GNOME 3 Printers tool and in the older `system-config-printer`. If the detection fails, you can use the GNOME 3 Printers tool, accessible from System Settings, to set up your printer.

KDE provides support for adding and configuring CUPS printers through the KDE System Settings ➤ Printer Configuration dialog. Select the Printer Configuration icon under Hardware. USB printers that are automatically detected will be listed in the KDE Printer Configuration dialog.

Printer URI (Universal Resource Identifier)

Printers can be local or remote. Both are referenced using Universal Resource Identifiers (URI). URIs support both network protocols used to communicate with remote printers and device connections used to reference local printers.

Remote printers are referenced by the protocol used to communicate with them, including `ipp` for the Internet Printing Protocol used for UNIX network printers, `smb` for the Samba protocol used for Windows network printers, and `lpd` for the older LPRng UNIX print servers. Their URIs are similar to a web URL, indicating the network addresses of the system the printer is connected to.

```
ipp://mytsuff.com/printers/queue1
smb://guest@lizard/myhp
```

For attached local printers, the URI will use the device connection and the device name. The `usb:` prefix is used for USB printers; `parallel:` is used for older printers connected to a parallel port; `serial:` is used for printers connected to a serial port; `scsi:` is used for SCSI-connected printers. For a locally attached USB printer, the URI would be something like the following:

```
usb://Canon/S330
```

> **Note** For many older HP printers, you must first install the `hpijs` package.

GNOME 3 Printers: System Settings

The GNOME 3 Printers tool, accessible from the System Settings dialog, lists installed printers, letting you turn them on or off and access their job queues (see Figure 16-1). If no printers are detected, an Add New Printer button is displayed, which you can use to detect your printer. Select a printer to display the printer name, model, location, and number of jobs. Click the Show button to list the current jobs for this printer (see Figure 16-2). To make the printer the default, click the Default check box. You can also print a test page.

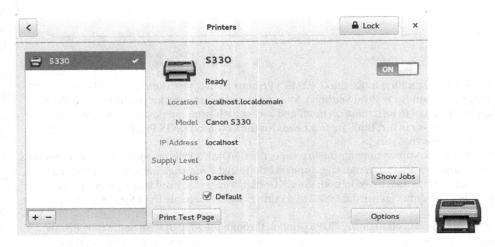

Figure 16-1. *GNOME 3 Printers tool*

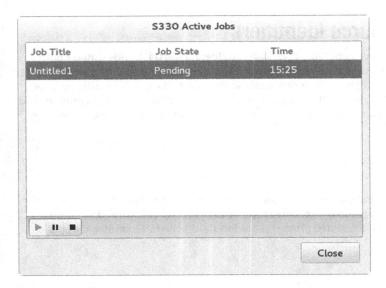

Figure 16-2. *GNOME 3 Printers tool: Jobs*

You can use the GNOME 3 Printers tool to configure your printer. Click the Options button to open the printer's options dialog (see Figure 16-3). From the options dialog, you can configure printer features, such as page setup, image, quality, and color. The Advanced tab lets you set specialized options, such as contrast, ink type, and saturation (see Figure 16-4).

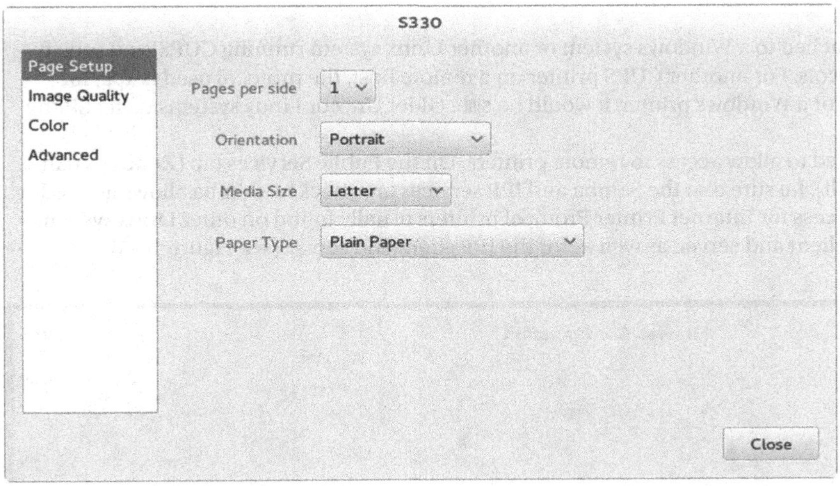

Figure 16-3. *GNOME 3 Printers tool: Options*

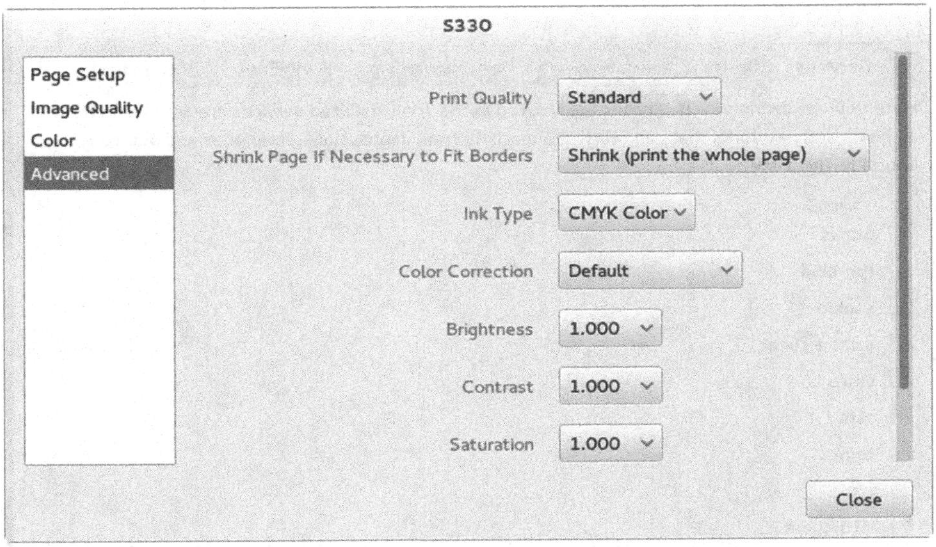

Figure 16-4. *GNOME 3 Printers tool: Advanced options*

On the Printers dialog, you can add or remove printers, using the plus and minus buttons below the list of printers. Click the plus button to open the Add a New Printer dialog, which lists printers attached to your system. They are detected automatically. If you know the address of a printer on your network, you can enter it in the search box at the bottom to have it detected and displayed.

On the Printers dialog, you can add or remove printers, using the plus and minus buttons below the list of printers. To remove a printer, select it and click the minus button. Printers attached to your system are detected and added automatically. You can use the plus button to add a remote printer.

Remote Printers

To install a remote printer that is attached to a Windows system or another Linux system running CUPS, you specify its location, using special URL protocols. For another CUPS printer on a remote host, the protocol used is ipp, for Internet Printing Protocol, whereas for a Windows printer, it would be smb. Older Unix or Linux systems using LPRng would use the lpd protocol.

Be sure your firewall is configured to allow access to remote printers. On the Public Services tab (Zones tab) in firewall-config (Sundry ➤ Firewall), be sure that the Samba and IPP services are checked. Samba allows access for Windows printers, and IPP allows access for Internet Printer Protocol printers usually found on other Linux systems. There will be entries for the Samba client and server, as well as for the IPP client and server (see Figure 16-5).

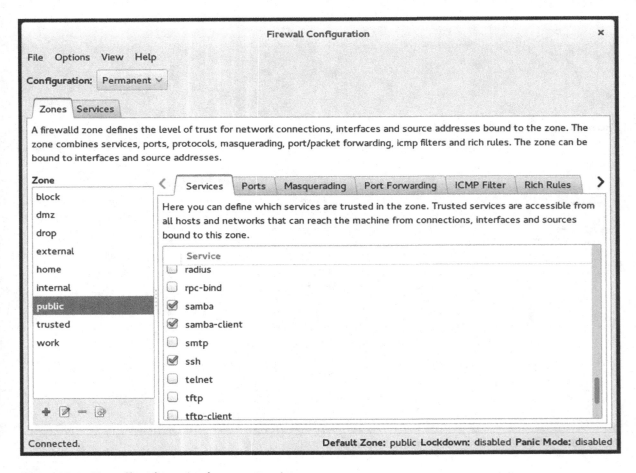

Figure 16-5. Firewall configuration for a remote printer

To access an SMB shared remote printer, you must install Samba and have the Server Message Block services enabled, using the smb and nmb daemons. The Samba service should be enabled by default. If not, you can enable it using the service command as the root user. Open a terminal window (Terminal), access the root user with the su command, and then enter a service command for the smb and nmb servers with the enable command.

```
su
service nmb enable
service smb enable
```

On the GNOME Printers dialog, click the plus button to open the Add a New Printer dialog listing Printers attached to your system (see Figure 16-6). If you know the address of a printer on your network, you can enter it in the search box at the bottom to have it detected and displayed. Remote systems that may have printers are also listed. Normally, these require authentication. Select the system you want to access and click the Authenticate button to open a dialog prompting you for a password (see Figure 16-7).

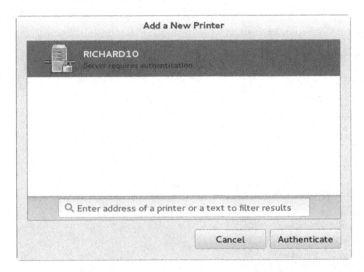

Figure 16-6. *GNOME 3 Printers tool: avaialable printers*

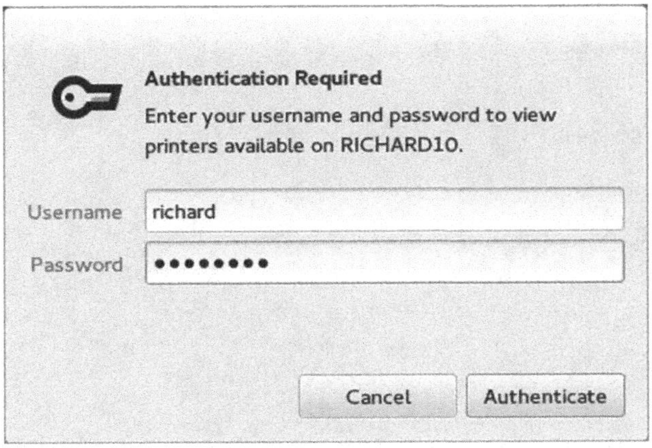

Figure 16-7. *GNOME 3 Printers tool: Authentication*

Once granted access, the printers available on that system are listed (see Figure 16-8). To add a printer, select it and then click the Add button. This opens the Select Printer Driver dialog, from which you choose the manufacturer and then the printer model (see Figure 16-9).

Figure 16-8. *GNOME 3 Printers tool: Added printers*

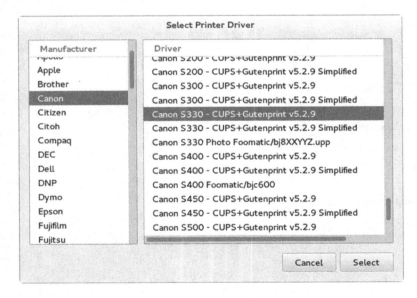

Figure 16-9. *GNOME 3 Printers tool: printer drivers*

Printer Settings: system-config-printer

You can also use the older system-config-printer tool to edit a printer configuration or to add a remote printer. You can install the system-config-printer package using PackageKit This utility enables you to select the appropriate driver for your printer, as well as set print options, such as paper size and print resolutions. You can configure a printer connected directly to your local computer or a printer on a remote system on your network. You can start system-config-printer by clicking the Print Settings icon from the Applications overview, Sundry subview. A printer configuration window is displayed, showing icons for installed printers. As you add printers, icons for them are displayed in the Printer configuration window (see Figure 16-10).

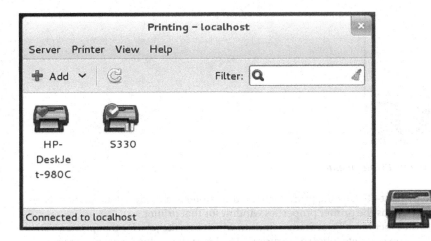

Figure 16-10. system-config-printer tool: multiple printers

To see the printer settings, such as printer and job options, access controls, and policies, double-click the printer icon or right-click and select Properties. The Printer Properties window opens with six tabs: Settings, Policies, Access Control, Printer Options, Job Options, and Ink/Toner Levels (see Figure 16-11).

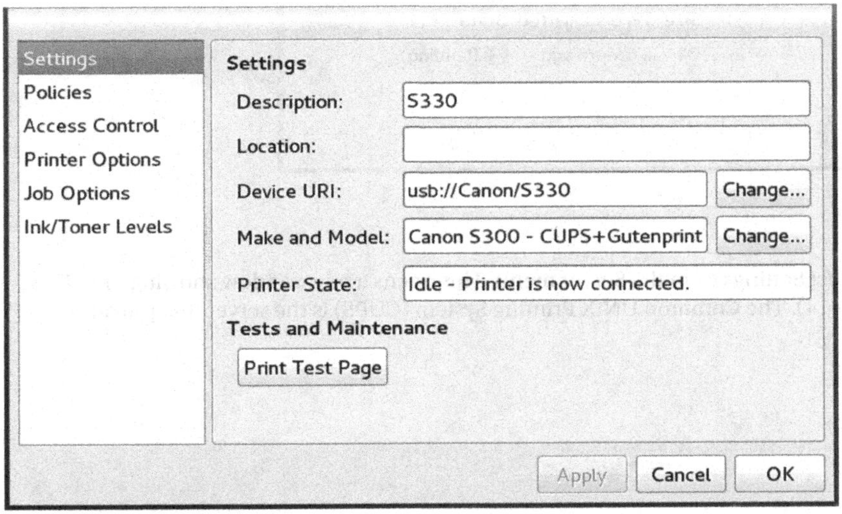

Figure 16-11. Printer Properties window

The Printer configuration window Printer menu lets you rename the printer, enable or disable it, and make it a shared printer. Select the printer icon and then click the Printer menu (see Figure 16-12). The Delete entry will remove a printer configuration. Use the Set As Default entry to make the printer a system-wide or personal default printer. There are also entries for accessing the printer properties and viewing the print queue.

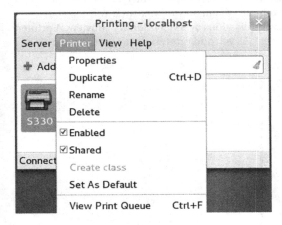

Figure 16-12. *Printer configuration window Printer menu*

The Printer icon menu is accessed by right-clicking the printer icon. If the printer is already a default, there is no Set As Default entry. The Properties entry opens the printer properties window for that printer.

The View Print Queue entry opens the Document Print Status window, which lists the jobs for that printer. You can change the queue position as well as stop or delete jobs (see Figure 16-13). From the toolbar, you can choose to display printed jobs and reprint them. You will be notified if a job should fail.

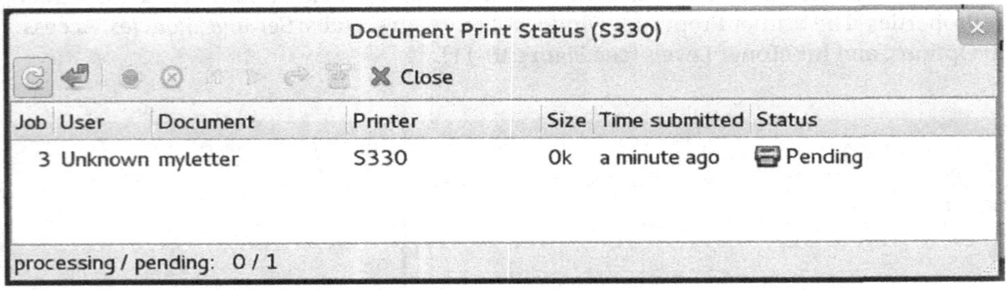

Job	User	Document	Printer	Size	Time submitted	Status
3	Unknown	myletter	S330	0k	a minute ago	Pending

processing / pending: 0 / 1

Figure 16-13. *Printer queue*

To check the server settings, select Settings from the Server menu. This opens a new window showing the CUPS printer server settings (see Figure 16-14). The Common UNIX Printing System (CUPS) is the server that provides printing services (www.cups.org).

Basic Server Settings

☑ Show printers shared by other systems   Problems?

☐ Publish shared printers connected to this system

☐ Allow printing from the Internet

☐ Allow remote administration

☐ Allow users to cancel any job (not just their own)

☐ Save debugging information for troubleshooting

▽ **Advanced Server Settings**

Job history

○ Do not preserve job history

◉ Preserve job history but not files

○ Preserve job files (allow reprinting)

Browse servers

Usually print servers broadcast their queues. Specify
print servers below to periodically ask for queues instead.

	Add
	Remove

Cancel   OK

Figure 16-14. *Server Settings*

To select a particular CUPS server, select the Connect entry in the Server menu. This opens a Connect to CUPS Server window with a drop-down menu listing all current CUPS servers from which to choose.

To add, edit, or remove printers requires root-level access. You have to enter your root user password (set up initially during installation) to edit a printer configuration, add a new printer, or remove an old one. For example, when you try to access the printer server settings, you will be prompted to enter the root user password.

Again, when you edit any printer's configuration settings, you will be prompted for authorization (see Figure 16-15). Whenever you try to change a printer setting, such as its driver or URI, you are prompted to enter the root password for device authorization.

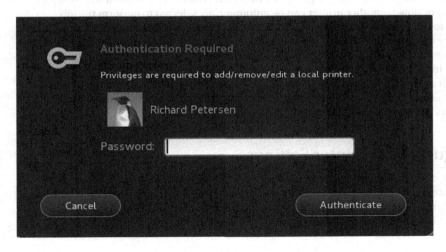

Authentication Required

Privileges are required to add/remove/edit a local printer.

Richard Petersen

Password: [   ]

Cancel   Authenticate

Figure 16-15. *Printer configuration authorization*

To make a printer the default , either right-click the printer icon and select Set As Default or single-click the printer icon and then, from the Printer configuration window's Printer menu, select the Set As Default entry. A Set Default Printer dialog opens with options for setting the system-wide default or setting the personal default. The system-wide default printer is the default for your entire network served by your CUPS server, not just your local system.

The system-wide default printer will have a green check mark emblem on its printer icon in the Printer configuration window.

Should you wish to use a different printer as your default, you can designate it as your personal default. To make a printer your personal default, select the entry Set as My Personal Default Printer in the Set Default Printer dialog. A personal emblem, a heart, will appear on the printer's icon in the Printer configuration window. In Figure 16-16, the S330 Windows printer is the system-wide default, whereas the HP DeskJet 980C printer is the personal default.

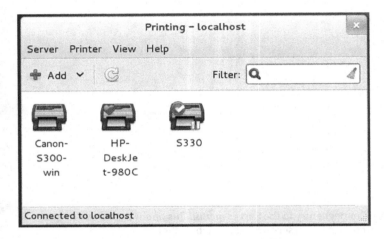

Figure 16-16. *System-wide and personal default printers*

If you have more than one printer on your system, you can make one the default by clicking the Make Default Printer button in the printer's properties Settings pane.

The Class entry in the New menu lets you create a printer class. You can access the New menu from the Server menu or from the New button. This feature lets you select a group of printers to print a job, instead of selecting just one. That way, if one printer is busy or down, another printer can be automatically selected to perform the job. Installed printers can be assigned to different classes. When you click the Class entry in the New menu, a New Class window opens. Here, you can enter the name for the class, any comments, and the location (your hostname is entered by default). On the right side, the next screen lists available printers (Other printers) and, on the left side, the printers you assigned to the class (Printers in this class). Use the arrow button to add or remove printers to the class. Click Apply when finished. The class will appear under the Local Classes heading on the main `system-config-printer` window. Panes for a selected class are much the same as for a printer, although with a Members pane instead of a Print Control pane. In the Members pane, you can change which printers belong to the class.

Editing Printer Configurations: Printer Settings

To edit an installed printer, double-click its icon in the Printer configuration window or right-click and select the Properties entry. This opens a Printer Properties window for that printer. A sidebar lists the configuration tabs. Click one to display that tab. There are configuration entries for Settings, Policies, Access Control, Printer Options, Job Options, and Ink/Toner Levels (see Figure 16-17).

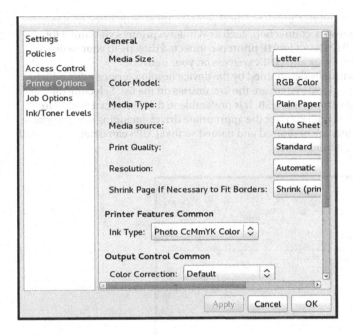

Figure 16-17. *Printer Options*

Once you have made your changes, you can click Apply to save your changes and restart the `printer` daemon. You can test your printer with a PostScript, A4, or ASCII test sheet selected from the Test menu.

On the Settings tab, you can change configuration settings, such as the driver and the printer name, enable or disable the printer, or specify whether to share it (see Figure 16-11. Should you have to change the selected driver, click the Change button next to the Make and Model entry. This will open printer model and driver windows such as those described in the Add New Printer Manually section. There, you can specify the model and driver you want to use, even loading your own driver.

The Policies tab lets you specify a start and end banner, as well as an error policy that specifies whether to retry or abort the print job or stop the printer, should an error occur. The Access Control tab allows you to deny access to certain users.

The Printer Options tab is where you set particular printing features, such as paper size and type, print quality, and the input tray to use (see Figure 16-17).

On the Job Options tab, you can select default printing features. A pop-up menu provides a list of printing feature categories to choose from. You then click the Add button to add the category, selecting a particular feature from a pop-up menu. You can set such features as the number of copies (copies); letter, glossy, or A4-sized paper (media); the kind of document, for example, text, PDF, PostScript, or image (document format); and single- or double-sided printing (sides).

Adding New Printers

To install a new printer, choose the Server ➤ New ➤ Printer menu entry or click the Add drop-down menu on the toolbar and select Printer. A New Printer window opens and displays a series of dialog boxes from which you select the connection, model, drivers, and printer name with location.

On the Select Device screen, you configure your printers. Connected local printers are already listed by name, whereas for remote printers, you specify the type of network connection, such as Windows printers via Samba for printers connected to a Windows system, AppSocket/HP Direct for HP printers connected directly to your network, and the Internet Printing Protocol (ipp) for printers on Linux and UNIX systems on your network.

For most connected printers, your connection is usually determined by the device hotplug service udev, which manages all devices. Printers already connected to your local system are the first entries on the list. Selecting the connected printer lists the kind of connections available for it, like USB. It is preferable to first connect a printer to your system before configuring it. A search will then be conducted for the appropriate driver, including downloadable drivers. Printer driver packages on the Fedora repository are organized and named so that CUPS can detect and install the correct driver automatically. If the driver is found, it is installed.

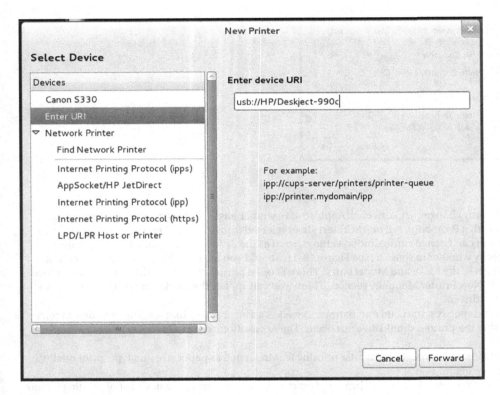

Figure 16-18. *Selecting a new printer device: connected printer*

The Choose Driver screen is then displayed with the appropriate driver manufacturer already selected for you. You need only click the Forward button (see Figure 16-19).

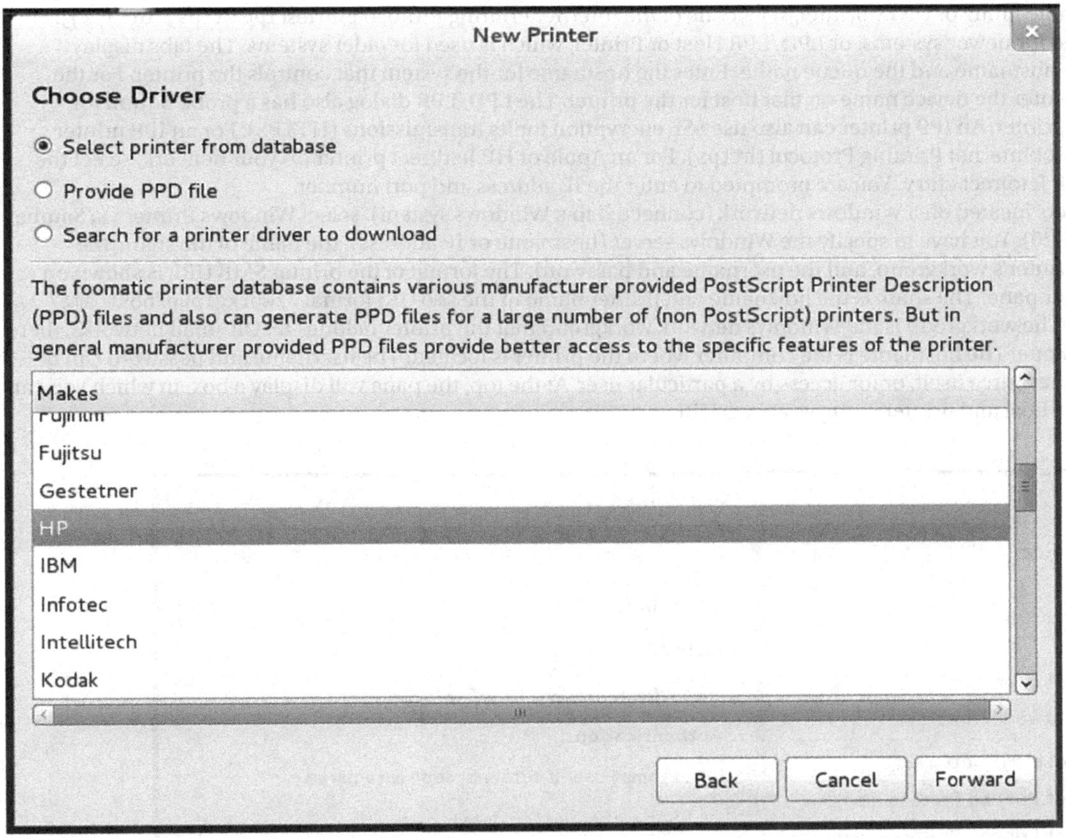

New Printer

Choose Driver

- ● Select printer from database
- ○ Provide PPD file
- ○ Search for a printer driver to download

The foomatic printer database contains various manufacturer provided PostScript Printer Description (PPD) files and also can generate PPD files for a large number of (non PostScript) printers. But in general manufacturer provided PPD files provide better access to the specific features of the printer.

Makes

Fujitsu
Fujitsu
Gestetner
HP
IBM
Infotec
Intellitech
Kodak

Back   Cancel   Forward

Figure 16-19. *Printer manufacturer for new printers*

On the next screen, also labeled Choose Driver, the printer models and drivers files will be listed, and the appropriate one will already be selected for you. Just click the Forward button again.

If your printer driver is not detected or detected incorrectly, then—on the Choose Driver screen—you have the options to choose the driver from the database, from a PPD driver file of your own, or from your own search of the OpenPrinting online repository. The selection display will change according to which option you choose. The database option lists possible manufacturers. Use your mouse to select the one you want.

The search option displays a search box for make and model. Enter both the make (printer manufacturer) and part of the model name. The search results are available in the Printer Model drop-down menu. Select the one you want. The PPD file option simply displays a file location button that, when clicked, opens a Select file dialog you can use to locate your PPD file on your system.

The Describe Printer screen is then displayed. From here, you can enter the printer name, description, and location. These are ways you can personally identify a printer. These will be entered for you using the printer model and your system's hostname. You can change the printer name to anything you want. When ready, click Apply. An icon for your printer is then displayed in the Printer configuration window.

You can use system-config-printer to set up a remote printer on Linux, UNIX, or Windows networks. When you add a new printer or edit one, the New Printer/Select Devices dialog will list possible remote connection types. When you select a remote connection entry, a pane will be displayed in which you can enter configuration information.

The location is specified using special URI protocols. For another CUPS printer on a remote host, the protocol used is ipp, for Internet Printing Protocol, whereas for a Windows printer, it is smb. Older UNIX and Linux systems using LPRng use the lpd protocol.

For a remote Linux or UNIX printer, select one of the Internet Printing Protocolentries(ipp,https, or ips)), which are used for newer systems, or LPD/LPR Host or Printer, which is used for older systems. The tabs display entries for the hostname and the queue name. Enter the hostname for the system that controls the printer. For the queue name, enter the device name on that host for the printer. The LPD/LPR dialog also has a probe button for detecting the printer. An IPP printer can also use SSL encryption for its transmissions (HTTPS). For an IPP printer using SSL, select Internet Printing Protocol (https). For an Apple or HP Jetdirect printer on your network, select the AppSocket/HP Jetdirect entry. You are prompted to enter the IP address and port number.

For printers located on a Windows network (connected to a Windows system), select Windows Printer via Samba (see Figure 16-20). You have to specify the Windows server (hostname or IP address), the name of the share, the name of the printer's workgroup, and the username and password. The format of the printer SMB URL is shown on the SMP Printer pane. The share is the hostname and printer name in the smb URI format //workgroup/hostname/ printername. The workgroup is the Windows network workgroup that the printer belongs to. On small networks, there is usually only one. The hostname is the computer where the printer is located. The username and password can be for the printer resource itself, or for access by a particular user. At the top, the pane will display a box, in which you can enter the share host and printer name as an smb URI.

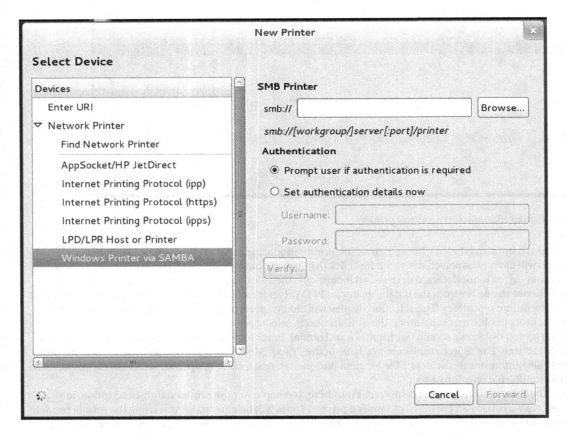

Figure 16-20. *Selecting a Windows printer*

If you do not see an entry for Samba, use the Find Network Printer tab to search for a printer. Enter the hostname of the system the printer is connected to.

You can click the Browse button to open a SMB Browser window, from which you can select the printer from a listing of Windows hosts on your network (see Figure 16-21). For example, if your Windows network is WORKGROUP, then the entry WORKGROUP will be shown, which you can then expand to list all the Windows hosts on that network (if your network is MSHOME, then that is what will be listed). Be sure that the remote system is running.

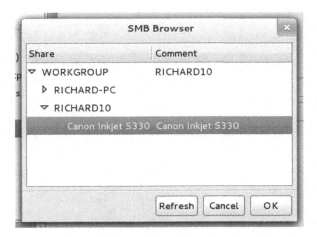

Figure 16-21. *SMB Browser, selecting a remote Windows printer*

When you make your selection, the corresponding URL will show up in the smb:// box. Make sure the firewall and SELinux are already configured to allow Samba access (see Chapter 15. Also on the tab, you can enter any needed Samba authentication, if required, such as username or password. Check Authentication Required to enter the Samba username and password.

You then continue with install screens for the printer model, driver, and name. Once installed, you can access the printer properties just as you would any printer (see Figure 16-22).

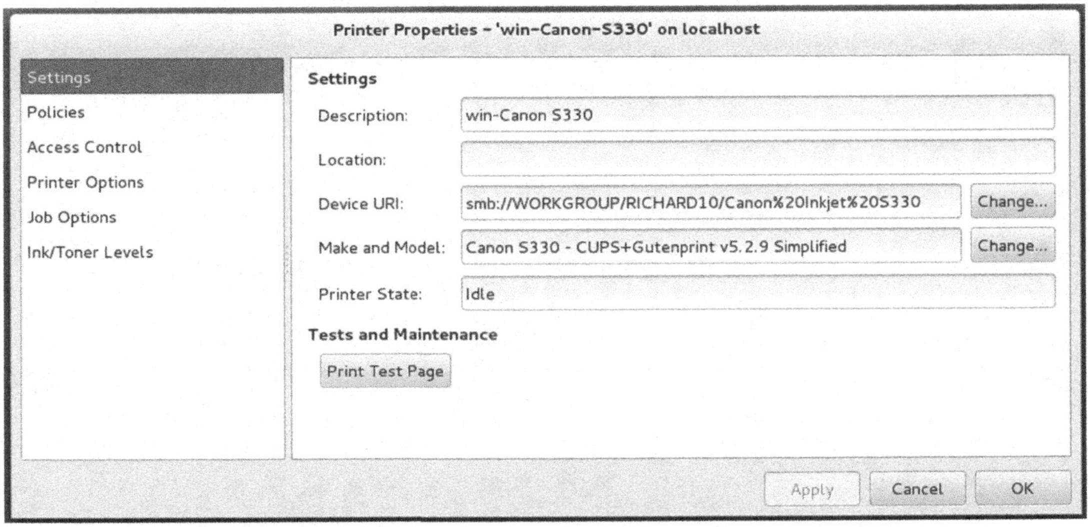

Figure 16-22. *Remote Windows printer settings*

To access an SMB shared remote printer, you must install Samba and have the Server Message Block services enabled, using the smb and nmb daemons. The Samba service will be enabled by default. The service is enabled using the service command as the root user. Open a terminal window (Terminal), access the root user with the su command, and then enter a service command for the smb and nmb servers with the enable command.

```
su
service nmb enable
service smb enable
```

Index

■ H

■ I

■ T